Music

FOR
SILENT
FILMS

1894–1929

Music
FOR
SILENT
FILMS
1894–1929

A GUIDE

Compiled and with an Introduction by

Gillian B. Anderson
MUSIC DIVISION

With a Foreword by Eileen Bowser

LIBRARY OF CONGRESS
Washington   1988

Library of Congress Cataloging-in-Publication Data

Anderson, Gillian B., 1943-
 Music for silent films, 1894-1929.

 Bibliography: p.
 Includes index.
 1. Silent film music—Bibliography—Union lists.
I. Title.
ML128.M7A5   1988   016.7828′5   87-26248
ISBN 0-8444-0580-9

For sale by the Superintendent of Documents
U.S. Government Printing Office
Washington, D.C. 20402

Foreword

Music for silent films is a fundamental part of the films themselves. Preservation of the scores and cue sheets should go hand-in-hand with preservation of the films. Unfortunately, this music has been too long neglected by film archives overwhelmed with the burden of transferring thousands of nitrate films to more durable safety stock before they deteriorate. The Music Division of the Library of Congress has performed an outstanding service by microfilming the silent film music of two very important collections, their own and that of the Museum of Modern Art in New York. The Music Division should be congratulated for its efforts to make music scores for the silent film more widely available. We hope the present publication will make it possible for silent films to be presented throughout the world in the way that they were originally shown, with musical accompaniment. This will lead to a better understanding of the art of the silent film, which we all know was never really silent.

EILEEN BOWSER
Curator
Department of Film
Museum of Modern Art

Unknown violinist and harmonium player provide mood music for Pauline Clarke and Conrad Nagel during the shooting of *Sun-Up* (1925). Courtesy of the Astoria Motion Picture and Television Center Foundation, Astoria, New York.

Contents

Preface

Sound has almost always been an indispensable element in motion picture presentations, but, until recently, the Museum of Modern Art (MOMA) Film Department was alone in keeping music and silent films together. The Museum collected, commissioned, and circulated scores and always screened silent films with some form of accompaniment. Almost always the accompanist was a lone pianist, for many years composer and arranger Arthur Kleiner. (There are still many people whose knowledge of early films was acquired not from film classes or videotapes but from Saturday afternoon screenings at MOMA.)

Francis Ford Coppola's commercial revival of Abel Gance's 1927 classic, *Napoleon,* exposed a large audience to the other extreme of the silent film accompaniment scale, the full orchestra. The *Napoleon* tour stimulated an increased interest in the original accompaniments to silent films. Simultaneously, the Library of Congress achieved bibliographic control over its holdings of silent film music and noted that its holdings complemented those at MOMA.

The scores and musical cue sheets in both collections were brittle with age and sometimes fragile from extensive use. Therefore, MOMA and the Library of Congress Music Division embarked on a joint preservation microfilming project. This guide is the second product of the collaboration, the first being the microfilm itself.

The purpose of this work is to provide a guide for locating scores and musical cue sheets made for films of the silent era, 1894-1929. An essay about the nature, history, and presentation of the musical accompaniments for silent films provides the context for these artifacts. The guide follows the introductory essay. All the entries are for microfilmed items found in the Library of Congress (LC) and Museum of Modern Art (MOMA) music collections. MOMA's collection is on permanent loan to the Library's Music Division.

Appendixes 3, 4, 5, and 6 contain items found at the University of Minnesota in the Arthur Kleiner Collection; the George Eastman House in Rochester, New York; the New York Public Library Music Division; and the Fédération Internationale des Archives du Film in Brussels, Belgium. The photographs show scores, cue sheets, famous film musicians, showmen, theater organs, film orchestras, movie theaters, and film music in the making. A number of photographs are stills from movies for which there are scores. The index is to names and titles found on the LC and MOMA scores and cue sheets, and consequently in the guide as well.

With the exception of sixteen items (which were located after the initial filming), the material in the main body of the guide is found on two sets of microfilm. Music 3212 consists primarily of scores and parts acquired by the Library through copyright registration and cataloged, classified, or located in storage by 1978. Music 3236 consists of scores, parts, and over six hundred cue sheets from the MOMA collection. The contents, reel numbers, and number of exposures of microfilms 3212 and 3236 are provided in Appendixes 1 and 2.

To make the material more accessible to students of silent film and its music, we have organized the guide alphabetically according to film title. Complete information for any item will be found under the name of the silent movie for which the music or cue sheet was intended. The names, titles, and dates in each entry are found on the cue sheets or scores. Alternate titles, additional names of producers or actors, and release dates are not provided.

When composer's names are not listed (particularly on MOMA scores), they are not known. Cue sheets for sound films occasionally appear among the MOMA cue sheets and are included in this guide. The scores by Browning, Huff, Kleiner, and Leyda were composed or compiled well after the silent film era ended, as were a number of the MOMA scores.

Film titles are listed as they appear on the scores or cue sheets. Thus, *Proud Heart,* which was copyrighted as *His People,* appears under *Proud Heart. Sunrice* may be *Sunrise,* but it appears under *Sunrice.* In instances where a cue sheet or score contains music for more than one film, the titles of all the related films have been listed in the index, but the main entry appears under the title on the score or cue sheet. See, for example, *German Short Films.*

Generally, the names of contributors, such as producers, actors, and screenwriters, appear on the cue sheets, but not on the musical scores. Therefore, John Barrymore does not appear in the index. However, there is a score for *Don Juan* (1926) in which he starred, but it does not mention his or any other actor's or producer's name. Thus, if a user of this guide is looking for scores or cue sheets for films by a certain star, he or she has to compile a list of film titles first and then look up each one.

The format for each main entry follows:

1. Entry number
2. Film title
3. Title as transcribed from title page
4. Literary source of film and its author
5. Adaptor
6. Author(s) of screenplay
7. Producer
8. Director
9. Film company
10. Distributor
11. Composer/compiler
12. Musical series title
13. Publisher of music, place and date of publication
14. Instrumentation (e.g., piano score, parts, etc.). Orchestral parts are noted in parentheses. They are listed in this order: flute, oboe, clarinet, bassoon; French horn, trumpet, trombone, tuba; percussion; strings. Thus (1,0,1,0; 0,1,1,0; drums; strings) means: 1 flute, 1 clarinet, 1 trumpet, 1 trombone, drums, and the usual 5 string parts.
15. Copyright registration and renewal information. This information was found in the *Catalog of Copyright Entries* published by the Library of Congress annually in book form. The absence of a copyright registration or renewal does not necessarily mean that an item is not under copyright protection. A copyright search for the status of copyright ownership is required by the Library of Congress Photoduplication Service before it can supply photocopies of a work.
16. Additional notes
17. Projection time and film footage
18. Library (MOMA or LC) and call number
19. Pagination and height (except in cases where the width is greater than the height, in which case both measurements are given, width by height)
20. Microfilm and item number

How to Order Copies

In order to purchase copies of any of this material, first the patron must write to the Copyright Office (Copyright Reference Search Section, Library of Congress, Washington, D.C. 20559) to obtain written verification of the item's copyright status. A fee of about ten dollars an hour is charged for this service. If the item is indeed in the public domain, the Copyright Office can certify it as such. If the item is still under copyright protection, the Copyright Office can usually supply the most up-to-date address of the copyright claimant, but one must specifically ask them to supply this information.

If the item is in the public domain, the patron should send the certification of this fact together with the request for the score or cue sheet to the Photoduplication Service, Library of Congress, Washington, D.C. 20540. The patron should be sure to supply full information with the request, that is, the title of the film, the composer if given, and the music microfilm and item numbers. If the desired item is protected by copyright, the patron must obtain a letter of permission for copying from the copyright claimant and must submit this letter of permission with the photoduplication request. If the material to be photocopied is for performance purposes, be sure to request that material be enlarged to its original size.

Many people contributed to the production of the microfilms and this guide. I would particularly like to thank Barbara Ringer, Eileen Bowser, Jon Gartenberg, Paul Spehr, David Parker, Madeline Matz, Pat Loughney, Scott Simmon, Kate Holum, Mrs. Arthur Kleiner, John Jensen, Clifford McCarty, Jon and Iris Newsom, Wayne Shirley, Martin Marks, Barbara Costelloe, Rob Miller, Lloyd Pinchback, and Rita Smith for their assistance.

The Normal Theater, Chicago, in 1909, piano and
drums to the left of the screen. Silent films were
always accompanied by at least one instrument—
originally to cover the sound of the projector and to
overcome the "ghostliness" of the images. By the end
of the silent era, there were ensembles ranging in size
from theater organ or piano to full ninety- to one
hundred-piece symphonic orchestras, and the music
was being used for a full range of effects. Prints and
Photographs Division, Library of Congress.

Introduction
A Warming Flame*—The Musical Presentation of Silent Films

Drawing heavily on recollections by the participants as well as on contemporary accounts, this introduction provides a context for the film scores and cue sheets of the silent era in America. Not surprisingly, these musical artifacts are only the tip of the iceberg, remnants of a vast music-making machine that took over thirty years to develop, but only two years to wipe out.

Music for the Earlier Silent Films

From the beginning, Thomas Edison saw the mechanical reproduction of sound and image as inextricably bound. His earliest motion pictures were visual recordings and even came in the same cylinder format as his sound recordings. Some of his moving pictures came with sound recordings, *Jack's Joke* (1913), for example. Other manufacturers also released moving pictures with a recording. *Poor John* and *Waiting at the Church* (Belcher and Waterson, 1907) featured the vaudevillian, Vesta Victoria, singing the songs "Poor John" and "Waiting at the Church." However, the successful presentation of a mechanically produced, synchronized sound track and image took over thirty years to develop—the span of the silent film era. In the meantime live music from vaudeville, ballet, symphony, and opera accompanied silent films, and the earliest days of silent movies saw a variety of combinations of music and image.

One combination resulted from films about musical works. For example, the French film *Mozart's Last Requiem* (Gaumont, 1909) described—in ten minutes—the composition of Mozart's final, unfinished work. *Mendelssohn's Spring Song* (Imp, 1910) purportedly told the story of Mendelssohn's composition of that work.

Another combination of music and image resulted from films that illustrated the stories in popular songs. For example, *Mother* (World, 1914) dramatized the temperance song, "Where Is My Wandering Boy Tonight." Edison released the picture songs *Love and War* and *The Astor Tramp,* which used several songs in sequence as well as stereopticon slides and reading matter. His catalog of 1906 announced:

> We have at last succeeded in perfectly synchronizing music and moving pictures. The following scenes are very carefully chosen to fit the words and the songs, which have been especially composed for these pictures…[*Love and War*] presents this beautiful song picture in six scenes, each of which has a separate song, making the entire series a complete and effective novelty…[1]

The musical accompaniment was a soloist, a quartet, or an orchestra.

The Astor Tramp was presented with or without music, the explanatory text being spoken or sung. Continuing the same tradition, but much later in the silent film era, popular songs on slides or films were accompanied by a theater organist and the audience. Max Fleischer's *My Old Kentucky Home* (Inkwell, 1926), for example, was an animated, follow-the-bouncing-ball film.

As the presentation of silent films became more set, two general styles of accompaniment became perceptible: simple and elaborate. They depended on the financial resources of each theater or theater chain, and these resources affected every aspect of film music presentation from synchronization to organ repair. Obviously, Edison had been concerned with a close synchronization of sound and image. However, such synchronization was hard to achieve, and as time went on, the numbers of theaters and performers

---

*"[Film] music is like a small flame put under the screen to help warm it." Aaron Copland, "Second Thoughts on Hollywood," *Modern Music,* April 1940.

xiii

involved in silent film presentation made it even more unlikely. In the classiest movie houses with the biggest staffs or in the large theater chains, close synchronization appears to have been both possible and practiced. In the smaller, less elaborate houses it probably was not.

Orchestral forces had been available for silent film accompaniment since the moving pictures were first presented in vaudeville theaters. However, D. W. Griffith's presentation of *The Birth of a Nation* (1914) with a full symphony orchestra playing a score that was extremely closely synchronized and based on the operatic compositional practice of leitmotifs was a watershed. Large orchestras became a necessity in fancy movie palaces.

Hollywood's Aspiration to the Ultimate in Theatrical Grandeur

Today, we associate star quality and dazzling effects with motion pictures. In the early days of film, however, the world of opera and opera singers occupied this position. Thomas Edison in his first printed statement about his new invention predicted that it would spread opera far and wide.[2] In 1904 he released a twenty-two-minute version of Richard Wagner's four-hour opera, *Parsifal*.[3] A slide show and lecture tied the eight filmed highlights together. A piano score was available for the accompaniment. Edison also distributed a shorter version of Friedrich von Flotow's opera, *Martha*.

> This film shows a quartette of well-known opera singers acting and singing their parts in this ever popular opera. The subjects are taken with the greatest care and the films manufactured by the Edison Manufacturing Company. Managers can arrange to produce this exhibition throughout the country, and can obtain a quartette of church singers to remain behind the scenes and sing the parts and produce a remarkably fine entertainment, besides giving a local interest to the same by utilizing local talent. If it is desired to do so, however, the quartette can be engaged to travel with the exhibition.[4]

Edison was not the only filmmaker with operatic aspirations. In 1916 Thomas Dixon's *The Fall of a Nation,* with its score by Victor Herbert, was advertised as the first grand opera cinema.

In 1915, Hollywood enjoyed one of its first encounters with the real world of opera singers. Agnes DeMille, niece of Cecil B. DeMille as well as a great choreographer in her own right, noted the results:

> Our second summer Uncle Cecil brought [Geraldine] Farrar to Hollywood to play *Carmen* and I had my first model to aspire to…Grand Opera meant far more in those days than it does now or possibly ever will again. It represented the ultimate in theatrical grandeur, honor, permanence and splendor and Farrar was among its most dazzling names…She visited…first on a Sunday morning and we were all on hand, the executives and their families…I was enthralled…The electricians, the carpenters, the cowboys also adored her. Everyone at the studio from executive to assistant prop-boy, spoke of her as "Our Gerry"…
>
> Once every summer she came to dinner at our house. I was not permitted, of course, to eat with her, but very nearly ran a temperature at the prospect of having her under our roof.
>
> After dinner there was music. Farrar…played the piano…brilliantly, improvising as she went, talking and laughing… The sound of the music and the laughter woke my sister and me and we crept in our nightgowns to the stairs and sat there with faces pressed against the ballustrade, shivering at the glory below.[5]

In 1915 Hollywood regarded a great opera singer as it regards a movie star today. Clearly, Hollywood aspired to opera's position, to use DeMille's words, "the ultimate in theatrical grandeur…and splendor," and music was used to realize this aspiration.

Ordinary and Deluxe Film Presentations

Rarely since the silent film era ended have film images and music shared equal prominence and worked as successfully together. Many accompaniments for sound films declare their role in the titles found on copyright deposits of the scores: "Background Musical Score for..." Before the silent film era ended, however, music was often in the foreground of an audience's attention. The following eloquent account by Jean Paul Sartre attests to this.

On rainy days, Anne Marie would ask me what I felt like doing. We would hesitate for a long time between the circus, the Chatelet, the Electric House, and the Grevin Museum. At the last moment, with calculated casualness, we would decide to go to the movies...The show had begun. We would stumblingly follow the usherette. I would feel I was doing something clandestine. Above our heads, a shaft of light crossed the hall; one could see dust and vapor dancing in it. A piano whinnied away....

Above all, I liked the incurable muteness of my heroes. But no, they weren't mute, since they knew how to make themselves understood. We communicated by means of music; it was the sound of their inner life. Persecuted innocence did better than merely show or speak of suffering: it permeated me with its pain by means of the melody that issued from it. I would read the conversations, but I heard the hope and bitterness; I would perceive by ear the proud grief that remains silent. I was compromised; the young widow who wept on the screen was not I, and yet she and I had only one soul: Chopin's funeral march; no more was needed for her tears to wet my eyes. I felt I was a prophet without being able to foresee anything: even before the traitor betrayed, his crime entered me; when all seemed peaceful in the castle, sinister chords exposed the murderer's presence. How happy were those cowboys, those musketeers, those detectives; their future was there, in that premonitory music, and governed the present. An unbroken song blended with their lives, led them on to victory or death by moving toward its own end. They were expected: by the girl in danger, by the general, by the traitor lurking in the forest, by the friend who was tied up near a powder-keg and who sadly watched the flame run along the fuse. The course of that flame, the virgin's desperate struggle against her abductor, the hero's gallop across the plain, the interlacing of all those images, of all those speeds, and, beneath it all, the demonic movement of the "Race to the Abyss," an orchestral selection taken from the *Damnation of Faust* and adapted for the piano, all of this was one and the same: it was Destiny. The hero dismounted, put out the fuse, the traitor sprang at him, a duel with knives began; but the accidents of the duel likewise partook of the rigor of the musical development; they were fake accidents which ill concealed the universal order. What joy when the last knife stroke coincided with the last chord! I was utterly content, I had found the world in which I wanted to live, I touched the absolute. What an uneasy feeling when the lights went on: I had been wracked with love for the characters and they had disappeared, carrying their world with them. I had felt their victory in my bones; yet it was theirs and not mine. In the street I found myself superfluous.[6]

Sartre's account describes an ordinary silent film presentation—piano and film, what most people still think of as the only form of musical accompaniment for silent films. However, between 1894 and 1929 the accompanying forces ranged from piano or organ to piano, violin and drums to twenty-two- to seventy-piece orchestras, and the relationship between film image and music ranged from entirely improvisational to minutely synchronized and orchestrated. The differences between the ordinary and deluxe presentations are described in an article entitled "South, South, South" published in 1926:

> We no longer go to see movin' pictures. We now see Presentations just like New York or Dodge City. There is a difference ...Movin' Pitchers mean an enclosure with or without a roof, seats or benches, a booth accommodating a youth called an "operator" and one or more devices that click like a roomful of telegraph instruments and from whence issue fitful shadows which appear on a white cotton sheet as horsemen riding frantically up the sides of canyons and shooting in the air with several pistols. At times the sheet becomes a blank and blinding white area while the operator joins a ruptured fillum. A custard comedy is included in the program which is followed by two cracked slides extolling the cooling qualities of the ice-cream at the Elite Drug Store and the wearing qualities of shoes obtained at Pinchem's Boot Shoppe. During the picture Miss Iva Rea Key plays Ben Hur's Chariot Race by E. T. Paull and other selections in keeping with the sentiment and action of the picture. She does this seven hours a day on a piano or if in towns as large as Butte, on a Unit Orchestra [theater organ], Largest in the State, cost $75,000.[7]

This account, while violating the letter, no doubt is true to the spirit of most performances in small movie theaters. The account goes on to describe how deluxe theaters worked by comparison.

> A Presentation is divided into Units which are reclassified as DeLuxe Shows and just shows. Here also is a difference. The plain show uses only the lesser talent at the organ while the orchestra lolls in the Green Room, while at stated intervals a DeLuxe performance is given which is supposed to be the peak of the entertainment. The Chief Organist is seated at the Organ, the right foot planted on the Grand Crescendo Pedal, the leader's baton (pronounced battongh) is poised aloft—and the Overture (unit No. 1) is under way. This is ended with a storm of applause, the Chief Conductor bows, retires, and the assistant conductor takes charge during the News Reel which is unit No. 2. After the President has thrown the first baseball and all the battleships are launched, we come to Unit No. 3. This is the Organ Novelty. A spotlight is turned on the Chief Organist, a slide is thrown on the screen announcing the name and the featured music number, which "Why don't you kiss me when I pucker my lips," in six slides and two choruses played on the Sleigh-bells, Tibia, and Vox Humana.
>
> The slides are beautifully colored cartoons of the Mutt and Jeff type with a portion of the poem on each.
>
> We now come to Unit No. 4, a piece de resistance including some wild acrobatic dancing and still wilder singing, and always a ballet dancer and her partner. Her regulation costume seems to be some beads, quantities of white powder, and what is known among African Explorers as a breach clout. We are now treading dangerous ground and will pass on to Unit No. 5 which is the Feature Picture costing $1,000,000 to produce and takes 30 minutes to introduce the cast, directors, writers, fillum cutters, and 300 others vitally concerned with the production or the Super-Special.
>
> There is not much shooting. Probably only once. This is in the big scene and is carefully cued by the drummer and followed by quivering silence. We hasten now to say that somebody is clinched in somebody else's arms at the end and we reach the conclusion of a Presentation.[8]

Hugo Riesenfeld's presentations at two of the largest theaters in New York, the Rialto and Rivoli, followed the deluxe pattern outlined in this account. On May 2, 1920, for each of the four shows the overture was Goldmark's *Sakuntala.*

The orchestra at New York City's Roxy Theater, one of the most elaborate motion picture palaces. In addition to their accompanying films, these orchestras often played four concerts a day. When they finished, the stage upon which they sat would sink down out of sight. Museum of Modern Art, Film Stills Archive.

The first picture was *Shakleton's South Polar Expedition.* It was followed by a violin solo, Stahl's *Indian Beauty.* The next picture was a current film news pictorial. Then came Meyerbeer's "O paradiso" for tenor solo, followed by the feature film, *The Dancin' Fool* (Wood, 1920), and a comedy. The program concluded with an organ solo, Theodore Dubois's *Toccata.*[9]

In several of the deluxe theaters the show business went well beyond the entr'actes and musical accompaniments. Here is an account of the presentation of *The Thief of Bagdad* (Fairbanks, 1924):

Once more that worthy showman Mr. Sid Grauman has proved his genius in the presentation of this most remarkable picture at his Hollywood Theater. From the first step into the large court of the theater Bagdad atmosphere is rampant, so to speak. Life size paper elephants stand here and there swinging their bulky ears and emitting strange noises, probably begging for the succulent tuber which the visitor is forbidden to offer. Veiled sheikesses are mounted on the gaily decorated howdahs and others entertain with palmistry or that "Wish it was over" look. The oriental flutist and his tom tom assistant produce atmospheric music including the popular oriental ballad "It ain't goin' to rain no more" in their scant repertoire. The interior of the theater has been practically rebuilt and one does not have to even bother his imagination to find himself in an oriental city looking out on a Bagdad street, for here Mr. Grauman has introduced another innovation—the curtain is up, the natives are strolling along the street, and one hears a hidden flutist long before the prologue is presented.

The somewhat lengthy prologue is splendidly staged and the singing and dancing in the scene were very entertaining and most commendable.[10]

First class theaters generally had more seats (the Roxy in New York had 6,214),[11] charged higher prices for admission, and had larger orchestras and better organs. The second and third class houses were small, charged lower prices, showed shortened versions of some films, had smaller (or no) orchestras, smaller organs, more slapstick comedies, and often got the films long after their premieres.[12]

The Schedule and Working Conditions in Deluxe Movie Theaters

Theaters, whether deluxe or ordinary, would open at noon and close at midnight. In the early 1920s there might have been four shows a day, seven days a week. Toward the end of the era, there were more likely to be two shows. In deluxe houses the same feature film might run for months, as happened in 1923, for example, with the film *The Covered Wagon* (Famous Players Lasky, 1923). In the bigger houses, however, the shows probably changed twice a week on average. In the smaller theaters they changed every day!

And remember that by the word *show* we mean the five- to eight-unit program that was repeated four times each day. In 1927 some of the Broadway theaters instituted a midnight show as well.[13]

The pit orchestras in 1929 at the best houses cost between $3,000 and $10,000 a week. At the Roxy Theater the bill was between $15,000 and $20,000 a week.[14] The average first class house had an orchestra of between twenty and eighty players plus organ. The small orchestras consisted of six violins, two violas, two cellos, one bass, flute, oboe, clarinet, two horns, two trumpets, one trombone, drums, and piano. The large orchestras had full woodwind and brass sections, larger numbers of strings, harp, and percussion, and no piano.[15]

In 1920 the salaries of theater organists ranged from $1.50 to $2.50 an hour for from thirty to fifty hours of work a week.[16] In 1921 in New York all the movie palace musicians went on strike when the managers attempted to reduce their salaries to $56 a week, a 20 percent reduction. All the musicians were replaced. Only three of the six organists were rehired after the strike.[17] By 1926 the musicians in the Broadway houses were earning $83 a week, in the vaudeville houses $63 a week. It was said that one of the best New York theater organists had been offered $1,000 a week to play on the West Coast, but the average salary by 1929 was $75 to $125 a week. By that time only the famous Mr. and Mrs. Jesse Crawford, the organ playing team, commanded $500 to $1,000 a week.[18]

In 1922 Hugo Riesenfeld estimated that five hundred moving picture theaters had full orchestras.[19] The Rialto and Rivoli orchestras in New York each had forty-five players. Each theater had two organists. There were five conductors. In 1920, Riesenfeld's music budget for these two theaters and the Criterion Theater was $500,000. He estimated (perhaps on the high side) that five million people a year saw their productions. The public paid ten to fifty cents for admission[20] and over a dollar for deluxe presentations of special feature films like *The Thief of Bagdad*.[21]

Obviously, the instrumentalists at the Rialto and Rivoli could not play constantly for twelve hours a day. The schedule started at noon with two hours and ten minutes of solo organ. A five-minute break was followed by two hours of orchestra with organ. A fifteen-minute break was followed by organ alone for two hours. A thirty-minute break was followed by three hours of orchestra and organ followed by one and a half hours of organ alone. Additionally, during the orchestral periods the organ frequently gave the instrumentalists a fifteen- to thirty-minute break.

This schedule was followed regardless of what was on the screen, so it was common for the orchestra to stop in the middle of a film and for the organ to take up alone.[22] The switchover was disconcerting unless handled very carefully, which it frequently was not. No amount of care would allow a smooth transition between organ and orchestra if the organ had not been voiced properly. By 1921 the organ at the Rialto had been adjusted, but *The American Organist* reported that formerly it had been "10 feet out of tune" and that the woodwind section had turned purple in the face every time the organist had played the woodwind stops.[23]

It is not surprising that the six hours a day, seven days a week use caused the middle portions of the organ manuals at the Rialto to wear out and need replacement. It was estimated that in six months the average theater organ got as much use as a church organ did in twenty years.[24]

Theater Organs and Organists

During the First World War, droves of people used to go to the Rialto Theater in New York "just to hear and see Hugo Riesenfeld conduct a fine overture....the very best music for 50 cents a seat. This beat Carnegie Hall..."[25] As the silent film era progressed the unit orchestra or theater organ played an increasingly greater role in silent film accompaniment. Initially, the theaters with full orchestras employed church style pipe organs, known as "straight" organs, but eventually these organs were replaced by the dramatically more flexible Wurlitzer, Kimball, Morton, Moeller, and other makes of theater or "unit" organs.[26]

One difference between the two types of organ involved the unit organ's use of electrical circuitry to reuse part of a rank of pipes instead of adding another rank of pipes of the same size.[27] They frequently used a higher wind pressure, fewer ranks of pipes, and more percussion stops than comparable straight or church organs.

The heavily tremulated wind gave them their characteristic sound. The changeover from straight to unit organs was accompanied by a furious debate about the merits of unit versus straight organs.[28]

> Where the regular organ is dignified, sonorous, appealing, reverent, the theater organ shouts vengeance, frantically claws the enemy, wails with impassioned grief, screams with victory, sobs thickly with love, moans with remorse, cries like a baby, giggles like a young girl, does a Charleston, barks like a dog, and finally shoots itself with a bass drum.[29]

An increased reliance on the unit organ also brought several new musical developments, one of which was the original organ novelty. Before or between the films, the organist would accompany illustrated slides with a selection of popular tunes and would invite the audience to sing along.[30] Audiences loved the sing-alongs, which after the First World War spread from the West Coast all over the United States. In addition, many players of the unit organ film accompaniments drew more on popular songs and dance music than on the classical repertory. Their musical style was more generally accessible and associated with vaudeville. Many Easterners deplored these developments, the taste of West Coast theater organists, and the unit organ:

> The tones of this organ were...the kind you hear in the merry-go-round affair that makes you think the pipes must be screwed into the wind chest to keep them from blowing out. The whole sound a riot of immodest vulgarity that was an absolute shock to the senses and that made it impossible to fix your attention on the picture.[31]

Western organists on the other hand accused the Easterners of elitist snobbery.

> Some day, before long, there will be organized in the grand and glorious West from where I came a society of theater organists who will stand for the best in organs, music for the people and

S. L. ("Roxy") Rothapfel (1882-1931) and the Roxy Theater Organ. Gaudily decorated, these huge instruments could duplicate the sounds of bells, cymbals, castanets, tambourines, tom-toms, gongs, banjos, harpsichords and mandolins, and they would perfume the air with music. Museum of Modern Art, Film Stills Archive.

a helping hand instead of suppression such as this bunch of insects of New York City who are taking up banners under that magic word Society of Theater Organists—nice ladies all of you must be.[32]

Even theaters which had relied on the ubiquitous piano (or piano, drum set, and occasional violinist) began to purchase organs and feature an organ accompaniment. As a result, the demand for trained theater organists exceeded the supply. A school for theater organists was started in Chicago in 1921;[33] later one opened in Boston and two in New York.[34] In the twenties in the deluxe theaters the organs and the orchestras were placed on separate lifts which rose and fell for dramatic effect.

The impact of the first Organ solo presentation I heard [Jesse Crawford] play there [New York Paramount Theatre in

Times Square] over 40 years ago is indelibly imprinted on my memory. I had been brought up in a small Canadian town, and in January 1929 I went to New York to take a six month electrical course. The bright lights of Broadway fascinated me, but my first visit to the Paramount was without doubt one of my life's most memorable events. The lofty lobby with its beautiful staircase and the marble pillars was crowded, but I pushed on through to a seat in the center of the orchestra section. The picture had just finished, when from the left side of the orchestra pit rose a gorgeous ivory and gold Organ console, illuminated by brilliant arc spots. At the massive console, on the Howard seat, was the one and only Jesse Crawford. It seemed that I was completely surrounded by the most beautiful music. He took over the same musical number with which the picture had just finished, but the contrast in the tone quality was almost unbelievable. The gorgeous sound of this the greatest of all the Wurlitzers, in the full stereo of these shallow chambers, a near perfect acoustical environment, made the puny sounds of the screen characteristic of that period seem like a collection of tin cans by comparison.[35]

Organists like Iris Vining (San Francisco) improvised an accompaniment to each picture; others like Jesse Crawford played original scores or scores compiled from popular songs, dance tunes, and the light and serious classics. They played their accompaniments—whether improvisational or written out—before, during and after the pictures. C. Roy Carter of Los Angeles, California made the following claim:

> The tremendous popularity of the Pipe Organ in the Moving-Picture Theatre has undoubtedly put this wonderful instrument in the first place to stay as the most perfect accompaniment to the Silent Drama. Its superiority over the orchestra for this means is undisputed,

not only because of the Organs greater flexibility and range of tonal expression but because under the control of an artist it can do all and much more than a large orchestra, greatly surpassing it in power and grandeur and even variety of tone.[36]

Carter went on to describe how to imitate the following effects on the organ: "The Snore, Laughter, Yell or Scream, The Kiss, R.R. Train, Aeroplane, Thunder and Rain Storm, Steam Whistle, Policeman's or Other Shrill Whistle, Prize-Fight, Gong, Dog Bark, Dog Yelp, Cat Meow, Lion Roar, Cow's Moo, Rooster Crow, Pig Grunt, Cuckoo, Bag Pipes, Music Box, Banjo, Hand Organ, Accordion-Harmonica, Telegraph-Typewriter."[37]

By 1924 many organists from the deluxe theaters were featured regularly on the radio.[38] After 1929, some theater organists continued as accompanists for radio.

The Music Director in Deluxe Theaters—Hugo Riesenfeld

During the silent film era the music director of a theater played an important role in determining the quality of the film accompaniment. In the deluxe theaters the music director controlled a large staff of musicians. Several conductors and accompanists helped with the selection of music as well as with its performance. In the smaller theaters the music director might be the only musician, either an organist or a pianist. Those that had the time controlled the selection of music and its execution, particularly its volume and synchronization. Hugo Riesenfeld described the process of musical selection in his deluxe theaters:

> I resort mainly for themes to the songs of the period of the particular film for which I am arranging the score. For instance, with the *Rough Riders,* I have taken "Hot Time in the Old Town Tonight," "Break the News to Mother," "Good-Bye Dolly Gray," and "The Blue and The Gray," as themes. Some of these, to be sure, were old before the [Spanish-American] war, but the others sprang into popularity during it... When arranging a certain score, I usually

Hugo Riesenfeld (1879-1939), Viennese-born music director and composer. In the United States he was perhaps the most prominent of the musicians who worked with silent films. Before becoming the musical director of the Rialto, Rivoli, and Criterion Movie Theaters in New York, he had been a violinist in the Vienna Opera Orchestra and concertmaster for the Manhattan Opera House Orchestra. *The American Organist* (May 1920) labelled his movie music productions "photoplays deluxe." An estimated five million people a year attended his performances, and his orchestras achieved a distinction which, according to Riesenfeld's assessment, equalled that of the New York Philharmonic. Music Division, Library of Congress.

divide the film into sections according to moods. For instance, sentimental, pastoral, dramatic, heavy...ominous, or—even every day life. Then I have hundreds of compositions representative of the pastoral, the dramatic, etc. My course is to go through these and eliminate. My leading themes come in between these miscellaneous selections and may be as elaborate or as simple as the action requires. Once, perhaps, they are heroic; again sentimental, then allegro—all sorts of variations of the same theme...[39]

In this very general account Riesenfeld alludes to the theme songs associated with silent film accompaniments. Sometimes these songs were not just "of the period of the particular film" but original compositions. They became quite popular, just as they do today, and were used to sell the picture (although sometimes the picture sold them). "Charmaine" from *What Price Glory* (Fox, 1926) and "Diane" from *7th Heaven* (Fox, 1927) sold over a million copies. "Ramona" was credited with contributing to *Ramona*'s (Inspiration Pictures, 1928) $1 million gross.[40] The sheet music covers of the theme songs often featured photographs of the actors or stills from the movies themselves.

Riesenfeld's account is not very specific about either theme songs or what went into the synchronization of music and movies. T. Scott Buhrman, editor of *The American Organist,* describes Riesenfeld's selection and synchronization procedures in far more detail:

To visit a projection room during the musical scoring of a film is an interesting experience. At one end of a twelve by thirty-foot room is a screen possibly six feet square; in the wall at the opposite end are two holes for the machines and two for the operators to peep through or stick their heads through for an occasional conference with the director: directly under these holes are half a dozen comfortable wicker chairs with a long table-like bench conveniently in front and a swinging phone within grabbing distance; to the right is an upright piano; around the walls are cabinets of piano scores and violin scores all carefully assorted under proper heads, "love scenes," "home scenes," "waltzes," "Russian," "Overtures," "suites," "military marches," etc., ad infinitum; and in the ceiling is an electric light of excellent power which keeps going full force through the entire operation.

"There are millions of ways," says Hugo Riesenfeld, who scores all the pictures of the Rialto, Rivoli, and Criterion programs, "of selecting music to serve as accompaniment for a picture, but there are only two ways that a good musician would choose. One is to select beautiful music that is appropriate for the scenes of the picture, and the good musician, inexperienced in motion picture presentation would undoubtedly follow this course. The second course, and the one that requires the hardest work, is to select music such as would be chosen in the first mentioned way, but with an ear to subjugation. There may be half a hundred waltzes that would go prettily with certain scenes, but the experienced scorer of motion pictures will, after listening to the piece, know whether it is too striking—or even too beautiful." And all through the few hours when I had the privilege of observing the scoring process under Mr. Riesenfeld's magic hand, I witnessed this "subjugation" in actual fact. "Not so fast," "Slower, please," "Oh, not so fast," "Take it this way," and the director would hum the tune or whistle it or beat it out on the table with his thumb; in every case the music was "toned down," "subjugated" to the picture. Had it not been done I imagine the effect would have been one of frivolity, if not completely grotesque; but subjugated in this way, and ultimately in many other ways of which only Hugo Riesenfeld can give the clue, music of the most attractive kind—attractive to musicians—lends itself admirably to the screen.

The success of the Riesenfeld productions is not only a matter of the films selected; I question if the films

have even fifty per cent of the credit. In fact I know of one case where Mr. Riesenfeld scored a picture, after cutting up the film and showing it as he wanted instead of as the producers photographed it, with success, while the same picture in its original form under the management of other producers in other houses fell a failure.

At half after ten on a Monday night, when most people were beginning to seal up their day as well done and turn their thoughts to hot or cold showers according to taste, and feather pillows, I got safely by the guards (an iron gate that works with difficulty) and climbed two flights of stairs at Broadway and 42nd Street. In the director's private projection room were already gathered the operators, conductors, pianist, and librarian, with Mr. Riesenfeld seated in his comfortable chair ready to "make" another Riesenfeld production. Mr. Riesenfeld had already seen the picture once, of course, so he began his search for music of a certain well defined type. Piece after piece (only a little of each, of course) was played on the piano as this or that conductor would pick out one as a suggestion, and all that could be gotten out of Mr. Riesenfeld was "No," "Not that," "No, that won't do," "Oh, no, not that" — and all the while the cameras were waiting to click their first inch of the film, not a picture as yet having gone to the screen; the director had his head stuck deep in a folio of possibly two hundred selections of a given type, every one of which he glanced through in his search for the "right" one. Finally it was found; and what a relief. "Slower; oh, not so fast," then "Ah, that's it, that's it," and the ready amanuensis jotted down a few abbreviations to show that when the picture was ready to begin the music would be this piece, and that so much of it would be used. A mark was put lightly on the score. All that work for about sixty seconds' worth of music! To the question, "What is Hugo Riesenfeld.?" we might answer, "Infinite capacity for taking pains." The piece, before being laid aside, was again played on the piano at proper tempo, that is at Mr. Riesenfeld's own tempo; the director pushed the button, the picture announcement began, and I almost thought I was going to see a free picture show this time. But no, I read some words announcing the title of the picture, and some other words telling who photographed it, and still more words advising me all about the people who acted in it; and then the fatal button was pressed and the "show" stopped. Then the search for music began all over again. Soon something was tried which pleased Director Riesenfeld and as the pianist started to play it again the button was pressed and the picture resumed its course just where it left off. That is, resumed it for another two seconds till the emotions of the screen drama changed and with it changed the emotions of this highly-strung bit of human machinery who controlled the fatal button — and the picture went dead again till some new bit of music could be found to suit the new emotions…And this only tells a small part of the story; it forgets all about the cuts, the arrangements, the slides and glides and skips and hops through all musicdom in order to make these things go together in a proper sequence of keys as one piece.

After little snatches of the film are thus projected and music fitted intimately with the moods of each, with proper record made of each separate bit of film and the music corresponding with it, Mr. Riesenfeld takes the music under his wing and spends laborious hours over it, marking, timing, cutting, trimming, fitting and preparing it to time rightly with the film. When this is done and the librarians and orchestrators have arranged and written such things as are needed for the film, the film itself is taken in hand for revision. Projection machines can be made to

run at variable speeds to suit the occasion, and these speeds can be arbitrarily set by a projector without interfering in any way with the picture; I doubt if any but a very skilled man would be able to detect the many changes Mr. Riesenfeld must get from his operators. Many times the titles and joints in the film are deleted to just the right amount to make the film time exactly with the music, while at other times, the speed accomplishes the result. Thus after the music is first fitted to the picture, the picture is then fitted exactly to the music.[41]

Riesenfeld's library consisted of 6,000 orchestral scores and thousands of pieces of unorchestrated music. In the scoring of the film *Everywoman* (Paramount, 1919) he and his four conductors "worked four full hours merely on the selection of music for one of the eight reels, one eighth of the film."[42] At the peak of the silent film era, the Loew's Theater chain employed six hundred orchestral musicians and two hundred organists of which almost a hundred organists were in New York City. Their music library alone consisted of 50,000 scores, and their music department sent out 167 compiled scores with parts per week.[43]

Musical Repertory in the Deluxe Movie Palaces

In addition to the accompaniments for the films, deluxe theaters presented every kind of music imaginable before and between the films. A list follows of the orchestral overtures conducted by Hugo Riesenfeld between 1918 and 1921. They were played at the beginning of each of the four shows, seven days a week, either by the orchestra, the organ, or both.

Orchestral Overtures Played at the Rialto Theater New York, 1918–July 1921[44]

Von Suppe—Pique Dame	January 6, 1918
Wagner—Lohengrin	January 13
Goldmark—Queen of Sheba	January 20
Wagner—Tannhaeuser	January 27

Liszt—Symphonic Poem No. 3	February 3
Rimsky-Korsakov—Capriccio Espagnol	February 10
Goldmark—In the Spring	February 24
Tchaikowsky—Capriccio Italien	March 3
Tchaikowsky—Romeo and Juliet	April 7
Verdi—Aida	April 21
Liszt—Mazeppa	April 28
Rimsky-Korsakov—Semiramide	May 5
Rimsky-Korsakov—Scheherazade	May 19
Verdi—Sicilian Vespers	May 26
Massenet—Manon	June 23
Tchaikowsky—Symphony No. 4 (movements 2, 4)	August 4
Verdi—Rigoletto	August 11
Tchaikowsky—Solonelle [1812]	September 8
Dvorak—New World Symphony (movement 2, finale)	September 15
Rimsky-Korsakov—Capriccio Espagnol	October 6
Tchaikowsky—Pathetique finale	October 13
Rossini—William Tell	October 20
Liszt—Second Rhapsody	October 27
Liszt—Sixth Rhapsody	December 1
Saint-Saëns—Danse Macabre	December 8
Goldmark—Sakuntala	December 15
Beethoven—Leonora No. 3	January 19, 1919
Liszt—First Rhapsody	January 26
Tchaikowsky—March Slav	February 9
Sibelius—Finlandia	February 16
Gounod—Faust	February 23
Thomas—Mignon	March 2
Liszt—Les Preludes	April 6
Herbert—Natoma	April 13
Liszt—Second Rhapsody	April 20
Balfe—Bohemian Girl	May 4
Tchaikowsky—Romeo and Juliet	May 18
Weber—Euryanthe	June 1
Mendelssohn—Midsummer Night's Dream	June 15
Liszt—Thirteenth Rhapsody	July 6
Massenet—Manon	July 13
Weber—Freischuetz	August 3
Verdi—Aida	August 10
Saint-Saëns—Spinning Wheel [Le Rouet d'Omphale	August 17
Liszt—Ideale	August 31

Wagner—Tannhauser	September 21
Tchaikowsky—1812 Overture	September 28
Rossini—William Tell	October 5
Goldmark—Sakuntala	October 12
Verdi—La Traviata	October 19
Liszt—Sixth Rhapsody	November 16
Tchaikowsky—March Slav	November 23
Weber—Oberon	November 30
Liszt—In Vienna	December 14
Liszt—First Rhapsody	December 28
Wagner—Rienzi	January 4, 1920
Dvorak—Carneval	February 15
Mascagni—Hymn to Sun	March 14
Liszt—Les Preludes	April 11
Liszt—Sixth Rhapsody	April 18
Mendelssohn—Ruy Blas	April 25
Tchaikowsky—Capriccio Italien	May 16
Liszt—Second Rhapsody	May 23
Wagner—Tristan	June 6
Massenet—Phaedre	June 20
Thomas—Mignon	June 27
Mendelssohn—Midsummer Night's Dream	July 4
Rimsky-Korsakov—Scheherazade	July 11
Massenet—Manon	July 18
Goldmark—Queen of Sheba	August 29
Liszt—Fourth Rhapsody	September 5
Verdi—Aida	September 12
Rossini—William Tell	September 19
Wagner—Tannhauser	October 3
Weber—Euryanthe	October 10
Tchaikowsky—March Slav	October 17
Mortimer Wilson—New Orleans (A $500 first prize overture composed by Mr. Wilson for the Hugo Riesenfeld competition, conducted by Mr. Wilson at the first presentation of this week)	[October 24?]
Wagner—Lohengrin	October 31
Goldmark—Sakuntala	November 7
Liszt—Thirteenth Rhapsody	November 28
Wagner—Die Meistersinger	December 5
Wagner—Rienzi	January 2, 1921
Elgar—Pomp and Circumstance	February 6
Tchaikowsky—1812 Overture	February 13
Liszt—Les Preludes	February 20
Weber—Freischuetz	February 27

Liszt—First Rhapsody	March 20
Liszt—Ideale	March 27
Rossini—Barber of Seville	April 3
von Suppé—Poet and Peasant	April 10
Liszt—Sixth Rhapsody	April 17
Liszt—Second Rhapsody	May 29
Gounod—Faust	June 19
Massenet—Phèdre	June 26
Auber—Masaniello	July 10
Verdi—La Forza del Destino	July 17
Massenet—Manon	July 24
von Suppé—Beautiful Galatea	July 31

In addition to these overtures, in 1920 Riesenfeld presented fifteen-minute operatic selections.[45] At other times there were xylophone novelties, barber shop quartets, Miss Ruth Brewer playing fourteen instruments,[46] Ben Bernie and his jazz band in 1925 at the Rialto for a half-hour entertainment, and Eddie Elkins's jazz band in 1926.[47] There was a piano trio (three pianists) playing Rimsky-Korsakoff's *Song of India* and Ray Henderson's *Georgette*.[48] Sometimes drummer Max H. Manne would be the featured soloist; sometimes it would be a harmonica player.[49]

On one occasion a pianist, Carlo Marx, was featured playing Liszt's *Concerto in E Flat* which the reviewer reported was "applauded more heartily than any of the more or less elaborate opera excerpts have been for many months."[50] Percy Grainger played and sold Duo-Art pianos for a week at the Capitol Theater in 1921.[51] On another occasion, in 1925, Hugo Riesenfeld had a string quartet play on rare instruments for a week during a New York convention of violin makers.[52]

Some of the most famous musical interludes played between films were Riesenfeld's own arrangements of what he called "Classical Jazz." For the program of March 26, 1923,

> Riesenfeld staged a "Classical Jazz" performance that showed the close connection of Jazz with what is known popularly as "the classics"—…Mr. Riesenfeld dug up four good melodies from Chopin, Gounod, and Puccini, had his orchestra play them as scored by "legitimate" musicians, and then had the

orchestra play Jazz selections which were apparently built wholesale on them.[53]

These performances were often elaborately staged and lighted. The following is another account from 1923:

> One of the players…was playing a sweet little solo tune accompanied by the rest of the orchestra, and he was required to stand while playing, the spot light being thrown on his musicianly form. When he finished, the spot-light went out and he sat down; but then the composer began playing with the theme the soloist had just finished, treating it contrapuntally and chasing snatches of it hither and thither among the various instruments and groups of instruments; as each player or group of players got the melody or snatch to play, they bobbed up double quick, played their snatch, the spot-light picked them up with a shot and went out as they finished the snatch and sat down; the whole thing going like lightning, with players bobbing up all around, and spot-lights shooting out like fire-flies, brought down the house with a roar.[54]

The Failings of Films and Accompanists

Theater musicians could change the film directors' intentions by varying the speed of the projectors, by reorganizing the films' sequences or by deleting whole scenes. More frequently, however, through their choice of the entr'actes and movie accompaniments photoplayers could reinforce or contradict intended dramatic context, emotional effects, film rhythms, scenic structure, and the overall pacing of films. Their accompaniments could simulate speech patterns, accents, calls and responses, and could move people and conjure up associations; in other words, they could become an almost living, independent character commenting on the pantomimed drama on the screen. At their best, film accompaniments could intensify the effects and reinforce the inherent structures of a good film. For the average film, however, the desired effect for music was different, according to an article in *The Metronome.*[55]

> What the enthusiastic protagonists of musical intepretation of motion pictures persist in overlooking really is the crux of the whole situation. Motion picture masterpieces are exceedingly rare, while the lurid "hoakum" of the picture screen is plastered in a thick and viscid layer over a large part of the habitable globe. It is right here that the lavish application of music truly justifies itself—as an anaesthetic. At the present stage of enlightenment of motion picture patrons, the experienced picture showman does not dream of opening his program until the audience has been rendered insensible to pain. He can't very well chloroform his paying patrons, so he employs the seductive, and equally efficacious, anaesthetic known as music. By the time the screen reveals the first sticky close-up of the brave and noble-minded hero, Hercules Hoakum, and of our very own precious sweet and tearful heroine, Lotta Bunk, the audience has been filled so full of the Bach-Gounod Ave Maria or In the Gloaming that it actually would enjoy an operation for appendicitis where it sits. From this on, comparatively small quantities of musical anaesthetic are guaranteed to transform what normally would be the most unbearable mental anguish into a condition of celestial beatitude.

Most film accompanists were not as patient, thorough, or gifted as Hugo Riesenfeld or as organized as the Loew's theater music department. Not unexpectedly, their musical mistakes were numerous.[56] Under the heading "Misfits," May Meskimen Mills warned novice theater organ players about such pitfalls:

> If you are playing pictures, do so intelligently. To give you an idea of how easily a wrong number can be chosen for a scene, a man and a woman were shown on the screen in each other's embrace. The organist began playing a silly love song, only to find that the couple were brother and sister. Here is another

example: during the late war, an army of soldiers were shown marching in the distance. Immediately the organist began playing "Three Cheers for the Red, White and Blue." Naturally the audience rose to their feet only to find that they were greeting an army of German soldiers instead. The audience seeing the mistake gradually slipped into their seats but the organist tore madly through the number not noticing the difference. I once heard in a prominent theatre in one of the Eastern cities, an organist play "I Am Always Chasing Rainbows" when Salome was chasing John the Baptist in the picture. There is no logical reason for one playing a drinking song such as "How Dry I Am" on an echo or catherdral chimes. Yet you hear it done and many other things equally as ridiculous. Persons of good taste would not be seen in a bathing suit at a church wedding, yet players do just as absurd things in the fitting of pictures.[57]

There were often complaints about incompetent organists.[58] Orchestras and organs were often accused of being too loud.[59] Brass often did not play during the feature films on Broadway because they could not play softly enough. Strings were considered the one tone quality most audiences could stand for any length of time.[60] Some claimed that the average theater orchestra could be beaten by any live theater organist with a halfway acceptable organ.[61] Vocalists were vilified:

> The vocal solos were diaphramatic writings on da-me-ni-po, or some equally intelligent sounds, so over-accompanied by the orchestra that it was fortunately not compulsory to listen to the vocal gurglings much of the time.[62]

The changeover between the playing by the orchestra and that by the organ could be ghastly:

> Some conductors stop the orchestra anywhere in a number, like applying the

emergency brakes at full speed. Sometimes, not trusting the men to watch
them, they snap out the lights suddenly
which makes the score a series of jolts
and jars.[63]

And the synchronization could be terrible:

> The music should be as closely joined to
> the picture as in the Phono-film, where
> the two cannot become separated…We
> often hear the organist, after the cue for
> a change has appeared, end the previous
> number rather indecisively, ramble
> around in a few aimless chords, fix the
> stops and finally float into something fit-
> ting the scene—when it is half over.[64]

On the other hand, the conditions for photoplayers were not ideal either.

> The conservatories which turned out
> graduates for the theater…overlooked
> some important details. [The graduates]
> had never been taught under the condi-
> tions which [they] had to face later in
> actual experience. [They] had never
> been taught to play a Chopin Nocturne
> "with great feeling" while accompanied
> by extraneous sounds such as peanut
> cracking, ribald jeers, and popping
> gum…[65]

There were some directors, like D. W. Griffith
and Douglas Fairbanks, Sr., who controlled the
musical accompaniments that went with their
films and thereby attempted to control the affect
their films had on the public. More often than
not, however, movie directors had almost no time
to think about music, and individual musicians
had no time to do anything but keep playing.
Through the amount of time and money they had
and were willing to spend, music directors and
theater managers, more than any other people,
controlled the type and quality of accompaniment given to each picture. From the accounts of
the Rialto and Rivoli theaters in New York, it is
clear that Hugo Riesenfeld exemplified the outstanding music director.

Theater Managers and Film Music

Some of the theater managers also are
legends: S. L. Rothapfel ("Roxy") in New York
and Sid Grauman in Los Angeles. Rothapfel, when
at the Capitol Theater in New York, employed the
then unknown Eugene Ormandy, first as the
concert master of his orchestra and then as its
conductor.[66] Later he opened the enormous and
short-lived cathedral of movie palaces, the Roxy,
where his musical expenses were as elephantine
as everything else about the theater's operations.
In 1927 he offerred classical violinist Fritz
Kreisler $12,500 for one week's appearance.[67]

These legendary managers were exceptional.
The problems presented by the run-of-the-mill
theater managers are summarized in an article
entitled "Managers of Heavenly Descent: Photoplaying isn't an art but the enjoyment of an
investment. They bought the darned things and
pay us to use them. Full steam ahead and no pax
vobiscum."[68]

> there is, sad to say, a larger class about
> whom nothing praiseworthy can be said
> except that they know the film market.
> These are the Bad Boys who make the
> organist take to drink, go back to the
> dance orchestra, or start selling vacuum
> cleaners at back doors…
>
> My first indictment against them is
> that they think the organ is a great deal
> like the furnace; once bought you need
> do nothing more to it than engage
> someone to run it. Maybe tune it once
> every two years or so, and then again
> maybe not. Who can tell the difference?
> …The only thing that will make a dent in
> his code of laisser faire is a cipher on
> the 16' Trombone, assuming for the
> moment the unlikely possibility that the
> organ has a 16' Trombone…
>
> The luckless organist innocently
> enters [the manager's office] with a
> confident request for service to get this
> Trombone cipher fixed…"What!" yells
> the outraged boss, "I should pay five dol-
> lars for a one pipe to fix? What kind
> organist are you that don't know how to
> fix one pipe?"…
>
> This unexpected cataclysm presents
> three alternatives to the organist. He can

either go back to the job and pretend the cipher is the noise of some motor on the premises, or he can play all his music in that key and pretend it requires a sustained Pedal Point on that note, or he can leave the picture flat while he climbs into the organ chamber, tears his pants, bumps his head, gets dirt all over his hands and clothes and a smudge on his nose, and wrastles with the Grampa of Trombone pipes, knocking the tuning slide a minor third out of pitch, stepping on a few small pipes getting in and out, and leaving an eight-inch pressure leak that will be handy for the tornado episodes in the picture but slightly annoying the rest of the time…

Managers who thus reduce overhead by eliminating necessary organ repairs can logically do so on no other grounds than that music is a necessary evil endured only so that the show will not be run in dead silence. Granting this assumption, it then becomes good business to keep the music going at a minimum of expense, with quality a perfectly extraneous factor…

The whole philosophy is similar to that of a manager I once knew who installed a ventilating system that proved to be more expensive than efficient. Instead of an indirect system which unobtrusively freshened and renewed the air, there was an enormous fan above the proscenium which blew such a draft down upon the heads of the patrons that it was no uncommon thing to see strong men sitting there with overcoats on and collars turned up, and even hats on if there was no one directly behind to object. It is a fact that heavy velvet draperies at the front of the house were blown out and held at a conspicuous angle from the floor. Furthermore, the air, which was sucked in from the roof, was hot in hot weather and cold in cold weather, with the natural result that the fan could always be relied on to make the inside temperature more uncomfortable than that on the street. …"Hadn't we better stop the fan, sir?"

said the electrician one chilly day. "The house is down to 65, and we're getting complaints." I herewith append the [manager's] reply for what it is worth: "Keep that fan going. I'm going to give 'em their twenty thousand dollars' worth of ventillation if I have to freeze 'em to their seats." Thus with the music.[69]

Clearly, music in the silent film era was as prominent as the images, for better or for worse.

At the beginning of the silent film era, music had been used to mask the sound of the projector and to offset the "ghostliness" of the images. For the most part the accompaniments were a stream of accompanying sound.[70] Often they were a string of popular tunes or what some people uncharitably referred to as commercialized noise.[71] By the 1920s in many theaters sophisticated accompaniments were being used to achieve a full range of effects, and direct control over a film's accompaniment could be achieved through the distribution of cue sheets, compiled scores, and original scores.

Cue Sheets

In 1909 the *New York Daily Mirror* reported that the Edison and Vitagraph companies had been circulating printed programs of instrumental music suitable as accompaniment to their films.[72] Between 1910 and 1912 movie companies, music publishers, and the trade press began to make and distribute musical cue sheets for films.[73] Cue sheets presented a list of film actions and intertitles in the order in which they appeared in the film. After each cue or title there was a timed reference to a specific musical composition which in a sort of shorthand referred to a specific publication. Vast series of incidental music, timed and classified by mood and tempo (such as "Highly dramatic agitato" and "Agitato furioso"), were published to meet the needs of photoplayers.[74] Cue sheet compilers relied heavily on these series.[75]

Cue sheets thus could save time and provide a modicum of musical control. However, the quality of the cue sheets was a source of debate among experienced photoplayers, some of whom

Thematic Music Cue Sheet

M. J. MINTZ (PATENT)
JULY 31, 1923

RAMON NOVARRO
in
ACROSS TO SINGAPORE

with

Joan Crawford and Ernest Torrence
A William Nigh Production
From the book "All the Brother Were Valiant"
By Ben Ames Williams
Adaptation by Ted Shane
Continuity by Richard Schayer
Directed by William Nigh
Compiled by Ernst Luz

A METRO-GOLDWYN-MAYER PICTURE
Length of film 7 reels (6720 feet)   Maximum projection time 1 hour, 22 minutes

1 AT SCREENING ....Symphonic Color Classic No. 5 (Marquardt) (YELLOW)....1½ Min.

Comodo

Copyr. 1925 Music Buyers Corp.

2 (Title) AMONG THE UNSUNG DEEDS ....A. B. C. Dram. Set No. 13-A1 (Luz) ....1¼ Min.

Allo viro

Copyr. 1916 Photo Play Mus. Co

3 (Title) SWIM ....A. B. C. Dram. Set No. 13-B2 (Luz) ....½ Min.

Adagio

Copyr. 1916 Photo Play Mus. Co

4 (Title) IT WAS THE BEST ....Symphonic Color Classic No. 5 (Marquardt) (GREEN).......1 Min.

Modo

Copyr. 1925 Music Buyers Corp.

5 (Action) LOVERS STAND UP—SHIP SHOWS...........Ship Ahoy (Frey) ....1¼ Min.

March

Copyr. 1927 Robbins Music Corp.

6 (Title) THE LOG OF ....Mariette (Sterny) ....1 Min.

Allo

Copyr. 1911 Ed. B. Marks & Co

7 (Title) MARSE CROWNINSHIELD IS HERE...../....Dutch Fishergirls (Fresco) ....2 Min.

Valse

Copyr. 1925 Belwin Inc

NOTE: Play introduction and Waltz.

8 (Action) BOY UPSETS GLASS OF WINE ....Social Chat (Eugene) ....2 Min.

Alleo

Copyr. 1926 Em. Ascher

**9 (Action) FATHER CARRIES BOY FROM DINING
ROOM** ....Symphonic-Color Classic No. 5 (Marquardt) (DK. BLUE)...1½ Min.

Allo

Copyr. 1925 Music Buyers Cor

XXX

argued that cue sheets were only useful to the completely inexperienced movie accompanist and then only if they were by cue sheet compiler S. M. Berg.[76]

The cue sheets did have drawbacks. If a musician did not have a piece cited by the cue sheet, a substitution had to be made. An enormous library of incidental music was required. All the music needed to be assembled and arranged. Often only two minutes of a five-minute piece were called for and harmonic transitions from one key to another were lacking. The arrangement process took time. Sometimes the cue sheet was incomplete, and sometimes the taste of the cue sheet's compiler would differ from that of the photoplayer. Often the cue sheets appeared in print too late for big city screenings of the films.[77] And if the same music library was used over and over again, the accompaniments became monotonous.

The cue sheet for Ramon Novarro's *Across to Singapore* (MGM, 1928) is an example of the shorthand employed by cue sheet compilers to present the organization of the film and the music that was to fit it. The cue sheet begins with the notation "1 AT SCREENING...*Symphonic Color Classic No. 5* (Marquardt) (YELLOW)...1½ Min." Six measures of music follow and conclude with "Copyr. 1925 Music Buyers Corp." Item 2 is "(Title) AMONG THE UNSUNG DEEDS...*A.B.C. Dram. Set No. 13-A1* (Luz)...1¼ Min." Another six measures of music follow and conclude with "Copyr. 1916 Photo Play Mus. Co." Item 3 is "(Title) SWIM...*A.B.C. Dram. Set No. 13-B2* (Luz)...½ Min." Seven measures of music follow and conclude with "Copyr. 1916 Photo Play Mus. Co." Item 4 is "(Title) IT WAS THE BEST...*Symphonic Color Classic No. 5* (Marquardt) (GREEN)...1 Min." which is followed by seven

Cue sheet for *Across to Singapore* (1928). Upon receipt of this cue sheet, a theater organist or pianist could either improvise an accompaniment, using the themes and timings provided, or could compile a score by assembling the listed sources, such as *Symphonic Color Classic No. 5* and *A.B.C. Dramatic Set No. 13-B2*. Such sources were individual numbers in the vast collections of incidental music for theater orchestras. Museum of Modern Art, Film Music Collection.

measures of music and concludes with "Copyr. 1925 Music Buyers Corp." and so on for forty-seven segments.

These shorthand notations translate into the following:

AT SCREENING—P. A. Marquardt. *A Twentieth Century Romance* (N.Y., Music Buyers Corp., 1925; No. 5 in the Series *Symphonic Color Classics*), fifth movement (YELLOW). Over 80 measures of music to fit 90 seconds of film. Arranged for full or small orchestra (the latter: flute, clarinet, 2 cornets, trombone, timpani/drums, violin I and II, viola, cello, bass, and piano).

AMONG THE UNSUNG DEEDS—Ernst Luz. *Agitato-Hurry* (N.Y., Photoplay Music Co., 1916; No. 13 in the series *A.B.C. Dramatic Set*), first section. 117 measures to fit 75 seconds of film. Arranged for flute, clarinet, 2 cornets, trombone, drums/timpani, violins I and II, viola, cello, bass, piano, and organ.

SWIM—Ernst Luz. *Plaintive* (N.Y., Photoplay Music Co., 1916; No. 13 in the series *A.B.C. Dramatic Set*), second section. 16 measures to fit 30 seconds of film. With published parts as above for AMONG THE UNSUNG DEEDS.

IT WAS THE BEST—P. A. Marquardt. *A Twentieth Century Romance* (N.Y., Music Buyers Corp., 1925; No. 5 in series *Symphonic Color Classics*), fourth movement (GREEN). 48 measures to fit 60 seconds of film. Arranged for full or small orchestra with published parts as above in cue AT SCREENING.

and so forth.

With such cue sheets and a vast library of incidental music (the *A.B.C. Dramatic Set* exceeded twenty-five numbers and many series had over one hundred separate numbers), theater musicians could concoct the musical accompaniments specified by the movie producers, music publishers, or the makers of cue sheets. If they had a full orchestra and all the printed parts, they could put together a compilation of music that followed the cue sheet exactly. They could use as many or as few instruments as they had on hand, or they could even improvise on the themes that were printed on some cue sheets instead of sticking to the printed arrangements.

Cue sheets left a lot of room for individual variation, but they also left a lot to be desired. For the photoplayer who performed four shows a day in a theater whose pictures changed every day or two, there could never be enough time to put together a compiled score of any sort, much less to screen each new film before accompanying it. Often, too, during their travels through the theaters, films were damaged. The damaged sections were cut, and the remaining sections were spliced together. After a while cue sheets no longer contained an accurate representation of the films' timings or even of their organization.

Compiled and Original Scores

A few directors obtained a somewhat greater degree of control over their musical accompaniments by commissioning and circulating scores with their films. This practice may have begun quite early. Charles Gilbert reported that the Film Division of the Australian National Library in Canberra was presented with the original score written for *Soldiers of the Cross,* a 3000-foot film made by the Salvation Army in Melbourne in 1900. T. M. F. Steen submits that the earliest example of original film music must be Gaston Paulin's 1892 score for Emile Reynaud's *Pantomimes Lumineuses.* Camille Saint-Saëns wrote an original score for the ten-minute *L'Assassinat du Duc de Guise* (1908). Thomas Dixon may have been the first American producer to commission an original score (from Victor Herbert for *The Fall of a Nation* in 1916). However, Walter Cleveland Simon may have been the first American to compose an original film score, for *Arrah Na Pough* (1911).[78]

The practice of hiring a composer to compile a score from preexisiting classical and popular music and of circulating the score with the picture was continued most notably in the late teens and early twenties by D. W. Griffith. Like cue sheets, these scores were liberally sprinkled with action and intertitles. Instead of the timings (one and one-half minutes of x music, 30 seconds of y,

etc.), there were metronome markings (Section X will go at the quarter note equals 120, Section Y at eighth note equals 96, etc.). All these devices were intended to help the conductor stay in sync with the film.

D. W. Griffith, *The Birth of a Nation,* and *Way Down East*

D. W. Griffith was one of the first American directors to maintain careful control over the selection and distribution of the musical accompaniment for his films.[79] They premiered in only one city at a time. He travelled with the film and the orchestral parts to each new theater, overseeing the whole presentation of each new premiere. He participated in the selection of the music, and then organized the images, the music, and the sound effects for his film presentations. He firmly established the practice of using a full orchestral accompaniment in American movie theaters. Musically, he also may have been the most knowledgeable of the early directors. Karl Brown in *Adventures with D. W. Griffith* tells many stories about Griffith's knowledge of music:

> Griffith's personal habits of shadowboxing, dancing whenever Miss Geesh [Lillian Gish] was available, or singing at the top of his lungs went on as usual. Up to this picture he had been content to sing the most effective parts of the more flamboyant operatic arias. Canio's famous "Vesti la giubba," from *I Pagliacci,* got a thorough working over, but only in open tones, not Italian. He would sometimes also observe, in full voice, that the stars were brightly shining, this from *Tosca.*
>
> Another time Griffith's obsession with music showed itself was when we took a very long shot of the battlefield strewn with dead and with Lillian Gish running from corpse to corpse, looking for her beloved. Correction: she fluttered from corpse to corpse. A lot of little quick steps, a pause, a look, then some more quick little fluttering steps, another look, and so on. It was during the making of this scene that Griffith exclaimed, with a sense of sudden inspiration, that the Lohengrin Wedding March, the

Joseph Carl Breil (1870-1926), composer of scores for D. W. Griffith's *Birth of a Nation* and *Intolerance,* as well as one of the first American scores composed for a screen drama, *Queen Elizabeth* (1912). Prints and Photographs Division, Library of Congress.

familiar "Here comes the bride," was in exactly the same time and rhythm of the equally familiar Funeral March from the Chopin sonata. It seemed to astonish him that two such opposite sentiments, the extreme of happiness and extreme grief, should be couched in exactly the same musical terms, except that one was in the major mode, the other in the minor.[80]

On the opening night of *The Birth of a Nation* (1914), Brown heard both of these tunes in the accompaniment for this scene.

Griffith not only knew a lot about music, he knew enough to be able to articulate his desires to composer Joseph Carl Breil during the production of *The Birth of a Nation*.

The two men had many disagreements over the scoring of the film. "If I ever kill anyone," Mr. Griffith once said, "it won't

be an actor but a musician." The greatest dispute was over the Klan call, which
was taken from "The Ride of the Valkyries" by Richard Wagner. Mr. Griffith
wanted a slight change in the notes. Mr.
Breil fought against making it.

　　"You can't tamper with Wagner!" he
protested. "It's never been done!"

　　This music wasn't *primarily* music,
Mr. Griffith explained. It was music for
motion pictures.[81]

Art historian Irwin Panofsky elegantly summarized these problems of collaboration:

> It might be said that a film, called into
> being by a cooperative effort in which all
> contributions have the same degree of
> permanence, is the nearest modern
> equivalent of a medieval cathedral…And
> if you speak to any one of [the] colla-
> borators he will tell you, with perfect
> bona fides, that his is really the most
> important job—which is quite true to
> the extent that it is indispensible…[82]

Karl Brown, apprentice cameraman to D. W.
Griffith during the shooting of *The Birth of a
Nation,* had read Thomas Dixon's novel, *The
Clansman,* upon which the movie is based.
Throughout the shooting he had doubted that
Griffith could make this racist story into a suc-
cessful film. However, his account of opening
night speaks worlds about the impact of a musi-
cal accompaniment (although his description
may be in error on certain points):

> My first inkling that this was not to be
> just another movie came when I heard,
> over the babble of the crowd, the famil-
> iar sound of a great orchestra tuning up.
> First the oboe sounding A, then the oth-
> ers joining to produce an ever-changing
> medley of unrelated sounds, with each
> instrument testing its own strength and
> capability through this warming-up pre-
> liminary. Then the orchestra came
> creeping in through that little doorway
> under the proscenium apron and I tried
> to count them. Impossible. Too many.

But there were at least seventy, for
that's where I lost count, so most if not
all of the Los Angeles Symphony orchestra had been hired to "play" the picture.

Not that I hadn't known about a special
score having been prepared for the production. Joseph Carl Breil had been
around the studio a lot, talking with
Griffith, so I knew what was up. But Carl
Breil was no Beethoven. Thus far he had
produced only one song, "The Song of
the Soul," which had become a great
favorite among those who like that kind
of music, but he was no great shakes as
a composer in the grand manner. Oh, he
was capable enough in his own limited
way. He was a musician, there was no
denying that. He could arrange, he was
good at instrumentation, and he could
conduct. He could do just about anything known to music except think up
tunes. Well, maybe Griffith had supplied
that lack. We'd soon find out, because
the orchestra pit was crammed to over-
flowing with the finest performers in
Los Angeles and more, many more
instruments of different kinds than I
had seen anywhere before except at full-
dress, all-out symphony concerts. He
had the big doghouses, as we called the
double basses, and a lot of little doghouses, as the cellos were called, with as
many fiddles as there was room for and
enough brass to make up a full brass
band all by itself. And as for the kitchen,
or hardware shop, as the drum section
was called, there was everything known
to percussion, while at the console of
the massive pipe organ sat a little man
lost in a maze of stops and manuals,
ready to turn on the full roar of that
monster at the tip of a baton. Yes, it was
a complete orchestra, all right. I even
glimpsed two or three banjos in that
crowded orchestra pit, but what they
could be doing there was more than I
could imagine.

The house lights dimmed. The audience
became tensely silent. I felt once again,
as always before, that strange all-over

chill that comes with the magic moment of hushed anticipation when the curtain is about to rise.

The title came on, apparently by mistake, because the curtain had not yet risen and all I could see was the faint flicker of the lettering against the dark fabric of the main curtain. But it was not a mistake at all, because the big curtain rose slowly to disclose the title, full and clear upon the picture screen, while at the same moment Breil's baton rose, held for an instant, and then swept down, releasing the full impact of the orchestra in a mighty fanfare that was all but out-roared by the massive blast of the organ in an overwhelming burst of earth-shaking sound that shocked the audience first into a stunned silence and then roused them to a pitch of enthusiasm such as I had never seen or heard before…

The orchestra sort of murmured to itself during the titles, as though to assure the audience that they couldn't last forever. And then…the picture, gliding along through its opening sequences on a flow of music that seemed to speak for the screen and to interpret every mood. The audience was held entranced,…

What unfolded on that screen was magic itself. I knew there were cuts from this and to that, but try as I would, I could not see them. A shot of the extreme far end of the Confederate line flowed into another but nearer shot of the same line, to be followed by another, and another, until I could have sworn that the camera had been carried back by some sort of impossible carrier that made it seem to be all one unbroken scene. Perhaps the smoke helped blind out the jumps. I don't know. All I knew was that between the ebb and flow of a broad canvas of a great battle, now far and now near, and the roaring of that

gorgeous orchestra banging and blaring battle songs to stir the coldest bloke, I was hot and cold and feeling waves of tingling electric shocks racing all over me.

The Confederate charge was simply magnificent. Once again, there was nothing choppy about it, no sense of scenes being cut into another. That whole line of men simply flowed across the field, stumbling and dropping as they ran somehow into solid sheets of rifle fire from the Union entrenchments, while bombs, real bombs and not Fireworks Wilson's silly little powder puffs, burst with deafening roars among these charging heroes. Oh yes; I knew. I knew perfectly well that the backstage crew was working furiously to create these explosion effects just behind the screen, but I was too caught up in the magnificence of the spectacle to care how it was achieved.

And that scene with Walthall snatching up the flag and racing forward with it: holding it high and waving it defiantly as he ran with it in one hand and his drawn sword in the other straight at the cannon, to mount the parapet, and then—in a single, magnificent, overwhelming glimpse of one man, alone against a sky full of bursting bombs, thrusting that standard down the cannon's throat and shouting his defiant yell, while the trumpets in the orchestra split the air. Nor were those trumpets alone. I think every man in that packed audience was on his feet cheering, not the picture, not the orchestra, not Griffith but voicing his exultation at this man's courage—defiant in defeat, and all alone with only the heavens for his witness…

I was forced to admit to myself over again how pitifully little I knew about anything at all. There was that scene of Lillian Gish fluttering and running, fluttering and running over the death-strewn battlefield looking for her beloved, not as any human being would make such a search but as a ballet dancer might pictorialize it. I thought it was awful when it was being shot. But it was heartbreakingly effective on that night upon that screen before that particular audience, especially with the orchestra, that beautiful orchestra, interweaving the twin themes of love and death, just as Griffith had thought of them at that one magic moment on the battlefield. For she wasn't a woman at all but a spirit, a will-of-the-wisp, floating over the field of death. She was even more than that: she was the spirit of *all* the women of the Civil War, who still lived in the memories of their daughters and granddaughters, whose hearts had been searching among the dead for the living after every one of the many major battles...

And yet it wasn't the finish that worried me so much as the long dull, do-nothing stuff that I knew was slated for the bulk of the second half. Stuff like the hospital scenes, where Lillian Gish comes to visit Henry Walthall, she in demurest of dove gray, he in bed with a bandage neatly and evenly wrapped around his head. Now what in the world can anyone possibly do to make a hospital visit seem other than routine?...Since this was an army hospital, there had to be a sentry on guard...Well, Lillian passed before him and he looked after her and sighed. In the theater and on the screen, that sigh became a monumental, standout scene...Breil may not have been the greatest composer the world has ever known but he did know how to make an orchestra talk, and that sigh, uttered by the cellos and the muted trombones softly sliding down in a discordant glissando, drove the audience into gales of laughter...[83]

Brown cites a number of other such examples and then concludes:

Somewhere in this welter of...images came a new concept of Griffith...What

he really was—it seemed odd to think so—was a great composer of visual images instead of notes. What I had seen was not so much a motion picture but the equivalent of Beethoven's *Eroica* or his Fifth. That picture had been perfectly orchestrated and the instrumentation flawless.[84]

In 1914 *The Birth of a Nation* established the use of a full orchestra for film accompaniment in the United States. The East Coast premieres had a score that was a combination of original music by Breil and arrangements of popular and classical music. The score on the West Coast was by Carli Elinor and although it is lost, it must have contained a similar combination of music.[85] Griffith's *Way Down East* (1920) also had a specially fitted score that:

didn't consist of the usual hackneyed, thumb-worn numbers. Most of it seemed to have been written for the production, except the old tunes directly called for. Scores are apt to be slapped together in a hurry, a mechanical routine of publishers' lists and card-indexes. The storm and ice music was the weak spot—bald and crude of content. The fragments from Flying Dutchman and Les Preludes were the only blood and thunder touch in the score. There should have been the maximum sonority, but that of a symphonic orchestra—whirring strings relieving the boiler-factory din of the brass, and easing up on the huskies back-stage. The gatling-guns and bombs still surviving behind (or before) the scenes in some houses are a public menace.

Otherwise the music was a marvel of repose and placidity. No lashing of tempos, blurring of passage-work, hurrying-to-catch-a-train spirit. This hectic, neurasthenic style has a bad effect on the individual and collective playing of orchestra and organists. The pause was used often and effectively. The picture being well directed, it was possible to have a smooth and flowing score.

The leit-motif system was used to advantage, although it is capable of unlimited development, following the interweaving of emotions and mental states. A motif can be varied in instrumentation, introduced stealthily and subtly in one part, like the baleful movements of the villain. But the course of this story is simple and direct, far from metaphysics or psychoanalysis. The gossip's theme was characteristic and expressive. Especially appealing were the several themes for the mishaps and tribulations of Anna. The youthful Innocence motif was delightful. How much better than using some sentimental melody already played to death...

The music of "Way Down East" seemed written for this play alone; the next time we went the play seemed written for the music. The music and the story were like ivy clinging to a tree. The score was always on the job, fitting the action, like skin-tights, all the time, not like a hoop-skirt, touching only here and there. Score-makers, conductors, and organists, should throw themselves into the work as the great actors do, and make themselves the creators of the characters and story, till it becomes a living flesh and blood organism. But they need better pictures to project themselves into...

The natural evolution of the picture business then points to a renaissance of the Greek drama, with Wagnerian music-setting. The screen reveals the actors, dialogue, and stage-settings, the orchestra gives a continuous tonal version of the story.[86]

Clearly, the carefully chosen and well synchronized music of William Frederick Peters and Louis Silvers, although rather lightweight musically, was refreshing and impressive to a musically sensitive, frequent filmgoer.[87] One can infer from this account that the constant reuse of the same music was common and tedious and that sloppy synchronization or abrupt transitions between keys detracted at least a little from some people's enjoyment.

A British presentation of *Way Down East* in 1923 elicited a totally negative reaction to the music:

most of the music was of such undistinguished character that [Mr. Albert Marchbank, conductor of the orchestra at the Tower Cinema, Rye Lane, Peckham, London] had to practically rescore the musical fitting...The music for the big storm-scene especially was bad, and this was replaced entirely by him. In addition to the music being of a low standard, the score is "peppered" with leit-motifs for each of the six main characters. The airs of "I love you" and "Believe me" are scored each time the heroine appears. There is a further theme announcing the arrival of the chatterbox neighbour, and this theme alone appears forty times in the original score. If this is supposed to be the latest advancement in film-music, I look with apprehension to its future! It is appalling to see these blundering attempts at imitating great masters. Truly, a little knowledge is dangerous. I am glad Mr. Marchbank refused to perform this rubbish and made a clean sweep of both the music supplied with the film and the innumerable cues which appeared about every ten bars or so. The inevitable result was a veritable musical victory, for the house has been playing to capacity night after night and thousands of people had to be turned away as there was no further accommodation. This success was due in a large measure to the masterly musical setting by Mr. Marchbank. The storm-music provided the greatest sensation, and this, together with the wonderful effects supplied with the film, absolutely "brought the house down." There were, for instance, realistic lightning effects for which a special electric installation had been laid on.

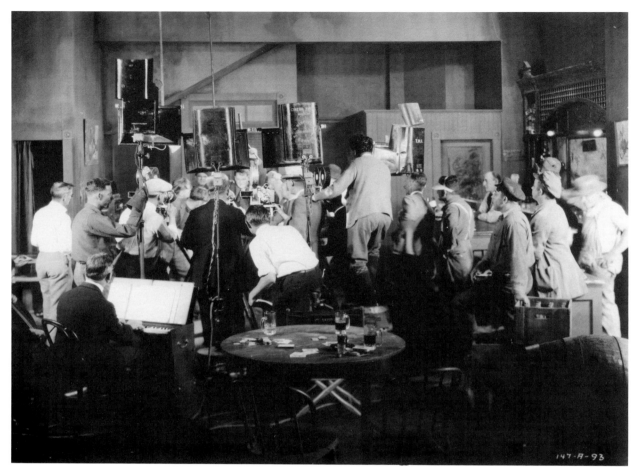

Production shot from *Anna Christie* (1923). The organ helped set the mood for the shooting of this melodrama about a girl with a shady past, her sea captain father, and the sailor she falls in love with. Museum of Modern Art, Film Stills Archive.

This lightning Mr. Marchbank—like Zeus—controlled (from the organ), evoking thunderous replies from the lower regions of the orchestra. There were also ice-breaking machines, waterfall, rain, wind effects and what-not. All these effects, manipulated in the right way, combined with the wonderful setting of the music, played superbly by the orchestra, as a musical illustration of the drama on the screen, produced a whole which was a stunning triumph of perfect film-presentation and worthy of the highest praise.[88]

D. W. Griffith never could leave any of his pictures alone. After their initial release, he constantly cut and rearranged them. (Even after he gave his collection to the Museum of Modern Art, he still recut the films in the projection booth after each screening until finally the Museum ordered the projection booth locked.) By 1923, probably as much as 25 percent of *Way Down East* had been cut or changed. Cut marks through the score and parts testify to the constant tinkering. In all probability, the score no longer fit the 1923 version like "skin-tights" or "ivy clinging to a tree," and Mr. Marchbank was well advised to use different music. Although the tastes in the two reviews differ with respect to the Peters-Silvers score, the ideal for film music is the same—"continuous tonal version of the story" and "musical illustration of the drama on the screen."

The scores for D. W. Griffith's films were compiled, arranged, and created by knowledgeable composers, but the majority of the scores for his films relied heavily on arrangements of preexisting music. *Intolerance* (1916), for example, uses an entire chorus from Verdi's *Aida* (twice), a vocal quartet version of "My Wild Irish Rose," and music from Delibes's ballets. By comparison, the commissioning of totally original scores, especially for feature films, became increasingly common in the 1920s. It led to such landmark scores as Mortimer Wilson's for *The Thief of Bagdad* (1924), William Axt's for *Don Juan* (1926) and Leo Pouget and Victor Alix's for *La Passion de Jean D'Arc* (1928).

The Thief of Bagdad

There were those, however, who preferred scores compiled from preexisting material.

> Something the professional critics have kindly failed to mention is the ultra oriental music score accompanying this wonder picture [*The Thief of Bagdad*]. Marcelli and his orchestra and Mr. Scholl worked for many weeks preparing the music written by Mr. Mortimer Wilson and their performance of the score is above criticism. They are all able, conscientious musicians and capable of handling even worse scores than this one though I hope it will never be necessary for them to do so. The press agent has termed the score a "harmonic

fealty," "a vital emotional symphony," "a fitting note for every gesture," "written like a grand opera," "a motive for every theme" reminiscent of an intended quotation we once saw on the screen reading "And never the two shall twain."

> Foibles of art and music are excusable at times but a valid excuse for this Bagdad music score must be extraordinary, if any. When the music of the world is at the disposal of an arranger and the libraries are rich in beautiful numbers, written by renowned composers, suitable for accompanying such a delightfully fantastic picture, why worry any one man to write a new "note for every gesture?" Strains from the modern writings of Ravel, Debussy, Korsakow, Puccini, Ornstein, Grainger, Irvin Cobb or Paul Whiteman would have been welcomed, somewhere a few beautiful harmonic passages from MacDowell would have been enjoyable and made more fitting contrast for some of the bizarre extensions, augmentations, depleted sixteenths, vigorous minor forte passages and other incongruous music idioms under the guise of oriental music...Technically the score may be symphonic, but most successful symphonies have melodies that have lived for a considerable period...A few good rich dominant seventh chords might have saved part of the wreck of "Bagdad" but perhaps they never used such implements in Bagdad. When there are such successful arrangers in the field as Luz, Schertzinger, Bradford and others whose scores are a pleasure to play and easy to hear, why issue such a potpourri as this "Bagdad" music and expect any one capable of music appreciation to enjoy listening to it even in the hands of the most capable musicians?...Unless an original score is such that it can be handled by small orchestras or organists on short notice, it is liable to be a detriment to the picture, as the musician conscientiously wishes to use an accompanying score. I feel quite sure that there is going to be some wonderful first night atmospheric creations when

Doug comes to town with his "harmonic fealty."[89]

This review was followed by T. S. Buhrman's editorial postscript:

Mr. Medcalfe does not appear to like Mr. Wilson's score. That's too bad. The New York critics, if we may be pardoned for mentioning these creatures, were unanimous in according the Wilson "Bagdad" score the highest praise. Perhaps the incident merely emphasizes the age-old difference in taste between N.Y. and L.A. Anyway, it has been said in these pages—modesty forbids my saying who said it—that a N.Y. organist could not make good in L.A. nor an L.A. organist make good in N.Y. I'd be tickled beyond my ability to endure if a score of mine were to be praised as highly as Mr. Wilson's was and by men of the reputation these acclaimers enjoy.

In one respect the biased Los Angeles reviewer was correct. The score to *The Thief of Bagdad* was not something that just any orchestra could field. It was technically extremely difficult, particularly for the string players, and there were virtuoso solos on the trumpet and French horn. A cue sheet was concocted to accompany the film,[90] and it must have been used instead of the original score in many theaters.

As the editor of *The American Organist* pointed out, the high quality of Mortimer Wilson's score for *The Thief of Bagdad* received immediate recognition from the New York critics. The veteran music critic of the *New York Evening Post* thought it a masterwork:

Where the eyes are kept so busy every second, it is difficult to listen to every detail of the music, but I have learned to do so, and it was with increasing admiration that I followed the evolution of Mr. Wilson's score, noting the freshness and inexhaustible variety of the musical invention, its appropriateness to every situation and the clever avoidance of awkward gaps. Everything synchronized to perfection, Mr. Wilson to some extent uses leading motives; he is a master of orchestral coloring, and yesterday, he

conducted the score as only the creator of a work—if he happens to be also a born leader—can conduct it.[91]

Theodore Stearns, writing in the *New York Morning Telegraph,* shared this view: "The score is undeniably beautiful. It has lofty sentiment, warmth and tenderness, and feelingly portrays the fundamental idea of *The Thief of Bagdad,* that true happiness must be earned." He especially admired the continuity of the music, contrasting it with the patchwork effect of the usual silent-film accompaniments, especially those using snippets of preexisting music:

What has handicapped the few real composers of original scores to accompany a big movie, up to date, has been that producers and directors eternally insist upon the music changing instantly with the changes in the picture. Inasmuch as *The Thief of Bagdad* is made up of some 2,000 "cut-ins," [that] would mean changing the musical idea at the rate of once a minute for two and a half hours. This attempt is made, however, in most moving-pictures, and the result— nine times out of ten—is a hodgepodge of something commenced, nothing ever satisfactorily finished...[92]

Wilson's music for *The Thief of Bagdad* provides numerous examples of the composer's inventiveness, melodic gifts, and skill at musical development and scoring. Stearns's review in the *Telegraph* is gratifyingly specific:

In the Shiraz bazaar—in the Isle of Wak—in all the subsequent adventures of the Thief searching for the magic casket Mr. Wilson logically develops his former musical ideas, altering them and fitting them to the symbolism of the picture rather than to the tempo of the camera.

But characteristic gestures—even expressions—of Douglas Fairbanks are nicely mirrored in the orchestra. As the flying carpet is brought forth, just a single flute trill delicately portrays it. There is no "Flying Dutchman" hurry and bustle—no inane tremolos on the cymbal or strings.

As the Thief is passing through the ordeal by fire and slays a dragon that would turn Siegfried green with envy, there is no Ride of the Valkyries idea—merely a restless movement in the music. The snake and the magic apple are coldly pictured by a ponticello on the strings—which always gives a shiver down the spine.

The final reunion of the Thief and the Princess is marked by the highly artistic return of the Mosque music. Ordinarily, a composer—certainly the general run of movie directors—would naturally insist upon using the former love duet or barcarolle music. But, in a sense, the happiness of the lovers was earned through sacrifice and pain. Moonlight and magic carpets did not bring them together so much as did renunciation and patience.[93]

Mortimer Wilson (1876-1932), American organist and composer, studied and taught with Max Reger for two years in Leipzig before returning to the United States where he composed a number of the finest silent film scores. Courtesy of Clyde Allen and Mortimer Wilson, Jr.

The Los Angeles critic aside, Wilson's score is a landmark in the history of motion picture music.

According to Wilson's son, Mortimer Wilson, Jr., the composer had to use some preexisting music for the first performance of the work because of pressure from someone who disliked the idea of a completely original score. Gradually he slipped all his original music back into the work, and nobody noticed. The first edition of the score and parts contains a number of ossias (additional pages) that are meant to substitute for some of the numbers, and in every case the additions are musically more effective. The second edition of the score and parts incorporated all these changes, and paid more careful attention to bad page turns in the parts. However, for the entrance of the magic army at the end of the film the first edition corresponds to the longer, premiere print of the film. The second edition corresponds to the shorter print that was distributed throughout the country. In any event the battle between compiled and original scores was never resolved during the silent era.

In the meantime a vast industry had been generated to supply movie theaters with trained musicians, theater organs, music scores, music libraries, and cue sheets. Many of the production companies, through their house periodicals—Paramount's *Progress-Advance* (1914–20), for example—published cue sheets. The motion picture trade journals similarly printed cue sheets, *The Motion Picture Exhibitor* (1918+), for example. *The American Organist* instituted a regular "Photoplaying" column in 1920 which carried articles by noted theater organists, reviews of theater orchestra and organist performances, and cue sheets. George Eastman founded the Eastman School of Music in 1921 to train theater organists. Many of the major music publishers established special movie music departments and published vast libraries of incidental music, organized by mood, tempo, and duration.

Music Played During the Shooting of Silent Films

Starting in the late teens music also played a role during the shooting of films. Geraldine Farrar may have introduced this practice:

> I asked Mr. DeMille if we might have music during our scenes, as I was so accustomed to orchestral accompaniment for certain tempi and phrasings, I felt I could better pantomime the rhythm of the effects. A little piano was hastily wheeled on the set and the talented Melville Ellis…inspired all my scenes with his impromptu playing. I believe this started the habit for music "off stage" for all later aspirants to emotional appeal. At any rate, from that time on I always had a musician at my elbow whose soulful throbs did more to start my tears than all the glycerine drops or onions more frequently employed by less responsive orbs.[94]

Abel Gance, the French director of *Napoleon* (1927), agreed:

> "I always had music on the set," said Gance, who employed an organist, a violinist and a cellist, "not only to give the mood, but to keep everyone quiet. You can capture their attention more easily by the use of music. In the scene where

the young Napoleon lies on the cannon …he had to cry in that scene. He couldn't, until the musicians played Beethoven's *Moonlight Sonata.*'[95]

Joseph von Sternberg used music during the shooting of his last silent film, *The Docks of New York* (1928):

> From the darkness behind the big sun-arcs a violin wailed and a harmonium grunted like a passionate duet between a musical hyena and a melodious warthog. The director allowed a few moments for this stimulus to work on the feelings of the actors, then through the megaphone, bellowed "Go!" The actors sprang into motion. But von Sternberg was not satisfied. He bellowed "Stop" through the megaphone, and, turning the instrument towards the musicians, shouted, "That tune's no good. Stir us up a bit. Put more battle spirit into it. Gee, nobody feels like fighting to a damned waltz![96]

Music was not used during the shooting of Carl Dreyer's *La Passion de Jeanne D'Arc* (1928) nor during the shooting of D. W. Griffith's films, but by the 1920s it was standard on most movie lots. Lillian Gish, whose orbs were surely as responsive as Geraldine Farrar's, was initially surprised and distracted by such music when after leaving D. W. Griffith's employ, she started acting for Paramount:

> I could not impose my kind of rehearsal on the others, nor could I object when they wanted music for their scenes. I had never had music before, and I simply had to close my ears and continue working. The music was fine, of course, when I wasn't trying to concentrate on a scene.[97]

Occasionally, a large ensemble was used, for example, Rudolph Berliner's Palm Court Orchestra for Cecil B. DeMille's *The Ten Commandments* (1923).

> The film's most dangerous scene was the giant pursuit of the Exodus by the charioted army of Egypt, played by members of the Eleventh Cavalry. They

made a heroic spectacle in their golden tunics, metal cuirasses gleaming in the sun, their gilded helmets tossing with multicolored plumes. In the van of the chase was a span of black thoroughbreds which DeMille had bought in Kansas City for fifty thousand dollars. When the stampede was over, four men lay in the sand, severely injured. Horses were lamed. Sand swirled with the wreckage of broken chariots ground up by the horses' hooves. One horse ran screaming about, its flesh flapping like a red scarf.

DeMille had insisted upon a thirty-piece Palm Court orchestra, playing martial music, to sit in a special enclosure just off camera "to keep everyone in the right mood." It was conducted by the unfortunate Rudolph Berliner, DeMille's childhood friend who had been installed comfortably as Director of the Palm Court orchestra of the Ritz-Carlton in New York for the past few years. The flying horses headed, many of them riderless, straight for the band, which gallantly went on playing in evening dress, seemingly more frightened of DeMille than of the advancing horde. A moment later the chariots and horses crashed into them, leaving a heap of broken instruments and badly bruised men and women.

Even when they were not being subjected to severe bruises and cuts, Berliner and his orchestra were constantly in distress, playing in the teeth of a gale which blew sand into the trombones and trumpets, clogging them up, and into ears, and mouths.[98]

MGM estimated that it spent $52,000 on set musicians in 1927. By 1928, phonograph records had replaced these musicians (records cost only $1,500 a year).[99]

While film music was not absolutely always present during the silent era,[100] the vast majority of films were accompanied by some sort of music, which, for better or worse, played an important part in a film's presentation. It also played an increasing role in setting the mood during the shooting of silent films.

Sound on Film

In 1923 the phonofilm was demonstrated at the Rivoli by Dr. Lee De Forest. The reviewer's reactions were:

> It sounds like a phonograph. For certain purposes, and even for certain portions of feature film, now and then, the device could be of practical use; but anything that sounds like reproduced music instead of like the original is inferior and not to be accepted.[101]

In 1926 the Warner Theater presented the feature film *Don Juan* (Warner Bros.). The music by William Axt was recorded on a Vitaphone disc which was synchronized to the film. Admission was two dollars. *The American Organist*'s reviewer reported that some thought the sound a very great improvement over De Forest's phonofilm. Others thought that it was "still the product of the tin-can and can not compete with music."[102] Most reviewers still focused on the music; they had yet to see the great potential of the new medium for the reproduction of speech.

By 1928, the handwriting was on the wall. An article appeared entitled "Vitaphone et al. An examination of the results of filmized music and a few reflections on the whole pack of inventions." After discussing the various drawbacks of the sound film, the writer said:

> On the other hand, anyone who saw Richard Dix in the baseball picture and heard the film's results in reproducing the contagious racket of the Yankee Stadium, will agree that here the device has produced something that is entirely beyond the realm of possibility for organist and orchestra...There is to be said, further, in behalf of the vocalized film, that when a picture is made and a score set by a man like Hugo Riesenfeld, and played for records by an adequate orchestra under such a man's direction, the resultant audible and visible film is infinitely superior to the accompaniments of the piano-drum-fiddle combinations so universally used in smaller houses.[103]

Emil Jannings and Esther Ralston dancing the polka in
Betrayal (1929), a picture that was released in both
sound and silent versions. The Paramount Famous
Lasky Corporation claimed that the sound of the film
musical score was "of unequalled beauty and [the]
sound effects startling in their realism." In spite of
such claims, it would be many years before the new
sound technology had improved sufficiently to approx-
imate a good live movie music orchestra. Museum of
Modern Art, Film Stills Archive.

At the end of 1929, the Loew's Theater chain announced there would be no organists in their theaters in the future.[104] One of the major New York theater organists, J. van Cleft Cooper, "acquired the duty of creating cross-word puzzles, at the rate of two a day, for a newspaper service that reaches 1100 papers."[105] A few of the major Broadway houses retained their organists to play in case the sound system failed, or between the films, or along with the sound films to boost their volume.[106] Many composers, arrangers, and songwriters moved to Hollywood.[107] Between 1928 and 1930, 10,000 musicians, half of all those playing in movie houses, lost their jobs.[108]

There were some who felt that the photoplayers were getting what they deserved:

> The present invasion of the Vitaphone and canned music into our picture theaters is causing the organists and orchestral musicians a great deal of worry as to the future. Most of these good people brought the storm down on their heads by their own action. The miserable so-called organ playing and the poor type of orchestral music undoubtedly caused a reaction in favour of the canned variety of a better type. Still, after talking with many men of the theatrical and musical professions, I feel that though the speaking picture is probably here to stay, the music accompaniment will again be given by the organists and instrumentalists. Only let us hope that they have learned their lesson, that the public will no longer tolerate the faking of standard compositions and the ruthless murder of classics which we have been compelled to endure in the past.[109]

Undoubtedly, well-synchronized performances of well-selected music or brilliantly improvised music could be heard throughout the 1920s. However, the average performance in the average theater was probably not well synchronized and not well played. The music did not intensify the film experience, which was enjoyed probably as often as not in spite of the music and even the film. Sound film brought sound effects not possible from an instrumental ensemble, and the sound of voices. It brought the standardization of the accompanying forces—that is, large instrumental ensembles. Gone were the improvised piano and organ accompaniments and even the smaller orchestral ensembles. Sound film also made exact synchronization the standard instead of the exception. It may even have accelerated the development of original scoring for films.

During the silent film era two methods of scoring were established, compiling from preexisting material and composing an original score. Before 1929 the former type of score predominated. Original scores were really the exception. After 1929 original scores became the rule although low budget films continued to use preexisting public domain music. Whether compiled or original, silent film accompaniments fell into two compositional traditions, vaudeville and operatic, and these traditions continued into the sound era.[110]

The silent era also established a continuum between two ideals for the relationship between the images and the music—subordinate and equally prominent. This continuum carried over into the sound era even though the introduction of the spoken word drastically affected the relationship between music and image.

> Photoplay accompaniments have gradually evolved into an integral part of the picture, and it is possible to be so perfect that one finds it difficult to concentrate upon the music itself. This is the sole mission of music, to take the place of the spoken word so completely that we become absorbed in the subject matter presented on the screen. Here is the final test of the accompaniment, and until this test is passed it cannot be considered a success.[111]

> There are various lights in which the art of picture playing is regarded. Many persons regard the music as an accompaniment to the picture—to overcome the awful silence that can almost be felt when a picture is run without music. Others regard the music as a frame, a

setting, or a background for a picture. In my opinion the music is neither of these, but is a component part of a photoplay production, taking the place, psychologically, of the spoken word, expressing…through the medium of the ear the mood that the picture seeks to express through the medium of the eye. Both are equally important to a satisfactory expression of the playwright's thought.[112]

It is possible to absorb histrionic impressions through the eye and ear simultaneously, without either dominating, on condition that both synchronously provide emotional stimuli of the same genus and intensity. In picture presentation we have the same combination of music, drama, and scenic arts as in opera, the only difference being the absence of the speaking or singing voice.[113]

Sound has always been an indispensable element in motion picture presentations. During the sound era, however, *music* in films went from the foreground to the background of people's attention. At times it was totally absent. In televised or filmed versions of operas and ballets it reassumes the prominence it has not had since the silent film era ended. Music was and still is most prominent when there is no talking.

GILLIAN B. ANDERSON
Music Specialist

NOTES

1. *Edison Films, No. 288.* Orange, N.J., Thomas A. Edison, July 1906, p. 13.
2. Paul Spehr, *The Movies Begin: Making Movies in New Jersey 1887–1920* (Newark, N.J.: The Newark Museum, 1977), pp. 25–26. The *New York Times,* May 13, 1893, quoted in Gordon Hendricks, *Origins of the American Film* (New York: Arno Press and the *New York Times,* 1972), pp. 104–5. "My intention is to have such a happy combination of photography and electricity that a man can sit in his own parlour and see depicted upon a curtain the forms of the players in opera upon a distant stage, and hear the voices of the singers." This intention finally became a reality in the age of television and home videotapes.
3. *Edison Films, No. 288.* Orange, N.J., Thomas A. Edison, July 1906, pp. 50–51. *The New York Clipper* (November 12, 1904): 895.
4. Ibid., p. 2.
5. *Dance to the Piper* (Boston: Little, Brown and Co., 1952), pp. 22–24. *Carmen* was the Cecil B. DeMille film released November 1, 1915.
6. Jean-Paul Sartre, "Childhood Memories," reprinted from *The Words* (New York: George Braziller, Inc., 1964) in Harry M. Geduld, ed., *Authors on Film* (Bloomington: Indiana University Press, 1972), pp. 42–46.
7. James E. Scheirer, *The American Organist* (vol. 9, no. 9, 1926): 267.
8. Ibid.
9. T. Scott Buhrman, "Photoplays DeLuxe," *The American Organist* (vol. 3, no. 5, 1920): 164.
10. Roy L. Medcalfe, "Hollywood Theater," *The American Organist* (vol. 7, no. 11, 1924): 642–43.

11. Ben M. Hall, *The Golden Age of the Movie Palace: The Best Remaining Seats* (New York: Clarkson N. Potter, Inc., 1961), p. 8.
12. Rollo F. Maitland, "Photoplaying in the Stanley [Philadelphia]," *The American Organist* (vol. 3, no. 4, 1920): 120–21.
13. General Notes. Midnight Shows," *The American Organist* (vol. 11, no. 3, 1928): 115.
14. Buhrman, "From New York," *The American Organist* (vol. 12, no. 5, 1929): 293.
15. Walter Wild, "Variety in the Music Score," *The American Organist* (vol. 5, no. 12, 1922): 546.
16. Maitland, "Photoplaying in the Stanley," *The American Organist* (vol. 3, no. 4, 1920): 122.
17. M. M. Hansford, "Strikes and Some Suggestions," *The American Organist* (vol. 4, no. 11, 1921): 386.
18. Buhrman, "From New York," *The American Organist* (vol. 12, no. 5, 1929): 293.
19. Hugo Riesenfeld, "Musical Classics for Millions," in James Francis Cooke, *Great Men and Famous Musicians on the Art of Music* (Philadelphia, Theodore Presser Co., 1925), p. 410–11; Dorothea B. Herzog, "Smiling His Way to the Goal of His Ambition," *The National Brain Power Monthly* (Nov., 1922), p. 24.
20. Buhrman, "Photoplays DeLuxe," *The American Organist* (vol. 3, no. 9, 1920): 157–58.
21. Medcalfe, "Hollywood Theater," *The American Organist* (vol. 7, no. 11, 1924): 642.
22. Buhrman, "Photoplays DeLuxe," *The American Organist* (vol. 3, no. 9, 1920): 157–58.
23. Hansford, "Picturegraphs," *The American Organist* (vol. 4, no. 4, 1921): 132.

24. Buhrman, "Photoplays DeLuxe," *The American Organist* (vol. 3, no. 5, 1920): 164.

25. Hansford, "Picturegraphs," *The American Organist* (vol. 10, no. 5, 1927): 129.

26. [Hansford], "Wurlitzerizing in the Rialto," *The American Organist* (vol. 5, no. 7, 1922): 292.

27. Geoffrey Wyatt, *At the Mighty Organ* (Oxford: Oxford Illustrated Press, 1974), p. 7.

28. "Unit vs. Straight," *The American Organist* (vol. 7, no. 1, 1924): 18-26.

29. Harry J. Colwell, "Give the New Baby a Chance," *The American Organist* (vol. 10, no. 5, 1927): 130.

30. Theodore Merson, "Here and There and Everywhere," *The American Organist* (vol. 9, no. 3, 1926): 74.

31. Ernest M. Skinner, "Cinema Music," *The American Organist* (vol. 1, no. 8, 1918): 417. See also J. van Cleft Cooper, "'The Vagabond'—A Vagabond," *The American Organist* (vol. 6, no. 2, 1923): 110.

32. Kenneth Baylan, "Points and Viewpoints: Our Terrifying Ignorance," *The American Organist* (vol. 6, no. 4, 1923): 251. This outburst elicited the following response: "I was under the impression that T.A.O. [*The American Organist*] was a really fine publication…Now I find that T.A.O. is a 'foolish and narrow magazine' run by a 'bunch of insects' in New York City. How could you deceive us guileless and trusting little fellows out here in the tall grass?" T. L. R., "We're Discovered at Last," *The American Organist* (vol. 6, no. 6, 1923): 382.

33. [Hansford], "American Conservatory Theater School," *The American Organist* (vol. 6, no. 7, 1923): 444-50.

34. "White Institute," *The American Organist* (vol. 12, no. 4, 1929): 252.

35. Clealan Blakely in the Preface to John W. Landon, *Jesse Crawford Poet of the Organ, Wizard of the Mighty Wurlitzer* (New York, The Vestal Press, 1974), p. vii.

36. C. Roy Carter, *Theatre Organist's Secrets: A Collection of Successful Imitations, Tricks and Effects for Motion Picture Accompaniment on the Pipe Organ* (Los Angeles: C. Roy Carter, 1926), p. 1.

37. Ibid.

38. General Notes. The Capitol Theater," *The American Organist* (vol. 7, no. 8, 1924): 482; "Radio Broadcasting," *The American Organist* (vol. 8, no. 7, 1925): 297.

39. "Hugo Riesenfeld Tells How He Scores a Film," *Musical Courier* (vol. 94, no. 7, Feb. 17, 1927): 48. *Rough Riders,* directed by Victor Fleming, was premiered in New York on March 15, 1927. Kenneth Munden, *The American Film Institute Catalog of Motion Pictures Produced in the United States: Feature Films 1921-1930* (New York and London: R. R. Bowker Co., 1971), p. 668.

40. Alexander Walker, *The Shattered Silents* (New York: William Morrow and Co., Inc., 1979), p. 82.

41. "Photoplays DeLuxe," *The American Organist* (vol. 3, no. 5, 1920): 171-73; see also "The Loew Music System," *The American Organist* (vol. 7, no. 6, 1924): 332-36.

42. Op. cit. (vol. 3, no. 5, 1920): 175.

43. "The Loew Music System," *The American Organist* (vol. 7, no. 6, 1924): 332 and 334.

44. "Rialto Overtures," *The American Organist* (vol. 4, no. 10, 1921): 351-52.

45. These were roundly criticized because they were in a foreign language and the orchestra drowned out the singers, a not infrequent problem for singers in these completely carpeted theaters. "Film Facts and Fancies," *The American Organist* (vol. 3, no. 9, 1920): 339.

46. "Rialto and Rivoli," *The American Organist* (vol. 9, no. 6, 1926): 182.

47. Ibid., no. 2, p. 40 and no. 6, p. 182.

48. "As Broadway Does It. In the Rivoli," *The American Organist* (vol. 6, no. 2, 1923): 107.

49. "Rialto and Rivoli," *The American Organist* (vol. 9, no. 2, 1926): 40; "Photoplaying. Critiques. Rivoli," *The American Organist* (vol. 6, no. 3, 1923): 167.

50. "News and Notes. The Rivoli," *The American Organist* (vol. 5, no. 2, 1922): 79.

51. Hansford, "Picturegraphs," *The American Organist* (vol. 4, no. 5, 1921): 169.

52. "The Theater World," *The American Organist* (vol. 8, no. 2, 1925): 69.

53. "Critiques. Rivoli," *The American Organist* (vol. 6, no. 6, 1923): 366.

54. "Ideas Going to Waste," *The American Organist* (vol. 6, no. 8, 1923): 505.

55. Quoted in "Mr. Curtis Dunham," *The American Organist* (vol. 4, no. 6, 1921): 209.

56. "There used to be current an anecdote about a man in a cinema audience who had been sitting in long-suffering silence while a very bad pianist accompanied the film. When the heroine was about to seek an end of her troubles by plunging to a watery grave, he called out to her image on the screen, in a voice full of disgust: 'Take the pianist with you, while you're about it!'" Kurt London, *Film Music: A Summary of the Characteristic Features of Its History, Aesthetics, Technique; and Possible Developments,* trans. Eric S. Bensinger (London: Faber and Faber Ltd., 1936), p. 41. *Moving Picture World* (July 3, 1909), in an editorial entitled "The Musical End," echoed this sentiment: "Half the pianists whom we have heard these last six months deserve to lose their jobs…The pianos should be either burnt or put into tune or replaced with better ones…" Quoted in Charles Hofmann, *Sounds for Silents* (New York: Drama Book Specialists, 1970), p. [15].

57. May Meskimen Mills, *The Pipe Organist's Complete Instruction and Reference Work on the Art of Photo-playing* (n.p.: May Meskimen Mills, 1922), p. 7. An even earlier example of such mistakes was reported in the *New York Daily Mirror* (October 9, 1909): "Bad judgement in the selection of music may ruin an exhibition as much as a good programme may help it. Imagine a pathetic scene showing a husband mourning his dead wife accompanied by the strains of 'No wedding bells for me!' And yet this exact circumstance was noted by the writer recently…" Quoted in Charles Hofmann, *Sounds for Silents* (New York: Drama Book Specialists, 1970), p. [13].

58. Ernest M. Skinner, "Cinema Music," *The American Organist* (vol. 1, no. 8, 1918): 418; John Scott, "Entertainment the Solution," *The American Organist* (vol. 13, no. 2, 1930): 104.

59. Hansford, "Picturegraphs," *The American Organist* (vol. 9, no. 12, 1926): 364.

60. A Contrib., "Roaming the Big Town," *The American Organist* (vol. 8, no. 2, 1925): 25.

61. "Critiques of a New Art. Loew Family," *The American Organist* (vol. 8, no. 6, 1925): 231.

62. "Critiques. Brooklyn-Strand," *The American Organist* (vol. 4, no. 8, 1921): 280.

63. Frank Stewart Adams, "On Time or Not at All," *The American Organist* (vol. 9, no. 1, 1926): 14.

64. Ibid.

65. E. Nigma, "Sic Semper Tyrannis," *The American Organist* (vol. 10, no. 3, 1927): 65.

66. "The Capitol, New York," *The American Organist* (vol. 6, no. 11, 1923): 694; "As Broadway Does It. The Capitol," *The American Organist* (vol. 6, no. 10, 1923): 623. See also Ben M. Hall, *The Golden Age of the Movie Palace: The Best Remaining Seats* (New York: Clarkson N. Potter, Inc., 1961), pp. 57-68 and 76-90 about the Capitol and Roxy Theaters respectively; pp. 206-8 about Sid Grauman.

67. Alanson Weller, "New York," *The American Organist* (vol. 10, no. 6, 1927): 161.

68. L. G. del Castillo, "Managers of Heavenly Descent," *The American Organist* (vol. 10, no. 4, 1927): 102-4.

69. Ibid.

70. Kurt London, *Film Music,* p. 40. [See note 56 for the full citation.]

71. *Moving Picture World* (March 13, 1909) reported on a screening of the Biograph film *A Fool's Revenge:* "A pleasant variation from the eternal ragtime was a refined deliverance of classical music corresponding to the character of the picture, including Schumann's 'Traumerei' and Beethoven's 'Moonlight Sonata.' The first time, indeed, we ever heard Beethoven in a five-cent theater…" Quoted in Hofmann, *Sounds for Silents,* p. [13].

72. Hofmann, *Sounds for Silents,* p. [13].

73. Max Winkler, "The Origin of Film Music," in James Limbacher, *Film Music* (Metuchen, N.J.: The Scarecrow Press, 1974), pp. 15-24. See also Max Winkler, *A Penny from Heaven* (New York: Appleton-Century Crofts, 1951). Winkler's claim that he invented the cue sheet is disputed by Bert Ennis in a manuscript account, "Music Cues—Without Aid of Riesenfeld" in the files of the Department of Film, Museum of Modern Art, New York. Quoted in Hofmann, *Sounds for Silents,* pp. [18-20].

74. Kurt London credits the Italian Giuseppe Becce with the idea of publishing a cinema music library (under the name Kinothek, a contraction of the German word Kinobibliothek) in 1919. London, *Film Music,* pp. 51 and 54.

75. Ibid., pp. 55-57. See also Erno Rapee, *Encyclopaedia of Music for Pictures* (New York: Arno Press and the *New York Times,* 1970).

76. L. G. del Castillo, "Cue Sheets and Something Better," *The American Organist* (vol. 5, no. 10, 1922): 453; Maitland, "Photoplaying in the Stanley," *The American Organist* (vol. 3, no. 4, 1920): 120; see also Edith Lang and J. Harold Weisel, "Cue Sheets: Two Discussions," *The American Organist* (vol. 5, no. 7, 1922): 289-91.

77. J. van Cleft Cooper, "'The Vagabond'—A Vagabond," *The American Organist* (vol. 6, no. 2, 1923): 109.

78. I am indebted to Clifford McCarty for this information. *Films in Review* (June-July 1960): 379; and (Aug.-Sept. 1960): 445. Wayne D. Shirley, "'A Bugle Call to Arms for National Defense!': Victor Herbert and His Score for *The Fall of a Nation,*" *Wonderful Inventions: Motion Pictures, Broadcasting, and Recorded Sound at the Library of Congress,* ed. Iris Newsom (Washington, D.C.: Library of Congress, 1985), pp. 173-85.

79. His own copies of the scores and parts to a number of his films, particularly the feature-length ones, are part of the Museum of Modern Art Film Score Collection which is on permanent loan to the Music Division of the Library of Congress.

80. (New York: Farrar, Strauss, and Giroux, 1973), pp. 79 and 80. Brown's accounts capture the excitement of the original presentation and the effect of the music. However, they have many inconsistencies and must be taken with a grain of salt. For example, Brown claimed that Joseph Carl Breil wrote the music for the Los Angeles premiere when in fact the music was compiled by Carli Elinor; the Los Angeles Symphony could not have been the orchestra at the Los Angeles premiere; and so forth. Clyde Allen's notes for *The Birth of a Nation* Label X, LXDR-701-2 recording, 1986. See also Martin Marks, soon to be completed doctoral dissertation on film music for Harvard University.

81. Lillian Gish with Ann Pinchot, *The Movies, Mr. Griffith and Me* (London: W. H. Allen, 1969), p. 152.

82. "Style and Medium in the Motion Pictures," in *Film: An Anthology,* ed. Daniel Talbot (Berkeley: University of California Press, 1975), pp. 29-30.

83. Brown, *Adventures with D. W. Griffith,* pp. 86-92.

84. Ibid., p. 96.

85. Seymour Stern, *Film Culture* (no. 36, Spring/Summer 1965): 103-32.

86. Frank Stewart Adams, "'Way Down East' and the Future," *The American Organist* (vol. 4, no. 1, 1921): 25-26.

87. The exact contribution of each of the two composers can be ascertained because Peters' wife copyrighted her husband's music by submitting a score with Silvers' sections crossed or cut out. Compare entries 981 and 982, MUSIC 3212, Item 144 and MUSIC 3236, Item 78.

88. Hansford, "Picturegraphs," *The American Organist* (vol. 6, no. 4, 1923): 234.

89. Medcalfe, "Hollywood Theater," *The American Organist* (vol. 7, no. 11, 1924): 642-44.

90. George C. Pratt, "Cue Sheets for Silent Films [in the Department of Film at the George Eastman House]," *Image* (vol. 25, no. 1, March 1982): 23. See Appendix 4 of this guide for a reprint.

91. Quoted in *The Literary Digest* (vol. 82, July 19, 1924): 27.

92. Ibid., p. 26.

93. Ibid.

94. Geraldine Farrar, *Such Sweet Compulsion* (Nw York: Greystone Press, 1928), p. 169.

95. Quoted in Kevin Brownlow, *Napoleon: Abel Gance's Classic Film* (New York: Alfred A. Knopf, 1983), p. 73.

96. Jan and Cora Gordon, *Star-Dust in Hollywood* (London: George G. Harrap & Co., 1930), p. 78, quoted in Alexander Walker, *The Shattered Silents: How the Talkies Came to Stay* (New York: William Morrow and Co., Inc., 1979). p. 34.

97. Lillian Gish with Ann Pinchot, *The Movies, Mr. Griffith and Me* (New York: Avon Books, 1969), p. 279.

98. Charles Higham, *Cecil B. DeMille* New York: Charles Scribner's Son's 1973), p. 119.

99. Alexander Walker, *The Shattered Silents,* p. 95.

100. Carl Dreyer preferred silence to the Baroque music supplied for his *La Passion de Jeanne D'Arc* in the 1950s and also to any other form of accompaniment that he had heard, but there is no evidence that the film was actually screened silent in 1928 and 1929. Silences between musical sections of a film score were not uncommon (Cooper, "Creation of Atmosphere," *The American Organist* (vol. 5, no. 6, 1922): 241). For dramatic effect D. W. Griffith kept the orchestra silent for up to ninety seconds in *Way Down East* and *Intolerance*. Occasionally, films were shown silent because of a musicians' strike (Adams, "'Way Down East' and the Future," *The American Organist* (vol. 4, no. 1, 1921): 25.), but more often a victrola would be used to substitute for an organist on break or musicians on strike. ("Film Facts and Fancies," *The American Organist* (vol. 3, no. 8, 1920): 298–99.)

101. "Critiques. Ideas Going to Waste," *The American Organist* (vol. 6, no. 8, 1923): 504.

102. S. O. Mebody, "New York City Notes," *The American Organist* (vol. 9, no. 11, 1926): 330. See also Walker, *The Shattered Silents,* p. 10.

103. "Vitaphone et al.," *The American Organist* (vol. 11, no. 10, 1928): 443.

104. "New York," *The American Organist* (vol. 12, no. 12, 1929): 756.

105. "J. van Cleft Cooper," *The American Organist* (vol. 12, no. 6, 1929): 358.

106. Buhrman, "Here We Are," *The American Organist* (vol. 13, no. 1, 1930): 34; "Organ Again. The Rivoli Organists Find a Way to Keep Alive," *The American Organist* (vol. 12, no. 6, 1929): 358.

107. Walker, *The Shattered Silents,* p. 112.

108. Ibid., p. 67.

109. Frederick W. Goodrich, "A Review of the Times," *The American Organist* (vol. 12, no. 6, 1929): 370.

110. Maitland, "Photoplaying in the Stanley," *The American Organist* (vol. 3, no. 4, 1920): 119.

111. George Lee Hamrick, "Photoplaying. Fundamentals," *The American Organist* (vol. 3, no. 1, 1920): 21.

112. Maitland, "Photoplaying in the Stanley," *The American Organist* (vol. 3, no. 4, 1920): 120.

113. Adams, "Photoplaying. Dynamic Values," *The American Organist* (vol. 3, no. 8, 1920): 280.

The Guide to Music for Silent Films

1
Abie's Irish Rose
Original compositions and arrangements from *Abie's Irish Rose. Music by:* J. S. Zamecnik, E. Kilenyi, and C. Rybner. *Published by:* Sam Fox Publ. Co., Cleveland, 1928. *Instrumentation :* Violin. *Copyright:* © C1 E 699725, September 26, 1928; R 161671, December 16, 1955, Sam Fox Pub. Co., Inc. (PWH)
LC M1357.Z 20 p., 30 cm.
Music 3212, Item 0

2
Ach wie ist's möglich dann
Ach wie ist's möglich dann. Scenario by: Hans Forsten. *Music by:* Bruno Müller, Opus 109. *Published by:* Münchener Kunstfilm P. Ostermayr, Munich, 1914. *Instrumentation:* Piano. *Copyright:* © C1 E 350244, March 28, 1914, B. Müller, Munich.
LC M1527.M75A3 90 p., 34 cm.
Music 3212, Item 1

3
Across to Singapore
Thematic music cue sheet. Ramon Novarro in *Across to Singapore* with Joan Crawford and Ernest Torrence. *Production by:* William Nigh. *Directed by:* William Nigh. *Film company:* Metro-Goldwyn-Mayer. *Music compiled by:* Ernst Luz. *Note:* Music incipits. "Sunday Feb 24" marked in pencil. *Number of reels:* 7. *Footage:* 6720. *Maximum projection time:* 1 hour, 22 minutes.
MOMA 4 p., 31 cm.
Music 3236, Item 86

4
Adoration
Thematic music cue sheet. Richard A. Rowland presents Billie Dove in *Adoration. Story by:* Lajos Biro. *Production by:* Frank Lloyd. *Film company:* First National. *Music compiled by:* James C. Bradford. *Note:* Music incipits.
MOMA 4 p., 31 cm.
Music 3236, Item 87

5
The Adventurer
Thematic music cue sheet. Tim McCoy in *The Adventurer* with Dorothy Sebastian and Charles Delaney. *Story by:* Leon Abrams. *Screenplay by:* Jack Cunningham. *Film company:* Metro-Goldwyn-Mayer. *Music compiled by:* Ernst Luz.
Note: Music incipits. Two copies. Copy 1 marked in pencil "Sunday Dec 16." *Footage:* 4160. *Maximum projection time:* 48 minutes.
MOMA 4 p., 31 cm.
Music 3236, Item 88

6
The Adventurer
Thematic music cue sheet. Tim McCoy in *The Adventurer* with Dorothy Sebastian and Charles Delaney. *Story by:* Leon Abrams. *Screenplay by:* Jack Cunningham. *Film company:* Metro-Goldwyn-Mayer. *Music compiled by:* Ernst Luz. *Note:* Music incipits. *Number of reels:* 5. *Footage:* 4660. *Maximum projection time:* 48 minutes.
MOMA 4 p., 31 cm.
Music 3236, Item 89

7
Afraid to Love
Afraid to Love. Note: Typescript cue sheet. No music.
MOMA 1 p., 28 cm.
Music 3236, Item 91

8
Afraid to Love
Thematic music cue sheet. Adolph Zukor and Jesse L. Lasky present Florence Vidor in *Afraid to Love* with Clive Brook, Jocelyn Lee and Norman Trevor. *Directed by:* Edward H. Griffith. *Screenplay by:* Doris Anderson and Joseph Jackson. *Film company:* Paramount. *Music compiled by:* James C. Bradford. *Note:* Music incipits. "Thursday April 28/29" marked in pencil. *Footage:* 6199.
MOMA 4 p., 32 cm.
Music 3236, Item 92

9
After the Storm
Thematic music cue sheet. Columbia Pictures presents Hobart Bosworth in *After the Storm* with Eugenia Gilbert, Charles Delaney, Maude George, George Kuwa and Linda Loredo. *Scenario by:* Will M. Ritchey. *Production by:* George B. Seitz. *Copyrighted and distributed by:* Columbia Pictures Corporation. *Music compiled by:* James C. Bradford. *Note:* Music incipits. "Th Fri Sat June 14-15-16." marked in pencil.
MOMA 2 p., 32 cm.
Music 3236, Item 90

10
The Air Legion
Thematic music cue sheet. William Le Baron presents *The Air Legion* with Ben Lyon and Antonio Moreno. *Story by:* James Ashmore Creelman. *Directed by:* Bert Glennon. *Distributed by:* F B O Pictures Corporation. *Music compiled by:* James C. Bradford. *Note:* Music incipits.
MOMA   4 p., 32 cm.
Music 3236, Item 93

11
Alice Brown Derby
Alice Brown Derby. Note: Typescript cue sheet. No music.
MOMA   1 p., 28 cm.
Music 3236, Item 94

12
All Aboard
Thematic music cue sheet. C. C. Burr presents Johnny Hines in *All Aboard. Screenplay by:* Matt Taylor. *Directed by:* Charles Hines. *Film company:* First National. *Music compiled by:* Dr. Edward Kilenyi. *Note:* Music incipits. "Monday April 25/27" marked in pencil.
MOMA   4 p., 31 cm.
Music 3236, Item 95

13
All Around Frying Pan
Thematic music cue sheet. F. B. O. presents Fred Thomson and his famous horse Silver King in *All Around Frying Pan. Story by:* Frank Richardson Pierce. *Directed by:* David Kirkland. *Distributed by:* Film Booking Offices of America, Inc. *Music compiled by:* Eugene Conte. *Note:* Music incipits. "Sunday Jan 24" marked in pencil.
MOMA   4 p., 30 cm.
Music 3236, Item 96

14
All at Sea
Thematic music cue sheet. Karl Dane and George K. Arthur in *All at Sea* with Josephine Dunn. *Story by:* Byron Morgan. *Continuity by:* Ann Price and Byron Morgan. *Directed by:* Alf Goulding. *Film company:* Metro-Goldwyn-Mayer. *Music compiled by:* Ernst Luz. *Note:* Music incipits. *Number of reels:* 6. *Footage:* 5314. *Maximum projection time:* 1 hour.
MOMA   2 p., 31 cm.
Music 3236, Item 97

15
Aloha Oe
Musical setting for the photoplay *Aloha Oe. Production by:* Thomas H. Ince. *Music arranged and adapted by:* Wedgewood Nowell. *Series title:* Triangle plays. *Published by:* G. Schirmer for the Triangle Film Corp., New York, 1915. *Instrumentation:* Piano conductor. *Copyright:* © Cl E 377031, November 26, 1915.
LC M1357.N   89 p., 30 cm.
Music 3212, Item 2

16
Alt-Heidelberg
Alt-Heidelberg. Film-Schauspiel in 6 Akten (Cserépy-Film der Ufa) nach Wilhelm Meyer-Foerster. *Screenplay and direction by:* Hans Behrendt. *Music by:* Marc Roland. *Published by:* Drei-Masken Verlag, A. G., Berlin, 1923. *Instrumentation:* Piano conductor. *Copyright:* © Cl E 567848, April 19, 1923.
LC M1527.R63A5   99 p., 33 cm.
Music 3212, Item 3

17
America
D. W. Griffith presents *America. Story by:* Robert W. Chambers. *Film company:* D. W. Griffith, Inc. Albert L. Grey, Gen. Mgr. *Music arranged and synchronized by:* Joseph Carl Breil and Adolph Fink. *Published by:* D. W. Griffith, Inc., 1924. *Instrumentation:* Orchestral parts (1,1,2,1,: 2,2,1; drums; strings).
MOMA   31 cm.
Music 3236, Item 1

18
America
Incidental music for the film *America. Music by:* Manuel Klein as produced at the New York Hippodrome. *Published by:* M. Witmark & Sons, New York, 1914. *Instrumentation:* Piano score. *Copyright:* © Cl E 339319, May 14, 1914; R 97155, May 22, 1941, Helen Klein, Hollywood, California.
LC M176.A5   61 p., 34 cm.
Music 3212, Item 4

19
American Beauty
Thematic music cue sheet. Richard A. Rowland presents Billie Dove in *American Beauty* with Lloyd Hughes. *Film company:* First National. *Music compiled by:* James C. Bradford. *Note:* Music incipits. "Monday Oct 31/27" marked in pencil.
MOMA   4 p., 31 cm.
Music 3236, Item 98

20

American Pluck

Thematic music cue sheet.Chadwick Pictures
Corporation presents George Walsh in *American
Pluck* from the novel *Blaze Derringer. Story by:*
Eugene P. Lyle, Jr. *Music compiled by:* James C.
Bradford. *Note:* Music incipits. "Mon & Tues Feb.
8-9" marked in pencil.

MOMA   4 p., 30 cm.
Music 3236, Item 99

21

The Ancient Highway

Thematic music cue sheet. Adolph Zukor and
Jesse L. Lasky present James Oliver Curwood's
The Ancient Highway, an Irvin Willat Production
with Jack Holt, Billie Dove and Montagu Love.
Screenplay by: James S. Hamilton and Eve Unsell.
Film company: Paramount. *Music compiled by:*
James C. Bradford. *Note:* Music incipits. "Saturday
Jan. 2" marked in pencil. Footage: 6034

MOMA   2 p., 31 cm.
Music 3236, Item 100

22

The Angel of Broadway

Thematic music cue sheet. William Sistrom presents Leatrice Joy in *The Angel of Broadway* with
Victor Varconi, May Robson and Clarence Burton.
Story by: Lenore J. Coffee. *Directed by:* Lois
Weber. *Produced by:* DeMille Pictures Corporation. *Distributed by:* Pathe Exchange, Inc. *Music
compiled by:* Rudolph Berliner. *Note:* Music
incipits. "Monday Nov 14" marked in pencil.

MOMA   4 p., 31 cm.
Music 3236, Item 101

23

Annapolis

Thematic music cue sheet. Pathe presents *Annapolis. Scenario by:* F. McGrew Willis. *Story by:*
Royal S Pease. *Directed by:* Christy Cabanne.
Produced by: F. McGrew Willis for Pathe Studios,
Inc. *Distributed by:* Pathe Exchange, Inc. *Music
compiled by:* James C. Bradford. *Note:* Music
incipits.

MOMA   4 p., 31 cm.
Music 3236, Item 102

24

Antony and Cleopatra

Special music for the Kleine-Cines Production
Antony and Cleopatra. Music composed by:
George Colburn. *Published by:* George Kleine

Attractions, Chicago, 1914. *Instrumentation:*
Piano score. *Copyright:* © C1 E 334026, February
9, 1914.

LC M176.A55   39 p., 34 cm.
Music 3212, Item 5

25

Anybody Here Seen Kelly?

Thematic music cue sheet. Carl Laemmle pres-
ents *Anybody Here Seen Kelly? Production by:*
Universal. *Music compiled by:* James C. Bradford.
Note: Music incipits.

MOMA   2 p., 32 cm.
Music 3236, Item 103

26

The Apostle of Vengeance

The Apostle of Vengeance. Produced by: W. S.
Hart and Th. H. Ince, 1916. *Note:* Music incipits.
Cue sheet.

MOMA   2 p., 28 cm.
Music 3236, Item 104

27

An Arabian Tragedy

Special piano music for *An Arabian Tragedy.
Music compiled by:* Walter C. Simon. *Published
by:* Kalem Co., New York, 1912. *Instrumentation:*
Piano. *Copyright:* © E 297641, June 19, 1912; R
86888, April 27, 1940, Walter C. Simon, New York.

LC M176.A65   11 p., 32 cm.
Music 3212, Item 6

28

The Arizona Sweepstakes

Thematic music cue sheet. Carl Laemmle presents Hoot Gibson in *The Arizona Sweepstakes.
Story by:* Charles Logue. *Directed by:* Clifford S.
Smith. *Film company:* Universal-Jewel. *Music
compiled by:* James C. Bradford. *Note:* Music
incipits. "Sunday & Monday 3/14/15" marked in
pencil.

MOMA   2 p., 33 cm.
Music 3236, Item 105

29

Arsenal

Music cues on *Arsenal. Note:* Cue sheet. typate-
script. No music.

MOMA   1 p., 28 cm.
Music 3236, Item 106

30

Arsenal

Cue sheet for *Arsenal*. *Note:* Typsecript. No
music.

MOMA   1 p., 28 cm.

Music 3236, Item 107

31

Arsenal

Music for *Arsenal*. *Music composed by:* Ivan
Belza. *Published by:* The Museum of Modern Art
Film Library. *Instrumentation:* Piano score.

MOMA   55 p., 32 cm.

Music 3236, Item 2

32

As We Forgive

As We Forgive. Story based on: Epistle of Paul to
Philemon. *Music composed by:* Alexander
Savine. *Published by:* Pictorial Clubs, Inc., New
York, 1926. *Instrumentation:* Piano score. *Copy-
right:* © C1 E 641093, March 15, 1926.

LC M1527.S26A7   28 p., 31 cm.

Music 3212, Item 7

32A

L'Assassinat du duc de Guise

L'Assassinat du duc de Guise. Opus 128; tableaux d'histoire. *Scenario by:* Henri Lavedan.
Music composed by: Camille Saint-Saëns. *Published by:* A. Durand & Fils, Paris, 1908. *Instrumentation:* Piano score.

LC M1513.S15A7   34 p., 27 cm.

Music 3449-supp., Item 1166

33

Autum Fire

Autumn Fire. Note: Cut sheet. No music. Manuscript. Cue sheet divided into two parts—Score A
and Score B; written on The Coliseum House
letterhead.

MOMA   1 p., 24 cm.

Music 3236, Item 108

34

Avalanche

Thematic music cue sheet. Adolph Zukor and
Jesse L. Lasky present Zane Grey's *Avalanche*
with Jack Holt, Doris Hill, and Baclanova.
Directed by: Otto Brower. *Adaptation and
screenplay by:* Sam Mintz and J. Walter Ruben.
Production by: West Coast Productions, B. P.
Schulberg, General Manager. *Film company:*
Paramount. *Music compiled by:* James C. Brad-
ford. *Note:* Music incipits. *Footage:* 6099.

MOMA   4 p., 31 cm.

Music 3236, Item 109

35

The Avenging Rider

Musical synopsis for *The Avenging Rider. Music
compiled by:* James C. Bradford. *Note:* Cue sheet.
Two copies. No music.

MOMA   1 p., 28 cm.; 32 cm.

Music 3236. Item 110

36

The Awakening

Thematic music cue sheet. Samuel Goldwyn pres-
ents Vilma Banky in *The Awakening* by Frances
Marion with Louis Wolheim and Walter Byron.
Production by: Victor Fleming. *Film company:*
United Artists. *Music compiled by:* Ernst Luz.
Note: Music incipits. Two copies. *Number of reels:*
9. *Footage:* 7930. *Maximum projection time:* 1
hour, 22 minutes.

MOMA   6 p., 31 cm.

Music 3236, Item 111

37

The Baby Cyclone

Thematic music cue sheet. Lew Cody and Aileen
Pringle in *The Baby Cyclone* with Robert Armstrong and Gwen Lee. *Production by:* Edward
Sutherland. *Based on the play by:* George M.
Cohan. *Adaptation and continuity by:* F. Hugh
Herbert. *Directed by:* Edward Sutherland. *Film
company:* Metro-Goldwyn-Mayer. *Music compiled by:* Ernst Luz. *Note:* Music incipits. *Number
of reels:* 7. *Footage:* 5305. *Maximum projection
time:* 57 minutes.

MOMA   2 p., 31 cm.

Music 3236, Item 112

38

The Bachelor Daddy

The Bachelor Daddy. Note: Cue sheet. No music.
Typescript.

MOMA   1 p., 28 cm.

Music 3236, Item 113

39

Back to God's Country

Thematic music cue sheet. Carl Laemmle presents *Back to God's Country. Film company:*
Universal-Jewel. *Music compiled by:* James C.
Bradford. *Note:* Music incipits. "Lyceum—Dec.
26-27-192[7]" marked in pencil.

MOMA   2 p., 32 cm.

Music 3236, Item 114

40
Ballet Mecanique
Ballet Mecanique, Leger. Note: Cue sheet. No music. Typescript.
MOMA   1 p., 28 cm.
Music 3236, Item 115

41
Barbed Wire
Barbed Wire. Note: Cue sheet. No music. Typescript.
MOMA   2 p., 28 cm.
Music 3236, Item 116

42
Bare Knees
Musical setting for *Bare Knees* featuring Virginia Lee Corbin. *Production by:* Gotham. *Music arranged by:* Joseph E. Zivelli. *Note:* Cue sheet. Music incipits. Copy mutilated.
MOMA   1 p., 33 cm.
Music 3236, Item 117

43
Baree, Son of Kazan
An original tax free piano-organ score for *Baree, Son of Kazan* by James Oliver Curwood starring Anita Stewart. *Production by:* David Smith. *Film company:* Vitagraph. *Music composed by:* Michael Hoffman. *Published by:* Michael Hoffman, New York, 1925. *Instrumentation:* Piano/organ. *Copyright:* © C1 E 618211, recieved May 23, 1925.
LC M1527.H7B3   40 p., 34 cm.
Music 3212, Item 156

44
Barefoot Boy
Barefoot Boy. Note: Cue sheet. No music. Typescript.
MOMA   1 p., 28 cm.
Music 3236, Item 118

45
The Barrier
The Barrier. Music by: Sol P. Levy and Frederick O. Hanks. *Published by:* The Rex Beach Pictures Co., New York. *Instrumentation:* Piano.
LC M1527.L657B4   109 p., 31 cm.
Music 3212, Item 8

46
The Barrier
Thematic music cue sheet. *The Barrier* by Rex Beach with Norman Kerry, Lionel Barrymore and Henry B. Walthall. *Directed by:* George Hill. *Scenario by:* Harvey Gates. *Film company:* Metro-Goldwyn-Mayer. *Music compiled by:* Ernst Luz. *Note:* Music incipits. "Wed July 17" marked in pencil. *Number of reels:* 7. *Footage:* 6480. *Maximum projection time:* 1 hour, 17 minutes.
MOMA   4 p., 32 cm.
Music 3236, Item 119

47
The Bat
The Bat. Note: Cue sheet. No music. Typescript.
MOMA   1 p., 28 cm.
Music 3236, Item 120

48
The Battle Cry of Peace
Special musical setting for the patriotic photoplay drama *The Battle Cry of Peace. Film company:* The Vitagraph Company of America. *Music selected and adapted by:* S. L. Rothapfel. *Music edited by:* Ivan Rudisill & S. M. Berg. *Published by:* G. Schirmer, New York, 1915. *Instrumentation:* Piano conductor. *Copyright:* ©C1 E 373407, November 10, 1915.
LC M1527.R68B3   105 p., 31 cm.
Music 3212, Item 9

49
The Battle Cry of Peace
Special musical setting for the patriotic photoplay drama *The Battle Cry of Peace. Film company:* The Vitagraph Company of America. *Music selected and adapted by:* S. L. Rothapfel. *Music edited by:* Ivan Rudisill and S. M. Berg. *Published by:* G. Schirmer, New York, 1915. *Instrumentation:* Piano conductor; (1,1,2,1; 2,2,1,0; tympani and drums; strings). *Copyright:* © C1 E 376042, October 15, 1915.
LC M1357.R   105 p., 31 cm.
Music 3212, Item 10

50
The Battling Bookworm
Suggested musical setting *The Battling Bookworm. Note:* Cue sheet. No music. "Fri & Sat Dec 7–8" marked in pencil. Photographs and advertising information for the film on the verso.
MOMA   1 p., 32 cm.
Music 3236, Item 121

51

Beau Broadway

Thematic music cue sheet. Lew Cody and Aileen Pringle in *Beau Broadway* with Sue Carol. *Production by:* Malcolm St. Clair. *Story by:* Malcolm St. Clair. *Adapted by:* F. Hugh Herbert. *Film company:* Metro-Goldwyn-Mayer. *Music compiled by:* Ernst Luz. *Note:* Music incipits. *Number of reels:* 7. *Footage:* 9010. *Maximum projection time:* 1 hour, 10 minutes.

MOMA   4 p., 32 cm.
                              Music 3236, Item 122

52

Beau Geste

Beau Geste. Note: Cue sheet. No music. Typescript. "Paramount Famous Lasky Corp. Production Department. File No. 891—Bea. Entered 5/24/27 F" stamped on top of each page. Several cues are original composition by Hugo Riesenfeld.

MOMA   5 p., 28 cm.
                              Music 3236, Item 123

53

Beau Geste

Music score of *Beau Geste. Directed by:* Herbert Brenon. *Music compiled and synchronized by:* Hugo Riesenfeld. *Printed by:* Robbins-Engel, Inc. *Published by:* Famous Players-Lasky Corp., New York, 1927. *Instrumentation:* Piano conductor: (1,1,2,1; 2,2,1,0; drums, strings). *Copyright:* © C1 E 653262, January 20, 1927; R 125424, February 8, 1954, Hugo Riesenfeld (A).

LC M1357.R; M1357.R.Pf. copy 2;   140 p., 31 cm
M1527.R56B3   Music 3212, Item 11

54

Beau Geste

Selected themes from *Beau Geste. Music composed and compiled by:* Hugo Riesenfeld. *Orchestration:* D. Savino. *Published by:* Robbins-Engel, Inc., New York, 1927. *Instrumentation:* Piano conductor; (1,0,1,0; 0,2,1,0; drums and tympani; strings) *Copyright:* © C1 E 661451, April 5, 1927; R 129807, May 3, 1954, Robbins Music Corp. (PWH of D. Savino); R 131790, June 14, 1954, Mabel Riesenfeld (W).

LC M1357.R   3 p., 31 cm.
                              Music 3212, Item 12

55

Beau Geste

Chanson Algerian from the super-photoplay production *Beau Geste. Music by:* James C. Bradford & Hans Spialek. *Series title:* Sam Fox Paramount Edition for Orchestra No. 1 (Series A). *Published by:* Sam Fox Pub. Co., Cleveland, 1926. *Instrumentation:* Piano conductor; (1,1,2,1; 2,2,1,0; drums, tympani; strings) *Copyright* © C1 E 652519, December 17, 1926.

LC M1357.B   3 p., 31 cm.
                              Music 3212, Item 13

56

Beau Geste

Marching song of the Foreign Legion from the super-photoplay production *Beau Geste. Music by:* James C. Bradford. *Music arranged by:* Hans Spialek. *Series title:* Sam Fox Paramount Edition for Orchestra No. 2 (Series B). *Published by:* Sam Fox Pub. Co., Cleveland, 1926. *Instrumentation:* Piano conductor; (1,1,2,1; 2,2,1,0; drums, tympani; strings) *Copyright:* ©C1 E 652518, December 17, 1926.

LC M1357.B   3 p., 27 cm.
                              Music 3212, Item 14

57

Beau Sabreur

Thematic music cue sheet. Adolph Zuker [sic] and Jesse L. Lasky present *Beau Sabreur* the answer to *Beau Geste* by Percival C. Wren with Gary Cooper, Evelyn Brent, Noah Beery and William Powell. *Directed by:* John Waters. *Adapted by:* Tom J. Geraghty. *Produced by:* B. P. Schulberg, Associate Producer. *Film company:* Paramount. *Music compiled by:* James C. Bradford. *Note:* Music incipits. *Footage:* 6536.

MOMA   4 p., 32 cm.
                              Music 3236, Item 124

58

The Beautiful Cheat

Thematic music cue sheet. Carl Laemmle presents Laura LaPlante in *The Beautiful Cheat. Directed by:* Edward Sloman. *Written by:* Nina Wilcox Putman. *Film company:* Universal-Jewel. *Music compiled by:* Eugene Conte. *Note:* Music incipits. "Thurs & Friday May 13-14" marked in pencil.

MOMA   2 p., 32 cm.
                              Music 3236, Item 125

59

Beautiful Waters

Beautiful Waters. Note: Cue sheet. No music, Typescript.

MOMA   1 p., 28 cm.
                              Music 3236, Item 126

60

The Beckoning Flame

Musical setting for the photoplay *The Beckoning Flame* (P. 30). *Production by:* Thomas H. Ince. *Music composed and selected by:* Victor L. Schertzinger. *Published by:* G. Schirmer for the Triangle Film Corp., New York, 1915. *Instrumentation:* Piano conductor. *Copyright* © C1 E 377030, December 29, 1915.

LC M1357.S · 40 p., 30 cm.
Music 3212, Item 15

61

Before Midnight

Thematic music cue sheet. Royal Pictures presents *Before Midnight* by William Russell with a distinguished cast including Barbara Bedford. *Directed by:* John Adolfi. *Distributed by:* Henry Ginsberg Distributing Corporation. *Music compiled by:* James C. Bradford. *Note:* Music incipits. "Jan 3-4 Sun & Mon" marked in pencil.

MOMA · 2 p., 31 cm.
Music 3236, Item 127

62

Beggars of Life

Thematic music cue sheet. Adolph Zukor and Jesse L. Lasky present *Beggars of Life* with Wallace Beery, Richard Arlen and Louise Brooks. *Production by:* William A. Wellman. *Story by:* Jim Tully. *Adapted and supervised by:* Benjamin Glazer, B. P. Schulberg, Associate Producer. *Film company:* Paramount. *Note:* Music incipits. *Footage:* 7504.

MOMA · 4 p., 31 cm.
Music 3236, Item 128

63

Behind Closed Doors

Thematic music cue sheet. Columbia Pictures presents *Behind Closed Doors* with Virginia Valli, Gaston Glass, Otto Matiesen and Andre De Segurola. *Production by:* R. William Neill. *Copyrighted and distributed by:* Columbia Pictures Corporation. *Music compiled by:* James C. Bradford. *Note:* Music incipits. "Thursday 3/14" marked in pencil.

MOMA · 2 p., 32 cm.
Music 3236, Item 129

64

Behind the Front

Thematic music cue sheet. Adolph Zukor and Jesse L. Lasky present an Edward Sutherland Production *Behind the Front* with Wallace Beery, Raymond Hatton and Mary Brian. *Story from:* *Spoils of War* by Hugh Wiley. *Adapted by:* Monty Brice. *Screenplay by:* Ethel Doherty. *Film company:* Paramount. *Music compiled by:* James C. Bradford. *Note:* Music incipits. Thermofax copy. *Footage:* 5555.

MOMA · 4 p., 36 cm.
Music 3236, Item 130

65

The Belle of New York

Musical setting for *The Belle of New York. Music compiled by:* Max Winkler. *Note:* Cue sheet. Two songs from the original music written for the play *The Belle of New York* by G. Kerker: Love theme, "Teach me how to kiss," and Salvation Army theme, "They all follow me." Music for the Salvation Army theme on verso of cue sheet.

MOMA · 2 p., 30 cm.
Music 3236, Item 131

66

Below the Deadline

Musical synopsis for *Below the Deadline. Production by:* Chesterfield. *Music compiled by:* Motion Pictures Synchronization Service, Inc., 1650 Broadway, New York City. *Note:* Cue sheet. No music. "Fri & Sat Feb 21-22" marked in pencil.

MOMA · 1 p., 30 cm.
Music 3236, Item 132

67

Ben Hur

Music score for Fred. Niblo's Metro-Goldwyn-Mayer Production of *Ben Hur. Story by:* Gen. Lew Wallace. *Filmed by arrangement with:* A. L. Erlanger. *Music adapted and arranged by:* David Mendoza and William Axt. *Published by:* Photo Play Music Co., Inc., New York, n.d. *Instrumentation:* 1st violin.

MOMA · 80 p., 31 cm.
Music 3236, Item 3

68

Betrayal

Original compositions from *Betrayal. Music score by:* J. S. Zamecnik and L. DeFrancesco. *Published by:* Sam Fox Publishing Co., Cleveland, 1929. *Instrumentation:* Piano conductor. *Copyright:* © C1 Ep 5886, May 14, 1929; R 174210, July 17, 1956, Sam Fox Pub. Co., Inc. (PWH)

LC M1527.B56 · 32 p., 31 cm.
Music 3212, Item 16

69
Between Men

Musical setting for the photoplay *Between Men*. *Production by:* Thomas H. Ince. *Music composed and selected by:* Joseph E. Nurnberger, Victor Schertzinger and Wedgewood Nowell. *Published by:* G. Schirmer for the Triangle Film Corp., New York, 1915. *Series title:* Triangle Plays. *Instrumentation:* Piano conductor. *Copyright:* ©C1 E 377036, December 11, 1915.

LC M1357.N 52 p., 31 cm.
Music 3212, Item 17

70
Beware of Blondes

Thematic music cue sheet. Columbia Pictures presents *Beware of Blondes* with Matt More [sic], Roy D'Arcy, Dorothy Revier. *Story by:* Harvey Thew and George C. Hull. *Scenario by:* Peter Milne. *Production by:* George B. Seitz. *Music compiled by:* James C. Bradford. *Note:* Music incipits. *Copyrighted and distributed by:* Columbia Pictures Corporation.

MOMA 2 p., 31 cm.
Music 3236, Item 133

71
Beware of Married Men

Warner Bros. present *Beware of Married Men* starring Irene Rich. *Note:* Cue sheet. No music. *Projection time:* About an hour, based on a speed of 11 minutes per 1000 feet.

MOMA 1 p., 35 cm.
Music 3236, Item 134

72
Beware of Widows

Thematic music cue sheet. Carl Laemmle presents *Beware of Widows*. *Film company:* Universal-Jewel. *Music compiled by:* James C. Bradford. *Note:* Music incipits. Two copies. "Monday June 27/27" marked in pencil on copy 1. "June 27th" marked in pencil on copy 2.

MOMA 2 p., 32 cm.
Music 3236, Item 135

73
Beyond the Rockies

Musical synopsis for Bob Custer in *Beyond the Rockies*. *Music compiled by:* James C. Bradford. *Note:* Cue sheet. No music. "Wednesday 4/14" marked in pencil.

MOMA 1 p., 30 cm.
Music 3236, Item 136

74
Beyond the Sierras

Thematic music cue sheet. Tim McCoy in *Beyond the Sierras*. *Story by:* John Thomas Neville. *Screenplay by:* Robert Lord. *Directed by:* Nick Grinde. *Film company:* Metro-Goldwyn-Mayer. *Music compiled by:* Ernst Luz. *Note:* Music incipits. *Number of reels:* 6. *Footage:* 5850. *Maximum projection time:* 1 hour, 10 minutes.

MOMA 4 p., 31 cm.
Music 3236, Item 137

75
The Big Killing

The Big Killing. *Note:* Cue sheet. No music. Typescript.

MOMA 1 p., 28 cm.
Music 3236, Item 138

76
The Big Killing

Thematic music cue sheet. Adolph Zukor and Jesse L. Lasky present Wallace Beery and Raymond Hatton in *The Big Killing* with Mary Brian and Lane Chandler. *Story by:* Grover Jones. *Screenplay by:* Gilbert Pratt and Grover Jones. *Production by:* F. Richard Jones; B. P. Schulberg, Associate Producer. *Film company:* Paramount. *Music compiled by:* James C. Bradford. *Note:* Music incipits. *Footage:* 5930.

MOMA 4 p., 31 cm.
Music 3236, Item 139

77
The Big Noise

Thematic music cue sheet. Robert Kane presents Allan Dwan's Production of *The Big Noise* with Chester Conklin. *Story by:* Ben Hecht. *Adaptation by:* Tom Geraghty. *Directed by:* Allan Dwan. *Film company:* First National. *Music compiled by:* Eugene Conte. *Note:* Music incipits.

MOMA 4 p., 32 cm.
Music 3236, Item 140

78
The Big Parade

Music score for King Vidor's Metro-Goldwyn-Mayer Production of *The Big Parade* Starring John Gilbert featuring Renee Adorée. *Screen story by:* Laurence Stallings. *Music adapted and arranged by:* David Mendoza and William Axt with original compositions by William Axt. *Published by:* Photo Play Music Co., Inc., New York, n.d. *Instrumentation:* 1st violin.

MOMA 80 p., 31 cm.
Music 3236, Item 4

79
The Birth of a Nation

D. W. Griffith presents *The Birth of a Nation.*
Music composed by: Joseph Carl Breil. *Instru-
mentation:* Parts (0,1,2,1; 2,2,2, tuba; drums; harp;
1st violin, 1st violin-second desk, 2nd violin, viola)
Note: Cover of oboe part is stamped "LARGE
ORCHESTRA: SET F"; clarinet "LARGE ORCHES-
TRA: SET A"; and viola "MEDIUM ORCHESTRA:
SET NO. 1."
MOMA   35 cm.
                                Music 3236, Item 5

80
The Birth of a Nation

D. W. Griffith presents *The Birth of a Nation.*
Property of: Epoch Producing Corporation, New
York. *Music composed by:* Joseph Carl Breil.
Instrumentation: Parts (1,0,1,0; 0,1,1; drums;
strings). *Note:* All parts headed on first page
"Music score of *The Birth of a Nation.*"
MOMA   31 cm.
                                Music 3236, Item 6

81
The Birth of a Nation

Small orchestra. D. W. Griffith presents *The Birth
of a Nation. Music composed by:* Joseph Carl
Breil. *Instrumentation:* Parts (1,0,1,0; 0,1,1; drums
and tympani; 1st violin, cello, bass).
MOMA   31 cm.
                                Music 3236, Item 7

82
The Birth of a Nation

The Birth of a Nation. Music composed by:
Joseph Carl Breil. *Instrumentation:* Piano conductor. *Note:* Carbon typescript with contents attached (3 p.).
MOMA   151 p., 31 cm.
                                Music 3236, Item 8

83
Bismarck

Bismarck. Story by: R. Schott. *Music composed
by:* Ferdinand Hummel for the Eiko-Film G.m.b.H.
Published by: Eiko Film, G.m.b.H, Berlin, 1914.
Instrumentation: Piano score. *Copyright:* ©C1 E
341671, February 10, 1914.
LC M176.B55   63 p., 33 cm.
                                Music 3212, Item 18

84
Bitter Apples

Warner Bros. present *Bitter Apples* starring
Monte Blue & Myrna Loy. *Note:* Cue sheet. No
music. "Lyceum—Fri. & Sat. Dec.—23–24. 1927"
marked in pencil. *Number of reels:* 6½. *Projection
time:* 61 minutes based on a speed of 11 minutes
per 1000 feet.
MOMA   1 p., 31 cm.
                                Music 3236, Item 141

85
Black Butterflies

Black Butterflies. Note: Cue sheet. No music.
Copy slightly mutilated. Various descriptions and
advertisements for the film on verso.
MOMA   1 p., 40 cm.
                                Music 3236, Item 142

86
The Black Crook

Special piano music for *The Black Crook* in five
parts. *Music composed by:* Walter C. Simon. *Published by:* Kalem Co., New York, 1916. *Instrumentation:* Piano. *Copyright:* © C1 E 376817, January
10, 1916; R 120871, September 2, 1943, Walter C.
Simon, New York.
LC M176.B6   39 p., 33 cm.
                                Music 3212, Item 19

87
Black Jack

Thematic music cue sheet. William Fox feature
film production. Buck Jones in *Black Jack.*
Music compiled by: Michael P. Krueger. *Note:*
Music incipits. "Sun. Oct. 28" marked in pencil.
MOMA   2 p., 31 cm.
                                Music 3236, Item 143

88
Black Paradise

Thematic music cue sheet. William Fox Produc-
tion *Black Paradise. Music compiled by:*
Michael P. Krueger. *Note:* Music incipits. "Mon &
Tuesd Sept 6-7" marked in pencil.
MOMA   2 p., 34 cm.
                                Music 3236, Item 144

89
The Black Pirate

Douglas Fairbanks in *The Black Pirate. Music
by:* Mortimer Wilson, Op. 76. *Instrumentation:*
Orchestral parts (piccolo, 1,1,2,1;2,2,1; percussion;
harp, strings)
MOMA   32 cm., Ms.
                                Music 3236, Item 9

Douglas Fairbanks, Sr. in *The Black Pirate* (1926),
one of the earliest full-length, two-color Technicolor
films. Museum of Modern Art, Film Stills Archive.

90
The Blackguard

Thematic music cue sheet. Lee-Bradford Corporation, Arthur A. Lee President, presents Jane Novak in *The Blackguard. Story by:* Raymond Paton. *Directed by:* Graham Cutts. *Music compiled by:* James C. Bradford. *Note:* Music incipits. "Thurs & Friday 3/25–26" marked in pencil.

MOMA　　　　　　　　　　　　2 p., 31 cm.
Music 3236, Item 145

91
Blind Alleys

Thematic music cue sheet. Adolph Zukor and Jesse L. Lasky present Thomas Meighan in *Blind Alleys* with Evelyn Brent and Greta Nissen. *Story by:* Owen Davis. *Screenplay by:* Emmet Grozier. *Production by:* Frank Tuttle. *Film company:* Paramount. *Music compiled by:* James C. Bradford. *Note:* Music incipits. Two copies. *Footage:* 5477.

MOMA　　　　　　　　　　　　4 p., 32 cm.
Music 3236, Item 146

92
Blindfold

Thematic music cue sheet. William Fox special production George O'Brien and Lois Moran in *Blindfold. Music compiled by:* Michael P. Krueger. *Note:* Music incipits.

MOMA　　　　　　　　　　　　4 p., 31 cm.
Music 3236, Item 147

93
Blockade

Thematic music cue sheet. William Le Baron presents Anna Q. Nilsson in *Blockade. Production by:* George B. Seitz. *Distributed by:* F. B. O. Pictures Corporation. *Music compiled by:* James C. Bradford. *Note:* Music incipits.

MOMA　　　　　　　　　　　　4 p., 31 cm.
Music 3236, Item 148

94
A Blonde for a Night

Thematic music cue sheet. Pathe presents Marie Prevost in *A Blonde for a Night* with Franklin Pangborn, Harrison Ford, T. Roy Barnes and Lucien Littlefield. *Story by:* Willson Collison. *Adapted by:* F. McGrew Willis. *Continuity by:* Rex Taylor. *Directed by:* E. Mason Hopper. *Production by:* DeMille Studio. *Distributed by:* Pathe Exchange, Inc. *Music compiled by:* Rudolph Berliner. *Note:* Music incipits.

MOMA　　　　　　　　　　　　4 p., 31 cm.
Music 3236, Item 149

95
The Blonde Saint

Thematic music cue sheet. Samuel E. Rork presents *The Blonde Saint* with Lewis Stone and Doris Kenyon. *Film company:* First National. *Music Compiled by:* James C. Bradford. *Note:* Music incipits. "Monday Jan 17/26" marked in pencil. Two copies.

MOMA　　　　　　　　　　　　4 p., 32 cm.
Music 3236, Item 150

96
Blood and Sand

Blood and Sand. Note: Cue sheet. No music. Typescript and six copies.

MOMA　　　　　　　　　　　　2 p., 28 cm.
Music 3236, Item 151

97
The Blood Ship

The Blood Ship. Note: Cue sheet. No music.

MOMA　　　　　　　　3 p., 21 cm., Ms.
Music 3236, Item 152

98
Blue Blazes

Musical setting for *Blue Blazes. Music compiled by:* Max Winkler. Theme, "Love's Declaration." (Romance) Baron. *Note:* Cue sheet. No music. "Wednesday 3/24" marked in pencil.

MOMA　　　　　　　　　　　　1 p., 30 cm.
Music 3236, Item 153

99
Blue Blood

A Chadwick Picture musical setting for *Blue Blood. Music arranged by:* Joseph Zivelli. *Note:* Cue sheet. No music. Copy mutilated. "Sat. Feb. 20" marked in pencil.

MOMA　　　　　　　　1 p., 35 by 53 cm.
Music 3236, Item 154

100
Blue Skies

Thematic music cue sheet. William Fox Film Production *Blue Skies. Music compiled by:* Michael P. Krueger. *Note:* Music incipits.

MOMA　　　　　　　　　　　　4 p., 32 cm.
Music 3236, Item 155

101
The Border Sheriff
Musical setting for *The Border Sheriff. Music compiled by:* M. Winkler. "My Madeline" theme by Maurice Baron. *Note:* Cue sheet. No music. "Saturday May 8" marked in pencil.
MOMA   1 p., 31 cm.
                            Music 3236, Item 156

102
Born to the West
Thematic music cue sheet. Adolph Zukor and Jesse L. Lasky present Zane Grey's *Born to the West* with Jack Holt, Margaret Morris, Raymond Hatton, Arlette Marchal and George Siegman. *Adaptation and screenplay by:* Lucien Hubbard. *Directed by:* John Waters. *Film company:* Paramount. *Music compiled by:* James C. Bradford. *Note:* Music incipits. *Footage:* 6403.
MOMA   4 p., 32 cm.
                            Music 3236, Item 157

103
Borrowed Finery
Thematic music cue sheet. Tiffany presents *Borrowed Finery. Story by:* George Bronson Howard. *Directed by:* Oscar Apfel. *Music compiled by:* James C. Bradford. *Note:* Music incipits. "Mon & Tuesday Jan 18–19" marked in pencil.
MOMA   4 p., 32 cm.
                            Music 3236, Item 158

104
Boy Blue
Boy Blue. Note: Cue sheet. No music. Typescript.
MOMA   1 p., 28 cm.
                            Music 3236, Item 159

105
Branded Sombrero
Thematic music cue sheet. Buck Jones in *Branded Sombrero. Production by:* William Fox Feature Film. *Music compiled by:* Michael P. Krueger. *Note:* Music incipits. "Sunday Dec 23" marked in pencil.
MOMA   2 p., 32 cm.
                            Music 3236, Item 160

106
Breezy Bill
A Syndicate Picture musical setting for *Breezy Bill* featuring Bob Steele. *Type of film:* Western comedy drama. *Music arranged by:* Joseph E. Zivelli. *Note:* Cue sheet. No music. "Wed & Thurs Apr 22 & 23 Plaza Theatre" marked in pencil. *Number of reels:* 5.
MOMA   1 p., 32 cm.
                            Music 3236, Item 161

107
Bride of the Storm
Warner Bros. present *Bride of the Storm* starring Dolores Costello and Tyrone Power. *Note:* Cue sheet. No music. "Sat & Sun Sept 3–4" marked in pencil. *Projection time:* 1 hour, 13 minutes based on a speed of 11 minutes per 1000 feet. *Number of reels:* 7.
MOMA   1 p., 35 cm.
                            Music 3236, Item 162

108
La Briere
La Briere. Scènes Cinématographiques. *Inspired by the film by:* Léon Poirier. *Based on the novel by:* A. de Châteaubriant. *Published by:* Éditions Musicales Évette, Paris, 1927. *Music by:* Paul Ladmirault. *Instrumentation:* Piano conductor: (1,1,1,1: 1,2,1,0; tympani, harmonium; strings) *Copyright:* © Cl E 684118, November 1, 1927.
LC M1527.L15B5   14 cues, 29 cm.
                            Music 3212, Item 20

109
The Broadway Boob
Thematic music cue sheet. Associated Exhibitors, Inc., Oscar A. Price, Pres., presents Glen Hunter in *The Broadway Boob* with Mildred Ryan. *From the story by:* C. Gardner Sullivan. *Directed by:* Joseph Henabery. *Released by:* Associated Exhibitors, Inc. *Music compiled by:* James C. Bradford. *Note:* Music incipits. "Wed July 14" marked in pencil.
MOMA   4 p., 32 cm.
                            Music 3236, Item 163

110
Broadway Fever
Broadway Fever. Note: Cue sheet. No music. Ms.
MOMA   2 p., 28 cm.
                            Music 3236, Item 164

111
The Broadway Gallant
Thematic music cue sheet. A. Carlos presents Richard Talmadge in *The Broadway Gallant. Directed by:* Mason Noel. *Production by:* Richard Talmadge. *Distributed by:* Film Booking Offices of America, Inc. *Music compiled by:* James C.

Bradford. *Note:* Music incipits. "Sunday May 16"
marked in pencil.

MOMA   4 p., 32 cm.
                                Music 3236, Item 165

112
Broadway Nights
Thematic music cue sheet. Robert Kane presents
Broadway Nights with Lois Wilson, Sam Hardy,
Louis John Bartels and Phillip Strange. *Adapted
for the screen by:* Forrest Halsey. *From the orig-
inal story by:* Norman Houston. *Directed by:*
John C. Boyle. *Film company:* First National.
Music compiled by: James C. Bradford. *Note:*
Music incipits. "Thursday July 14/27" marked in
pencil. Copy mutilated.

MOMA   4 p., 32 cm.
                                Music 3236, Item 166

113
Broken Blossoms
D. W. Griffith's *Broken Blossoms. Adapted from a
story by:* Thomas Burke. *Produced by:* D. W. Griffith. *Music by:* Louis F. Gottschalk. *Instrumentation:* Piano conductor; (1,1,2,1; 2,2,1,0; drums
[Prologue I° missing]; harp [Prologue I° only],
strings). *Note:* Prologue I° bound separately.

MOMA   13, 55 p., 31 cm.
                                 Music 3236, Item 10

114
The Broken Gate
Thematic music cue sheet. Tiffany Productions
presents *The Broken Gate. By:* Emerson Hough,
author of *The Covered Wagon. Directed by:*
James C. McKay. *Music compiled by:* James C.
Bradford. *Note:* Music incipits. "Monday April
4/27" marked in pencil. Three copies.

MOMA   4 p., 32 cm.
                                Music 3236, Item 167

115
Broken Hearts
Jaffe Art Film *Broken Hearts. Note:* Cue sheet. No
music. "Wed Thurs & Frid. May 19-20-21"
marked in pencil. Typescript. *Footage:* 8060.

MOMA   2 p., 28 cm.
                                Music 3236, Item 168

116
Brotherly Love
Thematic music cue sheet. Karl Dane and
George K. Arthur in *Brotherly Love. Based on
the story* Big Hearted Jim *by:* Petterson Marzoni.
Screenplay by: Earl Baldwin. *Continuity by:* Earl
Baldwin and Lew Lipton. *Directed by:* Charles F.

Reisner. *Film company:* Metro-Goldwyn-Mayer.
Music compiled by: Ernst Luz. *Note:* Music incipits. *Number of reels:* 7. *Footage:* 6495. *Maximum
projection time:* 1 hour, 12 minutes.

MOMA   4 p., 30 cm.
                                Music 3236, Item 169

117
The Brown Derby
Thematic music cue sheet. C. C. Burr presents
Johnny Hines in *The Brown Derby. Film com-
pany:* First National. *Music compiled by:* Dr.
Edward Kilenyi. *Note:* Music incipits. Two copies.
"Sat & Sun Aug 14-15" marked in pencil on
copy 1. "Sat & Sunday Aug 14-15" marked on
copy 2.

MOMA   4 p., 32 cm.
                                Music 3236, Item 170

118
The Brute
Warner Bros. presents *The Brute* starring Monte
Blue. *Note:* Cue sheet. No music. Two copies.
"Monday May 9/27" marked in pencil on copy 2
which is also mutilated. *Number of reels:* 10. *Projection time:* 1 hour, 14 minutes based on a speed
of 10 minutes per 1000 feet.

MOMA   1 p., 32 cm.
                                Music 3236, Item 171

119
Buck Privates
Thematic music cue sheet. Carl Laemmle pre-
sents *Buck Privates. Film company:* Universal-
Jewel. *Music compiled by:* James C. Bradford.
Note: Music incipits.

MOMA   4 p., 31 cm.
                                Music 3236, Item 172

120
The Bugler of Battery B &
Hungry Hanks Hallucination
Special piano music for *The Bugler of Battery B
& Hungry Hanks Hallucination. Music by:* Walter C. Simon. *Published by:* Kalem Co., New York,
1912. *Instrumentation:* Piano. *Copyright:* © C1 E
288312, June 20, 1912.

LC M176.B83   13 p., 32 cm.
                                 Music 3212, Item 21

15

121
Burning Daylight
Thematic music cue sheet. Richard A. Rowland presents Milton Sills in *Burning Daylight* with Doris Kenyon. *Produced by:* Wid Gunning. *Production by:* Charles J. Brabin. *Film company:* First National. *Music compiled by:* Eugene Conte. *Note:* Music incipits. Two copies. "5/28/28" marked in pencil on copy 1.
MOMA   5 p., 31 cm.
                                Music 3236, Item 173

122
Burning the Wind
Thematic music cue sheet. Carl Laemmle presents *Burning the Wind*. *Production by:* Universal. *Music compiled by:* James C. Bradford. *Note:* Music incipits.
MOMA   2 p., 33 cm.
                                Music 3236, Item 174

123
The Bush Leaguer
Warner Bros. presents *The Bush Leaguer* starring Monte Blue. *Note:* Cue sheet. No music. "Aug 29/27 Monday" marked in pencil. *Projection time:* 1 hour, 8 minutes based on a speed of 10 minutes per 1000 feet.
MOMA   1 p., 30 cm.
                                Music 3236, Item 175

124
Bustin' Thru
Musical setting for *Bustin' Thru*. *Music compiled by:* M. Winkler. "Scented Floweret" theme by Zivelli. *Note:* Cue sheet. No music. "Saturday 12/19" marked in pencil.
MOMA   1 p., 30 cm.
                                Music 3236, Item 176

125
The Butter and Egg Man
Thematic music cue sheet. Richard A. Rowland presents *The Butter and Egg Man* with Jack Mulhall and Greta Nissen. *From the play by:* George S. Kaufman. *Production by:* Richard Wallace. *Film company:* First National. *Music compiled by:* James C. Bradford. *Note:* Music incipits.
MOMA   4 p., 32 cm.
                                Music 3236, Item 177

126
Butterflies in the Rain
Thematic music cue sheet. Carl Laemmle presents Laura LaPlante and James Kirkwood in *Butterflies in the Rain*. *Directed by:* Edward Slo-

man. *Film company:* Universal-Jewel. *Music compiled by:* James C. Bradford. *Note:* Music incipits.
MOMA   2 p., 34 cm.
                                Music 3236, Item 178

127
Buttons
Thematic music cue sheet. Jackie Coogan in *Buttons* with Lars Hanson, Gertrude Olmsted and Paul Hurst. *From the story by:* George Hill. *Adapted by:* Hayden Talbot. *Continuity by:* Marian Constance Blackton. *Production by:* George Hill. *Directed by:* George Hill. *Film company:* Metro-Goldwyn-Mayer. *Music compiled by:* Ernst Luz. *Note:* Music incipits. *Number of reels:* 7. *Footage:* 6020. *Maximum projection time:* 1 hour, 10 minutes.
MOMA   4 p., 32 cm.
                                Music 3236, Item 179

128
By the Law
Music for *By the Law*. *Published by:* The Museum of Modern Art Film Library, New York. *Instrumentation:* Piano score.
MOMA   98 p., 32 cm.
                                Music 3236, Item 11

129
Cabaret
Cabaret. *Note:* Cue sheet. No Music. Typescript.
MOMA   2 p., 28 cm.
                                Music 3236, Item 180

130
The Cabinet of Dr. Caligari
The Cabinet of Dr. Caligari. *Instrumentation:* Piano conductor. *Note:* Typescript with contents attached.
MOMA   140 p., 30 cm.
                                Music 3236, Item 12

131
Caïn
Caïn, Aventure des Mers Exotique. *Film by:* Léon Poirier C.U.C. *Music composed by:* André Petiot. *Music arranged by:* Ph. Pares. *Published by:* Editions Musicales Sam Fox, Paris, 1930. *Instrumentation:* Piano score. *Copyright:* © C1 E for. 17072, received February 26, 1931.
LC M1527.P6C3   95 p., 31 cm.
                                Music 3212, Item 157

To accompany the cracked and grotesque setting of
The Cabinet of Dr. Caligari (1919) for its showing at
the Roxy Theater, Erno Rapee and S. L. ("Roxy")
Rothapfel selected thematic material from the music of
modern composers, Schoenberg, Debussy, Stravinsky,
Prokofieff and Richard Strauss. Museum of Modern
Art, Film Stills Archive.

132

California Straight Ahead

Thematic music cue sheet. Carl Laemmle presents Reginald Denny in *California Straight Ahead* by Byron Morgan. *Production by:* Harry Pollard. *Film company:* Universal-Jewel. *Music compiled by:* Eugene Conte. *Note:* Music incipits. "Saturday 3/6" marked in pencil.

MOMA   2 p., 36 cm.
                          Music 3236, Item 181

133

The Call of Courage

Musical setting for *The Call of Courage. Music compiled by:* Max Winkler. "Adolescence" (Entre Act) theme by Collinge. *Note:* Cue sheet. No music "Mon & Tuesday Feb 1–2" marked in pencil.

MOMA   1 p., 30 cm.
                          Music 3236, Item 182

134

Call of the Desert

A Syndicate Picture musical setting for *Call of the Desert* featuring Tom Tyler. *Character of film:* Western drama. *Music arranged by:* Joseph E. Zivelli. Love theme, "When the right one comes along" (Feist); Plot theme, "The Crook" by Peele (Belwin). *Note:* Cue sheet. No music. "Nov. 28 & 29, 1930 Plaza Theatre" marked in ink. *Number of reels:* 5.

MOMA   1 p., 32 cm.
                          Music 3236, Item 183

135

Canyon of Missing Men

Musical setting for *Canyon of Missing Men. Film company:* Syndicate. *Music arranged by:* Joseph E. Zivelli. Love theme, "Amorita," by Zamecnik (Fox); Gang theme, "The conspirators," by Santos (Belwin). *Note:* Cue sheet. No music. "Plaza Theatre Bayonne, N.J. Fri. & Sa. Oct. 10 & 11—1930" marked in ink. Includes descriptive and promotional material for *Canyon of Missing Men. Number of reels:* 5.

MOMA   1 p., 32 cm.
                          Music 3236, Item 184

136

Captain Careless

Musical synopsis for *Captain Careless. Music compiled by:* James C. Bradford. Theme, "Ain't that a grand and glorious feeling." *Note:* Cue sheet. No music.

MOMA   1 p., 32 cm.
                          Music 3236, Item 185

137

Captain Lash

Thematic music cue sheet. Victor McLaglen in *Captain Lash. Production by:* William Fox. *Music compiled by:* Michael P. Krueger. *Note:* Music incipits.

MOMA   6 p., 32 cm.
                          Music 3236, Item 186

138

Captain Swagger

Thematic music cue sheet. Pathe presents Rod La Rocque in *Captain Swagger* with Sue Carol. *From an original story by:* Leonard Praskins. *Adapted by:* Adelaide Heilbron. *Production by:* Hector Turnbull. *Directed by:* Edward H. Griffith. *Distributed by:* Pathe Exchange, Inc. *Music compiled by:* James C. Bradford. *Note:* Music incipits.

MOMA   4 p., 31 cm.
                          Music 3236, Item 187

139

The Captive God

The Captive God, 1916, W. S. Hart. *Note:* Cue sheet. No music.

MOMA   2 p., 28 cm., Ms.
                          Music 3236, Item 188

140

Captured by Bedouins

Special piano music for *Captured by Bedouins. Music composed by:* Walter C. Simon. *Published by:* Kalem Co., New York, 1912. *Instrumentation:* Piano. *Copyright:* ©C1 E 296671, June 6, 1912; R 86887, April 27, 1940, Walter C. Simon, New York.

LC M176.C25   14 p., 32 cm.
                           Music 3212, Item 22

141

Carmen

Carmen. Opera-drama in English. *Music by:* Georges Bizet. *Translated and adapted by:* Jeannette Kretschmer Templeton. *Published by:* G. Schirmer, Inc., New York, 1923. *Instrumentation:* Piano/vocal score.

LC M1527.B62C3   391, 37 p., 28 cm., Ms. and printed
                          Music 3212, Item 158

World famous opera singer, Geraldine Farrar, in De
Mille's *Carmen* (1915), one of the earliest films to use
musical accompaniment during the production to help
set the mood. Geraldine Farrar Collection, Music Division, Library of Congress.

142
Carmen

Paramount photoplay music (P 123) for *Carmen* as produced by the Jesse L. Lasky Feature Play Co. featuring Geraldine Farrar by special arrangement with Morris Gest. Special musical setting used in the original presentation at Symphony Hall, Boston under the direction of S. L. Rothapfel. *Music arranged by:* Hugo Riesenfeld. *Published by:* G. Schirmer, New York, 1915. *Series title:* Schirmer's Photoplay Series. *Instrumentation:* Piano conductor; (1,0,2,0; 0,2,1,0; drums; strings). *Copyright:* © C1 E 373892, received by LC November 24, 1915.

LC M1357.R   92 p., 31 cm.
                              Music 3212, Item 23

143
The Case of Lena Smith

Thematic music cue sheet. Adolph Zukor and Jesse L. Lasky present *The Case of Lena Smith* with Esther Ralston and James Hall. *From the story by:* Samuel Ornitz. *Adapted by:* Jules Furthman. *Production by:* Josef von Sternberg. *Film company:* Paramount. *Music compiled by:* James C. Bradford. *Note:* Music incipits. *Footage:* 7229.

MOMA   4 p., 32 cm.
                             Music 3236, Item 189

144
Casey at the Bat

Casey at the Bat. Note: Cue sheet. No music. Typescript.

MOMA   1 p., 28 cm.
                             Music 3236, Item 190

145
Casey at the Bat

Thematic music cue sheet. Adolph Zukor and Jesse L. Lasky present Wallace Beery in *Casey at the Bat* with Ford Sterling, ZaSu [sic] Pitts and Sterling Holloway. *Screenplay by:* Jules Furthman. *Production by:* Hector Turnbull. *Directed by:* Monte Brice. *Film company:* Paramount. *Music compiled by:* James C. Bradford. *Note:* Music incipits. "Coming Thursday May 12/27" marked in pencil. *Footage:* 6040.

MOMA   4 p., 32 cm.
                             Music 3236, Item 191

146
The Cavalier

Thematic music cue sheet. Tiffany-Stahl presents *The Cavalier* with Richard Talmadge, Barbara Bedford, Nora Cecil, David Torrence, Stuart Holmes and David Mir. *Suggested from the novel* The Black Rider *by:* Max Brand. *Production by:* James C. Bradford. *Note:* Music incipits. Two copies.

MOMA   4 p., 31 cm.
                             Music 3236, Item 192

147
The Cave Man

Warner Brothers presents *The Cave Man* starring Marie Prevost and Matt Moore. *Note:* Cue sheet. No music. "Saturday 4/10" marked in pencil. Mutilated. *Number of reels:* 7. *Projection time:* 1 hour, 16 minutes based on a speed of 11 minutes per 1000 feet.

MOMA   1 p., 35 cm.
                             Music 3236, Item 193

148
Celebrity

Thematic music cue sheet. Pathe presents *Celebrity* with Lina Basquette, Robert Armstrong and Clyde Cook. *From the stage play by:* William Keefe. *Adapted by:* Elliott Clawson. *Screenplay by:* Tay Garnett and George Dromgold. *Production by:* Ralph Block. *Directed by:* Tay Garnett. *Distributed by:* Pathe Exchange, Inc. *Music compiled by:* Howard T. Wood. *Note:* Music incipits. Two copies.

MOMA   4 p., 31 cm.
                             Music 3236, Item 194

149
Cendrillon

Cendrillon. (Berger) *Music score by:* M. Lucien-Marie Aubé. *Note:* Cue sheet. No music. In French and English.

MOMA   1 p., 31 cm. by 21 cm., Ms.
                             Music 3236, Item 195

150
La Chaîne d'Amour

La Chaine d'Amour. Pièce d'Ombre. *Poem by:* Gabriel Montoya. *Music by:* Jules Bouval. *Published by:* Alphonse Leduc, Paris, 1898. *Instrumentation:* Piano/vocal score. *Copyright:* No. 75167-2, 1898, Alphonse Leduc (received December 23, 1898 by the LC)

LC M176.C43   39 p., 24 cm.
                             Music 3212, Item 24

151
Champion of Lost Causes

Music cue sheet. Edmund Lowe in *Champion of Lost Causes. Production by:* William Fox. *Music compiled by:* Michael P. Krueger. *Note:* No music. Typescript.

MOMA   2 p., 36 cm.

Music 3236, Item 196

152
Chang

Chang. Note: Cue sheet. No music. Two copies.

MOMA   3 p., 28 cm.

Music 3236, Item 197

153
The Chaplin Revue

Score *The Chaplin Revue. Music by:* Charles Chaplin. *Published by:* Bourne Inc., New York, 1959. *Instrumentation:* Piano conductor. *Copyright:* EP 134955, November 2, 1959.

LC M1527.C46C37   132 p., 31 cm.

Music 3212, Item 25

154
The Charge of the Gauchos

Thematic music cue sheet. William Le Baron presents The Ajuria Production *The Charge of the Gauchos* with Jacqueline Logan and Francis X. Bushman. *From the story by:* Julian Ajuria. *Directed by:* Albert Kelly. *Distributed by:* F B O Pictures Corporation. *Music compiled by:* James C. Bradford. *Note:* Music incipits.

MOMA   4 p., 32 cm.

Music 3236, Item 198

155
The Charlatan

Thematic music cue sheet. Carl Laemmle presents *The Charlatan. Production by:* Universal. *Music compiled by:* James C. Bradford. *Note:* Music incipits.

MOMA   2 p., 32 cm.

Music 3236, Item 199

156
Chasing Trouble

Musical setting for *Chasing Trouble. Music compiled by:* Max Winkler. Theme, "Clara" (Valse Amoureuse) by Winkler. *Note:* Cue sheet. No music. Two copies. "Sunday June 20" marked in pencil on both copies.

MOMA   1 p., 31 cm.

Music 3236, Item 200

157
Cheating Cheaters

Thematic music cue sheet. Carl Laemmle presents *Cheating Cheaters. Film company:* Universal-Jewel. *Music compiled by:* Eugene Conte. *Note:* Music incipits. "Thursday Feb 2/28" marked in pencil.

MOMA   2 p., 34 cm.

Music 3236, Item 201

158
The Cheerful Fraud

Thematic music cue sheet. Carl Laemmle presents Reginald Denny in *The Cheerful Fraud* by K. R. G. Browne. *Production by:* William Seiter. *Film company:* Universal-Jewel. *Music compiled by:* Eugene Conte. *Note:* Music incipits. "Thursday Jan 13, '27" marked in pencil.

MOMA   2 p., 32 cm.

Music 3236, Item 202

159
Chess Fever

Music for *Chess Fever. Published by:* The Museum of Modern Art Film Library, New York. *Instrumentation:* Piano score.

MOMA   39 p., 32 cm.

Music 3236, Item 13

160
Chicago

Thematic music cue sheet. Pathe presents *Chicago* with Phyllis Haver. *From the play by:* Maurine Watkins. *Adaptation and continuity by:* Lenore J. Coffee. *As produced on the stage by:* Sam H. Harris. *Production by:* DeMille Studio. *Directed by:* Frank Urson. *Distributed by:* Pathe Exchange, Inc. *Music compiled by:* Rudolph Berliner. *Note:* Music incipits. Two copies. "May-6-to-9" marked in pencil on copy 1. "Sat 4/12" marked in pencil on copy 2.

MOMA   4 p., 32 cm.

Music 3236, Item 203

161
Chicago After Midnight

Thematic music cue sheet. Joseph P. Kennedy presents *Chicago After Midnight* with Ralph Ince and Helen Jerome Eddy. *Story by:* Charles K. Harris. *Production by:* Ralph Ince. *Distributed by:* F B O Pictures Corporation. *Music compiled by:* James C. Bradford. *Note:* Music incipits. "Wed. Thurs. Fri. Sat. 3/-21-22-23-24/27 Lyceum Theatre Bayonne, N.J." marked in pencil.

MOMA   4 p., 31 cm.

Music 3236, Item 204

162
Children of Divorce

Children of Divorce. Note: Cue sheet. No music. Typescript.

MOMA 1 p., 28 cm.
Music 3236, Item 205

163
China Bound

Thematic music cue sheet. Karl Dane and George K. Arthur in *China Bound* with Josephine Dunn and Polly Moran. *Story by:* Sylvia Thalberg and Frank Butler. *Continuity by:* Peggy Kelly. *Directed by:* Charles F. Reisner. *Film company:* Metro-Goldwyn-Mayer. *Music compiled by:* Ernst Luz. *Note:* Music incipits. *Number of reels:* 7. *Footage:* 5621. *Maximum projection time:* 1 hour, 5 minutes.

MOMA 4 p., 31 cm.
Music 3236, Item 206

164
Chinatown Charlie

Thematic music cue sheet. C. C. Burr presents Johnny Hines in *Chinatown Charlie. Film company:* First National. *Music compiled by:* James C. Bradford. *Note:* Music incipits.

MOMA 4 p., 32 cm.
Music 3236, Item 207

165
The Chinese Parrot

Greater thematic music cue sheet for *The Chinese Parrot* with Marian Nixon, Edmund Burns and Hobart Bosworth. *Film company:* Universal. *Music compiled by:* James C. Bradford. *Note:* Music incipits. Two copies. "Mon. Feb 20" marked in pencil on copy 1. "Lyceum—Thurs. Fri. Sat. Jan. 12-13-14-1927" marked in pencil on copy 2. Copy one incomplete.

MOMA 6, 8 p., 31 cm.
Music 3236, Item 208

166
Chip of the Flying U

Thematic music cue sheet. Carl Laemmle presents Hoot Gibson in *Chip of the Flying U. From the novel by:* B. M. Bowers. *Directed by:* Lynn Reynolds. *Film company:* Universal-Jewel. *Note:* Music incipits. "Saturday 3/27" marked in pencil.

MOMA 2 p., 40 cm.
Music 3236, Item 209

167
Circumstancial [sic] Evidence

A Chesterfield Attraction. Musical setting for Helen Foster in *Circumstancial Evidence. Music arranged by:* Joseph E. Zivelli. Lucy theme, "She's a mean Job," (Remick); Love theme, "Remember, I love you," (Mills). *Note:* Cue sheet. No music. "Wed & Thurs Feb 26-27 also 1 reel comedy & Trailer" marked in pencil.

MOMA 1 p., 30 cm.
Music 3236, Item 210

168
The Circus Kid

Thematic music cue sheet. William Le Baron presents *The Circus Kid* with Joe E. Brown, Frankie Darro, Helene Costello, Poodles Hanneford and Troupe. *From the story by:* James Ashmore Creelman. *Production by:* George B. Seitz. *Distributed by:* F B O Pictures Corporation. *Music compiled by:* Howard T. Wood. *Note:* Music incipits.

MOMA 4 p., 31 cm.
Music 3236, Item 211

169
Circus Rookies.

Thematic music cue sheet. Karl Dane and George K. Arthur in *Circus Rookies* with Louise Lorraine. *Story by:* Edward Sedgwick and Lew Lipton. *Continuity by:* Richard Schayer. *Production by:* Edward Sedgwick. *Directed by:* Edward Sedgwick. *Film company:* Metro-Goldwyn-Mayer. *Music compiled by:* Ernst Luz. *Note:* Music incipits. *Number of reels:* 6. *Footage:* 5605. *Maximum projection time:* 1 hour, 10 minutes.

MOMA 4 p., 31 cm.
Music 3236, Item 212

170
The City Gone Wild

Thematic music cue sheet. Adolph Zukor and Jesse L. Lasky present Thomas Meighan in *The City Gone Wild* with Marietta Millner and Louise Brooks. *Story by:* Charles and Jules Furthman. *Screenplay by:* Jules Furthman. *Production by:* James Cruze; B. P. Schulberg, Associate Producer. *Film company:* Paramount. *Music compiled by:* James C. Bradford. *Note:* Music incipits. "Thursday Feb 9/28" marked in pencil. *Footage:* 5408.

MOMA 4 p., 32 cm.
Music 3236, Item 213

Virginia Cherrill and Charlie Chaplin in *City Lights* (1931). Chaplin, with the help of trained composers, wrote his own musical accompaniments. He was one of the only directors who continued to make silent films after the introduction of sound films. Museum of Modern Art, Film Stills Archive.

171
City Lights—Les Lumières de la Ville

City Lights—Les Lumières de la Ville. Music by: Charles Chaplin. *Published by:* Editions Campbell, Connelly, Paris, 1931. *Instrumentation:* Piano. *Copyright:* ©Eu 54286, December 4, 1931. LC M1527.C46C4.

131 p., 30 cm.
Music 3212, Item 26

172
The City Without Jews

Music cue sheet *The City Without Jews. Music arranged by:* Saunders Kurtz. *Note:* No music. "Thurs. Fri. Sat." marked in pencil. Typescript.
MOMA

1 p., 28 cm.
Music 3236, Item 214

173
Civilization

Musical score for Thos. H. Ince's million dollar cinema spectacle *Civilization. Music composed and arranged by:* Victor L. Schertzinger. *Published by:* Leo Feist, Inc. for Thos. H. Ince, Inc., New York, 1916. *Instrumentation:* Piano conductor. *Copyright:* © C1 E 388905, August 11, 1916; R 130640, August 4, 1944, Julia E. Schertzinger, Los Angeles.
LC M1357.S

112 p., 30 cm.
Music 3212, Item 27

174
Civilization

From Thos. H. Ince's million dollar cinema spectacle *Civilization* Peace March. *Music composed by:* Victor L. Schertzinger, arranged by Lee Orean Smith. *Published by:* Leo Feist, Inc., New York, 1916. *Instrumentation:* Piano; (1,1,0,0; 2 sax; 2,1,0; strings; drums, tympani in 2, tenor and alto sax). *Copyright:* © C1 E 388794, received by LC July 31, 1916.
LC M1357.S

3 p.
No microfilm

175
Clancy's Kosher Wedding

Thematic music cue sheet. Joseph P. Kennedy presents *Clancy's Kosher Wedding* with George Sidney. *Directed by:* A. E. Gilsprom. *Distributed by:* F B O Pictures Corporation. *Note:* Music incipits.
MOMA

4 p., 31 cm.
Music 3236, Item 215

176
Clash of the Wolves

Warner Brothers presents Rin-Tin-Tin in *Clash of the Wolves. Note:* Cue sheet. No music. "Sat Feb 13" marked in pencil. *Footage:* 6700. *Projection time:* 1 hour, 13 minutes based on a speed of 11 minutes per 1000 feet.
MOMA

1 p., 36 cm.
Music 3236, Item 216

177
Clear the Decks

Greater thematic music cue sheet. Carl Laemmle presents Reginald Denny in *Clear the Decks. Directed by:* Joseph Henabery. *Production by:* Universal Denny-Jewel. *Music compiled by:* James C. Bradford. *Note:* Music incipits.
MOMA

8 p., 32 cm.
Music 3236, Item 217

178
Clearing the Trail

Thematic music cue sheet. Carl Laemmle presents *Clearing the Trail. Production by:* Universal. *Music compiled by:* James C. Bradford. *Note:* Music incipits. Two copies.
MOMA

1 p., 31 cm.
Music 3236, Item 218

179
The Clever Dummy

The Clever Dummy. Music arranged by: Alden Beach. *Instrumentation:* Piano score. *Note:* Typescript with contents attached.
MOMA

42 p., 31 cm.
Music 3236, Item 14

180
The Cloak

Music for *The Cloak. Published by:* The Museum of Modern Art Film Library, New York. *Instrumentation:* Piano score.
MOMA

59 p., 32 cm.
Music 3236, Item 15

181
Clothes Make the Woman

Clothes Make the Woman. Note: Cue sheet. No music. Typescript.
MOMA

1 p., 28 cm.
Music 3236, Item 219

Thomas Ince's *Civilization* (1916) was reissued in
1930 with a musical score and talking sequences, a not
uncommon practice which radically altered the
rhythm of the original photoplay. Museum of Modern
Art, Film Stills Archive.

182

The Cohens and Kellys in Paris

Thematic music cue sheet. Carl Laemmle presents George Sidney and J. Farrell McDonald in *The Cohens and Kellys in Paris* with Vera Gordon and Kate Price. *Production by:* William Beaudine. *Film company:* Universal. *Music compiled by:* James C. Bradford. *Note:* Music incipits. Two copies "Saturday 3/3/28" marked in pencil on copy 1. "April 3–4" marked in pencil on copy 2. Copy 2 incomplete.

MOMA   8, 4 p., 31 cm.
Music 3236, Item 220

183

Cohens and Kellys in Scotland

Cohens and Kellys in Scotland. Note: Cue sheet. No music. Two completely different copies with two separate sets of cues.

MOMA   6 p., 33 cm.
Music 3236, Item 221 and 221a

184

La Colère des Dieux

La Colère des Dieux. Music arranged by: M. Marcel Devaux. *Note:* Cue sheet. No music. In French.

MOMA   1 p., 27 by 21 cm., Ms.
Music 3236, Item 222

185

College

Thematic music cue sheet. Buster Keaton in *College. Film company:* United Artists. *Music compiled by:* Ernst Luz. *Note:* Music incipits. Thermofax.

MOMA   4 p., 36 cm.
Music 3236, Item 223

186

Combat

Thematic music cue sheet. Carl Laemmle presents House Peters in *Combat* by J. G. Hawks and Edward Montaigne. *Directed by:* Lynn Reynolds. *Film company:* Universal-Jewel. *Music compiled by:* Eugene Conte. *Note:* Music incipits. "Wednesday June 16" marked in pencil.

MOMA   2 p., 34 cm.
Music 3236, Item 224

187

Come and Get It

Musical synopsis for *Come and Get It. Music compiled by:* James C. Bradford. *Note:* Cue sheet. No music.

MOMA   1 p., 30 cm.
Music 3236, Item 225

188

Compromise

Warner Brothers presents Irene Rich-Clive Brook-Louise Fazenda in *Compromise. Note:* Cue sheet. No music. "Saturday 2/27" marked in pencil. *Number of reels:* 7. *Projection time:* 1 hour, 17 minutes based on a speed of 11 minutes per 1000 feet.

MOMA   1 p., 36 cm.
Music 3236, Item 226

189

Comtesse Ursel

Comtesse Ursel, ein Film-Lustspiel. Starring Henry Porten. *Film company:* Messter-Film G.m.b.H., Berlin. *Music by:* G. Becce. *Published by:* Ed. Bote & G. Bock, Berlin, 1913. *Instrumentation:* Piano score. *Copyright:* ©C1 E 325426, October 24, 1913; R 10017, October 7, 1941, G. Becce, Berlin.

LC M176.C735   48 p., 33 cm.
Music 3212, Item 28

190

The Confederate Ironclad

Special piano music for *The Confederate Ironclad. Music by:* Walter C. Simon. *Published by:* Kalem Co., New York, 1912. *Instrumentation:* Piano. *Copyright:* © C1 E 293449, September 1, 1912; R 87446, May 24, 1940, Walter C. Simon, New York.

LC M176.C74   18 p., 32 cm.
Music 3212, Item 29

191

Confessions of a Wife

Thematic music cue sheet. Samuel Zierler presents Helene Chadwick in *Confessions of a Wife. Adapted from the stage play by:* Owen Davis. *Music compiled by:* Howard T. Wood. *Note:* Music incipits.

MOMA   2 p., 32 cm.
Music 3236, Item 227

192

The Conqueror

Musical setting for the photoplay *The Conqueror* (P. 35). *Production by:* Thomas H. Ince. *Music composed and arranged by:* Victor L. Schertzinger and Wedgewood Nowell. *Published by:* G. Schirmer for the Triangle Film Corp., New York, 1916. *Series title:* Triangle Plays. *Instrumentation:* Piano conductor. *Copyright:* © C1 E 377027, January 12, 1916.

LC M1357.S 40 p., 30 cm.
Music 3212, Item 30

193
The Convoy

Thematic music cue sheet. Robert Kane presents *The Convoy* with Dorothy Mackaill and Lowell Sherman, Lawrence Gray, Wm. Collier, Jr. and Ian Keith. *Adapted from* The Song of the Dragon *by:* John Painter [sic, Tainter] Foote. *Directed by:* Joseph C. Boyle. *Film company:* First National. *Music compiled by:* Eugene Conte. *Note:* Music incipits. "Thursday June 23/27" marked in pencil.

MOMA 6 p., 32 cm.
Music 3236, Item 228

194
The Cop

Thematic music cue sheet. Pathe presents William Boyd in *The Cop* with Alan Hale, Jacqueline Logan and Robert Armstrong. *Screenplay by:* Tay Garnett. *From the story by:* Elliott Clawson. *Produced by:* Ralph Block for DeMille Pictures Corporation. *Production by:* Donald Crisp. *Distributed by:* Pathe Exchange, Inc. *Music compiled by:* Rudolph Berliner. *Note:* Music incipits. Two copies.

MOMA 4 p., 32 cm.
Music 3236, Item 229

195
The Corner

Musical setting for the photoplay *The Corner* (P. 29). *Music selected and arranged by:* George W. Beynon. *Published by:* G. Schirmer, New York, 1915. *Instrumentation:* Piano conductor. *Series title:* Triangle Plays. *Copyright:* © C1 E 377038, December 23, 1915.

LC M1357.B 48 p., 30 cm.
Music 3212, Item 31

196
Corner in W

Corner in W. Note: Cue sheet. No music.

MOMA 1 p., 28 cm., Ms.
Music 3236, Item 230

John Gilbert and Renee Adoree on the cover of the sheet music for the theme song of MGM's *The Cossacks* (1928). Pop songs were used to advertise movies and vice-versa, then as now. Music Division, Library of Congress.

196a
Corner in Wheat
Corner in Wheat. Published by: Kalmus Filmusic Edition, N.Y., 1928. *Instrumentation:* Piano conductor score. *Note:* This is a photocopy of a printed score.
MOMA   18 p., 28 cm.
                                                        no microfilm

197
The Cossacks
Thematic music cue sheet. John Gilbert in *The Cossacks* with Renee Adorée and Ernest Torrence. *Based on the novel by:* Lyoff N. Tolstoi. *Adaptation and continuity by:* Frances Marion. *Production by:* George Hill. *Directed by:* George Hill. *Film company:* Metro-Goldwyn-Mayer. *Music compiled by:* Ernst Luz. *Note:* Music incipits. *Number of reels:* 10. *Footage:* 8480. *Maximum projection time:* 1 hour, 42 minutes.
MOMA   4 p., 31 cm.
                                                        Music 3236, Item 231

198
Counsel for the Defense
Thematic music cue sheet. Associated Exhibitors, Inc., Oscar A. Price, Pres., presents Betty Compson in *Counsel for the Defense* with House Peters and Jay Hunt. *Film company:* Encore. *Released by:* Associated Exhibitors, Inc. *Music compiled by:* James C. Bradford. *Note:* Music incipits. "Sat Jan 16" marked in pencil.
MOMA   4 p., 30 cm.
                                                        Music 3236, Item 232

199
The Covered Wagon
Music score *The Covered Wagon. Music arranged by:* Hugo Riesenfeld. *Instrumentation:* Piano conductor. *Note:* Typescript attached.
MOMA   127 p., 30 cm.
                                                        Music 3236, Item 16

199A
The Covered Wagon
"1849"; overture to the motion picture photoplay *The Covered Wagon. Music composed by:* Mortimer Wilson. *Published by:* J. Fischer & Bro., New York, 1923. *Instrumentation:* Piano conductor and orchestral parts (1,1,2,1; 2,2,1,0; tympani, drums; harp; strings). *Copyright:* © E 568026, J. Fischer & Bro., July 20, 1923.
LC M1004.W74E4p.Boxed   20 p., 32 cm.
                                                        Music 3449, Item 1133

200
Covered Wagon Trails
Musical setting for *Covered Wagon Trails* featuring Bob Custer. *Film company:* Syndicate. *Character of film:* Western drama. *Music arranged by:* Joseph E. Zivelli. Smugglers theme, "The Smugglers," by Axt (Robbins). [Love theme, "That wonderful something is love," (Robbins).] *Note:* Cue sheet. No music. "Plaza Bayonne, N.J. Oct 31–Nov 1–1930" marked in ink and in pencil. *Number of reels:* 5.
MOMA   1 p., 32 cm.
                                                        Music 3236, Item 233

201
The Cowboy and the Countess
Thematic music cue sheet. Buck Jones in *The Cowboy and the Countess. Production by:* William Fox. *Music compiled by:* Michael P. Krueger. *Note:* Music incipits. "Sunday & Monday 4/4–5" marked in pencil.
MOMA   1 p., 33 cm.
                                                        Music 3236, Item 234

202
Craig's Wife
Thematic music cue sheet. Pathe presents *Craig's Wife* with Irene Rich and Warner Baxter. *From the stage play by:* George Kelly. *Adapted by:* Clara Beranger. *Production by:* William C. DeMille. *Distributed by:* Pathe Exchange, Inc. *Music compiled by:* Howard T. Wood. *Note:* Music incipits.
MOMA   4 p., 32 cm.
                                                        Music 3236, Item 235

203
Cranquebille
Cranquebille. Note: Cue sheet. No music. Typescript.
MOMA   1 p., 28 cm.
                                                        Music 3236, Item 236

204
The Crash
Thematic music cue sheet. Richard A. Rowland presents Milton Sills in *The Crash* with Thelma Todd. *Film company:* First National. *Music compiled by:* James C. Bradford. *Note:* Music incipits. "Fri. Sat Dec 21–22" marked in pencil. Two copies.
MOMA   4 p., 31 cm.
                                                        Music 3236, Item 237

205
The Crazy Ray
The Crazy Ray (Paris qui dort). *Instrumentation:* Piano score.
MOMA   90 p., 30 cm.
                                    Music 3236, Item 17

206
The Crimson Canyon
Musical setting for *The Crimson Canyon. Music compiled by:* M. Winkler. Theme, "Moonlight shadows" (Valse Tendre), by Baron. *Note:* Cue sheet. No music. "Thursday 3/28" marked in pencil.
MOMA   1 p., 30 cm.
                                    Music 3236, Item 239

207
The Crimson City
Warner Bros. present *The Crimson City* starring Myrna Loy and John Miljan. *Note:* Cue sheet. No music. "Sunday Feb 3" marked in pencil. *Projection time:* About an hour based on speed of 11 minutes per 1000 feet.
MOMA   1 p., 30 cm.
                                    Music 3236, Item 238

208
The Crippled Hand
Musical setting to the Bluebird Photoplay No. 15. Robert Leonard and Ella Hall in *The Crippled Hand. Music selected and arranged by:* M. Winkler and F. Rehsen. *Series title:* Carl Fischer Photo-Play Series. *Published by:* Carl Fischer, New York, 1916. *Instrumentation:* Piano conductor; (1,1,2,1; 2,2,1,0; drums; strings) *Copyright:* © C1 E 386351, May 13, 1916.
LC M1357.W   61 p., 31 cm.
                                    Music 3212, Item 32

209
The Crisis
Reel 3 No. 3. Scene: A quiet Sunday in Locust Street. Original music written and composed expressly for the photoplay *The Crisis.* Reel 6 No. 6. Scene: The quarrel between Judge Whipple and Col. Carvel. *Presented by:* Elliot & Scherman. Minneapolis, Minn., December 24, 1916. *Music by:* A. Carrano. *Instrumentation:* Short score. *Copyright:* © C1 E 393948, December 26, 1916. and © C1 E 393949, December 26, 1916.
LC M1357.C   22 p., 34 cm.
                                    Music 3212, Item 33

Johnny Fox and Ernest Torrence on the cover of "Oh! Susanna," the Stephen Foster song used by Hugo Riesenfeld throughout his musical accompaniment for *The Covered Wagon* (1923). Music Division, Library of Congress.

210
Crooks Can't Win

Thematic music cue sheet. Joseph P. Kennedy presents *Crooks Can't Win* with Ralph Lewis and Joe E. Brown. *Directed by:* George M. Arthur. *Distributed by:* F B O Pictures Corporation. *Music compiled by:* James C. Bradford. *Note:* Music incipits. "Lyceum Theatre Thu Fri Sat June 7-8-9-1928" marked in pencil.

MOMA   4 p., 31 cm.
                               Music 3236, Item 240

211
Cross Currents

Musical setting for the photoplay *Cross Currents*. *Production by:* Fine-Arts Feature Co. *Music arranged and selected by:* J. A. Raynes. *Published by:* G. Schirmer for the Triangle Film Corporation, New York, 1915. *Series title:* Triangle Plays. *Instrumentation:* Piano conductor. *Copyright:* © C1 E 377034, December 17, 1915.

LC M1357.R   59 p., 30 cm.
                                Music 3236, Item 34

212
The Crowd

Thematic music cue sheet. *The Crowd* with James Murray, Eleanor Boardman, and Bert Roach. *Screenplay by:* King Vidor and John V. A. Weaver. *Production by:* King Vidor. *Directed by:* King Vidor. *Film company:* Metro-Goldwyn-Mayer. *Music compiled by:* Ernst Luz. *Note:* Music incipits. *Number of reels:* 9. *Footage:* 8375. *Maximum projection time:* 1 hour, 35 minutes.

MOMA   6 p., 31 cm.
                               Music 3236, Item 241

213
The Crown of Lies

Adolph Zukor and Jesse L. Lasky present Pola Negri in *The Crown of Lies*. *From the story by:* Ernest Vajda. *Screenplay by:* Hope Loring and Louis Lighton. *Production by:* Dimitri Buchowetzki. *Music compiled by:* James C. Bradford. *Published by:* Cameo Music Service Corp., New York, 1926. *Note:* Cue sheet.

LC M176.C95   2 p., 31 cm.
                                Music 3212, Item 35

214
The Crystal Cup

Thematic music cue sheet. *The Crystal Cup*. *Film company.* First National. *Music compiled by:* James C. Bradford, *Note:* Music incipits. Two copies. "Monday Dec 12/27" marked in pencil on copy 1 which is mutilated.

MOMA   4 p., 31 cm.
                               Music 3236, Item 242

215
Czar Ivan the Terrible

Czar Ivan the Terrible. *Note:* Cue sheet. No music. Ms.

MOMA   1 p., 28 cm.
                               Music 3236, Item 243

216
Dame Chance

Thematic music cue sheet. American Cinema Association presents *Dame Chance* with Robert Frazer, Julianne Johnston, Gertrude Astor, Mary Carr. *Production by:* David Hartford. *Directed by:* Bertram Brocken. *Film company:* ACA Pictures. *Music compiled by:* James C. Bradford. *Note:* Music incipits. Slightly multilated.

MOMA   2 p., 34 cm.
                               Music 3236, Item 244

217
Dame Chance

Non-Taxable musical cue sheet for *Dame Chance*. *Film company:* ACA Pictures. *Note:* No music. This picture was cued August 23, 1926.

MOMA   1 p., 34 cm.
                               Music 3236, Item 245

218
Dames Ahoy

Musical setting for *Dames Ahoy* with Glenn Tryon. *Film company:* Universal Pictures Corp. *Music selected and compiled by:* M. Winkler. *Note:* Cue sheet. No music.

MOMA   3 p., 28 cm.
                               Music 3236, Item 246

219
Dan

Dan. Incidental music to the motion picture *Dan* by Hal Reid. A comedy drama of Civil War days, featuring Lew Dockstader and an all-star cast. *Produced by:* The All Star Feature Corp. *Music composed by:* Manuel Klein, musical director of the New York Hippodrome. *Published by:* M. Witmark & Sons, New York, 1914. *Instrumentation:* Piano. *Copyright:* © C1 E 343166, July 10, 1914; R 98787, July 11, 1941, Helen Klein, Hollywood.

LC M176.D16   8 p., 35 cm.
                                Music 3212, Item 36

220
Dance Magic
Thematic music cue sheet. Robert Kane presents The Halperin Production *Dance Magic* with Ben Lyon, Pauline Starke and Louis John Bartels. *Adapted from the novel:* Clarence Budington Kelland. *Directed by:* Victor Halperin. *Film company:* First National. *Music compiled by:* James C. Bradford. *Note:* Music incipits. "Monday Aug 15/27" marked in pencil.

MOMA   4 p., 32 cm.

Music 3236, Item 247

221
The Dancer of Paris
Thematic music cue sheet. Robert Kane presents Michael Arlen's *The Dancer of Paris. Film company:* First National. *Music compiled by:* Eugene Conte. *Note:* Music incipits. "Thurs & Frid July 29–30" marked in pencil.

MOMA   4 p., 32 cm.

Music 3236, Item 248

222
The Danger Signal
Thematic music cue sheet. Columbia Pictures presents *The Danger Signal,* a drama of love amid great railroad thrills featuring Jane Novak with a great cast. *Directed by:* Erle C. Kenton. *Copyrighted and released by:* Columbia Pictures Corporation. *Music compiled by:* James C. Bradford. *Note:* Music incipits. "Saturday Dec 26" marked in pencil.

MOMA   2 p., 32 cm.

Music 3236, Item 249

223
Danger Street
Thematic music cue sheet. Joseph P. Kennedy presents *Danger Street* with Warner Baxter and Martha Sleeper. *From the story* The Beautiful Bullet *by:* Harold MacGrath. *Production by:* Ralph Ince. *Distributed by:* F B O Pictures Corporation. *Music compiled by:* James C. Bradford. *Note:* Music incipits.

MOMA   4 p., 32 cm.

Music 3236, Item 250

224
Daring Days
Musical setting for *Daring Days. Music selected and compiled by:* M. Winkler. Theme, "Love's sweet hour," (Dram.). *Note:* Cue sheet. No music. "Thurs & Friday Jan 7–8" marked in pencil.

MOMA   1 p., 30 cm.

Music 3236, Item 251

225
The Darling of New York
Musical setting for Baby Peggy's first feature *The Darling of New York. Production by:* Universal Jewel. *Music selected and compiled by:* M. Winkler. Theme, "Baby Peggy" Waltz, by J. Titlebaum. *Note:* Cue sheet. No music. Music for the "Baby Peggy" theme by J. Titlebaum on verso of cue sheet.

MOMA   2 p., 46 cm.

Music 3236, Item 252

226
D'Artagnan
Musical setting for the photoplay *D'Artagnan* (P. 32). *Production by:* Thomas Ince. *Music composed and arranged by:* Joseph E. Nurnberger, Victor L. Schertzinger and Wedgewood Nowell. *Series title:* Triangle Plays. *Published by:* G. Schirmer for the Triangle Film Corp., New York, 1915. *Instrumentation:* Piano conductor. *Copyright:* © C1 E 377029, December 31, 1915.

LC M1357.N   59 p., 30 cm.

Music 3212, Item 37

227
A Daughter of the Gods
Music score by the photoplay *A Daughter of the Gods* with Annette Kellermann. *Produced by:* The Fox Film Corporation. *Music compiled by:* Robert Hood Bowers. *Published by:* William Fox, New York, 1916. *Instrumentation:* Piano conductor. *Copyright:* © C1 E 398556, October 17, 1917, William Fox, New York; R 122211, October 25, 1943, 20th Century-Fox Film Corp., New York.

LC M1357.B   208 p., 30 cm.

Music 3212, Item 38

228
A Daughter of the Gods
Music score for *A Daughter of the Gods* film production with Annette Kellermann. *Music compiled by:* Robert Hood Bowers. *Published by:* William Fox, New York, 1916. *Instrumentation:* Piano or organ score. *Copyright:* © C1 E 398556, October 17, 1917, William Fox, New York; R122211, October 25, 1943, 20th Century-Fox Film Corp., New York.

LC M1527.B696D4.   208 p., 30 cm.

Music 3212, Item 39

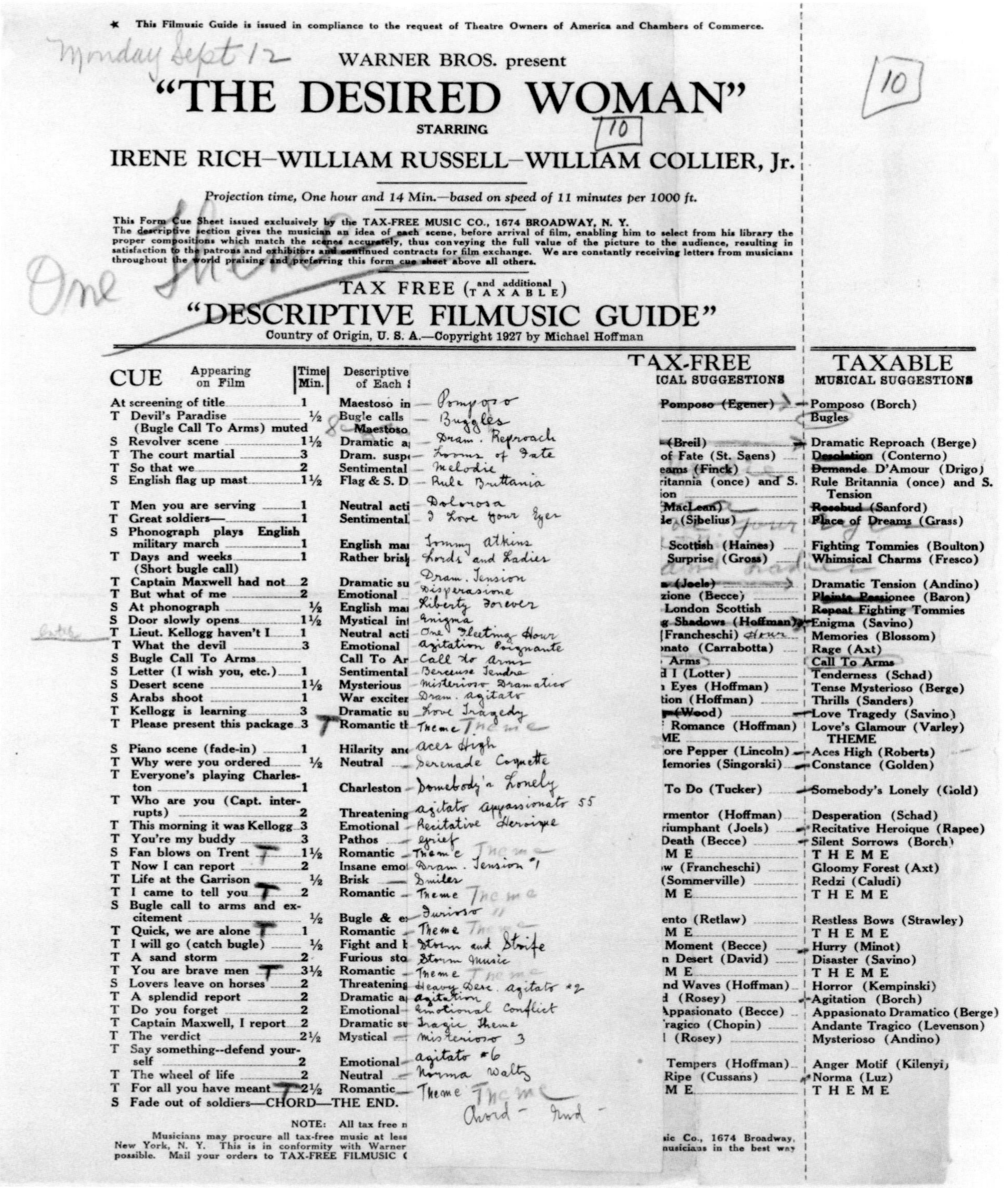

Monday Sept 12 [handwritten] [10] [handwritten, boxed]

WARNER BROS. present
"THE DESIRED WOMAN"
STARRING
[10] [handwritten, boxed]
IRENE RICH—WILLIAM RUSSELL—WILLIAM COLLIER, Jr.

Projection time, One hour and 14 Min.—based on speed of 11 minutes per 1000 ft.

This Form Cue Sheet issued exclusively by the TAX-FREE MUSIC CO., 1674 BROADWAY, N. Y. The descriptive section gives the musician an idea of each scene, before arrival of film, enabling him to select from his library the proper compositions which match the scenes accurately, thus conveying the full value of the picture to the audience, resulting in satisfaction to the patrons and exhibitors and continued contracts for film exchange. We are constantly receiving letters from musicians throughout the world praising and preferring this form cue sheet above all others.

One Sheet [handwritten]

TAX FREE (and additional TAXABLE)
"DESCRIPTIVE FILMUSIC GUIDE"
Country of Origin, U. S. A.—Copyright 1927 by Michael Hoffman

CUE	Appearing on Film	Time Min.	Descriptive of Each S	[handwritten notes]	TAX-FREE MUSICAL SUGGESTIONS	TAXABLE MUSICAL SUGGESTIONS
	At screening of title	1	Maestoso in	Pomposo	Pomposo (Egener)	Pomposo (Borch)
T	Devil's Paradise	½	Bugle calls	Bugles		Bugles
	(Bugle Call To Arms) muted		Maestoso			
S	Revolver scene	1½	Dramatic a	Dram. Reproach	(Breil)	Dramatic Reproach (Berge)
T	The court martial	3	Dram. susp	Forms of Fate	of Fate (St. Saens)	Desolation (Conterno)
T	So that we	2	Sentimental	Melodie	eams (Finck)	Demande D'Amour (Drigo)
S	English flag up mast	1½	Flag & S. D	Rule Brittania	ritannia (once) and S.	Rule Britannia (once) and S. Tension
T	Men you are serving	1	Neutral acti	Dolorosa	(MacLean)	Rosebud (Sanford)
T	Great soldiers—	1	Sentimental	I Love Your Eyes	e (Sibelius)	Place of Dreams (Grass)
S	Phonograph plays English military march	1	English mar	Tommy Atkins	Scottish (Haines)	Fighting Tommies (Boulton)
T	Days and weeks (Short bugle call)	1	Rather brisk	Lords and Ladies	Surprise (Gross)	Whimsical Charms (Fresco)
T	Captain Maxwell had not	2	Dramatic su	Dram. Tension	(Joels)	Dramatic Tension (Andino)
T	But what of me	2	Emotional	Disperasione	zione (Becce)	Plainte Passionee (Baron)
S	At phonograph	½	English mar	Liberty Forever	London Scottish	Repeat Fighting Tommies
S	Door slowly opens	1½	Mystical inf	Enigma	g Shadows (Hoffman)	Enigma (Savino)
T	Lieut. Kellogg haven't I	1	Neutral acti	One Fleeting Hour	(Francheschi)	Memories (Blossom)
T	What the devil	3	Emotional	Agitation Poignante	nato (Carrabotta)	Rage (Axt)
S	Bugle Call To Arms		Call To Ar	Call to Arms	Arms	Call To Arms
S	Letter (I wish you, etc.)	1	Sentimental	Berceuse Tendre	d I (Lotter)	Tenderness (Schad)
S	Desert scene	1½	Mysterious	Misterioso Dramatico	Eyes (Hoffman)	Tense Mysterioso (Berge)
S	Arabs shoot	1	War exciter	Dram. agitato	tion (Hoffman)	Thrills (Sanders)
T	Kellogg is learning	3	Dramatic su	Love Tragedy	(Wood)	Love Tragedy (Savino)
T	Please present this package	3	Romantic th	Theme	Romance (Hoffman)	Love's Glamour (Varley)
						THEME
S	Piano scene (fade-in)	1	Hilarity and	Aces High	ore Pepper (Lincoln)	Aces High (Roberts)
T	Why were you ordered	½	Neutral	Serenade Coquette	lemories (Singorski)	Constance (Golden)
	Everyone's playing Charleston		Charleston	Somebody's Lonely	To Do (Tucker)	Somebody's Lonely (Gold)
T	Who are you (Capt. interrupts)	2	Threatening	Agitato Appassionato 55	rmentor (Hoffman)	Desperation (Schad)
T	This morning it was Kellogg	3	Emotional	Recitative Heroique	riumphant (Joels)	Recitative Heroique (Rapee)
T	You're my buddy	3	Pathos	Grief	Death (Becce)	Silent Sorrows (Borch)
S	Fan blows on Trent	1½	Romantic	Theme	M E	THEME
T	Now I can report	2	Insane emot	Dram. Tension #1	w (Francheschi)	Gloomy Forest (Axt)
T	Life at the Garrison	½	Brisk	Smiles	(Sommerville)	Redzi (Caludi)
T	I came to tell you	2	Romantic	Theme	M E	THEME
S	Bugle call to arms and excitement	½	Bugle & ex	Furioso	ento (Retlaw)	Restless Bows (Strawley)
T	Quick, we are alone	1	Romantic	Theme	M E	THEME
T	I will go (catch bugle)	½	Fight and b	Storm and Strife	Moment (Becce)	Hurry (Minot)
T	A sand storm	2	Furious sto	Storm Music	n Desert (David)	Disaster (Savino)
T	You are brave men	3½	Romantic	Theme	M E	THEME
S	Lovers leave on horses	2	Threatening	Heavy Desc. agitato #2	nd Waves (Hoffman)	Horror (Kempinski)
T	A splendid report	2	Dramatic a	Agitation	d (Rosey)	Agitation (Borch)
T	Do you forget	2	Emotional	Emotional Conflict	Appasionato (Becce)	Appasionato Dramatico (Berge)
T	Captain Maxwell, I report	2	Dramatic su	Tragic Theme	ragico (Chopin)	Andante Tragico (Levenson)
T	The verdict	2½	Mystical	Misterioso 3	l (Rosey)	Mysterioso (Andino)
T	Say something--defend yourself	2	Emotional	Agitato #6	Tempers (Hoffman)	Anger Motif (Kilenyi)
T	The wheel of life	2	Neutral	Norma Waltz	Ripe (Cussans)	Norma (Luz)
T	For all you have meant	2½	Romantic	Theme	M E	THEME
S	Fade out of soldiers—CHORD—THE END.			Chord — End —		

NOTE: All tax free m

Musicians may procure all tax free music at less
New York, N. Y. This is in conformity with Warner
possible. Mail your orders to TAX-FREE FILMUSIC (

...ic Co., 1674 Broadway,
...nusicians in the best way

Cue sheet for *The Desired Woman* (1927). The printed suggestions made for musical accompaniment were often changed by theater organists or pianists to suit their own tastes. Museum of Modern Art, Film Music Collection.

229
Daughters Who Pay
Thematic music cue sheet. Banner Productions, Inc. presents *Daughters Who Pay* featuring John Bowers and Margaret De La Motte. *Directed by:* George Terwilliger. *Music compiled by:* Eugene Conte. *Note:* Music incipits. "Thurs & Fri Dec 24–25" marked in pencil.
MOMA   2 p., 34 cm.
Music 3236, Item 253

230
The Dawn Maker
The Dawn Maker, W. Simart. *Note:* Cue sheet. No music. Ms. *Number of reels:* 5.
MOMA   2 p., 28 cm.
Music 3236, Item 254

231
The Dead Line
Musical synopsis for Bob Custer in *The Dead Line. Music by:* James C. Bradford. Theme, "Habanera" (from Natoma), by Herbert. *Note:* Cue sheet. No music. "Wed Aug 4" marked in pencil.
MOMA   1 p., 31 cm.
Music 3236, Item 255

232
Deliverance
Music selections to accompany *Deliverance.* 40 cues. *Instrumentation:* Flute; drums; violins 1 and 2, viola, cello, bass. *Note:* Ms. and printed.
LC M1527.M8   40 cues, 33 cm.
Music 3212, Item 159

233
The Desired Woman
Warner Bros. present *The Desired Woman* starring Irene Rich, William Russell, William Collier, Jr. *Note:* Cue sheet. No music. "Monday Sept 12" marked in pencil. *Projection time:* 1 hour, 14 minutes based on a speed of 11 minutes per 1000 feet.
MOMA   1 p., 35 cm.
Music 3236, Item 256

234
The Desperate Game
Musical setting for *The Desperate Game. Music selected and compiled by:* M. Winkler. Theme. "Serenade Lointaine" (Mod.), by Bergee. *Note:* Cue sheet. No music. "Sunday Feb 14" marked in pencil.
MOMA   1 p., 30 cm.
Music 3236, Item 257

235
A Desperate Moment
Royal Productions present Wanda Hawley & Theodore Von Eltz in *A Desperate Moment. Production by:* Royal. *Music compiled by:* Michael Hoffman. *Note:* Cue sheet. No music. "Monday May 3" marked in pencil.
MOMA   1 p., 31 cm.
Music 3236, Item 258

236
The Despoilers
Musical setting for the photoplay *The Despoilers* (P. 34). *Production by:* Thomas H. Ince. *Music composed and selected by:* Louis F. Gottschalk. *Series title:* Triangle Plays. *Published by:* G. Schirmer for the Triangle Film Corp., New York, 1916. *Instrumentation:* Piano conductor. *Copyright:* © C1 E 377028, January 5, 1916.
LC M1357.G   80 p., 30 cm.
Music 3212, Item 40

237
Destiny
Destiny. Note: Cue sheet. No music. Ms.
MOMA   7 p., 28 cm.
Music 3236, Item 259

238
Destiny
Destiny. Note: Cue sheet. No music. Ms.
MOMA   9 p., 28 cm.
Music 3236, Item 260

239
The Devil Dancer
Thematic music cue sheet. Samuel Goldwyn presents Gilda Gray in *The Devil Dancer* by Harry Hervey with Clive Book. *Production by:* Fred Niblo. *Film company:* United Artists. *Music compiled by:* Ernst Luz. *Note:* Music incipits. Two copies. "Thur & Fri & Sat Nov 8–9–10" marked in pencil on copy 1. "Sunday Monday Tuesday Jan 22, 23, 24" marked in pencil on copy 2 which is incomplete. *Number of reels:* 8. *Footage:* 6705. *Maximum projection time:* 1 hour, 18 minutes.
MOMA   6 p., 32 cm.
Music 3236, Item 261

240
The Devil's Skipper
Thematic music cue sheet. Tiffany-Stahl presents *The Devil's Skipper* with Belle Bennett, Montagu

Love. *Suggested by:* Jack London. *Adapted for the screen by:* Robert Dillon. *Production by:* Tiffany-Stahl. *Directed by:* John G. Adolphi. *Music compiled by:* James C. Bradford. *Note:* Music incipits.
MOMA   4 p., 32 cm.
                                  Music 3236, Item 262

241
The Devil's Trademark
Thematic music cue sheet. Joseph P. Kennedy presents Belle Bennett in *The Devil's Trademark. From the story* Pedigree *by:* Calvin Johnston. *Production by:* Leo Meehan. *Produced and distributed by:* F B O Pictures Corporation. *Music compiled by:* James C. Bradford. *Note:* Music incipits.
MOMA   4 p., 32 cm.
                                  Music 3236, Item 263

242
Diplomacy
Thematic music cue sheet. Adolph Zukor and Jesse L. Lasky present Marshall Neilan's *Diplomacy* with Blanche Sweet. *From the play by:* Victorian [sic] Sardou. *Screenplay by:* Benjamin Glazer. *Music compiled by:* James C. Bradford. *Note:* Music incipits. "Thurs. Oct 21, 22, 23, 24" marked in pencil. *Footage:* 6811.
MOMA   4 p., 32 cm.
                                  Music 3236, Item 264

243
The Dixie Merchant
Thematic music cue sheet. William Fox special production *The Dixie Merchant. Music compiled by:* Michael P. Krueger. *Note:* Music incipits. "Thurs & Friday May 13–14" marked in pencil.
MOMA   2 p., 34 cm.
                                  Music 3236, Item 265

244
Do Your Duty
Thematic music cue sheet. First National Pictures, Inc. presents Charlie Murray in *Do Your Duty* with Doris Dawson and Lucien Littlefield. *Production by:* William Beaudine. *Film company:* First National. *Music compiled by:* James C. Bradford. *Note:* Music incipits. Two copies. "Sunday Dec 7" marked in pencil on copy 1.
MOMA   4 p., 32 cm.
                                  Music 3236, Item 266

245
The Doctor's Secret
The Doctor's Secret by Méliès. *Instrumentation:* Piano score.
MOMA   20 p., 31 cm.
                                  Music 3236, Item 18

246
Dog Law
Musical synopsis for *Dog Law. Music compiled by:* James C. Bradford. Theme, "There'll never be another you," by Bergner. *Note:* Cue sheet. No music.
MOMA   1 p., 32 cm.
                                  Music 3236, Item 267

247
Dog of the Regiment
Warner Bros. present *Dog of the Regiment* starring Rin-Tin-Tin. *Note:* Cue sheet. No music. Two copies. *Projection time:* About an hour based on a speed of 11 minutes per 1000 feet.
MOMA   1 p., 34 cm.
                                  Music 3236, Item 268

248
Dogs
Dogs. Note: Cue sheet. No music. Typescript.
MOMA   1 p., 28 cm,
                                  Music 3236, Item 269

249
Don Juan
Don Juan at Screening. *Music composed by:* William Axt. *Instrumentation:* Orchestral score. *Note:* Holograph.
LC M1527.A9D7   174 p., 34 cm.
                                  Music 3212, Item 41

250
Don Q, Son of Zorro
Douglas Fairbanks in *Don Q, Son of Zorro. Music by:* Mortimer Wilson, Opus 75. *Copyright:* The Elton Corporation, 1925. *Instrumentation:* Orchestral parts (1,1,2,1; 2,2,1,0; drums; strings)
MOMA   31 cm.
                                  Music 3236, Item 19

251
Le Donne Di Buon Umore
Le Donne Di Buon Umore. Commedia Coregrafica. *The Good Humored Ladies,* Choreographic [sic] Comedy. *Les Femmes De Bonne Humeur,* Comédie Chorégraphique. *Music by:* Domenico Scarlatti, arranged by Vincenzo Tommasini.

John Barrymore and Mary Astor in *Don Juan* (1926).
William Axt prepared one of the most sophisticated
silent film scores for this romantic drama about the
great Spanish lover. It was performed by the New York
Philharmonic, Henry Hadley conducting, and was
recorded for the new Vitaphone sound film system.
Museum of Modern Art, Film Stills Archive.

First page of the complete score for *Don Juan* (1926). With increasing frequency in the 1920s, film directors commissioned original scores for their films, but original scores remained an exceptional form of accompaniment until the arrival of the sound film. Music Division, Library of Congress.

Cover by: A. P. Allinson. *Published by:* J. & W. Chester, London, 1919. *Instrumentation:* Piano. *Copyright:* © C1 E 460605, received by the LC October 9, 1919.
LC M1527.S32D62   72 p., 32 cm.
Music 3212, Item 160

252
The Donovan Affair

Thematic music cue sheet. Columbia Pictures presents *The Donovan Affair* with Jack Holt, Dorothy Revier and Wm. Collier, Jr. *Production by:* Frank R. Capra. *Copyrighted and distributed by:* Columbia Pictures Corporation. *Note:* Music incipits.
MOMA   2 p., 32 cm.
Music 3236, Item 270

253
Don't Marry

Thematic music cue sheet. Lois Moran in *Don't Marry.* *Production by:* William Fox. *Music compiled by:* Michael P. Krueger. *Note:* Music incipits.
MOMA   4 p., 31 cm.
Music 3236, Item 271

254
Don't Tell the Wife

Warner Bros. present *Don't Tell the Wife* starring Irene Rich. *Note:* Cue sheet. No music. "Thursday Mar. 3/27" marked in pencil. *Projection time:* 1 hour, 16 minutes based on a speed of 11 minutes per 1000 feet. *Number of reels:* 7.
MOMA   1 p., 37 cm.
Music 3236, Item 272

255
Doomsday

Doomsday. *Note:* Cue sheet. No music. Typescript.
MOMA   1 p., 28 cm.
Music 3236, Item 273

256
Doomsday

Thematic music cue sheet. Adolph Zukor and Jesse L. Lasky present Florence Vidor in *Doomsday* with Gary Cooper. *From the novel by:* Warwick Deeping. *Adaptation by:* Doris Anderson. *Screenplay by:* Donald W. Lee. *Production by:* Roland V. Lee; B. P. Schulberg, Associate Producer. *Film company:* Paramount. *Music compiled by:* James C. Bradford. *Note:* Music incipits. "Monday April 30/28" marked in pencil. *Footage:* 5665
MOMA   4 p., 31 cm
Music 3236, Item 274

257
Double Trouble

Musical setting for the photoplay *Double Trouble* featuring Douglas Fairbanks. *Production by:* Fine-Arts Feature Co. *Music arranged and adapted by:* J. C. Breil. *Series title:* Triangle Plays. *Published by:* G. Schirmer, Inc. for the Triangle Film Corp., New York, 1915. *Instrumentation:* Piano conductor; (1,0,2,0; 0,2,1,0; drums; strings). *Note:* Cornet part in M176.D(Box). *Copyright:* © C1 E 373895, November 22, 1915.
LC M1357.B   93 p., 30 cm.
Music 3212, Item 42

258
The Dove

The Dove. *Note:* Cue sheet. No music. Typescript.
MOMA   1 p., 28 cm.
Music 3236, Item 275

259
The Dove

Thematic music cue sheet. Joseph M. Schenck presents Norma Talmadge in *The Dove* with Noah Beery and Gilbert Roland. *Film company:* United Artists. *Music compiled by:* Ernst Luz. *Note:* Music incipits. Two copies. *Number of reels:* 9. *Footage:* 8285. *Maximum projection time:* 1 hour, 35 minutes.
MOMA   6 p., 31 cm.
Music 3236, Item 276

260
The Drag Net

Thematic music cue sheet. Adolph Zukor and Jesse L. Lasky present George Bancroft in *The Drag Net* with Evelyn Brent and William Powell. *Story by:* Oliver H. P. Garrett. *Adaptation and screenplay by:* Jules and Charles Furthman. *Directed by:* Josef von Sternberg. *Produced by:* B. P. Schulberg, Associate Producer. *Film company:* Paramount. *Music compiled by:* James C. Bradford. *Note:* Music incipits. *Footage:* 7866.
MOMA   4 p., 31 cm.
Music 3236, Item 277

261
The Drag Net

The Drag Net. *Note:* Cue sheet. No music. Typescript.
MOMA   1 p., 28 cm.
Music 3236, Item 278

262
Drake's Love Story
Incidental music to *Drake's Love Story*. Mr. E. Hay Plumb as Sir Francis Drake. *Production by:* The Hepworth M'f'g Co. *Music by:* Victor Montefiore, Op. 33. *Published by:* Weeks & Co., London, 1913. *Instrumentation:* Piano. *Copyright:* © C1 E 303920, April 14, 1913.

LC M176.D76   24 p., 32 cm.
Music 3212, Item 43

263
Dream of Love
Thematic music cue sheet. Fred Niblo's Production *Dream of Love* with Joan Crawford, Nils Asther and Aileen Pringle. *Screenplay by:* Dorothy Farnum. *Based on the play* Adrienne Lecouvreur *by:* Eugene Scribe and Ernest Legouve. *Directed by:* Fred Niblo. *Film company:* Metro-Goldwyn-Mayer. *Music compiled by:* Ernst Luz. *Note:* Music incipits. *Number of reels:* 9. *Footage:* 7949. *Maximum projection time:* 1 hour, 30 minutes.

MOMA   4 p., 31 cm.
Music 3236, Item 279

264
Dream Street
D. W. Griffith presents *Dream Street* based on characters of Thomas Burke's stories. *Film company:* D. W. Griffith, Inc., Albert L. Grey, Gen. Mgr. *Instrumentation:* Piano conductor (1st and 2nd editions); (1,1,2,1; 2,2,1,0; drums; harp; strings; all parts except oboe, horns and trumpets are stamped "2nd Edition").

MOMA   156 p., 31 cm.
Music 3236, Item 20

265
Dream Street
Dream Street. Music by: Louis Silvers. *Instrumentation:* Piano conductor. *Note:* Incomplete.

MOMA   130 p., 31 cm., Ms.
Music 3236, Item 21

266
Dress Parade
Thematic music cue sheet. William Sistrom presents William Boyd in *Dress Parade* with Bessie Love. *Screenplay by:* Douglas Z. Doty. *From the story by:* Major Robert Classburn, Major Alexander Chilton and Herbert David Walter. *Production by:* Donald Crist [sic]. *Produced by:* DeMille

Pictures Corporation. *Distributed by:* Pathe Exchange, Inc. *Music compiled by:* Rudolph Berliner. *Note:* Music incipits. "Thursday Nov. 24/27" marked in pencil.

MOMA   4 p., 31 cm.
Music 3236, Item 280

267
Driftin' Through
Thematic music cue sheet. Charles R. Rogers presents Harry Carey in *Driftin' Through*. *By:* Basil Dickey and Harry Haven. *Film company:* Pathé. *Music compiled by:* Eugene Conte. *Note:* Music incipits. "Sunday & Monday 3/28–29" marked in pencil.

MOMA   4 p., 31 cm.
Music 3236, Item 281

268
The Drummer Girl of Vicksburg
Special piano music for *The Drummer Girl of Vicksburg. Music by:* Walter C. Simon. *Published by:* Kalem Co., New York, 1912. *Instrumentation:* Piano. *Copyright:* © C1 E 285244, May 25, 1912.

LC M176.D79   9 p., 32 cm.
Music 3212, Item 44

269
Dry Martini
Thematic music cue sheet. William Fox film production *Dry Martini. Music compiled by:* Michael P. Krueger. *Note:* Music incipits.

MOMA   4 p., 32 cm.
Music 3236, Item 282

270
Easy Come, Easy Go
Easy Come, Easy Go. Note: Cue sheet. No music. Typescript.

MOMA   1 p., 28 cm.
Music 3236, Item 283

271
Easy Come, Easy Go
Thematic music cue sheet. Adolph Zukor and Jesse L. Lasky present Richard Dix in *Easy Come, Easy Go* with Nancy Carroll. *From the play by:* Owen Davis. *Scenario by:* Florence Ryerson. *Production by:* Frank Tuttle; B. P. Schulberg, Associate Producer. *Film company:* Paramount. *Music compiled by:* James C. Bradford. *Note:* Music incipits. "Tues. & Wed. Sept. 4–5" marked in pencil. *Footage:* 5364.

MOMA   4 p., 31 cm.
Music 3236, Item 284

272

The Edge of the Abyss

Musical setting for the photoplay *The Edge of the Abyss*. *Production by:* Thomas H. Ince. *Music composed by:* Victor Schertzinger and Joseph E. Nurnberger. *Series title:* Triangle Plays. *Published by:* G. Schirmer for the Triangle Film Corp., New York, 1915. *Instrumentation:* Piano conductor. *Copyright:* © C1 E 377032, November 26, 1915.

LC M1357.S 78 p., 30 cm.
Music 3212, Item 45

273

Emak Bakia

Partition musicale pour *Emak Bakia*. *Note:* Cue sheet. No music. Ms. In French.

MOMA 2 p., 27 cm.
Music 3236, Item 285

274

Emak Bakia

Emak Bakia. Note: Cue sheet. Ms. "Orig. cue sheet" marked in pencil.

MOMA 1 p., 28 cm.
Music 3236, Item 286

275

Emak Bakia

Emak Bakia. Note: Cue sheet. No music. Also includes music cues for the film *Etoile de Mer*.

MOMA 2 p., 28 cm.
Music 3236, Item 287

276

L'Empreinte

L'Empreinte. Mimodrame en ll Tableaux. *Music by:* Fernand Le Borne, Op. 55. *Series title:* Le Film D'Art. *Published by:* A. Zunz Mathot, Paris, 1908. *Instrumentation:* Piano. *Copyright:* © C1 E 196857, December 26, 1908.

LC M176.E55 38 p., 30 cm.
Music 3212, Item 46

277

Empty Hearts

Thematic music cue sheet. Banner Productions, Inc. presents *Empty Hearts* with Clara Bow, John Bowers, Lillian Rich, Charles Murray. *Production by:* Ben Verschleiser. *Directed by:* Al Santell. *Music compiled by:* Edward Kilenyi. *Note:* Music incipits. "Mon & Tuesday Jan 25–26" marked in pencil.

MOMA 2 p., 32 cm.
Music 3236, Item 288

278

The Enchanted Hill

Thematic music cue sheet. Adolph Zukor and Jesse L. Lasky present An Irvin Willat Production *The Enchanted Hill* with Jack Holt, Florence Vidor, Noah Beery, George Bancroft and Mary Brian. *Adapted from the novel by:* Peter B. Kyne. *Screenplay by:* James S. Hamilton. *Film company:* Paramount. *Music compiled by:* James C. Bradford. *Note:* Music incipits. "Friday 2/12" marked in pencil. *Footage:* 6377.

MOMA 2 p., 33 cm.
Music 3236, Item 289

279

Enemies of Women

Enemies of Women. Production by: Cosmopolitan Corporation. *Music composed by:* Wm. Frederick Peters. *Instrumentation:* Violin. *Copyright:* © C1 E 695548, July 7, 1928, Julia Peters, Englewood, N.J.

LC M1527.P55E 90 p., 30 cm.
Music 3212, Item 162

280

Enemy of Men

Thematic music cue sheet. Waldorf Pictures presents *Enemy of Men,* an all star production featuring Dorothy Revier and Cullen Landis. *Copyrighted and released by:* Columbia Pictures Corporation. *Music compiled by:* James C. Bradford. *Note:* Music incipits. "Thurs & Frid May 27–28" marked in pencil.

MOMA 2 p., 32 cm.
Music 3236, Item 290

281

Enoch Arden

Enoch Arden Parts IV, V. *Instrumentation:* Piano.

MOMA 33 p., 30 cm.
Music 3236, Item 22

282

The Escape

Musical setting for *The Escape. Music compiled by:* M. Winkler. Theme, "You and I," (Romance) by Lotter. *Note:* Cue sheet. No music. "Wed July 21" marked in pencil.

MOMA 1 p., 30 cm.
Music 3236, Item 291

283
The Escape
Thematic music cue sheet. Virginia Valli in *The Escape. Production by:* William Fox. *Music compiled by:* Michael P. Krueger. *Note:* Music incipits. "Sat Feb 16 Embassy Theatre One day only D. Feature." marked in pencil.
MOMA   4 p., 31 cm.
                              Music 3236, Item 292

284
L'Etoile de Mer
Note: Cue sheet. No music. Ms. "Orig. Cue Sheet" marked in pencil. Arthur Kleiner, compiler?
MOMA   1 p., 28 cm.
                              Music 3236, Item 293

285
Etoile de Mer
Etoile de Mer. Note: Cue sheet. No music. Also includes music cues for the film *Emak Bakia.*
MOMA   2 p., 28 cm.
                              Music 3236, Item 294

286
Eton Boys
Eton Boys. Note: Cue sheet. No music. Typescript.
MOMA   1 p., 28 cm.
                              Music 3236, Item 295

287
Excess Baggage
Thematic music cue sheet. William Haines in *Excess Baggage* with Josephine Dunn and Ricardo Cortez. *Based on the play by:* John McGowan. *Continuity by:* Frances Marion. *Production by:* James Cruze. *Directed by:* James Cruze. *Film company:* Metro-Goldwyn-Mayer. *Music compiled by:* Ernst Luz. *Note:* Music incipits. Two copies. "Sun Nov 18" marked in pencil on copy 1. *Number of reels:* 8. *Footage:* 7145. *Maximum projection time:* 1 hour, 22 minutes.
MOMA   6 p., 32 cm.
                              Music 3236, Item 296

288
The Execution of Mary Queen of Scots
Musical accompaniment [for] *The Execution of Mary Queen of Scots, Wash Day Troubles, A Trip to the Moon, The Great Train Robbery, Faust,* and *Queen Elizabeth. Music arranged by:* Alden Beach & T. Huff. *Instrumentation:* Piano score. *Note:* Typescript, 2 p., with contents attached.
MOMA   117 p., 31 cm.
                              Music 3236, Item 23

289
Eyes of the Underworld
Musical setting for *Eyes of the Underworld. Music compiled by:* M. Winkler. Theme, "Rendezvous D'Amour," (Mod.) by Edwards. *Note:* Cue sheet. No music. "Thursday 4/18" marked in pencil.
MOMA   1 p., 30 cm.
                              Music 3236, Item 297

290
Fabiola
Musical score. Fabiola Photoplay Corporation presents photo drama production of Nicholas Cardinal Wiseman's *Fabiola. Music score composed and arranged by:* Alexander Henneman. *Published by:* Alexander Henneman, Chicago, 1923. *Instrumentation:* Piano conductor; (1,1,2,1; 2,2,1,0; drums, timp., organ; strings). *Copyright:* © C1 E 560449, February 27, 1923.
LC M1357.H   135 p., 32 cm.
                              Music 3212, Item 47

291
The Fakir
Thematic music cue sheet. Columbia Pictures presents *The Fakir* with Jacqueline Logan, Charles E. Delaney, Warner Oland and Gaston Glass. *Directed by:* Phil Rosen. *Copyrighted and distributed by:* Columbia Pictures Corporation. *Music compiled by:* James C. Bradford. *Note:* Music incipits. "Thursday 3/28" marked in pencil.
MOMA   2 p., 32 cm.
                              Music 3236, Item 298

291A
The Fall of a Nation
The Fall of a Nation; motion picture score. *Music composed by:* Victor Herbert. *Note:* Autograph ms. score and sketches. Several printed pages also included, with emendations. [1916] Score not in order.
Victor Herbert Collection   597 p., 33 cm.
                              Music 3449, Item 371A

291B
The Fall of a Nation
Piano Music Score of *The Fall of a Nation.* By Thomas Dixon. A Drama of the Origin and Destiny of Our Republic As Produced with great Success at the Liberty Theatre, New York, and the Illinois Theatre, Chicago. The First Original Score to a Great Picture Ever Made by an Eminent Composer. *Music composed by:* Victor Herbert. *Published by:* A. W. Tams Music Library, 1916.

Instrumentation: Piano score. *Copyright:* ©
Victor Herbert, 1916.

Victor Herbert Collection   112 p., 33 cm.
No microfilm

291C
The Fall of a Nation

[The Fall of a Nation] Devastation. Entrance of
the Heroes. Forebodings. Heart Throbs. Karma.
The Night's Tournament. Little Italy. Punch and
Judy. The Rabble. *Music composed by:* Victor
Herbert. *Published by:* Carl Fischer, New York,
1925-8. *Instrumentation:* Piano conductor and
orchestral parts (2,2,2,2; 2,4,3,1; tympani, drums,
harp; strings). *Note:* individual cues from the film
score, rescored and published.

M1350.H   300 p., 31 cm.
Music 3449, Item 371B

292
The Fall of the House of Usher

The Fall of the House of Usher. Instrumentation:
Piano score.

MOMA   86 p., 29 cm.
Music 3236, Item 24

293
The Farmer's Daughter

Thematic music cue sheet. William Fox Feature
Film Production *The Farmer's Daughter. Music
compiled by:* Michael P. Krueger. *Note:* Music
incipits. Two copies. "Sat Feb 23" marked in pencil on copy 1.

MOMA   4 p., 31 cm.
Music 3236, Item 299

294
Fashions for Women

Fashions for Women. Note: Cue sheet. No music.
Typescript.

MOMA   1 p., 28 cm.
Music 3236, Item 300

295
Fast and Furious

Fast and Furious. Note: Cue sheet. No music.
Typescript.

MOMA   1 p., 28 cm.
Music 3236, Item 301

296
The Fate of a Flirt

Thematic music cue sheet. Waldorf Pictures pre-
sents *The Fate of a Flirt* with Dorothy Revier and
Forrest Stanley, Tom Ricketts and Phillip Smalley.
Directed by: Frank R. Strayer. *Copyrighted and*

distributed by: Columbia Pictures Corporation.
Music compiled by: James C. Bradford. *Note:*
Music incipits. "Saturday June 26" marked in
pencil.

MOMA   2 p., 40 cm.
Music 3236, Item 302

297
Father Sergius

Music for *Father Sergius. Published by:* The
Museum of Modern Art Film Library, New York.
Instrumentation: Piano score.

MOMA   132 p., 32 cm.
Music 3236, Item 25

Faust,

See *The Execution of Mary Queen of Scots.*

298
Fazil

Thematic music cue sheet. Charles Farrell and
Greta Nissen in *Fazil. Production by:* William
Fox. *Music compiled by:* Michael P. Krueger.
Note: Music incipits. Three copies. "Frid & Sat
Nov. 23-24" marked in pencil on copy 1. "Neapoli-
tan Nights" by J. S. Zamecnik included. "Theme of
Fazil" marked in pencil. Copy 3 incomplete.

MOMA   6 p., 32 cm.
Music 3236, Item 303

299
Feel My Pulse

Feel My Pulse. Note: Cue sheet. No music.
Typescript.

MOMA   1 p., 28 cm.
Music 3236, Item 304

300
The Fifty-Fifty Girl

The Fifty-Fifty Girl. Note: Cue sheet. No music.
Typescript.

MOMA   1 p., 28 cm.
Music 3236, Item 305

301
The Fighting Boob

Music cue for Bob Custer in *The Fighting Boob.*
Music compiled by: Dr. Edward Kilenyi. *Note:*
Cue sheet. No music.

MOMA   1 p., 31 cm.
Music 3236, Item 306

302

The Fighting Buckaroo

Thematic music cue sheet. Buck Jones in *The Fighting Buckaroo. Production by:* William Fox. *Music compiled by:* Michael P. Krueger. *Note:* Music incipits. "Sat May 22" marked in pencil.

MOMA   2 p., 33 cm.
                                  Music 3236, Item 307

303

The Fighting Cub

The Fighting Cub. Music compiled by: Lee Zahler. Theme, "Suppose I had never met you" (Chorus only). *Note:* Cue sheet. Two copies. "Mon & Tues Jan 25–26" marked in pencil on copy 1. "Mon & Tues Jan 25–26" marked in pencil on copy 2.

MOMA   1 p., 36 cm., 28 cm.
                                  Music 3236, Item 308

304

Fighting Dan McCool

Fighting Dan McCool. Music by: M. Komroff. *Published by:* Kalem Co., New York, 1912. *Instrumentation:* Piano. *Copyright:* © C1 E 283733, April 21, 1912.

LC M176.F4   10 p., 31 cm.
                                   Music 3212, Item 48

305

The Fighting Dervishes of the Desert

Special piano music for *The Fighting Dervishes of the Desert. Music by:* Walter C. Simon. *Published by:* Kalem Co., New York, 1912. *Instrumentation:* Piano. *Copyright:* © C1 E 284864, May 17, 1912.

LC M176.F472   10 p., 32 cm.
                                   Music 3212, Item 49

306

The Fighting Edge

Warner Brothers presents *The Fighting Edge* starring Patsy Ruth Miller. *Note:* Cue sheet. No music. "Saturday May 1" marked in pencil. *Projection time:* 1 hour, 12 minutes based on a speed of 11 minutes per 1000 feet.

MOMA   1 p., 35 cm.
                                  Music 3236, Item 309

307

Fighting Youth

Musical synopsis for *Fighting Youth. Music compiled by:* James C. Bradford. *Note:* Cue sheet. No music. "Sat Jan 16" marked in pencil.

MOMA   1 p., 30 cm.
                                  Music 3236, Item 310

308

Finders Keepers

Thematic music cue sheet. Carl Laemmle presents *Finders Keepers. Production by:* Universal. *Music compiled by:* James C. Bradford. *Note:* Music incipits. Two copies. "Thursday Friday & S April 12–13–14" marked in pencil on copy 1. Slightly mutilated.

MOMA   2 p., 32 cm.
                                  Music 3236, Item 311

309

Fine Clothes

Thematic music cue sheet. Louis B. Mayer presents The John M. Stahl Production *Fine Clothes. Film company:* First National. *Music compiled by:* James C. Bradford. *Note:* Music incipits. "Tuesday 3/30" marked in pencil.

MOMA   4 p., 31 cm.
                                  Music 3236, Item 312

310

Fingerprints

Warner Bros. present *Fingerprints* starring Helene Costello and Louise Fazenda. *Note:* Cue sheet. No music. "Monday Jan 24/27" marked in pencil. *Projection time:* 1 hour, 13 minutes based on a speed of 11 minutes per 1000 feet.

MOMA   1 p., 38 cm.
                                  Music 3236, Item 313

311

Fireman Save My Child

Fireman Save My Child. Note: Cue sheet. No music. Typescript.

MOMA   1 p., 28 cm.
                                  Music 3236, Item 314

312

The First Kiss

The First Kiss. Note: Cue sheet. No music. Typescript.

MOMA   1 p., 28 cm.
                                  Music 3236, Item 315

313

The First Kiss

Thematic music cue sheet. Adolph Zukor and Jesse L. Lasky present Fay Wray and Gary Cooper in *The First Kiss. From the story* Four Brothers *by:* Tristram Tupper. *Adaptation and screenplay by:* John Farrow. *Production by:* Rowland V. Lee; B. P. Schulberg, Associate Producer. *Film company:* Paramount. *Music compiled by:* James C. Bradford. *Note:* Music incipits. *Footage:* 6134.

MOMA   4 p., 31 cm.
                                  Music 3236, Item 316

314
Fitzpatrick's Thanksgiving
Fitzpatrick's Thanksgiving. Note: Cue sheet. No music. Typescript.
MOMA 1 p., 28 cm.
Music 3236, Item 317

315
Flame of the Argentine
Thematic music cue sheet. Joseph P. Kennedy presents Evelyn Brent in *Flame of the Argentine. Directed by:* Eddie Dillon. *Distributed by:* Film Booking Offices of America, Inc. *Music compiled by:* James C. Bradford. *Note:* Music incipits. "Thurs & Frid Sept 9–10" marked in pencil.
MOMA 4 p., 31 cm.
Music 3236, Item 318

316
The Fleet's In!
Thematic music cue sheet. Adolph Zukor and Jesse L. Lasky present Clara Bow in *The Fleet's In!* with James Hall. *Story and screenplay by:* Monte Brice and J. Walter Ruben. *Production by:* Malcolm St. Clair; B. P. Schulberg, General Manager, West Coast Productions. *Film company:* Paramount. *Music compiled by:* James C. Bradford. *Note:* Music incipits. Two copies. *Footage:* 6918.
MOMA 4 p., 31 cm.
Music 3236, Item 319

317
The Flirt
Musical setting to the Bluebird Photo-Play No. 10. Marie Walcamp in *The Flirt. Produced by:* Phillips Smalley. *Music selected and arranged by:* M. Winkler. *Published by:* Carl Fischer, New York, 1916. *Series title:* Carl Fischer Photo-play Series. *Instrumentation:* Piano conductor or organ; (1,1,2,1; 2,2,1,0; drums; strings). *Copyright:* © C1 E 379349, March 24, 1916.
LC M1357.W 63 p., 31 cm.
Music 3212, Item 50

318
Flirting With Fate
Flirting With Fate 1916 Doug. Fairbanks. *Note:* Cue sheet. No Music. Ms.
MOMA 2 p., 28 cm.
Music 3236, Item 320

319
The Floating College
Thematic music cue sheet. Tiffany-Stahl presents *The Floating College* with Sally O'Neil and Wm. Collier, Jr. *Directed by:* George Crone. *Production by:* Tiffany-Stahl. *Music compiled by:* James C. Bradford. *Note:* Music incipits.
MOMA 4 p., 33 cm.
Music 3236, Item 321

320
The Flyin' Cowboy
Thematic music cue sheet. Carl Laemmle presents *The Flyin' Cowboy. Production by:* Universal. *Music compiled by:* James C. Bradford. *Note:* Music incipits.
MOMA 2 p., 31 cm.
Music 3236, Item 322

321
The Flying Fleet
Thematic music cue sheet. Ramon Novarro in *The Flying Fleet* with Ralph Graves, Anita Page and Edward Nugent. *Story by:* Lieutenant Commander Frank Wead, U.S.N. and Byron Morgan. *Screenplay by:* Richard Schayer. *Production by:* George Hill. *Directed by:* George Hill. *Film company:* Metro-Goldwyn-Mayer. *Music compiled by:* Ernst Luz. *Note:* Music incipits. *Number of reels:* 11. *Footage:* 9142. *Maximum projection time:* 2 hours.
MOMA 4 p., 32 cm.
Music 3236, Item 323

322
Flying Romeos
Thematic music cue sheet. Richard A. Rowland presents George Sidney and Charlie Murray in *Flying Romeos. Film company:* First National. *Music compiled by:* James C. Bradford. *Note:* Music incipits. "Monday April 16/28" marked in pencil.
MOMA 4 p., 31 cm.
Music 3236, Item 324

323
The Flying Torpedo
Musical setting for the photoplay *The Flying Torpedo* (P. 48). *Production by:* Fine-Arts Feature Co. *Music selected and arranged by:* J. A. Raynes. *Series title:* Triangle Plays. *Published by:* G. Schirmer for the Triangle Film Corp., New York, 1916. *Instrumentation:* Piano conductor. *Copyright:* © C1 E 377163, January 20, 1916.
LC M1357.R 47 p., 30 cm.
Music 3212, Item 51

Miss DuPont and Erich von Stroheim in *Foolish Wives* (1922); music by Sigmund Romberg. A number of famous composers of Broadway musicals wrote scores for silent films—Frederick Converse *(Puritan Passions)*, Henry Hadley *(Manon)*, Jerome Kern *(Gloria's Romance)*, and Victor Herbert *(Fall of a Nation)*. Museum of Modern Art, Film Stills Archive.

324
A Fool There Was

A Fool There Was. Musical accompaniment arranged by: Alden Beach. *Instrumentation:* Piano score. *Note:* Typescript contents attached.
MOMA   104 p., 31 cm.
Music 3236, Item 26

325
Foolish Wives

Part I music score. Universal Super-Jewel *Foolish Wives* by and with Erich von Stroheim. *Produced by:* The Universal Film Manufacturing Co. *Production by:* Carl Laemmle. *Written and directed by:* Erich von Stroheim. *Music composed by:* Sigmund Romberg. *Edited and adapted by:* J. Frank Cork. *Instrumentation:* Piano.
LC M1357.R   72 p., 31 cm.
Music 3212, Item 52

326
Fools for Luck

Fools for Luck. Note: Cue sheet. No music. Typescript.
MOMA   1 p., 28 cm.
Music 3236, Item 325

327
For Alimony Only

Thematic music cue sheet. John C. Flinn presents Leatrice Joy in *For Alimony Only* with Clive Brooks, Lilyan Tashman and Casson Ferguson. *Story and continuity by:* Lenore J. Coffee. *Production by:* William DeMille. *Produced by:* DeMille Pictures Corp. *Directed by:* William DeMille. *Released by:* Producers Distributing Corporation. *Music compiled by:* Rudolph Berliner. *Note:* Music incipits.
MOMA   4 p., 32 cm.
Music 3236, Item 326

328
For Wives Only

Thematic music cue sheet. John C. Flinn presents Marie Prevost in *For Wives Only* with Victor Varconi. *Adapted by:* Anthony Coldewey. *From the stage play* The Critical Year *by:* Rudolf Lothar and Hans Bachwitz. *Editorial supervision by:* F. McGrew Willis. *Produced by:* Producers Distributing Corporation. *Music compiled by:* Rudolph Berliner. *Note:* Music incipits. "Monday Dec 20/26" marked in pencil.
MOMA   4 p., 32 cm.
Music 3236, Item 333

Arthur Kleiner (1903-1980), composer and pianist, for many years the accompanist for the silent films at the Museum of Modern Art. He preserved and perpetuated the tradition of artful, effective accompaniments for early film. Courtesy of Mrs. Arthur Kleiner.

329
Foreign Devils

Thematic music cue sheet. Peter B. Kyne's *Foreign Devils* starring Tim McCoy with Claire Windsor. *Continuity by:* Marian Ainslee. *Directed by:* W. S. Van Dyke. *Film company;* Metro-Goldwyn-Mayer. *Music compiled by:* Ernst Luz. *Note:* Music incipits. *Number of reels:* 5. *Footage:* 4635. *Maximum projection time:* 55 minutes.

MOMA   4 p., 31 cm.
Music 3236, Item 327

330
The Foreign Legion

Greater thematic music cue sheet. Carl Laemmle presents *The Foreign Legion* with Lewis Stone, Mary Nolan, Norman Kerry and June Marlowe. *Production by:* Universal. *Music compiled by:* James C. Bradford. *Note:* Music incipits.

MOMA   8 p., 31 cm.
Music 3236, Item 328

331
Forgotten Faces

Forgotten Faces. Note: Cue sheet. No music. Typescript.

MOMA   1 p., 28 cm.
Music 3236, Item 329

332
Forgotten Faces

Thematic music cue sheet. Adolph Zukor and Jesse L. Lasky presents *Forgotten Faces* with Clive Brook, Mary Brian, William Powell and Baclanova. *Adapted by:* Oliver H. P. Garrett. *From a story by:* Richard Washburn Child. *Screenplay by:* Howard Estabrook. *Production by:* Victor Schertzinger; B. P. Schulberg, Associate Producer. *Film company:* Paramount. *Music compiled by:* James C. Bradford. *Note:* Music incipits. "Fri & Sat Dec 7–8" marked in pencil. *Footage:* 7640.

MOMA   4 p., 31 cm.
Music 3236, Item 330

333
Forlorn River

Thematic music cue sheet. Adolph Zukor and Jesse L. Lasky present Zane Grey's *Forlorn River* with Jack Holt, Raymond Hatton, Arlette Marchal and Edmund Burns. *Screenplay by:* George C. Hull. *Directed by:* John Waters. *Film company:*

Paramount. *Music compiled by:* James C. Bradford. *Note:* Music incipits. Two copies. *Footage:* 5631.

MOMA   4 p., 32 cm.
Music 3236, Item 331

334
Four Feathers

Four Feathers. Music score by: Wm. Frederick Peters. *Published by:* Sam Fox Pub. Co., Cleveland, 1929. *Instrumentation:* Violin. *Copyright:* © EP9298, September 23, 1929; R 191765, May 1, 1957, Mrs. Wm. Frederick Peters (W).

LC M1527.P55F5   32 p., 32 cm.
Music 3212, Item 53

335
The Four Horsemen of the Apocalypse

The Four Horsemen of the Apocalypse. Music compiled by: [Ernst Luz?] *Instrumentation:* Piano score. *Note:* Typescript contents attached.

MOMA   144 p., 30 cm.
Music 3236, Item 27

336
Four Sons

Thematic music cue sheet. William Fox special film production *Four Sons. Music compiled by:* Michael P. Krueger. *Note:* Music incipits. Two copies. "Frid & Sat Oct 26–27" and "Paul Norman Pianist and Organist" marked on one copy.

MOMA   6 p., 32 cm.
Music 3236, Item 332

337
Fragment of an Empire

Music for *Fragment of an Empire. Published by:* The Museum of Modern Art Film Library, New York. *Instrumentation:* Piano score.

MOMA   123 p., 32 cm.
Music 3236, Item 28

338
Free Lips

Musical setting for *Free Lips. Music arranged by:* Joseph E. Zivelli. *Note:* Cue sheet. No music. On verso, various advertisements for the film.

MOMA   1 p., 29 cm.
Music 3236, Item 334

339
Freedom of the Press

Greater thematic music cue sheet. Carl Laemmle presents Lewis Stone in *Freedom of the Press* with Marceline Day. *Production by:* Universal. *Music compiled by:* James C. Bradford. *Note:*

Rudolph Valentino and Alice Terry starred in the epic drama, *The Four Horsemen of the Apocalypse* (1921); music by Louis F. Gottschalk. The appearance of flute, clarinet, violin, hammered dulcimer, and bass players on screen might have suggested appropriate musical accompaniment, but the score did not call for any special instrumentation. Museum of Modern Art, Film Stills Archive.

Alice Terry and Rudolph Valentino on a sheet music cover of the song from *The Four Horsemen of the Apocalypse*. Music Division, Library of Congress.

Music incipits. Three copies. "Thursday Sept 20" marked in pencil on copy 3 which is also incomplete.

MOMA   8 p., 31 cm.
                        Music 3236, Item 335

340
French Dressing

Thematic music cue sheet *French Dressing*. *Film company:* First National. *Music compiled by:* James C. Bradford. *Note:* Music incipits. Two copies. "Thursday Jan. 26/28" marked in pencil on copy 1. "April 15–16" marked in pencil on copy 2.

MOMA   4 p., 32 cm.
                        Music 3236, Item 336

341
Fresh Every Hour

Thematic music cue sheet. Carl Laemmle presents *Fresh Every Hour. Production by:* Universal. *Music compiled by:* James C. Bradford. *Note:* Music incipits. Two copies. "Fresh Every Hour" crossed out in pencil on copy 2. "How to Handle Women" written in pencil as release title, q.v.

MOMA   2 p., 32 cm.
                        Music 3236, Item 337

342
The Freshman

Harold Lloyd in *The Freshman. Instrumentation:* Piano score.

MOMA   124 p., 31 cm.
                         Music 3236, Item 29

343
The Fugitive

Wm. S. Hart in *The Fugitive. Production by:* Thomas H. Ince. *Instrumentation:* Piano score. *Note:* Typescript contents attached.

MOMA   36 p., 31 cm.
                         Music 3236, Item 30

344
Fugitives

Thematic music cue sheet. William Fox Film Production. Madge Bellamy and Don Terry in *Fugitives. Music compiled by:* Michael P. Krueger. *Note:* Music incipits.

MOMA   4 p., 32 cm.
                        Music 3236, Item 338

345
La Galerie des Monstres

La Galerie des Monstres. Score by: Gaby Coutrot. *Note:* Cue sheet. No music. In French.

MOMA   2 p., 27 by 21 cm.
                        Music 3236, Item 339

346
The Galloping Fish

The Galloping Fish. Note: Cue sheet. No music. Ms.

MOMA   1 p., 29 cm.
                        Music 3236, Item 340

347
Galloping Fury

Thematic music cue sheet. Carl Laemmle presents *Galloping Fury. Film company:* Universal-Jewel. *Music compiled by:* James C. Bradford. *Note:* Music incipits. "Lyceum—Sat & Sun—Jan 29–30, 1928" marked in pencil.

MOMA   2 p., 32 cm.
                        Music 3236, Item 341

348
Gang War

Thematic music cue sheet. William Le Baron presents *Gang War* with Olive Borden, Jack Pickford, Eddie Gribbon and Walter Long. *From the story by:* James A. Creelman. *Directed by:* Bert Glennon. *Distributed by:* F B O Pictures Corporation. *Music compiled by:* James C. Bradford. *Note:* Music incipits. Two copies.

MOMA   4 p., 31 cm.
                        Music 3236, Item 342

349
Garden of Eden

Garden of Eden. Note: Cue sheet. No music. Typescript.

MOMA   1 p., 28 cm.
                        Music 3236, Item 343

350
The Gate Crasher

Thematic music cue sheet. Carl Laemmle presents Glenn Tryon in *The Gate Crasher. Production by:* Universal. *Directed by:* William J. Craft. *Music compiled by:* James C. Bradford. *Note:* Music incipits. Two copies.

MOMA   2 p., 32 cm.
                        Music 3236, Item 344

351
The Gay Lord Waring

Musical setting to the Bluebird Photoplay No. 14 *The Gay Lord Waring* featuring J. Warren Kerrigan. *Music selected and arranged by:* M. Winkler and F. Rehsen. *Series title:* Carl Fischer Photo-Play Series. *Published by:* Carl Fischer, New York, 1916. *Instrumentation:* Piano conductor; (1,1,2,1; 2,2,1,0; drums; strings). *Copyright:* © C1 E 383066, April 27, 1916.

LC M1357.W 59 p., 31 cm.
Music 3212, Item 54

352
The Gay Old Bird

Warner Bros. present *The Gay Old Bird* starring Louise Fazenda and John T. Murray. *Note:* Cue sheet. No music. "Coming Thur. March 31/27" marked in pencil. *Projection time:* 1 hour, 6 minutes based on a speed of 11 minutes per 1000 feet.

MOMA 1 p., 35 cm.
Music 3236, Item 345

353
The General

The General. Instrumentation: Piano score.

MOMA 99 p., 27 cm.
Music 3236, Item 31

354
The Gentle Cyclone

Thematic music cue sheet. Buck Jones in *The Gentle Cyclone. Production by:* William Fox. *Music compiled by:* Michael P. Krueger. *Note:* Music incipits. "Wednesday Aug 25/26" marked in pencil.

MOMA 2 p., 33 cm.
Music 3236, Item 346

355
The Gentleman from Indiana

Paramount Photoplay music (P 130 B 23) *The Gentleman from Indiana. Produced by:* Pallas Pictures. *Music selected and arranged by:* George W. Beynon. *Series title:* Schirmer's Photoplay Series. *Published by:* G. Schirmer, Inc., New York, 1915. *Instrumentation:* Piano conductor; (1,1,2,1; 2,2,1,0; tympani and drums; strings). *Copyright:* © C1 E 373891, November 22, 1915.

LC M1357.B 71 p., 31 cm.
Music 3212, Item 55

356
Gentlemen Prefer Blondes

Gentlemen Prefer Blondes. Note: Cue sheet. No music. Typescript.

MOMA 1 p., 28 cm.
Music 3236, Item 347

357
George Washington Cohen

Thematic music cue sheet. Tiffany-Stahl presents George Jessel in *George Washington Cohen. From the play* The Cherry Tree *by:* Aaron Hoffman. *Directed by:* George Archainbaud. *Production by:* Tiffany-Stahl. *Music compiled by:* James C. Bradford. *Note:* Music incipits.

MOMA 4 p., 31 cm.
Music 3236, Item 348

358
German Short Films

German Short Films: Primitive German Films by Skladanowsky, *Don Juan's Wedding, Misunderstood* with Henny Porten, and a sequence from *The Golem. Instrumentation:* Piano score. *Note:* Manuscript and typescript contents attached.

MOMA 77 p., 31 cm.
Music 3236, Item 32

359
Germania

Germania. Dramma Lirico di Luigi Illica. *Cinematography in six parts by:* Casa Savoja Film di Torino. *Music by:* Alberto Franchetti. *Arranged by:* R. Tenaglia. *Published by:* G. Ricordi & Co., Milan, 1914. *Instrumentation:* Orchestral score. *Copyright:* © C1 E 344876, August 28, 1914.

LC M1527.F73G2 582 p., 31 cm.
Music 3212, Item 56

360
Germania

Germania. Dramma lirico di Luigi Illica. Cinematografia in sei parti. *Film company:* Casa Savoja Film di Torino. *Music by:* Alberto Franchetti. *Arranged by:* R. Tenaglia. *Published by:* G. Ricordi & Co., 1914. *Instrumentation:* Piano. *Copyright:* © C1 E 344877, August 28, 1914.

LC M1527.F73G3 163 p., 31 cm.
Music 3212, Item 57

361
Gertie the Dinosaur

Gertie the Dinosaur by Winsor McCay. *Instrumentation:* Piano score.

MOMA   15 p., 32 cm.
Music 3236, Item 33

362
Die Geschichte des Prinzen Achmed

Die Geschichte des Prinzen Achmed, ein Silhouettenfilm von Lotte Reiniger. *Music by:* Wolfgang Zeller. *Instrumentation:* Piano conductor and orchestral parts (2,1,2,1; 2,2,1,0; percussion, celeste, and strings). *Note:* Two sets of orchestral parts; set "B," "Boston Symphony Orchestra" score, contains markings and timings. Set "E" is unmarked. The piano conductor part is marked "C," but the letter "B" has been added and the "C" crossed out.

MOMA   118 p., 34 cm.
Music 3236, Item 34

363
Gigolo

Thematic music cue sheet. Rod La Rocque in *Gigolo. From the story by:* Edna Ferber with Jobyna Ralston and Louise Dresser. *Adapted by:* Garrett Fort. *Continuity by:* Marion Orph. *Supervised by:* C. Gardner Sullivan. *Produced by:* DeMille Pictures Corp. *Directed by:* Wm K. Howard. *Released by:* Producers Distributing Corporation. *Music compiled by:* Rudolph Berliner. *Note:* Music incipits. "Thurs. Nov. 4/26" marked in pencil.

MOMA   6 p., 31 cm.
Music 3236, Item 349

364
Ginsberg the Great

Warner Bros. present *Ginsberg the Great* starring George Jessel. *Note:* Cue sheet. No music. *Projection time:* 1 hour, 2 minutes based on a speed of 11 minutes per 1000 feet.

MOMA   1 p., 35 cm.
Music 3236, Item 350

365
The Girl on the Barge

Thematic music cue sheet. Carl Laemmle presents *The Girl on the Barge. Production by:* Universal. *Music compiled by:* Howard T. Wood. *Note:* Music incipits.

MOMA   2 p., 32 cm.
Music 3236, Item 351

First page of the score for *Die Geschichte des Prinzen Achmed* (1926) by Wolfgang Zeller (1893-1967). Most film scores contain written cues which help the conductor keep the musicians in synch with the film. In this example, frames from the film itself appear over the appropriate measures of music. Museum of Modern Art, Film Music Collection.

366
Girl Shy Cowboy
Thematic music cue sheet. Rex Bell in *Girl Shy Cowboy. Production by:* William Fox. *Music compiled by:* Michael P. Krueger. *Note:* Music incipits. "Sunday Nov. 11" marked in pencil.
MOMA   2 p., 31 cm.
Music 3236, Item 352

367
The Girl Who Wouldn't Work
Thematic music cue sheet. B. P. Schulberg presents *The Girl Who Wouldn't Work. From the story by:* Gertie D. Wentworth-James. *Directed by:* Marcel DeSano with Lionel Barrymore. *Produced and distributed by:* B. P. Schulberg Productions, Inc. *Music compiled by:* James C. Bradford. *Note:* Music incipits. "Sunday June 27" marked in pencil.
MOMA   2 p., 31 cm.
Music 3236, Item 353

368
Give and Take
Greater thematic music cue sheet. Carl Laemmle presents George Sidney and Jean Hersholt in *Give and Take. Production by:* Universal. *Directed by:* William Beaudine. *Music compiled by:* James C. Bradford. *Note:* Music incipits. Two copies.
MOMA   8 p., 32 cm.
Music 3236, Item 354

369
Gloria's Romance
Incidental music for George Kleine's Production of Miss Billie Burke in *Gloria's Romance. Story by:* Mr. and Mrs. Rupert Hughes. *Music by:* Jerome Kern. *Published by:* T. B. Harms and Francis, Day & Hunter, New York, 1916. *Instrumentation:* Piano (1,0,1,0; 0,1,1,0; drums; strings). *Copyright:* © C1 E 383442, March 15, 1916; R 116235, March 15, 1943, Jerome Kern, Beverly Hills, Calif.
LC M1357.K   27 p., 33 cm.
Music 3212, Item 58

370
The Glorious Dead
The Glorious Dead. Music adapted and compiled by: Walter C. Simon. *Note:* Cue sheet. Music incipits.
MOMA   1 p., 32 cm.
Music 3236, Item 355

371
The Glorious Trail
Thematic music cue sheet. Charles R. Rogers presents Ken Maynard in *The Glorious Trail. Story by:* Marion Jackson. *Directed by:* Albert Rogell. *Supervised by:* Harry J. Brown. *Film company:* First National. *Music compiled by:* James C. Bradford. *Note:* Music incipits. Two copies, one marked in pencil "Sunday Jan 27."
MOMA   4 p., 32 cm.
Music 3236, Item 356

372
God Gave Me Twenty Cents
Thematic music cue sheet. Adolph Zukor and Jesse L. Lasky present a Herbert Brenon Production *God Gave Me Twenty Cents* with Lois Moran. *Story by:* Dixie Willson. *Adaptation by:* John Russell. *Screenplay by:* Elizabeth Meehan. *Film company:* Paramount. *Music compiled by:* James C. Bradford. *Note:* Music incipits. "Thursday Feb 24" marked in pencil.
MOMA   4 p., 32 cm.
Music 3236, Item 357

373
The Golden Claw
Music setting to *The Golden Claw* photoplay dramatization. *Music by:* Joseph E. Nurnberger, Victor Schertzinger and Wedgewood Nowell. *Published by:* G. Schirmer, Inc., New York, 1915. *Instrumentation:* Piano; (1,1,2,1; 2,2,1,0; drums; harp; strings). *Copyright:* © C1 E 373199, October 18, 1915.
LC M1357.N   47 p., 31 cm.
Music 3212, Item 59

374
The Golden Clown
Thematic music cue sheet. Pathe presents *The Golden Clown* featuring Gösta Ekman and Karima Bell. *Produced by:* Nordisk Film Co. *Directed by:* A. W. Sandberg. *Film company:* Pathépicture. *Music compiled by:* Dr. Edward Kilenyi. *Note:* Music incipits.
MOMA   4 p., 32 cm.
Music 3236, Item 359

375
The Golden Cocoon
Warner Brothers presents *The Golden Cocoon* starring Helene Chadwick and Huntley Gordon.

Note: Cue sheet. No music. "Wednesday 3/3" marked in pencil. Mutilated. *Projection time:* 1 hour, 17 minutes based on a speed of 11 minutes pe 1000 feet.
MOMA   1 p., 35 cm.
                                    Music 3236, Item 358

376
The Good-Bye Kiss
Thematic music cue sheet. Mack Sennett's personally directed romance *The Good-Bye Kiss* with Johnny Burke, Sally Eilers and Matty Kent. *Film company:* First National. *Music compiled by:* Rudolph Berliner. *Note:* Music incipits. Three copies. "Frid & Sat Nov–9–10" marked in pencil on copy 1.
MOMA   6 p., 32 cm.
                                    Music 3236, Item 360

377
Good Morning Judge
Greater thematic music cue sheet. Carl Laemmle presents *Good Morning Judge* with Reginald Denny. *Production by:* Universal. *Music compiled by:* James C. Bradford. *Note:* Music incipits. Two copies.
MOMA   8 p., 31 cm.
                                    Music 3236, Item 361

378
Good Time Charley
Warner Bros. presents *Good Time Charley* starring Helene Costello, Warner Oland, Montague [sic] Love. *Note:* Cue sheet. No music. "Sunday Feb 24" marked in pencil. *Projection time:* 1 hour, 9 minutes based on a speed of 11 minutes per 1000 feet.
MOMA   1 p., 30 cm.
                                    Music 3236, Item 362

379
The Goose Hangs High
The Goose Hangs High. Note: Cue sheet. No music. Typescript.
MOMA   1 p., 28 cm.
                                    Music 3236, Item 363

380
The Grand Duchess and the Waiter
Adolph Zukor and Jesse L. Lasky present A Malcolm St. Clair Production *The Grand Duchess and the Waiter* with Adolphe Menjou and Florence Vidor. *From the play by:* Alfred Savoir. *Screenplay by:* Pierre Collings. *Film company:* Paramount. *Music compiled by:* James C. Bradford. *Note:* Cue sheet. Music incipits. Page 1

slightly mutilated, missing uppermost portion of page. Thermofax copy. *Footage:* 6043.
MOMA   4 p., 33 cm.
                                    Music 3236, Item 364

381
The Gray Dawn
Thematic music cue sheet for *The Gray Dawn. Production by:* Benj. B. Hampton. *Film company:* Hodkinson Pictures. *Music compiled by:* James C. Bradford. *Note:* Music incipits.
MOMA   4 p., 32 cm.
                                    Music 3236, Item 365

382
Great Actresses of the Past
Music for *Great Actresses of the Past, Mme. Sans-Gêne* with Réjanne, *La Dame aux Camélias* with Sarah Bernhardt. *Vanity Fair* with Mrs. Fiske and *Cenere* with Duse. *Published by:* The Museum of Modern Art Film Library, New York. *Instrumentation:* Piano score.
MOMA   71 p., 32 cm.
                                    Music 3236, Item 35

383
The Great Love
D. W. Griffith's *The Great Love. Music set by:* Carli Densmore Elinor and Louis F. Gottschalk. *Published in:* Los Angeles, 1918. *Instrumentation:* Violin.
LC M1527.E45G7   77 p., 33 cm.
                                    Music 3212, Item 60

384
The Great Problem
Musical Setting to the Bluebird Photo-Play No. 13. Violet Mersereau in *The Great Problem. Music selected and arranged by:* M. Winkler and F. Rehsen. *Series title:* Carl Fischer Photo-Play Series. *Published by:* Carl Fischer, New York, 1916. *Instrumentation:* Piano or organ: (1,1,2,1; 2,2,1,0; drums; strings). *Copyright:* © C1 E 383013, April 18, 1916.
LC M1357.W   63 p., 30 cm.
                                    Music 3212, Item 61

385
The Great Sensation
Musical synopsis for *The Great Sensation. Music compiled by:* James C. Bradford. *Note:* Cue sheet. No music. "Monday & Tuesday May 17–18" marked in pencil.
MOMA   1 p., 31 cm.
                                    Music 3236, Item 366

The Great Train Robbery

See The Execution of Mary Queen of Scots.

386

The Greater Glory

Thematic music cue sheet. Richard A. Rowland presents *The Greater Glory* with Conway Tearle and Anna Q. Nilsson. *Production by:* June Mathis. *Directed by:* Curt Reahfeld [sic]. *Film company:* First National. *Music compiled by:* Dr. Edward Kilenyi. *Note:* Music incipits. "Thurs & Friday July 22–23" marked in pencil.

MOMA   6 p., 31 cm.
                              Music 3236, Item 367

387

The Greatest Question

D. W. Griffith presents *The Greatest Question*. *Music arranged by:* Albert Pesce. *Instrumentation:* Orchestral parts (1,1,2,1; 2,2,1,0; drums, strings).

MOMA   30 cm.
                              Music 3236, Item 36

388

Greed

Greed. Score arranged and composed by Theodore Huff. *Instrumentation:* Piano score.

MOMA   158 p., 30 cm.
                              Music 3236, Item 37

389

The Green Swamp

Musical setting for the photoplay *The Green Swamp* (P. 46). *Production by:* Fine-Arts Feature Co. *Music arranged and selected by:* William Furst and C. Herbert Kerr. *Series title:* Triangle Plays. *Published by:* G. Schirmer for the Triangle Film Corp., New York, 1916. *Instrumentation:* Piano conductor. *Copyright:* © C1 E 377162, January 21, 1916.

LC M1357.F   56 p., 31 cm.
                              Music 3212, Item 62

390

The Grip of Jealousy

Musical setting to the Bluebird Photo-Play No. 6 *The Grip of Jealousy* featuring Louise Welch, Lon Chaney, Grace Thompson, Marcia Moore, Hayward Mack. *Music selected and arranged by:* M. Winkler. *Series title:* Carl Fischer Photo-Play Series. *Published by:* Carl Fischer, New York, 1916.

Instrumentation: Piano conductor; (1,1,2,1; 2,2,1,0; drums; strings). *Copyright:* © C1 E 378846, February 26, 1916.

LC M1357.W   52 p., 31 cm.
                              Music 3212, Item 63

391

The Grip of the Yukon

Thematic music cue sheet. Carl Laemmle presents *The Grip of the Yukon*. *Film company:* Universal-Jewel. *Music compiled by:* James C. Bradford. *Note:* Music incipits. Three copies.

MOMA   2 p., 32 cm.
                              Music 3236, Item 368

392

Grit Wins

Musical setting for *Grit Wins*. *Music selected and compiled by:* M. Winkler. Theme, "Love's sweet hour." *Note:* Cue sheet. No music.

MOMA   1 p., 30 cm.
                              Music 3236, Item 369

393

Growth of the Soil

Score for *Growth of the Soil* by Jay Leyda, 282 West 4 Street. *Note:* Cue sheet. No music. Typescript. Mutilated, possibly incomplete.

MOMA   1 p., 16 cm.
                              Music 3236, Item 370

394

Gypsy of the North

Musical setting for *Gypsy of the North*. *Character of film:* Drama. *Music compiled by:* Joseph E. Zivelli. *Note:* Cue sheet. No music. Two copies. "May–27–28" marked in pencil on both copies. *Number of reels:* 6.

MOMA   1 p., 32 cm.
                              Music 3236, Item 371

395

Half a Bride

Thematic music cue sheet. Adolph Zukor and Jesse L. Lasky present Esther Ralston in *Half a Bride* with Gary Cooper. *Based on the story* White Hands *by:* Arthur Stringer. *Screenplay by:* Doris Anderson and Percy Heath. *Production by:* Gregory La Cava; B. P. Schulberg, Associate Producer. *Film company:* Paramount. *Music compiled by:* James C. Bradford. *Note:* Music incipits. *Footage:* 6263.

MOMA   4 p., 31 cm.
                              Music 3236, Item 372

Zasu Pitts in Erich von Stroheim's *Greed* (1923).
Museum of Modern Art, Film Stills Archive.

396

Ham and Eggs at the Front

Warner Bros. present *Ham and Eggs at the Front* starring Myrna Loy, Heine Conklin. *Note:* Cue sheet. No music. "Mon-Tue Dec 31–Jan 1" marked in pencil. *Projection time:* 1 hour, 2 minutes based on a speed of 11 minutes per 1000 feet.

MOMA   1 p., 31 cm.
Music 3236, Item 373

397

Hamlet

Hamlet, the last three reels. *Instrumentation:* Piano score.

MOMA   63 p., 31 cm.
Music 3236, Item 38

398

Hangman's House

Thematic music cue sheet. Victor McLaglen in *Hangman's House. Production by:* William Fox. *Music compiled by:* Michael P. Krueger. *Note:* Music incipits.

MOMA   4 p., 32 cm.
Music 3236, Item 374

399

Harold Teen

Thematic music cue sheet. Robert Kane presents Allan Dwan's Production of *Harold Teen* with Arthur Lake, Mary Brian, Lucien Littlefield and Alice White. *Film company:* First National. *Music compiled by:* James C. Bradford. *Note:* Music incipits.

MOMA   4 p., 32 cm.
Music 3236, Item 375

400

The Harvester

Thematic music cue sheet. Joseph P. Kennedy presents Jean [sic] Stratton Porter's Greatest novel, *The Sweetest Story Ever Told, The Harvester* with Orville Caldwell and Natalie Kingston. *Production by:* Leo Meehan. *Distributed by:* F B O Pictures Corporation. *Music compiled by:* James C. Bradford. *Note:* Music incipits.

MOMA   4 p., 31 cm.
Music 3236, Item 376

401

The Haunted House

Thematic music cue sheet. Richard A. Rowland presents *The Haunted House* with Chester Conklin and Thelma Todd. *Film company:* First

National. *Music compiled by:* James C. Bradford. *Note:* Music incipits.

MOMA   4 p., 32 cm.
Music 3236, Item 377

402

The Haunted Ship

Thematic music cue sheet. Tiffany-Stahl presents *The Haunted Ship* with Dorothy Sebastian. *Story suggested by White and Yellow by:* Jack London. *Adapted for the screen by:* E. Morton Hough. *Production by:* Tiffany-Stahl. *Directed by:* Forrest Sheldon. *Music compiled by:* James C. Bradford. *Note:* Music incipits.

MOMA   4 p., 32 cm.
Music 3236, Item 378

403

The Hawk's Nest

Thematic music cue sheet. Richard A. Rowland presents Milton Sills in *The Hawk's Nest* with Doris Kenyon. *Film company:* First National. *Music compiled by:* James C. Bradford. *Note:* Music incipits. Two copies.

MOMA   4 p., 32 cm.
Music 3236, Item 379

404

The Head Man

Thematic music cue sheet. Richard A. Rowland presents Charlie Murray in *The Head Man* with Loretta Young and Larry Kent. *Film company:* First National. *Music compiled by:* James C. Bradford. *Note:* Music incipits. Two copies.

MOMA   4 p., 31 cm.
Music 3236, Item 380

405

The Head of the Family

A Gotham Picture musical setting for *The Head of the Family. Character of film:* Comedy drama. *Music compiled by:* Joseph E. Zivelli. *Note:* Cue sheet. No music. Two copies. *Number of reels:* 7.

MOMA   1 p., 36 cm.
Music 3236, Item 381

406

The Heart of Broadway

A Rayart Picture musical setting for *The Heart of Broadway* with Pauline Garon and Robert Agnew. *Character of film:* Drama of Broadway. *Music compiled by:* Joseph E. Zivelli. *Note:* Cue sheet. No music. "May–13–14" marked in pencil. *Number of reels:* 6.

MOMA   1 p., 32 cm.
Music 3236, Item 382

407
Heart to Heart
Heart to Heart. Note: Cue sheet. No music.
Typescript.
MOMA   1 p., 28 cm.
Music 3236, Item 383

408
Heart to Heart
Thematic music cue sheet. First National Pic-
tures, Inc. presents *Heart to Heart* with Mary
Astor, Lloyd Hughes and Louise Fazenda. *Produc-
tion by:* William Beaudine. *Film company:* First
National. *Music compiled by:* James C. Bradford.
Note: Music incipits. Two copies. "Fri & Sat. Oct
19–20" marked in pencil on copy 1. "Tue & Wed
Oct 9–10" crossed out in pencil.
MOMA   4 p., 31 cm.
Music 3236, Item 384

409
Hearts Aflame
A Luz music score. Louis B. Mayer presents The
Reginald Barker production *Hearts Aflame. Film
company:* Metro; controlled by Loew's Inc. *Music
compiled by:* Ernst Luz. *Published by:* Photo-
play Music Co., New York, 1922. *Instrumentation:*
Piano. *Copyright:* © C1 E 555162, December 20,
1922.
LC M1527.L95H3   78 p., 30 cm.
Music 3212, Item 64

410
Hearts and Fists
Thematic music cue sheet. Associated Exhibitors,
Inc., presents *Hearts and Fists* with Marguerite
De La Motte and John Bowers. *From the* Ameri-
can Magazine *story by:* Clarence Budington Kel-
land. *Production by:* H. C. Weaver, Tacoma.
Released by: Associated Exhibitors, Inc. *Music
compiled by:* James C. Bradford. *Note:* Music
incipits. "Sunday May 2" marked in pencil.
MOMA   4 p., 32 cm
Music 3236, Item 385

411
Hearts of Men
A Crescent Picture musical presentation *Hearts
of Men. Music arranged by:* Gisdon True; Theme,
"Venetian Love Song," by Nevin. *Note:* Cue sheet.
No music.
MOMA   1 p., 31 cm.
Music 3236, Item 386

412
Hearts of the World
D. W. Griffith's *Hearts of the World. Management
of:* William Elliott, F. Ray Comstock and Morris
Gest. *Music selected and arranged by:* Carli
Densmore Elinor. *Instrumentation:* Piano
conductor.
MOMA   131 p., 31 cm.
Music 3236, Item 39

412A
Hearts of the World
D. W. Griffith's *Hearts of the World. Management
of:* William Elliott, F. Ray Comstock and Morris
Gest. *Music selected and arranged by:* Carli
Densmore Elinor. *Published by:* Tams Music
Library, New York. *Instrumentation:* Piano con-
ductor and instrumental parts (1,1,2,1; 2,2,2,1;
tympani; drums; harp; bells; strings). *Note:* There
are multiple copies of these parts.
MOMA   131 p., 31 cm.
No microfilm

413
Hearts of the World
D. W. Griffith's *Hearts of the World. Management
of:* William Elliott, F. Ray Comstock and Morris
Gest. *Music selected and arranged by:* Carli
Densmore Elinor. *Published by:* Tams Music
Library, New York. *Instrumentation:* Piano con-
ductor; (0,1,2,1; 2,2,2,1; tympani; drums; harp;
bells; strings).
LC M1527.E45H4   236 p., 30 cm.
Music 3212, Item 65

414
Hell Bent fer Heaven
Warner Bros. present *Hell Bent Fer Heaven* star-
ring Patsy Ruth Miller and John Harron. *Note:*
Cue sheet. No music. "Mon & Tues Aug 23–24"
marked in pencil. *Projection time:* 1 hour, 14
minutes at a speed of 11 minutes per 1000 feet.
MOMA   1 p., 36 cm.
Music 3236, Item 387

415
Hello Cheyenne
Thematic music cue sheet. Tom Mix in *Hello
Cheyenne. Production by:* William Fox. *Music
compiled by:* Michael P. Krueger. *Note:* Music
incipits. "Sunday Dec. 9" marked in pencil.
MOMA   4 p., 32 cm.
Music 3236, Item 388

Bulgarian born Carli Elinor, composer and music director, with Janet Gaynor. Elinor was the general music director for all D. W. Griffith's productions between 1915 and 1919, conductor of the orchestra at the California Theater in Los Angeles, 1915-1925, and musical director for the Carthay Circle Theater world premieres, 1926-1929. During this period he also created musical scores for Fox Film, MGM, Samuel Goldwyn, Charlie Chaplin, and United Artists. Music Division, Library of Congress.

416
Her Big Night
Thematic music cue sheet. Carl Laemmle presents Laura LaPlante in *Her Big Night by:* Peggy Cadeis. *Directed by:* Melville W. Brown. *Film company:* Universal-Jewel. *Music compiled by:* James C. Bradford. *Note:* Music incipits. "Dec 6/26 Monday" marked in pencil.

MOMA   2 p., 34 cm.
Music 3236, Item 389

417
Her Second Chance
Thematic music cue sheet. First National Pictures presents *Her Second Chance* with Anna Q. Nilssen [sic] and Huntley Gordon. *Film company:* First National. *Music compiled by:* James C. Bradford. *Note:* Music incipits. "Thurs & Friday 6/3-4" marked in pencil.

MOMA   4 p., 32 cm.
Music 3236, Item 390

418
Her Secret Hour
Her Secret Hour. Note: Cue sheet. No music. Typescipt.

MOMA   1 p., 28 cm.
Music 3236, Item 391

419
Hey Rube
Thematic music cue sheet. William Le Baron presents *Hey Rube* with Gertrude Olmsted and Hugh Trevor. *Production by:* George B. Seitz. *Distributed by:* F B O Pictures Corporation. *Note:* Music incipits. "Thursday April 4" marked in pencil.

MOMA   4 p., 32 cm.
Music 3236, Item 392

420
The High Flyer
Musical setting for *The High Flyer* featuring Reed Howes. *Film company:* Rayart. *Character of film:* Comedy drama. *Music compiled by:* Joseph E. Zivelli. *Note:* Cue sheet. No music. "Plaza Theatre. Aug. 11 & 12, 1930. Mon. & Tues." marked in ink. *Projection time:* 58¾ minutes.

MOMA   1 p., 32 cm.
Music 3236, Item 393

421
High School Hero
Thematic music cue sheet. William Fox Film Production *High School Hero. Music compiled by:* Michael P. Krueger. *Note:* Music incipits. Two copies.
MOMA   4 p., 32 cm.
                                Music 3236, Item 394

422
His Bitter Pill
His Bitter Pill by Mack Sennett. *Instrumentation:* Piano score.
MOMA   48 p., 31 cm.
                                Music 3236, Item 40

423
His First Command
His First Command. Note: Cue Sheet. No music. Typescript. Three copies.
MOMA   6 p., 33 cm.
                                Music 3236, Item 395

424
His Last Haul
Thematic music cue sheet. William Le Baron presents *His Last Haul* with Tom Moore and Seena Owen. *Directed by:* Marshall Neilan. *Distributed by:* F B O Pictures Corporation. *Music compiled by:* James C. Bradford. *Note:* Music incipits.
MOMA   4 p., 32 cm.
                                Music 3236, Item 396

425
His Master's Voice
Musical setting for *His Master's Voice. Music compiled by:* Joseph E. Zivelli. *Note:* Cue sheet. No music. "Wednesday & Thursday Dec. 30–31" marked in pencil. Mutilated.
MOMA   1 p., 25 by 27 cm.
                                Music 3236, Item 397

426
His Tiger Lady
His Tiger Lady. Note: Cue sheet. No music. Typescript.
MOMA   1 p., 28 cm.
                                Music 3236, Item 398

427
Hit of the Show
Thematic music cue sheet. Joseph P. Kennedy presents *Hit of the Show* with Gertrude Olmsted, Joe E. Brown, Gertrude Astor and Daphne Pollard. *From the story* Notices *by:* Viola Brothers Shore.

Production by: Ralph Ince. *Distributed by:* F B O Pictures Corporation. *Music compiled by:* James C. Bradford. *Note:* Music incipits.
MOMA   4 p., 32 cm.
                                Music 3236, Item 399

428
Hold 'Em Yale!
Thematic music cue sheet. Pathe presents Rod La Rocque in *Hold 'Em Yale!* with Jeanette Loff, Tom Kennedy, Joseph Cawthorn and Hugh Allen. *Original story* At Yale *by:* Owen Davis. *Adapted by:* George Dromgold. *Production by:* Hector Turnbull; DeMille Studio. *Directed by:* Edward H. Griffith. *Distributed by:* Pathe Exchange, Inc. *Music compiled by:* Rudolph Berliner. *Note:* Music incipits.
MOMA   4 p., 32 cm.
                                Music 3236, Item 400

429
Home James
Thematic music cue sheet. Carl Laemmle presents *Home James. Production by:* Universal. *Music compiled by:* James C. Bradford. *Note:* Music incipits. Two copies.
MOMA   2 p., 32 cm.
                                Music 3236, Item 401

430
Home Made
Thematic music cue sheet. C. C. Burr presents Johnny Hines in *Home Made. Directed by:* Charles Hines. *Film company:* First National. *Music compiled by:* James C. Bradford. *Note:* Music incipits. Two copies. "March 20–21" marked in pencil on copy 1.
MOMA   4 p., 32 cm.
                                Music 3236, Item 402

431
The Home Maker
Thematic music cue sheet. Carl Laemmle presents *The Home Maker* by Dorothy Canfield with Alice Joyce and Clive Brook. *Production by:* King Baggot. *Film company:* Universal-Jewel. *Music compiled by:* James C. Bradford. *Note:* Music incipits. *Footage:* 7754.
MOMA   2 p., 35 cm.
                                Music 3236, Item 403

432
Homesick
Thematic music cue sheet. William Fox Feature
Film Production Sammy Cohen and Marjorie
Beebe in *Homesick*. *Music compiled by:* Michael
P. Krueger. *Note:* Music incipits.
MOMA   4 p., 32 cm.
                              Music 3236, Item 404

433
Honeymoon
Thematic music cue sheet. *Honeymoon* with Polly
Moran, Harry Gribbon and Flash the dog extraor-
dinary. *Story by:* Lew Lipton. *Adaptation by:* E.
Richard Schayer. *Continuity by:* George O'Hara.
Directed by: Robert A. Golden. *Film company:*
Metro-Goldwyn-Mayer. *Music compiled by:*
Ernst Luz. *Note:* Music incipits. *Number of reels:*
6. *Footage:* 4956. *Projection time:* 56 minutes.
MOMA   4 p., 31 cm.
                              Music 3236, Item 405

434
Honeymoon Abroad
Thematic music cue sheet. World Wide Pictures,
Inc. presents *Honeymoon Abroad*. *Directed by:*
Tim Whelan. *Film company:* British Interna-
tional. *Music compiled by:* James C. Bradford.
Note: Music incipits. "Sunday [March?] 31"
marked in pencil.
MOMA   4 p., 32 cm.
                              Music 3236, Item 406

435
Honeymoon Flats
Thematic music cue sheet. Carl Laemmle presents
Honeymoon Flats. *Production by:* Universal.
Music compiled by: James C. Bradford. *Note:*
Music incipits. Two copies.
MOMA   2 p., 32 cm.
                              Music 3236, Item 407

436
Honeymoon Hate
Thematic music cue sheet. Adolph Zukor and
Jesse L. Lasky present Florence Vidor in *Honey-
moon Hate*. *Story by:* Alice M. Williamson. *Adap-
tation by:* Doris Anderson. *Screenplay by:* Ethel
Doherty. *Produced by:* B. P. Schulberg, Associate
Producer. *Directed by:* Luther Reed. *Film com-
pany:* Paramount. *Music compiled by:* James C.
Bradford. *Note:* Music incipits. *Footage:* 5415.
MOMA   4 p., 32 cm.
                              Music 3236, Item 408

437
Honor's Altar
Musical setting for the photoplay *Honor's Altar*
(P. 40). *Production by:* Thomas H. Ince. *Music
composed and selected by:* Louis F. Gottschalk.
Series title: Triangle plays. *Published by:* G.
Schirmer for the Triangle Film Corp., New York,
1916. *Instrumentation:* Piano conductor. *Copy-
right:* © C1 E 377024, January 11, 1916.
LC M1357.G   36 p., 30 cm.
                               Music 3212, Item 66

438
Hoofbeats of Vengeance
Musical setting for *Hoofbeats of Vengeance*.
Music specially selected and compiled by: M.
Winkler. Theme, Scene d'Amour, (Mod) by
Baron. *Projection time:* The timing is based on a
speed limit of 14 minutes per reel. *Note:* Cue
sheet. No music. "Norman R. McKeon" stamped
at top of page.
MOMA   1 p., 30 cm.
                              Music 3236, Item 409

439
Hook and Ladder No. 9
Thematic music cue sheet. Joseph P. Kennedy
presents *Hook and Ladder No. 9* with an all star
cast. *From the story by:* John Morosco. *Directed
by:* F. Harmon Weight. *Distributed by:* F B O Pictures Corporation. *Music compiled by:* James C.
Bradford. *Note:* Music incipits. "Lyceum Sat–Jan
28–1928" marked in pencil.
MOMA   4 p., 32 cm.
                              Music 3236, Item 410

440
Hop, the Devil's Brew
Musical setting to the Bluebird Photo-Play No. 4
Hop, the Devil's Brew. *From the story by:* Rufus
Steele. *Prepared for the screen and produced by:*
Lois Weber and Phillips Smalley. *Music selected
and arranged by:* M. Winkler. *Series title:* Carl
Fischer Photo-Play Series. *Published by:* Carl
Fischer, New York, 1916. *Instrumentation:* Piano
conductor: (1,1,2,1; 2,2,1,0; drums; strings). *Copy-
right:* © C1 E 377958, February 23, 1916.
LC M1357.W   59 p., 31 cm.
                               Music 3212, Item 67

441
Hotel Imperial
Hotel Imperial, 1st reel. *Instrumentation:* Piano
score.
MOMA   16 p., 31 cm.
                               Music 3236, Item 41

Mary Pickford in a production shot from *Hoodlum*
(1919). Museum of Modern Art, Film Stills Archive.

442
The Hottentot

Thomas H. Ince offers a music cue sheet for *The Hottentot. Prepared by:* Sol Cohen. *Note:* No music.

MOMA 2 p., 36 cm.
Music 3236, Item 411

443
How Baxter Butted In

Thematic music cue sheet. Warner Bros. classics of the screen *How Baxter Butted In. By:* Owen Davis. *Adapted from* Stuff of Heroes *by:* Harold Titus with Dorothy Devore. *Directed by:* William Beaudine. *Scenario by:* Julian Josephson. *Music compiled by:* James C. Bradford. *Note:* Music incipits. Cue sheet was prepared May 23, 1925.

MOMA 4 p., 32 cm.
Music 3236, Item 412

444
How to Handle Women

Thematic music cue sheet. Carl Laemmle presents *How to Handle Women. Production by:* Universal. *Music compiled by:* James C. Bradford. *Note:* Music incipits. *See Fresh Every Hour.* Released as *How to Handle Women.*

MOMA 2 p., 32 cm.
Music 3236, Item 413

445
Huntingtower

Thematic music cue sheet. Welsh-Pearson & Co. Ltd. present Sir Harry Lauder in *Huntingtower* with Vera Voronina. *Screenplay by:* Charles E. Whittaker. *From the novel by:* John Buchan. *Edited by:* T. Hayes Hunter. *Directed by:* George Pearson. *Film company:* Paramount. *Music compiled by:* James C. Bradford. *Note:* Music incipits. *Footage:* 5812.

MOMA 4 p., 32 cm.
Music 3236, Item 414

446
Husbands for Rent

Warner Bros. present *Husbands for Rent,* starring Owen Moore, Helene Costello, John Miljan. *Note:* Cue sheet. No music. *Projection time:* About an hour based on a speed of 11 minutes per 1000 feet.

MOMA 1 p., 35 cm.
Music 3236, Item 415

447
Idaho Red

Musical synopsis for *Idaho Red. Music compiled by:* James C. Bradford. *Note:* Cue sheet. No music.

MOMA 1 p., 32 cm.
Music 3236, Item 416

448
Im Kientopp

Im Kientopp, ein musikalischer Film. Grosses Potpourri zum Mitsingen. *Music by:* Otto Lindemann. *Published by:* Thalia-Theater Verlag, Berlin, 1912. *Instrumentation:* Piano/vocal score. *Copyright:* © C1 E 294372, September 5, 1912.

LC M176.I3 11 p., 34 cm.
Music 3212, Item 68

449
In Hollywood

Thematic music cue sheet. Samuel Goldwyn presents *In Hollywood* with Potash and Perlmutter. *Film company:* First National. *Music compiled by:* Eugene Conte, Musical Director, Plaza Theatre, N.Y. City. *Note:* Music incipits. Pages 1 and 2 are mutilated.

MOMA 4 p., 32 cm.
Music 3236, Item 417

450
In Mizzoura

In Mizzoura. Incidental music to the moving picture adaptation of Augustus Thomas' great play of rural life *In Mizzoura* featuring Burr McIntosh and an all star cast. *Produced by:* The All Star Feature Corporation. *Music composed by:* Manuel Klein, Musical Director of the New York Hippodrome. *Published by:* M. Witmark & Sons, N.Y., 1914. *Instrumentation:* Piano score. *Copyright:* © C1 E 335227, March 31, 1914; R 96679, April 2, 1941, Helen Klein, Hollywood, Calif.

LC M176.I35 16 p., 35 cm.
Music 3212, Item 69

451
In Old Siberia

In Old Siberia. Note: Ms. cue sheet. No music.

MOMA 1 p., 24 cm., Ms.
Music 3236, Item 418

452
L'Inondation

L'Inondation. Music arranged by: Gaby Coutrot. *Note:* Cue sheet. No music. In French.

MOMA 1 p., 27 cm. by 21 cm.
Music 3236, Item 419

453
Interference

Thematic music cue sheet. Adolph Zukor and Jesse L. Lasky present *Interference* with Evelyn Brent, Clive Brook, William Powell and Doris Kenyon. *Play by:* Roland Pertwee and Harold Dearden. *Adaptation by:* Hope Loring. *Production by:* West Coast Productions, B. P. Schulberg, General Manager. *Directed by:* Lothar Mendes. *Film company:* Paramount. *Music compiled by:* James C. Bradford. *Note:* Music incipits. *Footage:* 6643.

MOMA   4 p., 32 cm.
Music 3236, Item 420

454
Intolerance

D. W. Griffith presents *Intolerance. Instrumentation:* Orchestral parts (1,1,2,1; 2,2,2,0; drums; harp; strings).

MOMA   32 cm.
Music 3236, Item 42

455
Intolerance

D. W. Griffith's *Intolerance. Instrumentation:* Piano score.

MOMA   258 p., 30 cm.
Music 3236, Item 42a

456
Intolerance

Selection from the incidental music to D. W. Griffith's *Intolerance. Music by:* Joseph Carl Breil. *Published by:* Chappell & Co., Ltd., 1916. London. *Instrumentation:* Piano. *Copyright:* © E 391398, November 4, 1916; R 122566, November 4, 1943, Jean S. Breil, New York and Clarence Lucas, London.

LC M1527.B7315   52 p., 30 cm.
Music 3212, Item 70

457
Intolerance

Intolerance. Note: Cue sheet. No music. Typescript (photocopy). Pages are pieced together and held with tape.

MOMA   4 p., 36 cm.
Music 3236, Item 421

458
Iris

Iris, opera in tre atti di L. Illica e P. Mascagni, adattamento musicale per riproduzione cinematografica. *Music by:* L. Illica and P. Mascagni. *Published by:* Lux Artis (Esecuzione autorizzata da G. Ricordi & Co.), Rome, 1920. *Instrumentation:* Piano conductor; (1,pic.,2,0,0; 2,1,1,0; batteria, harmonium; strings). *Copyright:* © C1 E 484297, August 20, 1920.

LC M1527.M415P2   126 p., 27 cm.
Music 3212, Item 71

459
The Iron Mask

Conductor *The Iron Mask. Instrumentation:* Piano conductor, 10 volumes. *Note:* Each volume is music for a reel of film. Reel 11 is missing. Also includes letter addressed "To the Conductor" from C. Dunworth, United Artists Studio librarian, dated February 20, 1929, attributing the compilation to Dr. Hugo Riesenfeld.

MOMA   10 vols., 32 cm., 130 separate numbers
Music 3236, Item 84

460
L'Ironie du Destin

L'Ironie du Destin. Music compiled by: A. Leparcq. *Note:* Cue sheet. No music. In French.

MOMA   2 p., 27 cm. by 21 cm.
Music 3236, Item 422

461
The Irresistible Lover

Thematic music cue sheet. Carl Laemmle presents *The Irresistible Lover. Film company:* Universal-Jewel. *Music compiled by:* James C. Bradford. *Note:* Music incipits. Two copies. "Monday Dec 5/27" marked in pencil on both copies.

MOMA   2 p., 39 cm.
Music 3236, Item 423

462
Is Matrimony a Failure

Is Matrimony a Failure. Note: Cue sheet. No music. Typescript.

MOMA   1 p., 28 cm.
Music 3236, Item 424

463
Isn't Life Wonderful

D. W. Griffith presents *Isn't Life Wonderful. Produced by:* D. W. Griffith, Inc., Albert L. Grey, Gen. Mgr. *Music compiled and synchronized by:* Cesare Sodero and Louis Silvers. *Published by:* Robbins-Engel, Inc., New York, n.d. *Instrumentation:* Piano conductor and orchestral parts (1,1,2,1; 2,2,1,0; drums; strings).

MOMA   113 p., 30 cm.
Music 3236, Item 43

464
Isobel
Isobel. Music compiled by: James C. Bradford. *Note:* Cue sheet. No music. Scenes from the film on verso.
MOMA   1 p., 35 cm.
                          Music 3236, Item 425

465
It Can Be Done
Thematic music cue sheet. Carl Laemmle presents *It Can Be Done. Production by:* Universal. *Music compiled by:* James C. Bradford. *Note:* Music incipits. Two copies.
MOMA   2 p., 32 cm.
                          Music 3236, Item 426

466
The Italian Straw Hat
Music for *The Italian Straw Hat. Published by:* Museum of Modern Art Film Library, New York City. *Instrumentation:* Piano score.
MOMA   149 p., 32 cm.
                          Music 3236, Item 44

467
The Italian Straw Hat
Score for *The Italian Straw Hat. Music arranged by:* Jay Leyda. *Note:* Cue sheet. No music. Two copies. Typescript.
MOMA   1 p., 36 cm.
                          Music 3236, Item 427

468
Jane
Paramount photoplay music (P 131 B 24) *Jane. Produced by:* Pallas Pictures. *Music selected and arranged by:* George W. Beynon. *Series title:* Schirmer's Photoplay Series. *Published by:* G. Schirmer, New York, 1915. *Instrumentation:* Piano conductor. *Copyright:* © C1 E 377035, December 15, 1915.
LC M1357.B   84 p., 30 cm.
                          Music 3212, Item 72

469
Janice Meredith
Music score *Janice Meredith. Music by:* Deems Taylor. *Instrumentation:* Piano conductor.
LC M1527.T25J3   179 p., 31 cm.
                          Music 3212, Item 73

470
Jannings
Jannings. Note: Cue sheet. No music. Typescript (carbon). Also includes T. L. S. from Pauline A.

Grossman, Paramount Pictures Inc. to Florence West, Museum of Modern Art Film Library, July 24, 1936. Relates to cue sheet for Jannings.
MOMA   2 p., 28 cm.
                          Music 3236, Item 428

471
Jannings
Jannings. Note: Cue sheet. No music. "Last Laugh" marked in pencil. Typescript.
MOMA   1 p., 28 cm.
                          Music 3236, Item 429

472
Jeanne Dore
Musical setting to the Bluebird Photo-Play no. 1. Madame Sarah Bernhardt in a photo-play adaptation by Tristan-Bernard of *Jeanne Dore. Music selected and arranged by:* M. Winkler. *Series title:* Carl Fischer Photo-Play Series. *Published by:* Carl Fischer, New York, 1916. *Instrumentation:* Piano conductor; (1,1,2,1; 2,2,1,0; drums; strings). *Copyright:* © C1 E 378272, February 7, 1916.
LC M1357.W   60 p., 31 cm.
                          Music 3212, Item 74

473
Joan the Woman
Music score for the photoplay *Joan the Woman* with Geraldine Farrar as presented by Cecil B. DeMille. *Film company:* The Cardinal Film Corporation. *Music composed by:* William Furst. *Published by:* G. Schirmer, New York, 1917. *Instrumentation:* Piano or organ. *Copyright:* © C1 E 402122, March 10, 1917; R 129520, June 24, 1944, Paramount Pictures, Inc., New York.
LC M1527.F86J6   299 p., 31 cm.
                          Music 3212, Item 75

474
John Needham's Double
Musical setting to the Bluebird Photo-Play no. 12. Mr. Tyrone Power in *John Needham's Double. Produced by:* Phillips Smalley. *Music selected and arranged by:* M. Winkler and F. Rehsen. *Series title:* Carl Fischer Photo-Play Series. *Published by:* Carl Fischer, New York, 1916. *Instrumentation:* Piano conductor (1,1,2,1; 2,2,1,0; drums; strings). *Copyright:* © C1 E 379570, April 5, 1916.
LC M1357.W   52 p., 31 cm.
                          Music 3212, Item 76

475
Jordan Is a Hard Road

Musical setting to the photoplay *Jordan Is a Hard Road. Production by:* Fine-Arts Feature Co. *Music composed and arranged by:* J. A. Raynes. *Series title:* Triangle Plays. *Published by:* G. Schirmer, Inc. for The Triangle Film Corp., New York, 1915. *Instrumentation:* Piano conductor (1,0,2,0; 0,2,1,0; drum; strings). *Copyright:* © C1 E 373896, November 25, 1915.

LC M1357.R 81 p., 30 cm.
Music 3212, Item 77

476
Le Joueur d'Échecs

Le Joueur d'Échecs. Music by: Henri Rabaud. *Published by:* Max Eschig & Cie., Paris, 1927. *Instrumentation:* Piano score. *Copyright:* © C1 E 663325, April 20, 1927; R 146244, March 16, 1955, Jacqueline Rabaud (C).

LC M1527.R2J5 168 p., 30 cm.
Music 3212, Item 78

477
Judith of Bethulia

The following has bee[n] suggested as a musical program for *Judith of Bethulia.* The Biograph, April 3, 1915. *Note:* Cue sheet. No music. Typescript.

MOMA 1 p., 28 cm.
Music 3236, Item 430

478
The Jungle

The Jungle. Incidental music to the motion picture presentation of Upton Sinclair's story of the stockyards, *The Jungle. Produced by:* The All Star Feature Corporation. *Music composed by:* Manuel Klein. *Published by:* M. Witmark & Sons, New York, 1914. *Instrumentation:* Piano score. *Copyright:* © C1 E 339877, June 8, 1914; R 98070, June 25, 1941, Helen Klein, Hollywood, Calif.

LC M176.J95 11 p., 35 cm.
Music 3212, Item 79

479
Just Married

Thematic music cue sheet. Adolph Zukor and Jesse L. Lasky present Anne Nichols' *Just Married* with Ruth Taylor and James Hall. *Adaptation and screenplay by:* Frank Butler and Gilbert Pratt. *Produced by:* B. P. Schulberg, Associate Producer. *Directed by:* Frank Strayer. *Film company:* Paramount. *Music compiled by:* James C. Bradford. *Note:* Music incipits. Two

copies. "Sunday Nov 4" marked in pencil on copy 1. *Footage:* 6039.

MOMA 4 p., 31 cm.
Music 3236, Item 431

480
Just Married

Just Married. Note: Cue sheet. No music. Typescript.

MOMA 2 p., 35 cm.
Music 3236, Item 432

481
Just Off Broadway

Just Off Broadway, a Chesterfield Attraction. Musical synopsis. *Music compiled by:* Motion Pictures Synchronization Service, Inc., 1650 Broadway, New York City; Love Theme, "Marie," by Irving Berlin. *Note:* Cue sheet. No music. "Plaza 12/28/29" marked in pencil.

MOMA 1 p., 30 cm.
Music 3236, Item 433

482
Juve vs. Fantomas

Juve vs. Fantomas. Instrumentation: Piano score.

MOMA 81 p., 29 cm.
Music 3236, Item 45

483
Keep Smiling

Thematic music cue sheet. Howard Estabrook presents Monty Banks in *Keep Smiling. Released by:* Associated Exhibitors, Inc. *Physical distribution by:* Pathe Exchange, Inc. *Music compiled by:* James C. Bradford. *Note:* Music incipits. "Sun Jan 17" marked in pencil.

MOMA 4 p., 31 cm.
Music 3236, Item 434

484
Kettle Creek

Musical setting for Ken Maynard in *Kettle Creek* with Kathryn Crawford. *Film company:* Universal Pictures Corp. *Music compiled by:* M. Winkler. *Note:* Cue sheet. No music. Two copies.

MOMA 3 p., 28 cm.
Music 3236, Item 435

485
Kino-Pravda

Music for *Kino-Pravda: Kombrig Invanov Rebellion, Mutiny in Odessa. Published by:* The Museum of Modern Art Film Library, New York. *Instrumentation:* Piano score.

MOMA   22 p.; 19 p.; 4 p.
Music 3236, Item 46

486
Kit Carson

Thematic music cue sheet. Fred Thompson in *Kit Carson. Story by:* Paul Powell. *Directed by:* Lloyd Ingraham and Alfred L. Werker. *Film company:* Paramount. *Music compiled by:* James C. Bradford. *Note:* Music incipits. *Footage:* 7464.

MOMA   6 p., 31 cm.
Music 3236, Item 436

487
The Knockout

Thematic music cue sheet. Milton Sills in *The Knockout. Film company:* First National. *Music compiled by:* James C. Bradford. *Note:* Music incipits.

MOMA   4 p., 30 cm.
Music 3236, Item 437

488
Knockout Reilly

Knockout Reilly. Note: Cue sheet. No music. Typescript.

MOMA   1 p., 28 cm.
Music 3236, Item 438

489
Laddie

Thematic music cue sheet. Joseph P. Kennedy presents a gripping screen version of Gene Stratton Porter's best known novel *Laddie* with John Bowers. *Directed by:* James Leo Meehan. *Distributed by:* Film Booking Offices of America, Inc. *Music compiled by:* James C. Bradford. *Note:* Music incipits. "Thurs Fri Sat Feb 10–11–12" marked in pencil.

MOMA   4 p., 31 cm.
Music 3236, Item 439

490
Ladies Night in a Turkish Bath

Thematic music cue sheet. Asher, Small and Rogers presents *Ladies Night in a Turkish Bath* with Dorothy Mackaill and Jack Mulhall, by Charlton Andrews and Avery Hopwood. *Produced by:*
Edward Small. *Directed by:* Edward Cline. *Film company:* First National. *Music compiled by:* Eugene Conte. *Note:* Music incipits. Two copies. Copy 2 is a thermofax copy.

MOMA   4 p., 32 cm.
Music 3236, Item 440

491
Ladies of the Mob

Ladies of the Mob. Note: Cue sheet. No music. Typescript.

MOMA   1 p., 28 cm.
Music 3236, Item 441

492
Ladies of the Night Club

Thematic music cue sheet. Tiffany-Stahl presents *Ladies of the Night Club,* by Ben Grauman Kohn with Ricardo Cortez. *Directed by:* George Archainbaud. *Production by:* Tiffany-Stahl. *Music compiled by:* James C. Bradford. *Note:* Music incipits. "Lyceum Theatre Mon. Tues. Wed.—July 30, 31 and Aug. 2—1928" marked in pencil.

MOMA   4 p., 31 cm.
Music 3236, Item 442

493
Lady Be Good

Thematic music cue sheet. First National Pictures, Inc. presents *Lady Be Good* with Dorothy Mackaill and Jack Mulhall. *Production by:* Richard Wallace. *Film company:* First National. *Music compiled by:* James C. Bradford. *Note:* Music incipits.

MOMA   4 p., 32 cm.
Music 3236, Item 443

494
The Lady in Ermine

Thematic music cue sheet. Asher, Small and Rogers presents Corinne Griffith in *The Lady in Ermine. Screenplay by:* Benjamin Glazer. *Directed by:* James Flood. *Film company:* First National. *Music compiled by:* Eugene Conte. *Note:* Music incipits. "Thursday Jan. 27" marked in pencil.

MOMA   4 p., 31 cm.
Music 3236, Item 444

495
The Land

Music for the second program of the Film Society *The Land,* Harold Lloyd and Bebe Daniels. *Note:* Cue sheet. No music. Typescript (carbon).

MOMA   1 p., 28 cm.
Music 3236, Item 445

496
Land of the Silver Fox
Warner Bros. present *Land of the Silver Fox* starring Rin-Tin-Tin, John Miljan, Carroll Nye. *Note:* Cue sheet. No music. "Mon & Tues Dec 24–25" marked in pencil. *Projection time:* About an hour based on a speed of 11 minutes per 1000 feet.

MOMA   1 p., 33 cm.
Music 3236, Item 446

497
The Last Card
The Last Card. Instrumentation: Piano Score. *Note:* Typescript, 1 p., of contents attached.

MOMA   30 p., 31 cm.
Music 3236, Item 47

498
The Last Command
The Last Command. Instrumentation: Piano score.

MOMA   163 p., 30 cm.
Music 3236, Item 48

499
The Last Command
The Last Command. Note: Cue sheet. No music. Typescript.

MOMA   1 p., 28 cm.
Music 3236, Item 447

500
The Last Edition
Thematic music cue sheet. F. B. O. presents *The Last Edition* with Ralph Lewis. *Story and continuity by:* Emilie Johnson. *Production by:* Emory Johnson. *Distributed by:* Film Booking Offices of America, Inc. *Music compiled by:* James C. Bradford. *Note:* Music incipits. Two copies. "12/19" marked in pencil on copy 1. "Sat Dec 19" marked in pencil on copy 2.

MOMA   4 p., 31 cm.
Music 3236, Item 448

501
The Last Laugh
The Last Laugh. Instrumentation: Piano score.

MOMA   171 p., 31 cm.
Music 3236, Item 49

502
The Last Warning
Greater thematic music cue sheet for *The Last Warning* featuring Laura La Plante. *Production by:* Universal. *Music compiled by:* James C. Bradford. *Note:* Music incipits.

MOMA   8 p., 32 cm.
Music 3236, Item 449

503
The Law and the Man
A Rayart Picture musical setting for *The Law and the Man* featuring Gladys Brockwell and Tom Santschi. *Music arranged by:* Joseph E. Zivelli. *Character of film:* Drama. *Note:* Cue sheet. No music. *Number of reels:* 6.

MOMA   1 p., 32 cm.
Music 3236, Item 450

504
The Law of the Range
Thematic music cue sheet. Tim McCoy in *The Law of the Range* with Joan Crawford. *Story by:* Norman Houston. *Scenario by:* Richard Schayer. *Production by:* William Nigh. *Directed by:* William Nigh. *Film company:* Metro-Goldwyn-Mayer. *Note:* Music incipits. "Sat Oct 13" marked in pencil. *Number of reels:* 6. *Footage:* 5350. *Maximum projection time:* 1 hour, 12 minutes.

MOMA   4 p., 32 cm.
Music 3236, Item 451

505
Lawful Larceny
Lawful Larceny. Note: Cue sheet. No music. Typescript. Five copies.

MOMA   6 p., 33 cm.
Music 3236, Item 452

506
Der Lebende Leichnam
The Living Corpse. Note: About 50 separate compositions stamped "Schmidt-Boelcke," usually bearing pencilled cues or indications of excerpts to be performed. Mostly piano parts, order unknown. Several are in manuscript, others from published collections of incidental music. *See entry 523.*

MOMA   Music 3236, Item 85

507
Legion of the Condemned
Legion of the Condemned. Note: Cue sheet. No music. Typescript.

MOMA   1 p., 28 cm.
Music 3236, Item 453

508

The Legion of the Condemned

Thematic music cue sheet. Adolph Zukor and Jesse L. Lasky present *The Legion of the Condemned* with Fay Wray and Gary Cooper. *Story by:* John Monk Saunders. *Screenplay by:* John Monk Saunders and Jean de Limur. *Production by:* William A. Wellman; B. P. Schulberg, Associate Producer. *Film company:* Paramount. *Music compiled by:* James C. Bradford. *Note:* Music incipits. Two copies. "12/1" marked in ink on copy 1.

MOMA   6 p., 32 cm.

Music 3236, Item 454

509

The Leopard Lady

Thematic music cue sheet. Pathe presents *The Leopard Lady* with Jacqueline Logan, Alan Hale and Robert Armstrong. *Adaptation and continuity by:* Beulah Marie Dix. *From the story by:* Edward Childs Carpenter. *Supervised by:* Bertram Millhauser. *Production by:* DeMille Studio. *Directed by:* Rupert Julian. *Distributed by:* Pathe Exchange, Inc. *Music compiled by:* Rudolph Berliner. *Note:* Music incipits. "4/23/28" and "12/2" marked in pencil.

MOMA   4 p., 32 cm.

Music 3236, Item 455

510

Let 'Er Go, Gallegher!

Thematic music cue sheet. Pathe presents *Let 'Er Go, Gallegher!* with Junior Coghlan, Harrison Ford, Elinor Fair and Ivan Lebedeff. *Adaptation and continuity by:* Elliott Clawson. *From the story by:* Richard Harding Davis. *Produced by:* DeMille Pictures Corporation, Associate Producer, Ralph Block. *Directed by:* Elmer Clifton. *Distributed by:* Pathe Exchange, Inc. *Music compiled by:* Rudolph Berliner. *Note:* Music incipits. "Thur. Feb 16" marked in pencil.

MOMA   4 p., 32 cm.

Music 3236, Item 456

511

Let Katie Do It

Musical setting for the photoplay *Let Katie Do It.* *Production by:* Fine-Arts Feature Co. *Music composed by:* William Furst. *Series title:* Triangle Plays. *Published by:* G. Schirmer for the Triangle Film Corp., New York, 1915. *Instrumentation:* Piano conductor. *Copyright:* © C1 E 377026, December 29, 1915.

LC M1357.F   93 p., 30 cm.

Music 3212, Item 80

512

Let's Get Married

Thematic music cue sheet. Adolph Zukor and Jesse L. Lasky present Richard Dix in *Let's Get Married* with Lois Wilson. *Adapted by:* Luther Reed from *The Man from Mexico* by H. A. DuSouchet. *Screenplay by:* J. Clarkson Miller. *Directed by:* Gregory La Cava. *Film company:* Paramount. *Music compiled by:* James C. Bradford. *Note:* Music incipits. "Mon & Tues May 24–25" marked in pencil. *Footage:* 6800.

MOMA   4 p., 31 cm.

Music 3236, Item 457

513

The Life of Riley

Thematic music cue sheet. *The Life of Riley.* *Film company:* First National. *Music compiled by:* James C. Bradford. *Note:* Music incipits. "Thurs. Sept. [?] 9,27" marked in ink.

MOMA   4 p., 31 cm.

Music 3236, Item 458

514

Lightning Speed

Musical synopsis for *Lightning Speed.* *Music by:* James C. Bradford. *Note:* No music. Cue sheet.

MOMA   1 p., 32 cm.

Music 3236, Item 459

515

The Lily and the Rose

Musical setting for the photoplay *The Lily and the Rose.* *Production by:* Fine-Arts Feature Co. *Music arranged and adapted by:* Joseph C. Breil and J. A. Raynes. *Series title:* Triangle Plays. *Published by:* G. Schirmer for the Triangle Film Corp., New York, 1915. *Instrumentation:* Piano conductor; (1,0,2,0; 0,2,1,0; drums; strings). *Copyright:* © C1 E 373893, November 15, 1915.

LC M1357.B (Cornet, copy 2, in M176.L)   86 p., 31 cm.

Music 3212, Item 81

516

Lingerie

Thematic music cue sheet. Tiffany-Stahl presents *Lingerie* with Alice White, Malcolm McGregor and Mildred Harris. *Adapted by:* John F. Natteford. *Production by:* Tiffany-Stahl. *Directed by:* George Melford. *Music compiled by:* James C. Bradford. *Note:* Music incipits.

MOMA   4 p., 32 cm.

Music 3236, Item 460

Colleen Moore and Gary Cooper in a production shot
from *Lilac Time* (1928). Museum of Modern Art, Film
Stills Archive.

517

The Lion and the Mouse

Warner Bros. presents *The Lion and the Mouse* starring May McAvoy, Lionel Barrymore. *Note:* Cue sheet. No music. *Projection time:* 1 hour, 5 minutes based on a speed of 11 minutes per 1000 feet.

MOMA   1 p., 36 cm.
Music 3236, Item 461

518

The Little French Girl

The Little French Girl. Note: Cue sheet. No music. Typescript.

MOMA   1 p., 28 cm.
Music 3236, Item 462

519

The Little Giant

Thematic music cue sheet. Carl Laemmle presents Glenn Hunter in *The Little Giant* by Hugh McNair Kahler. *Production by:* Will Nigh. *Film company:* Universal-Jewel. *Note:* Music incipits. "Thurs & Friday 4/8-9" marked in pencil.

MOMA   2 p., 34 cm.
Music 3236, Item 463

520

Little Miss Bluebeard

Bebe Daniels in *Little Miss Bluebeard. Note:* Cue sheet. No music. Typescript.

MOMA   2 p., 28 cm.
Music 3236, Item 464

521

Little Old New York

Cosmopolitan Corporation presents Marion Davies in *Little Old New York* from Rida Johnson Young's stage play. *Adapted by:* Luther Reed. *Directed by:* Sidney Olcott. *Setting by:* Joseph Urban. *Music composed by:* William Frederick Peters. *Conducted by:* Frederick Stahlberg. *Instrumentation:* Piano.

LC M1527.P55L6   131 p., 34 cm.
Music 3212, Item 82

522

The Little Snob

Warner Bros. present *The Little Snob* starring May McAvoy. *Note:* Cue sheet. No music. *Projection time:* About an hour based on a speed of 11 minutes per 1000 feet.

MOMA   1 p., 35 cm.
Music 3236, Item 465

523

The Living Corpse

The Living Corpse. Note: Cue sheet. No music. Ms. *See* entry No. 506.

MOMA   2 p., 20 cm.
Music 3236, Item 466

524

The Lone Eagle

Thematic music cue sheet. Carl Laemmle presents *The Lone Eagle. Film company:* Universal-Jewel. *Note:* Music incipits. Two copies. "Lyceum Theatre Fri & Sat Feb-24-25-1928" marked in pencil on copy 1.

MOMA   2 p., 35 cm.
Music 3236, Item 467

525

Looking for Trouble

Musical setting for *Looking for Trouble. Music selected and compiled by:* M. Winkler. *Note:* Cue sheet. No music. "Sunday July 4" marked in pencil.

MOMA   1 p., 30 cm.
Music 3236, Item 468

526

The Lost Arrow

The Lost Arrow. Note: Cue sheet. No music. Typescript.

MOMA   1 p., 28 cm.
Music 3236, Item 469

527

Lost at Sea

Thematic music cue sheet. Carl Laemmle presents *The Lone Eagle. Film company:* Universal-*Suggested by:* Louis Vance's story *Main Spring. Production by:* Tiffany. *Directed by:* Louis J. Gasnier. *Music compiled by:* James C. Bradford. *Note:* Music incipits. "Lyceum" marked in pencil.

MOMA   4 p., 32 cm.
Music 3236, Item 470

528

Love and the Devil

First National Pictures, Inc. musical synopsis for *Love and the Devil. Music compiled by:* James C. Bradford. *Note:* Cue sheet. No music.

MOMA   1 p., 36 cm.
Music 3236, Item 471

529
The Love Flower

D. W. Griffith presents *The Love Flower. Music arranged and synchronized by:* Albert Pesce. *Instrumentation:* Orchestral parts (1,1,2,1; 2,2,1,0; tympani and drums; harp; strings).
MOMA   31 cm.
Music 3236, Item 50

530
The Love Gamble

Thematic music cue sheet. Banner Productions, Inc. presents *The Love Gamble* featuring Lillian Rich and Robert Frazer. *Production by:* Ben Verschleiser. *Directed by:* Edw. J. LeSaint. *Distributed by:* Henry Ginsberg Distributing Corporation. *Music compiled by:* James C. Bradford. *Note:* Music incipits. "Saturday Jan 23" marked in pencil.
MOMA   2 p., 33 cm.
Music 3236, Item 472

531
The Love of Jeanne Ney

The Love of Jeanne Ney. Instrumentation: Piano score.
MOMA   203 p., 29 cm.
Music 3236, Item 51

532
Love Over Night

Thematic music cue sheet. Pathe presents Rod La Rocque in *Love Over Night* with Jeanette Loff, Tom Kennedy and Mary Carr. *Production by:* Hector Turnbull. *Story and adaptation by:* George Dromgold and Sanford Hewitt. *Directed by:* Edward H. Griffith. *Distributed by:* Pathe Exchange, Inc. *Music compiled by:* Howard T. Wood. *Note:* Music incipits.
MOMA   4 p., 31 cm.
Music 3236, Item 473

533
The Love Thief

Thematic music cue sheet. Carl Laemmle presents Norman Kerry with Greta Nissen in *The Love Thief. From the play by:* Margaret Mayo. *Directed by:* John MacDermott. *Film company:* Universal-Jewel. *Music compiled by:* Eugene Conte. *Note:* Music incipits. "Thurs & Frid Aug 19–20" marked in pencil.
MOMA   2 p., 31 cm.
Music 3236, Item 474

534
The Love Thrill

Thematic music cue sheet. Carl Laemmle presents *The Love Thrill. Film company:* Universal-Jewel. *Music compiled by:* James C. Bradford. *Note:* Music incipits. Two copies. "Thur. June 16/27" marked in pencil on copy 1. "Thursday June 16/27" marked in pencil on copy 2.
MOMA   2 p., 33 cm.
Music 3236, Item 475

535
Lovers' Island

Thematic music cue sheet. Associated Exhibitors, Inc. presents *Lovers' Island* with Hope Hampton and James Kirkwood. *From the story by:* T. Howard Kelly. *Directed by:* Diamant-Berger. *Released by:* Associated Exhibitors, Inc. *Music compiled by:* Eugene Conte. *Note:* Music incipits. "Thurs & Friday March 4–5" marked in pencil.
MOMA   4 p., 30 cm.
Music 3236, Item 476

536
Loves of Casanova

Thematic music cue sheet. Metro-Goldwyn-Mayer presents *Loves of Casanova* with Ivan Mosjoukine. *Directed by:* Alexandre Volkoff. *Music compiled by:* Ernst Luz. *Note:* Music incipits. *Number of reels:* 8. *Footage:* 7310. *Maximum projection time:* 1 hour.
MOMA   4 p., 31 cm.
Music 3236, Item 477

537
The Lucky Lady

Thematic music cue sheet. Adolph Zukor and Jesse L. Lasky present a Raoul Walsh Production *The Lucky Lady* with Greta Nissen, Lionel Barrymore, William Collier, Jr., and Marc MacDermott. *From the story by:* Robert E. Sherwood and Bertram Bloch. *Screenplay by:* James T. O'Donohoe. *Film company:* Paramount. *Music compiled by:* James C. Bradford. *Note:* Music incipits. "Wed July 21" marked in pencil. *Footage:* 5942
MOMA   2 p., 34 cm.
Music 3236, Item 478

538
Lucrezia Borgia

Lucrezia Borgia. Note: Cue sheet. No music. Ms.
MOMA   1 p., 28 cm.
Music 3236, Item 479

539

Lumiere Films

Early Films by Lumiere with *The Runaway Horse. Instrumentation:* Piano.

MOMA 21 p., 30 cm.
Music 3236, Item 52

540

The Lunatic at Large

Thematic music cue sheet. First National Pictures, Inc. presents Leon Errol in *The Lunatic at Large* with Dorothy Mackaill. *Directed by:* Fred Newmeyer. *Film company:* First National. *Music compiled by:* Eugene Conte. *Note:* Music incipits.

MOMA 4 p., 32 cm.
Music 3236, Item 480

541

Lure of the Wild

Thematic music cue sheet. Columbia Pictures presents *Lure of the Wild* featuring Jane Novak and a great cast with The Wonder Dog. *Copyrighted and distributed by:* Columbia Pictures Corporation. *Music compiled by:* James C. Bradford. *Note:* Music incipits. "Wednesday May 5" marked in pencil.

MOMA 2 p., 33 cm.
Music 3236, Item 481

542

Lying Wives

Thematic music cue sheet. Ivan Players, Inc. presents *Lying Wives,* a dramatic presentation of troubled lives. *Written and directed by:* Ivan Abramson. *Music compiled by:* James C. Bradford. *Note:* Music incipits. "Sunday Jan 24" marked in pencil.

MOMA 4 p., 30 cm.
Music 3236, Item 482

543

Madame Pompadour

Madame Pompadour. Note: Cue sheet. No music. Typescript.

MOMA 1 p., 28 cm.
Music 3236, Item 483

544

Madame Récamier

Madame Récamier, Léon Moreau. Transcription pour Orchestre. *Music by:* Martin Garcias. *Published by:* Lucien de Lacour, Paris, 1928. *Instrumentation:* Piano conductor. *Copyright:* © E for. 2448, December 31, 1928.

LC M1527.M72M2 102, 114 p., 34 cm.
Music 3212, Item 83

545

Mademoiselle from Armentieres

Thematic music cue sheet. *Mademoiselle from Armentieres. From the story by:* Victor Saville. *Production by:* A. C. and R. C. Bromhead. *Directed by:* Maurice Elvey in conjunction with Victor Saville. *Controlled throughout the world by:* Gaumont Company, Ltd. *Distributed by;* Metro-Goldwyn-Mayer. *Music compiled by:* Ernst Luz. *Note:* Music incipits. "Fri & Sat Oct 5–6" marked in pencil. *Number of reels:* 6. *Footage:* 5435. *Maximum projection time;* 1 hour, 10 minutes.

MOMA 4 p., 31 cm.
Music 3236, Item 484

546

Mlle. Modiste

Thematic music cue sheet. Corinne Griffith in *Mlle. Modiste. Film company:* First National. *Music compiled by:* Eugene Conte. *Note:* Music incipits. "Thurs & Friday Aug 5–6" marked in pencil.

MOMA 4 p., 32 cm.
Music 3236, Item 485

547

The Magnificent Flirt

The Magnificent Flirt. Note: Cue sheet. No music. Typescript.

MOMA 1 p., 28 cm.
Music 3236, Item 486

548

The Main Event

Thematic music cue sheet. Vera Reynolds in *The Main Event* with Rudolph Schildkraut, Julia Faye, Charles Delaney and Robert Armstrong. *From the story* That Makes Us Even *by:* Paul Allison. *Continuity by:* Rochus Gliese. *Produced by:* DeMille Pictures Corporation. *Directed by:* William K. Howard. *Distributed by:* Pathe Exchange, Inc. *Music compiled by:* Rudolph Berliner. *Note:* Music incipits. Two copies. "Thur 22/27" marked in pencil on both copies.

MOMA .4 p., 31 cm.
Music 3236, Item 487

549

Man Crazy

Thematic music cue sheet. First National Pictures, Inc. presents *Man Crazy. Film company:* First National. *Music compiled by:* James C. Bradford. *Note:* Music incipits.

MOMA   4 p., 31 cm.

Music 3236, Item 488

550

The Man Four Square

Thematic music cue sheet. William Fox Production Buck Jones in *The Man Four Square. Music compiled by:* Michael P. Krueger. *Note:* Music incipits. "Saturday June 26" marked in pencil.

MOMA   2 p., 32 cm.

Music 3236, Item 489

551

The Man in Hobbles

Thematic music cue sheet. Tiffany-Stahl presents *The Man in Hobbles* with John Harron and Lila Lee. *Suggested by a story by:* Peter B. Kyne. *Production by:* Tiffany-Stahl. *Directed by:* George Archainbaud. *Note:* Music incipits.

MOMA   4 p., 30 cm.

Music 3236, Item 490

552

The Man in the Saddle

Thematic music cue sheet. Carl Laemmle presents Hoot Gibson in *The Man in the Saddle* by Charles Logue. *Film company:* Universal-Jewel. *Directed by:* Cliff Smith. *Music compiled by:* Dr. Edward Kilenyi. *Note:* Music incipits. Mutilated. "Mon & Tues Aug 9–10" marked in pencil.

MOMA   2 p., 31 cm.

Music 3236, Item 491

553

The Man Nobody Knows

The Man Nobody Knows, a film story of the life of Jesus, by Bruce Barton. *Music by:* Alexander Savine. *Published by:* Pictorial Clubs, Inc., New York, 1925. *Instrumentation:* Piano score. *Copyright:* © C1 E 641094, November 22, 1925.

LC M1527.S26M2   55 p., 31 cm.

Music 3212, Item 84

554

The Man Upstairs

Warner Brothers presents *The Man Upstairs* starring Monte Blue and Dorothy Devore. *Note:* Cue sheet. No music. "Wed. May 12" marked in

pencil. *Projection time:* 1 hour, 5 minutes based on a speed of 11 minutes per 1000 feet.

MOMA   1 p., 36 cm.

Music 3236, Item 492

555

Man, Woman and Wife

Thematic music cue sheet. Carl Laemmle presents *Man, Woman and Wife. Production by:* Universal. *Music compiled by:* James C. Bradford. *Note:* Music incipits. Two copies.

MOMA   2 p., 31 cm.

Music 3236, Item 493

556

Manhattan Cocktail

Thematic music cue sheet. Adolph Zukor and Jesse L. Lasky present *Manhattan Cocktail* with Nancy Carroll and Richard Arlen. *Story by:* Ernest Vajda. *Screenplay by:* Ethel Doherty. *Directed by:* Dorothy Arzner. *Film company:* Paramount. *Music compiled by:* James C. Bradford. *Note:* Music incipits. *Footage:* 6051

MOMA   4 p., 31 cm.

Music 3236, Item 495

557

The Manhattan Cowboy

Musical setting for Bob Custer in *The Manhattan Cowboy. Music arranged by:* Joseph Zivelli. *Character of film:* Western comedy drama. *Note:* Cue sheet. No music. "Plaza Theatre Fri & Sat June, 6 & 7" marked in ink.

MOMA   1 p., 31 cm.

Music 3236, Item 494

558

Manhattan Knights

Thematic music cue sheet. Samuel Zierler presents *Manhattan Knights* with Barbara Bedford, Walter Miller and an all star cast. *Music compiled by:* James C. Bradford. *Note:* Music incipits.

MOMA   2 p., 32 cm.

Music 3236, Item 496

559

Manhattan Madness

Manhattan Madness, 1916, Doug. Fairbanks. *Film company:* Triangle. *Note:* Cue sheet. No music. Ms. *Number of reels:* 5.

MOMA   2 p., 28 cm.

Music 3236, Item 497

Victor Schertzinger (1880-1941), a composer *(Civilization, Robin Hood)* and director *(Road to Zanzibar, Kiss the Boys Goodbye, The Fleet's In)*. Courtesy of Gillian Anderson.

Richard Arlen and Nancy Carroll on the cover of the song, "Gotta Be Good," from Victor Schertzinger's score to *Manhattan Cocktail* (1928). Music Division, Library of Congress.

560
Man-Made Women
Thematic music cue sheet. Pathe presents Leatrice Joy in *Man-Made Women* with H. B. Warner, John Boles and Seena Owen. *Screenplay by:* Alice D. G. Miller. *From the story by:* Ernest Pascal. *Produced by:* Ralph Block for DeMille Pictures Corporation. *Directed by:* Paul L. Stein. *Distributed by;* Pathe Exchange, Inc. *Music compiled by:* Rudolph Berliner. *Note:* Music incipits. Two copies.
MOMA   4 p., 32 cm.
Music 3236, Item 498

561
Manon
Manon. Music composed by: Henry Kimball Hadley. *Published by:* Vitaphone Corp., New York, 1926. *Instrumentation:* Piano score. *Copyright:* © C1 E 654019, November 19, 1926.
LC M1527.H13M2   232 p., 37 cm.
Music 3212, Item 85

562
Manpower
Manpower. Note: Cue sheet. No music. Typescript.
MOMA   1 p., 28 cm.
Music 3236, Item 499

563
Mark of Zorro
Mark of Zorro. Instrumentation: Piano score.
MOMA   141 p., 30 cm.
Music 3236, Item 53

564
Marriage by Contract
Thematic music cue sheet. Tiffany-Stahl presents *Marriage by Contract,* a John M. Stahl special with Patsy Ruth Miller. *Story by:* Edward Clark. *Production by:* Tiffany-Stahl. *Directed by:* James Flood. *Music compiled by:* James C. Bradford. *Note:* Music incipits.
MOMA   4 p., 32 cm.
Music 3236, Item 500

565
Martin Luther
Martin Luther His Life and Time. Music arranged and composed by: Edward Rechlin and H. Spielter. *Published by:* Lutheran Film Division, Inc., New York, 1925. *Instrumentation:* Organ score. *Copyright:* © C1 A 856052, May 1, 1925.
LC M1527.R32M3   64 p., 30 cm.
Music 3212, Item 86

Henry Hadley (1871-1937), who, like several distinguished American composers, tried his hand at writing one film score, *Manon* (1926). A. P. Schmidt Collection, Music Division, Library of Congress.

566
The Martyrs of the Alamo

Musical setting to *The Martyrs of the Alamo*. *Music selected and arranged by:* Joseph Carl Breil. *Published by:* G. Schirmer, New York, 1915. *Instrumentation:* Piano conductor; (1,1,2,1; 2,2,1,0; drums; harp; strings). *Copyright:* © C1 E 371505, October 16, 1915.

LC M1357.B   84 p., 31 cm.

Music 3212, Item 87

567
The Masked Woman

Thematic music cue sheet. First National Pictures, Inc. presents *The Masked Woman* with Anna Q. Nilsson and Holbrook Blinn. *Film company:* First National. *Music compiled by:* Eugene Conte. *Note:* Music incipits. Two copies. "Monday Feb 7/27" marked in pencil on copy 1.

MOMA   4 p., 31 cm.

Music 3236, Item 501

568
The Mating Call

Thematic music cue sheet. Howard R. Hughes presents Thomas Meighan in Rex Beach's *The Mating Call* with Evelyn Brent and Renee Adorée. *Production by:* Caddo. *Directed by:* James Cruze. *Film company:* Paramount. *Music compiled by:* James C. Bradford. *Note:* Music incipits.

MOMA   4 p., 32 cm.

Music 3236, Item 502

569
Matrimony

Musical setting to *Matrimony* photoplay dramatization. *Music selected by:* Joseph Nurnberger and Wedgwood Nowell. *Published by:* G. Schirmer, New York, 1915. *Instrumentation:* Piano conductor; (2,0,2,0; 0,2,1,0; drums; strings). *Copyright:* © C1 E 373198, October 25, 1915.

LC M1357.N   57 p., 31 cm.

Music 3212, Item 88

570
Mawas

Mawas. Instrumentation: Piano. *Copyright:* © C1 EU 13240, September 16, 1929, William Francis Dugan, Beverly Hills, Calif.

LC M1527.D6M2   51 p., 32 cm.

Music 3212, Item 89

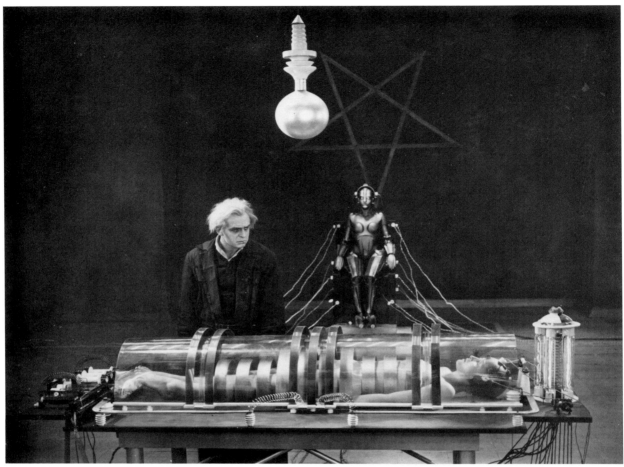

Rudolf Klein-Rogge and Brigitte Helm in *Metropolis* (1927). Museum of Modern Art, Film Stills Archive.

571

Me, Gangster

Thematic music cue sheet. William Fox Special Film Production *Me, Gangster. Music compiled by:* Michael P. Krueger. *Note:* Music incipits.
MOMA   4 p., 32 cm.
Music 3236, Item 503

572

Méliès Program

Music for *Méliès Program,* early French films [including: *The Conjurer, A Trip to the Moon, Palace of the Arabian Nights, The Doctor's Secret,* and *Conquest of the Pole]. Music compiled by:* Mortimer Browning. *Published by:* Museum of Modern Art Film Library, New York. *Instrumentation:* Piano score.
MOMA   80 p., 32 cm.
Music 3236, Item 54

573

Menilmontant

Menilmontant. Instrumentation: Piano score.
MOMA   48 p., 29 cm.
Music 3236, Item 55

574

The Merchant of Venice

The Merchant of Venice (Porten & Krauss). *Music by:* M. Lucien Marie Aubé. *Note:* Cue sheet. No music. In French.
MOMA   1 p., 31 cm.
Music 3236, Item 504

575

Messaline

Messaline, Ombre Lyriques en 17 Tableaux. Représentée pour la 1re fois aux Quat' Z-Arts, le 3 Mars 1913. Le Récitant, M. Gabriel Montoya. *Poem by:* Gabriel Montoya and Lionel Nastorg. *Piano accompaniment by:* M. L. Serez. *Music composed by:* Jean Messager. *Published by:* Max Eschig, Paris, 1915. *Instrumentation:* Piano/vocal score. *Copyright:* © C1 E 351515, February 27, 1915; R 105564, March 5, 1942, Jean Messager, Paris.
LC M176.M39   24 p., 26 cm.
Music 3212, Item 90

576

Metropolis

Metropolis. Instrumentation: Piano score.
MOMA   207 p., 30 cm.
Music 3236, Item 56

577

The Michigan Kid

Thematic music cue sheet. Carl Laemmle presents *The Michigan Kid. Production by:* Universal. *Music compiled by:* James C. Bradford. *Note:* Music incipits. Four copies.
MOMA   2 p., 32 cm.
Music 3236, Item 505

578

Mickey

Mickey. Note: Cue sheet. No music. Typescript. Three copies.
MOMA   1 p., 35 cm.
Music 3236, Item 506

579

The Midnight Flyer

Thematic music cue sheet. F. B. O. presents *The Midnight Flyer* with Dorothy Devore and Cullen Landis. *Story by:* Arthur Guy Empey. *Directed by:* Tom Forman. *Distributed by:* Film Booking Offices of America, Inc. *Music compiled by:* James C. Bradford. *Note:* Music incipits. "Wednesday Feb. 3" marked in pencil.
MOMA   4 p., 31 cm.
Music 3236, Item 507

580

Midnight Lovers

Thematic music cue sheet. First National Pictures, Inc. presents *Midnight Lovers* with Lewis Stone and Anna Q. Nilsson. *Film company:* First National. *Music compiled by:* James C. Bradford. *Note:* Music incipits. "Coming Monday Nov. 29/26" marked in pencil.
MOMA   4 p., 31 cm.
Music 3236, Item 508

581

Midnight Mystery

Midnight Mystery. Note: Cue sheet. No music. Typescript. Two copies.
MOMA   7 p., 33 cm.
Music 3236, Item 509

582

Midnight Mystery

Midnight Mystery. Note: Cue sheet. No music. Typescript. Seven copies. "Final cue sheet" marked on copy 1.
MOMA   7 p., 33 cm.
Music 3236, Item 510

583

Midnight Rose

Thematic music cue sheet. Carl Laemmle presents *Midnight Rose. Film company:* Universal-Jewel. *Music compiled by:* James C. Bradford. *Note:* Music incipits. "April 10-11" marked in pencil.

MOMA   2 p., 32 cm.
Music 3236, Item 511

584

The Midnight Sun

Thematic music cue sheet. Carl Laemmle presents *The Midnight Sun* with Laura La Plante and Pat O'Malley. *Production by:* Dimitri Buchowetzki. *Film company:* Universal-Jewel. *Music compiled by:* Dr. Edward Kilenyi. *Note:* Music incipits. "Thursday Oct 28/26" marked in pencil.

MOMA   4 p., 30 cm.
Music 3236, Item 512

585

Million Bid

Million Bid. Note: Cue sheet. No music. Typescript (carbon). Typed on "Publix Theatres Corportion Inter-Office Communication" letterhead. Dated "May 28-27."

MOMA   1 p., 28 cm.
Music 3236, Item 513

586

The Million Dollar Mystery

A Rayart Picture musical setting for *The Million Dollar Mystery. Character of film:* Mystery drama. *Music arranged by:* Joseph E. Zivelli. *Note:* Cue sheet. No music. "Saturday Nov. 5, 1927-Lyceum" marked in pencil. *Number of reels:* 6.

MOMA   1 p., 31 cm.
Music 3236, Item 514

587

Le Miracle des Loups

Le Miracle des Loups. Music by: Henri Rabaud. *Published by:* Max Eschig & Cie., Paris, 1924. *Instrumentation:* Piano score. *Copyright:* © C1 E 608237, December 31, 1924; R 98175, July 29, 1952, Jacqueline Rabaud (C).

LC M1527.R2M4.   161 p., 29 cm.
Music 3212, Item 91

588

Miss Nobody

Thematic music cue sheet. First National Pictures present Anna Q. Nilsson in *Miss Nobody. Film company:* First National. *Music compiled by:* Eugene Conte. *Note:* Music incipits. "Thurs & Frid Aug 26-27" marked in pencil.

MOMA   4 p., 32 cm.
Music 3236, Item 515

589

The Missing Links

Musical setting for the photoplay *The Missing Links* (P 31). *Production by:* Fine-Arts Feature Co. *Music selected and arranged by:* Joseph Carl Breil. *Series title:* Triangle Plays. *Published by:* G. Schirmer for the Triangle Film Corp., New York, 1916. *Instrumentation:* Piano conductor. *Copyright:* © C1 E 377240, January 7, 1916. *Note:* Inside title page says "Music selected and arranged by: George W. Beynon."

LC M1357.B   51 p., 31 cm.
Music 3212, Item 92

590

Moana

Moana. Note: Cue sheet. No music. Two copies. Typescript (carbon).

MOMA   2 p., 28 cm.
Music 3236, Item 516

591

The Model from Montmartre

Thematic music cue sheet. *The Model from Montmartre. Produced by:* Leonce Perret. *Film company:* Paramount. *Music compiled by:* James C. Bradford. *Note:* Music incipits.

MOMA   4 p., 31 cm.
Music 3236, Item 517

592

Modern Mothers

Thematic music cue sheet. Columbia Pictures presents *Modern Mothers* with Helene Chadwick, Douglas Fairbanks, Jr. *Story and scenario by:* Peter Milne. *Directed by:* Phil Rosen. *Copyrighted and distributed by:* Columbia Pictures Corporation. *Music compiled by:* James C. Bradford. *Note:* Music incipits.

MOMA   2 p., 31 cm.
Music 3236, Item 518

593

Modern Times

Score *Modern Times. Music by:* Charles Chaplin. *Published by:* Bourne, Inc. (Copyright assigned by Charles Chaplin), 1959. *Instrumentation:* Piano conductor. *Copyright:* © EP 139965, June 18, 1959.

LC M1527.C46M6   322 p., 32 cm.
Music 3212, Item 93

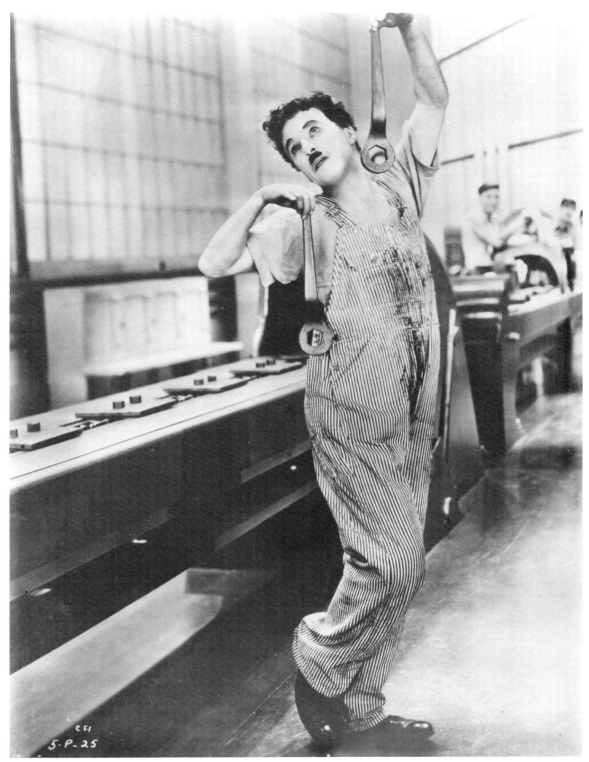

Charlie Chaplin in *Modern Times* (1936). Museum of
Modern Art, Film Stills Archive.

Rudolph Valentino in *Monsieur Beaucaire* (1924).
Museum of Modern Art, Film Stills Archive.

594

Moholy-Nagy

Moholy-Nagy. Note: Cue sheet. No music.
Typescript.

MOMA   1 p., 28 cm.
                        Music 3236, Item 519

595

Money Talks

Thematic music cue sheet. *Money Talks* with
Claire Windsor, Owen Moore and Bert Roach.
From the story by: Rupert Hughes. *Directed by:*
Archie Mayo. *Film company:* Metro-Goldwyn-
Mayer. *Music compiled by:* Ernst Luz. *Note:*
Music incipits. "Saturday July 3" marked in pen-
cil. *Number of reels:* 6. *Footage:* 6150. *Maximum
projection time:* 1 hour, 12 minutes.

MOMA   4 p., 31 cm.
                        Music 3236, Item 520

596

Monsieur Beaucaire

Monsieur Beaucaire. Instrumentation: Piano
score. *Note:* Pages at end bound out of order.

MOMA   166 p., 31 cm.
                        Music 3236, Item 57

597

Moon of Israel

Thematic music cue sheet. Joseph P. Kennedy
presents *Moon of Israel* starring Maria Corda and
Arlette Marchal. *From the famous novel by:* Sir
H. Rider Haggard. *Production by:* Sascha. *Distributed by:* F B O Pictures Corporation. *Music
compiled by:* James C. Bradford. *Note:* Music
incipits. "Nov 30–Dec 3, Lyceum Theatre" marked
in pencil.

MOMA   6 p., 31 cm.
                        Music 3236, Item 521

598

Moran of the Marines

Thematic music cue sheet. Adolph Zukor and
Jesse L. Lasky present Richard Dix in *Moran of
the Marines* with Ruth Elder. *Story by:* Lonton
Wells. *Production by:* West Coast Productions, B.
P. Schulberg, General Manager. *Directed by:*
Frank Strayer. *Film company:* Paramount.
Music compiled by: James C. Bradford. *Note:*
Music incipits. *Footage:* 5444.

MOMA   4 p., 32 cm.
                        Music 3236, Item 522

599

La Mort de Siegfried

La Mort de Siegfried. Score arranged by: M.
Szyfer. *Note:* Cue sheet. No music. Ms. In French.

MOMA   1 p., 31 cm. by 21 cm.
                        Music 3236, Item 523

600

Moscow Clad in Snow

Music for *Moscow Clad in Snow, The Revenge of
the Kinematograph Camerman* and *Moment
Musicale. Published by:* The Museum of Modern
Art Film Library, New York. *Instrumentation:*
Piano score.

MOMA   10 p., 14 p., 9 p., 32 cm.
                        Music 3236, Item 58

601

Mother

Music for Mother. Published by: The Museum of
Modern Art Film Library, New York. *Instrumentation:* Piano score.

MOMA   126 p., 32 cm.
                        Music 3236, Item 59

602

The Mother and the Law

D. W. Griffith presents *The Mother and the Law.
Music by:* Louis F. Gottschalk. *Instrumentation:*
Piano conductor.

MOMA   52 p., 30 cm.
                        Music 3236, Item 60

603

The Mother and the Law

D. W. Griffith presents *The Mother and the Law.
Music composed and adapted by:* Louis F.
Gottschalk, extracted from the super-picture
Intolerance. Music arranged by: Joseph Carl
Breil. *Printed by:* Felix Violé, Los Angeles, April
1919. *Instrumentation:* Orchestral parts (1,1,2,0;
2,2,1,0; drums; strings).

MOMA   30 cm.
                        Music 3236, Item 61

604

Mulhall's Great Catch

Thematic music cue sheet. Joseph P. Kennedy
presents Lefty Flynn in *Mulhall's Great Catch.
Story by:* Gerald Beaumont. *Produced by:* Harry
Garson. *Distributed by:* Film Booking Offices of
America, Inc. *Music compiled by:* James C.
Bradford. *Note:* Music incipits. "Wed. Sept 1st"
marked in pencil.

MOMA   4 p., 32 cm.
                        Music 3236, Item 524

605

My Best Girl

My Best Girl. Note: Cue sheet. No music.
Typescript.

MOMA   2 p., 28 cm.
Music 3236, Item 525

606

My Friend from India

Thematic music cue sheet. Pathe presents *My Friend from India* with Franklin Tangborn [sic Pangborn] and Elinor Fair. *From the play by:* H. A. de Souchet. *Supervised by:* F. McGrew Willis. *Produced by:* DeMille Pictures Corporation. *Directed by:* E. Mason Hopper. *Distributed by:* Pathe Exchange, Inc. *Music compiled by:* Rudolph Berliner. *Note:* Music incipits. "Monday Jan 16/28" marked in pencil.

MOMA   4 p., 31 cm.
Music 3236, Item 526

607

My Old Dutch

Thematic music cue sheet. Carl Laemmle presents *My Old Dutch* with Pat O'Malley and May McAvoy. *Production by:* Larry Trimble. *Film company:* Universal-Jewel. *Music compiled by:* James C. Bradford. *Note:* Music incipits. "Mon & Tues July 26-27" marked in pencil.

MOMA   4 p., 32 cm.
Music 3236, Item 527

608

Les Mysteries du Chateau de Dé

Disques pour *Les Mysteries du Chateau de Dé. Note:* Cue sheet. No music. Ms. In French.

MOMA   1 p., 25 cm.
Music 3236, Item 528

609

Name the Woman

Thematic music cue sheet. Columbia Pictures presents *Name the Woman* with Anita Stewart, Huntly Gordon and Gaston Glass. *Directed by:* Erle C. Kenton. *Copyrighted and distributed by:* Columbia Pictures Corporation. *Music compiled by:* James C. Bradford. *Note:* Music incipits.

MOMA   2 p., 31 cm.
Music 236, Item 529

610

Nameless Men

Thematic music cue sheet. Tiffany-Stahl presents *Nameless Men* with Antonio Moreno, Claire Windsor, Ray Hallor, Eddie Gribbon, Sally Rand and Charles Clary. *Story by:* E. Morton. *Directed by:* Christy Cabanne. *Production by:* Tiffany-Stahl. *Music compiled by:* James C. Bradford. *Note:* Music incipits. "Lyceum Theatre May 24-25-26-1927" marked in pencil.

MOMA   4 p., 31 cm.
Music 3236, Item 530

611

Nanook of the North

Nanook of the North. Note: Cue sheet. No music. Typescript (carbon).

MOMA   2 p., 28 cm.
Music 3236, Item 531

611A

Napoléon

Pas Accéléré. Exécuté au cours du film *Napoléon* réalisé par Abel Gance. *Directed by:* Abel Gance. *Music by:* Ch. Gourdin. *Published by:* Editions Musicales Sam Fox, Paris, 1927. *Instrumentation:* Piano conductor and instrumental parts (0,1,2,1; 2,2,3,1; percussion; strings). *Copyright:* © C1 E 685087, February 24, 1928.

LC M1350.G   2 p., 28 cm.
No microfilm

611B

Napoléon

Pas Cadencé des Sans-Cullottes. Exécuté au cours du film *Napoléon* réalisé par Abel Gance. *Directed by:* Abel Gance. *Music by:* Ch. Gourdin. *Published by:* Editions Musicales Sam Fox, Paris, 1927. *Instrumentation:* Piano conductor and instrumental parts (1,1,2,1; 2,2,2,1; percussion; strings). *Copyright:* © C1 E 685088, February 24, 1928.

LC M1350.G   2 p., 28 cm.
No microfilm

611C

Napoléon

[Napoléon]. Calme; La romance de violine; Danse des enfants; Interlude et finale; Chaconne de L'impératrice; Napoléon; Les ombres; Les mendiants de la gloire. *Music by:* Arthur Honegger. *Published by:* Editions Francis Salabert, Paris, 1927. *Instrumentation:* Piano conductor and instrumental parts (1,2,2,1; 2,2,3,1; percussion; strings; harmonium). *Copyright:* © C1 E 669239, 669242, 669240, 669241, Aug. 4, 1927; E 677050, November 9, 1927; E 685400, 685399, 685401, February 27, 1928.

LC M1350.H   various p.; 31 cm.
Music 3449, Item 384

612

Naughty Baby

Thematic music cue sheet. Richard A. Rowland presents *Naughty Baby* with Alice White and Jack Mulhall. *Directed by:* Mervyn LeRoy. *Film company:* First National. *Music compiled by:* James C. Bradford. *Note:* Music incipits.

MOMA   4 p., 31 cm.
                                    Music 3236, Item 532

613

Ned McCobb's Daughter

Thematic music cue sheet. Pathe presents *Ned McCobb's Daughter* with Irene Rich, Robert Armstrong, George Barraud and Theodore Roberts. *Adapted by:* Beulah Marie from Sidney Howard's Theatre Guild hit. *Directed by:* William J. Cowen. *Distributed by:* Pathe Exchange, Inc. *Music compiled by:* James C. Bradford. *Note:* Music incipits.

MOMA   4 p., 31 cm.
                                    Music 3236, Item 533

614

New Babylon

New Babylon. Note: Cue sheet. No music. Ms.

MOMA   1 p., 24 cm.
                                    Music 3236, Item 534

615

The New Commandment

Thematic music cue sheet. Robert T. Kane presents *The New Commandment. Film company:* First National. *Music compiled by:* Dr. Edward Kilenyi. *Note:* Music incipits. "Tuesday March 2" marked in pencil.

MOMA   4 p., 30 cm.
                                    Music 3236, Item 535

616

New Year's Eve

Thematic music cue sheet. William Fox special film production Mary Astor, Charles Morton and Earle Foxe in *New Year's Eve. Music compiled by:* Michael P. Krueger. *Note:* Music incipits. Two copies.

MOMA   4 p., 32 cm.
                                    Music 3236, Item 536

617

The New York Hat

The New York Hat. Note: Cue sheet. No music. Typescript (photocopy). Cue sheet is possibly incomplete. Also includes partial listing of music cues for the film, *Queen Elizabeth.*

MOMA   1 p., 26 cm.
                                    Music 3236, Item 537

618

The News Parade

Thematic music cue sheet. William Fox special film production *The News Parade. Music compiled by:* Michael P. Krueger. *Note:* Music incipits. "Fri Feb 22" marked in pencil.

MOMA   4 p., 31 cm.
                                    Music 3236, Item 538

619

The Night Bird

Greater thematic cue sheet. Carl Laemmle presents Reginald Denny in *The Night Bird. Production by:* Universal. *Directed by:* Fred Newmeyer. *Music compiled by:* James C. Bradford. *Note:* Music incipits. Two copies.

MOMA   8 p., 31 cm.
                                    Music 3236, Item 539

620

The Night Cry

Rin Tin Tin in *The Night Cry. Note:* Cue sheet. No music. Ms. and Typescript.

MOMA   1 p., 28 cm.
                                    Music 3236, Item 540

621

The Night Flyer

Thematic music cue sheet. James Cruze presents William Boyd in *The Night Flyer* with Jobyna Ralston. *Produced by:* James Cruze, Inc. *Directed by:* Walter Lang. *Distributed by:* Pathe Exchange, Inc. *Music compiled by:* Rudolph Berliner. *Note:* Music incipits. Two copies. "April–26–27–28" marked in pencil on copy 1.

MOMA   4 p., 31 cm.
                                    Music 3236, Item 541

622

Night Life of New York

Thematic music cue sheet. Adolph Zukor and Jesse L. Lasky present an Allan Dwan Production *Night Life of New York* with Rod La Rocque, Dorothy Gish, Ernest Torrence and George Hackathorne by Edgar Selwyn. *Screenplay by:* Paul Schofield. *Film company:* Paramount. *Music compiled by:* James C. Bradford. *Note:* Music incipits. Slightly mutilated. *Footage:* 6998.

MOMA   4 p., 30 cm.
                                    Music 3236, Item 542

623
The Night of Mystery
The Night of Mystery, Paramount, April 14, 1928.
Note: Cue sheet. No music. Typescript (carbon).
MOMA   2 p., 28 cm.
                                Music 3236, Item 543

624
Night Ride
Musical setting for *Night Ride* featuring Joseph
Schildkraut, Edward Robinson with Barbara Kent.
Film company: Universal Pictures Corporation.
Music selected and compiled by: M. Winkler.
Note: Cue sheet. No music. Two copies.
MOMA   3 p., 28 cm.
                                Music 3236, Item 544

625
The Night Watch
Thematic music cue sheet. Richard A. Rowland
presents Billie Dove in *The Night Watch. Produced by:* Ned Marin. *Directed by:* Alexander
Korda. *Film company:* First National. *Music
compiled by:* James C. Bradford. *Note:* Music
incipits. "Thur–Fri Oct 11–12" marked in pencil.
MOMA   4 p., 32 cm.
                                Music 3236, Item 545

626
Nightingale Scene
Nightingale Scene. Note: Cue sheet. No music.
Typescript.
MOMA   1 p., 28 cm.
                                Music 3236, Item 546

627
No Control
Thematic music cue sheet. John C. Flinn presents
No Control with Harrison Ford and Phyllis Haver.
Produced by: Metropolitan Pictures Corporation.
Directed by: Scott Sidney. *Released by:* Produc-
ers Distributing Corporation. *Music compiled by:*
Rudolph Berliner. *Note:* Music incipits. Two
copies. "Monday April 18" marked in pencil on
copy 1.
MOMA   4 p., 32 cm.
                                Music 3236, Item 547

628
No Man's Law
Thematic music cue sheet. Hal Roach presents
Rex the King of Wild Horses in *No Man's Law*
with Barbara Kent and James Finlayson. *Directed*

by: Fred Jackman. *Film company:* Pathépicture.
Music compiled by: James C. Bradford. *Note:*
Music incipits. "Lyceum Sat. Dec. 17, 1927"
marked in pencil.
MOMA   4 p., 31 cm.
                                Music 3236, Item 548

629
Nobody's Widow
Thematic music cue sheet. *Nobody's Widow.
Adapted by:* Clara Beranger and Douglas Z. Doty.
From the stage play by: Avery Hopwood. *Produc-
tion by:* Donald Crisp. *Produced by:* DeMille Pic-
tures Corporation. *Directed by:* Donald Crisp.
Released by: Producers Distributing Corporation.
Music compiled by: Rudolph Berliner. *Note:*
Music incipits. "Thursday Feb. 3/27" marked in
pencil.
MOMA   4 p., 32 cm.
                                Music 3236, Item 549

630
Noisy Neighbors
Thematic music cue sheet. Pathe presents *Noisy
Neighbors* with Eddie Quillan, The Quillan Family, Alberta Vaughn and Theodore Roberts. *From
an original story by:* F. Hugh Herbert. *Produced
by:* Paul Bern. *Directed by:* Charles Reisner. *Distributed by:* Pathe Exchange, Inc. *Music compiled by:* James C. Bradford. *Note:* Music incipits.
Two copies.
MOMA   4 p., 32 cm.
                                Music 3236, Item 550

631
None But the Brave
Thematic music cue sheet. William Fox special
film production Charles Morton, Sally Phipps and
Farrell MacDonald in *None But the Brave. Music
compiled by:* Michael P. Krueger. *Note:* Music
incipits.
MOMA   6 p., 31 cm.
                                Music 3236, Item 551

632
The Non-Stop Flight
Thematic music cue sheet. F. B. O. presents *The
Non-Stop Flight* with an all star cast. *Story and
continuity by:* Emilie Johnson. *Production by:*
Emory Johnson. *Distributed by:* Film Booking
Offices of America, Inc. *Music compiled by:*
Eugene Conte. *Note:* Music incipits.
MOMA   4 p., 32 cm.
                                Music 3236, Item 552

633
North of 36

North of 36. Note: Cue sheet. No music. Typescript.
MOMA   1 p., 28 cm.
Music 3236, Item 553

634
North Star

Thematic music cue sheet. Associated Exhibitors, Inc. presents Strongheart in *North Star. From the story by:* Rufus King. *Production by:* Howard Estabrook. *Directed by:* Paul Powell. *Film company:* Encore. *Released by:* Associated Exhibitors, Inc. *Music compiled by:* James C. Bradford. *Note:* Music incipits. "Sunday & Mon 3/7–8" marked in pencil.
MOMA   4 p., 31 cm.
Music 3236, Item 554

635
Not for Publication

Thematic music cue sheet. Joseph P. Kennedy presents *Not for Publication* starring Ralph Ince. *Production by:* Ralph Ince. *Distributed by:* Film Booking Offices of America, Inc. *Music compiled by:* James C. Bradford. *Note:* Music incipits. "Lyceum Theatre Bayonne, N.J. Thursday Friday & Saturday April 5-6-7" marked in pencil.
MOMA   4 p., 31 cm.
Music 3236, Item 555

636
Now We're in the Air

Now We're in the Air. Note: Cue sheet. No music. Typescript (carbon).
MOMA   3 p., 38 cm.
Music 3236, Item 556

637
Oh! What a Nurse

Warner Bros. present *Oh! What a Nurse* starring Syd Chaplin. *Note:* Cue sheet. No music. Slightly mutilated. *Number of reels:* 7. *Projection time:* 1 hour, 18 minutes based on a speed of 11 minutes per 1000 feet.
MOMA   1 p., 35 cm.
Music 3236, Item 557

638
The Oklahoma Sheriff

A Syndicate Picture musical setting for *The Oklahoma Sheriff* featuring Bob Steele. *Music arranged by:* Joseph E. Zivelli. *Note:* Cue sheet. No music. "Plaza Theatre Nov 21–22–1930" marked in pencil.
MOMA   1 p., 32 cm.
Music 3236, Item 558

639
Old Ironsides

Old Ironsides. Film company: Paramount. *Music score compiled by:* Hugo Riesenfeld. *Original themes by:* J. S. Zamecnik and Hugo Riesenfeld. *Published by:* Paramount Famous Lasky Corp. under the supervision of Sam Fox Publ. Co., New York, 1927. *Instrumentation:* Piano; (1,1,2,1; 2,2,1,0; drums; strings). *Copyright:* © C1 E 667546, June 17, 1927.
LC M1357.R   152 p., 31 cm.
Music 3212, Item 163

640
The Old Nest

The Old Nest. Production by: Goldwyn, Series 207. *Music composed by:* Firmin Swinnen. *Published by:* Synchronized Scenario Music Co., Chicago, 1921. *Instrumentation:* Piano or organ. *Note:* Score No. 207.
LC M1527.044   150 p., 30 cm.
Music 3212, Item 94

641
Old San Francisco

Warner Bros. present *Old San Francisco* starring Dolores Costello. *Note:* Cue sheet. No music. Two copies, both mutilated. *Projection time:* 1 hour, 25 minutes based on a speed of 10 minutes per 1000 feet.
MOMA   1 p., 35 cm.
Music 3236, Item 559

642
O'Malley Rides Alone

A Syndicate Picture musical setting for *O'Malley Rides Alone. Character of film:* Drama of the Northwest Mounted Police. *Music arranged by:* Joseph E. Zivelli. Plot theme, "The Plotters," Carozzini (Sonnemann). *Note:* Cue sheet. No music. "Fri & Sat Feb 28–Mar 1 1930 also comedy" marked in ink. *Number of reels:* 5.
MOMA   1 p., 32 cm.
Music 3236, Item 560

1st CLARINET

OLD IRONSIDES

A Paramount Picture

MUSIC SCORE

Compiled by Hugo Riesenfeld

ORIGINAL THEMES

by

J. S. Zamecnik *and* **Hugo Riesenfeld**

Published for

Paramount Famous Lasky Corporation

Under the supervision of

SAM FOX PUB. CO.

Cover for the score to *Old Ironsides* (1926), an adventure picture about the War of 1812; music compiled and composed by Hugo Riesenfeld and J. S. Zamecnik. The film has many shots of beautiful old ships like the *U.S.S. Constitution* under full sail. Music Division, Library of Congress.

643

On the Stroke of Twelve

Musical synopsis for *On the Stroke of Twelve*. *Music compiled by:* James C. Bradford. *Note:* Cue sheet. No music. "Sunday June 24" marked in pencil. "Jun 24 1928" stamped in ink.

MOMA   1 p., 31 cm.

Music 3236, Item 561

644

One Exciting Night

Large Orchestra. D. W. Griffith presents *One Exciting Night. Music arranged and synchronized by:* Albert Pesce, General Music Director for D. W. Griffith. *Published by:* D. W. Griffith, Inc., Los Angeles, 1922. *Instrumentation:* Piano conductor and orchestral parts; (1,1,2,1; 2,2,1,0; tympani and drums; harp; strings). *Note:* Copyright on piano part only.

MOMA   164 p., 31 cm.

Music 3236, Item 62

645

One Exciting Night

D. W. Griffith presents *One Exciting Night. Music arranged and synchronized by:* Albert Pesce, General Music Director for D. W. Griffith, Inc. *Published by:* D. W. Griffith, Inc., Los Angeles, 1922. *Instrumentation:* Piano. *Copyright:* © C1 E 553396, December 22, 1922.

LC M1527.P505   164 p., 30 cm.

Music 3212, Item 95

646

The Opening Night

Thematic music cue sheet. Columbia Pictures presents Claire Windsor in *The Opening Night* with John Bowers. *Screen adaptation by:* E. H. Griffith. *Directed by:* E. H. Griffith. *Copyrighted and distributed by:* Columbia Pictures Corporation. *Music compiled by:* James C. Bradford. *Note:* Music incipits. Two copies.

MOMA   2 p., 31 cm.

Music 3236, Item 562

647

Orphans of the Storm

D. W. Griffith presents *Orphans of the Storm. Film company:* D. W. Griffith, Inc., Albert L. Grey, Gen. Mgr. *Music composed and arranged by:* L. F. Gottschalk and Wm. Frederick Peters. *Instrumentation:* Piano conductor and orchestral parts (1,1,2,1; 2,2,1,0; tympani and drums; harp; strings).

MOMA   136 p., 31 cm.

Music 3236, Item 63

Lillian Gish in D. W. Griffith's *Orphans of the Storm* (1921), a melodrama about two sisters whose parents are killed by the plague which also leaves one of the sisters blind; music by Louis Gottschalk and William Frederick Peters. Museum of Modern Art, Film Stills Archive.

648
Orphans of the Storm
Dramatic numbers from D. W. Griffith's photoplay *Orphans of the Storm. Music composed by:* Wm. Frederick Peters. *Instrumentation:* Piano conductor. *Copyright:* © C1 E 695551, July 7, 1928; Julia Peters, Englewood, N.J.
LC M1527.P550   68 p., 34 cm., Ms.
Music 3212, Item 164

649
Out with the Tide
A Peerless Picture musical setting for *Out with the Tide. Music arranged by:* Joseph E. Zivelli. *Note:* Cue sheet. No music. "Sat Oct 13" marked in pencil.
MOMA   1 p., 30 cm.
Music 3236, Item 563

650
Over the Hill
Music cue sheet for William Fox Production all star cast in *Over the Hill,* a reissue. *Note:* No music.
MOMA   2 p., 35 cm.
Music 3236, Item 564

651
Over There
Over There, cue sheet. *Note:* No music. Typescript (carbon). "Made by E. Luz" marked in ink.
MOMA   3 p., 28 cm.
Music 3236, Item 565

652
Paid in Full
Incidental music to the motion picture presentation of Eugene Walter's greatest play *Paid in Full* featuring Tully Marshall and a Broadway cast. *Directed by:* Augustus Thomas. *Produced by:* The All Star Feature Corporation. *Music composed by:* Manuel Klein, Musical Director of the New York Hippodrome. *Published by:* M. Witmark & Sons, New York, 1914. *Instrumentation:* Piano score. *Copyright:* © C1 E 334229, February 24, 1914; R 93877, February 25, 1941, Helen Klein, Hollywood.
LC M176.P14   12 p., 35 cm.
Music 3212, Item 96

653
Pals
Pals. Note: Cue sheet. No music. Typescript (carbon). Typed on "Public Theatres Corporation Inter-Office Communication" letterhead, dated "Paramount 4/30/27."
MOMA   2 p., 28 cm.
Music 3236, Item 566

654
Paris qui dort
Paris qui dort. Music by: Gaby Coutrot. *Note:* Cue sheet. No music. In French. Ms.
MOMA   1 p., 31 cm. by 21 cm.
Music 3236, Item 567

655
The Part Time Wife
A Gotham Production musical setting for *The Part Time Wife. Character of film:* A story of movie life. *Music arranged by:* Joseph E. Zivelli. *Note:* Cue sheet. No music. "Thursday & Friday 3/18/19" marked in pencil. *Number of reels:* 5. *Projection time:* 50¾ minutes.
MOMA   1 p., 31 cm. by 26 cm.
Music 3236, Item 568

656
Partners in Crime
Partners in Crime. Note: Cue sheet. No music. Typescript.
MOMA   1 p., 28 cm.
Music 3236, Item 569

657
La Passion de Jeanne d'Arc
La Passion de Jeanne d'Arc. Directed by: Carl Dreyer. *Produced by:* Alliance Cinématographique. *Music composed by:* Léo Pouget and Victor Alix. *Instrumentation by:* E. Méthéhen. *Published by:* Editions Musicales Sam Fox, Paris, 1928. *Instrumentation:* Piano/vocal conductor, 4 strings. *Copyright:* © E for. 4975, December 31, 1928.
LC M1357.P   80 p., 32 cm.
Music 3212, Item 97

658
The Passion of Joan of Arc
Music for *The Passion of Joan of Arc. Published by:* Museum of Modern Art Film Library, New York. *Instrumentation:* Piano score. *Note:* Title page bears name Arthur Kleiner in pencil.
MOMA   65 p., 31 cm.
Music 3236, Item 64

Maurice Schutz (foreground), Renée Falconetti, and Antonin Artaud (background) in Dreyer's classic *La Passion de Jeanne D'Arc* (1927). The still shows Nicholas Loyeseleur (Schutz) praying as Joan of Arc (Falconetti) receives her final communion from Massieu (Artaud). Museum of Modern Art, Film Stills Archive. Although this particular shot does not appear in the film currently available through the Museum of Modern Art, it is plainly referred to in the musical score by Léo Pouget and Victor Alix ("Le prêtre pleure"). Music Division, Library of Congress.

659
The Patriot
Music score *The Patriot. Music by:* Domenico Savino, Gerard Carbonara and Max Bergunker. *Published by:* Famous Music Corp., New York, 1928. *Instrumentation:* Piano conductor. *Copyright:* © EP 723, November 2, 1928; R 159483, November 15, 1955, Paramount Pictures Corp. (PWH of D. Savino, G. Carbonara, M. Bergunker & Paramount Publix Music Dept.).
LC M1527.S28P2   175 p., 31 cm.
Music 3212, Item 98

660
The Patriot
The Patriot. W. S. Hart. *Note:* Cue sheet. No music. Ms. *Number of reels:* 5.
MOMA   2 p., 28 cm.
Music 3236, Item 570

661
Peacock Fan
Peacock Fan. A Chesterfield Attraction. *Musical synopsis by:* Motion Pictures Synchronization Service, Inc., 1650 Broadway, New York City. *Note:* Cue sheet. No music.
MOMA   1 p., 30 cm.
Music 3236, Item 571

662
Pearl of the Army
Pearl of the Army, Pearl White. *Note:* Cue sheet. No music. Typescript (carbon). Possibly incomplete.
MOMA   1 p., 28 cm.
Music 3236, Item 572

663
Peer Gynt
G. Schirmer's Paramount photo play music (P 110-MS) *Peer Gynt.* Musical setting for the photoplay dramatization. *Music selected, arranged, and composed by:* Geo. W. Beynon. *Published by:* G. Schirmer, Inc., New York, 1915. *Instrumentation:* Piano score; (1,1,0,0; 0,2,1,0; tympani and drums; strings). *Copyright:* © C1 E 373195, October 5, 1915.
LC M1357.B   74 p., 31 cm.
Music 3212, Item 99

664
Peg o' My Heart
A Luz music score. Metro presents Laurette Taylor in *Peg o' My Heart. Film company:* Metro (controlled by Loew's, Inc.). *Published by:* Photoplay Music Co., New York, 1922. *Instrumentation:* Piano leader. *Copyright:* © C1 E 554975, December 28, 1922.
LC M1527.L95P3   87 p., 30 cm.
Music 3212, Item 100

665
Los Penitentes
Musical setting for the photoplay *Los Penitentes* (The Penitents). *Production by:* Fine-Arts Feature Co. Production. *Music selected and arranged by:* Joseph Carl Breil. *Series title:* Triangle Plays. *Published by:* G. Schirmer for the Triangle Film Corp., New York, 1915. *Instrumentation:* Piano conductor. *Copyright:* © C1 E 377033, December 10, 1915.
LC M1357.B   99 p., 30 cm.
Music 3212, Item 101

666
The Perfect Crime
Thematic music cue sheet. Joseph P. Kennedy presents *The Perfect Crime* with Clive Brook and Irene Rich by William Le Baron. *Suggested by the story* The Big Bow Mystery *by:* Israel Zangwill. *Produced by:* William Le Baron. *Directed by:* Bert Glennon. *Distributed by:* F B O Pictures Corporation. *Music compiled by:* James C. Bradford. *Note:* Music incipits.
MOMA   4 p., 32 cm.
Music 3236, Item 573

667
Peter the Great
Peter the Great. Note: Cue sheet. No music. Typescript.
MOMA   1 p., 28 cm.
Music 3236, Item 574

668
The Phantom Bullet
Thematic music cue sheet. Carl Laemmle presents Hoot Gibson in *The Phantom Bullet. Written by:* Oscar Friend. *Directed by:* Clifford Smith. *Film company:* Universal-Jewel. *Music compiled by:* James C. Bradford. *Note:* Music incipits. "Saturday July 3" marked in pencil.
MOMA   2 p., 33 cm.
Music 3236, Item 575

Laurette Taylor and Ethel Grey Terry (men unidentified) in the comedy-drama, *Peg o' My Heart* (1922).
Museum of Modern Art, Film Stills Archive.

669
The Phantom of the Forest

A Gotham Production musical setting for *The Phantom of the Forest* with the famous dog Thunder. *Music arranged by:* Joseph E. Zivelli. *Note:* Cue sheet. No music. "Mon & Tues Aug 2–3" marked in pencil.

MOMA 1 p., 28 cm. by 25 cm.
Music 3236, Item 576

670
The Phantom of the Turf

Musical setting for *The Phantom of the Turf* featuring Helene Costello. *Music arranged by:* Joseph E. Zivelli. *Character of film:* Drama. *Note:* Cue sheet. No music. Two copies. "May–22–23" marked in pencil on copy 1. "Lyceum Theatre Sunday July 8–1928" marked in pencil on copy 2. *Number of reels:* 6.

MOMA 1 p., 32 cm.
Music 3236, Item 577

671
Phyllis of the Follies

Thematic music cue sheet. Carl Laemmle presents *Phyllis of the Follies. Production by:* Universal. *Music compiled by:* James C. Bradford. *Note:* Music incipits.

MOMA 2 p., 32 cm.
Music 3236, Item 578

672
Pierre of the Plains

Pierre of the Plains. Incidental music to the motion picture presentation of Edgar Selwyn in his own play *Pierre of the Plains. Produced by:* The All Star Feature Corp. *Music composed by:* Manuel Klein, Musical Director of the New York Hippodrome. *Published by:* M. Witmark & Sons, New York, 1914. *Instrumentation:* Piano score. *Copyright:* © C1 E 342121, May 25, 1914; R 98073, June 25, 1941, Helen Klein, Hollywood.

LC M176.P62 13 p., 35 cm.
Music 3212, Item 102

673
Pioneers of the West

Pioneers of the West. Note: Cue sheet. No music. Typescript (carbon). Slightly mutilated. Number of reels: 5.

MOMA 1 p., 28 cm.
Music 3236, Item 579

674
Plane Crazy

Plane Crazy, the first Mickey Mouse and music for John Rice, May Irwin *Kiss. Instrumentation:* Piano score.

MOMA 31 p., 31 cm.
Music 3236, Item 65

675
Plastered in Paris

Thematic music cue sheet. William Fox Film Production Sammy Cohen in *Plastered in Paris. Music compiled by:* Michael P. Krueger. *Note:* Cue sheet. Music incipits. Two copies. "Fri–Sat Dec 21–22" marked in pencil on copy 1.

MOMA 6 p., 31 cm.
Music 3236, Item 580

676
Points West

Thematic music cue sheet. Carl Laemmle presents *Points West. Production by:* Universal. *Music compiled by:* James C. Bradford. *Note:* Music incipits.

MOMA 2 p., 32 cm.
Music 3236, Item 581

677
The Poor Nut

Thematic music cue sheet. Jess Smith Productions, Inc. presents *The Poor Nut* with Jack Mulhall and Charlie Murray. *Production by:* Richard Wallace. *Production management by:* Henry Hobart. *Film company:* First National. *Music compiled by:* James C. Bradford. *Note:* Music incipits. "Thur. Aug 25/27" marked in pencil.

MOMA 4 p., 31 cm.
Music 3236, Item 582

678
Potemkin

Music for *Potemkin. Music composed by:* Arthur Kleiner. *Published by:* The Museum of Modern Art Film Library, New York. *Instrumentation:* Piano score.

MOMA 100 p., 32 cm.
Music 3236, Item 66

679
Potemkin

Potemkin. Music composed by: Edmund Meisel (1874–1930). *Music revised and edited by:* Arthur Kleiner. *Published by:* Arthur Kleiner,

Hopkins, MN., 1971. *Instrumentation:* Conductor's score. *Copyright:* © Eu 280711, Arthur Kleiner, August 31, 1971.

LC M1527.M52P67   224 p., 28 cm.
Music 3212, Item 103

680
Potemkin

Music for *Potemkin. Music composed by:* Arthur Kleiner. *Published by:* The Museum of Modern Art Film Library, New York, 1959. *Instrumentation:* Piano. *Copyright:* © Eu 603059 (rec'd November 20, 1959).

LC M1527.K55P7   100 p., 32 cm.
Music 3212, Item 103a

681
Power

Thematic music cue sheet. Pathe presents William Boyd in *Power* with Jacqueline Logan and Alan Hale. *Story and continuity by:* Tay Garnett. *Production by:* Ralph Block. *Directed by:* Howard Higgin. *Distributed by:* Pathe Exchange, Inc. *Music compiled by:* Howard T. Wood. *Note:* Music incipits. Two copies.

MOMA   4 p., 31 cm.
Music 3236, Item 583

682
The Power of Silence

Thematic music cue sheet. Tiffany-Stahl presents Belle Bennett in *The Power of Silence* by Frances Hyland. *Production by:* Tiffany-Stahl. *Directed by:* Wallace Worsley. *Music compiled by:* James C. Bradford. *Note:* Music incipits.

MOMA   4 p., 32 cm.
Music 3236, Item 584

683
Prep and Pep

Thematic music cue sheet. William Fox Feature Film Production David Rollins and Nancy Drexel in *Prep and Pep. Music compiled by:* Michael P. Krueger. *Note:* Music incipits. Two copies.

MOMA   4 p., 31 cm.
Music 3236, Item 585

684
The Price of Power

Musical setting for the photoplay *The Price of Power* (P. 42). *Production by:* Fine-Arts Feature Co. *Music selected and arranged by:* J. A. Raynes. *Series title:* Triangle Plays. *Published by:* G. Schirmer for the Triangle Film Corp., New York, 1916. *Instrumentation:* Piano conductor.

Copyright: © C1 E 377023, January 17, 1916.

LC M1357.R   67 p., 30 cm.
Music 3212, Item 104

685
The Price of Success

Thematic music cue sheet. Waldorf Pictures presents *The Price of Success* featuring Alice Lake. *Produced by:* Harry Cohn. *Directed by:* Antonio Gaudio. *Copyrighted and distributed by:* Columbia Pictures Corporation. *Music compiled by:* James C. Bradford. *Note:* Music incipits. "Sunday Feb 7" marked in pencil.

MOMA   2 p., 31 cm.
Music 3236, Item 586

686
The Prince of Pep

Thematic music cue sheet. A. Carlos presents Richard Talmadge in *The Prince of Pep. Continuity by:* James Bell Smith. *Production by:* Richard Talmadge. *Directed by:* Jack Nelson. *Distributed by:* Film Booking Offices of America, Inc. *Music compiled by:* Dr. Edward Kilenyi. *Note:* Music incipits. "Thurs & Friday Jan 14–15" marked in pencil.

MOMA   4 p., 29 cm.
Music 3236, Item 587

687
The Princess of the Dark

Thomas E. Ince presents Enid Bennett, the new Triangle-Kay-Bee star, in *The Princess of the Dark. Incidental music by:* Victor L. Schertzinger. *Published by:* Leo Feist, Inc. for New York Motion Picture Corp., New York, 1917. *Instrumentation:* Piano conductor (1,1,2,1; 2,2,1,0; drum and bells; strings. Nos. 2-3: strings; cl., fl.) *Copyright:* © C1 E 397275, February 1, 1917, Leo Feist, Inc. for New York Motion Picture Corp; R 134544, December 23, 1944, Julia E. Schertzinger, Los Angeles.

LC M1357.S   3 cues, 28 cm.
Music 3212, Item 105

688
A Prisoner of the Harem and Egyptian Sports

Special piano music for *A Prisoner of the Harem and Egyptian Sports. Music by:* Walter C. Simon. *Published by:* Kalem Co., New York, 1912. *Instrumentation:* Piano. *Copyright:* © C1 E 297642, July 19, 1912; R 87494, June 10, 1940, Walter C. Simon, New York.

LC M176.P95   13 p., 32 cm.
Music 3212, Item 106

689
The Private Life of Helen of Troy
Thematic music cue sheet. Richard A. Rowland presents *The Private Life of Helen of Troy* by John Erskine with Lewis Stone, Marie Corda and Ricardo Cortez. *Film company:* First National. *Music compiled by:* James C. Bradford. *Note:* Music incipits. "April–24–25" marked in pencil.
MOMA   6 p., 32 cm.
Music 3236, Item 588

690
Proud Heart
Thematic music cue sheet. Carl Laemmle presents Rudolph Schildkraut in *Proud Heart* by Isidor Bernstein. *Directed by:* Edward Sloman. *Film company:* Universal-Jewel. *Music compiled by:* Dr. Edward Kilenyi. *Note:* Music incipits. "Wed–Thurs–Fri 20-21-22" marked in pencil.
MOMA   2 p., 44 cm.
Music 3236, Item 589

691
Put 'Em Up
Musical setting for *Put 'Em Up. Music compiled by:* M. Winkler, Theme, "Ludicia" (Intermezzo) by Caludi. *Note:* Cue sheet. No music. "May-15-16" marked in pencil. *Projection time:* The timing is based on a speed limit of 14 minutes per reel.
MOMA   1 p., 30 cm.
Music 3236, Item 590

692
Quality Street
Thematic music cue sheet. Marion Davies in *Quality Street* with Conrad Nagel. *From the play by:* James M. Barrie. *Adaptation and scenario by:* Hans Kraly and Albert Lewin. *Production by:* Marion Davies. *Directed by:* Sidney Franklin. *Film company:* Metro-Goldwyn-Mayer. *Music compiled by:* Ernst Luz. *Note:* Music incipits. "78 mins." marked in pencil. *Number of reels:* 8. *Footage:* 7870. *Maximum projection time:* 1 hour, 32 minutes.
MOMA   8 p., 31 cm.
Music 3236, Item 591

693
Queen Elizabeth
Queen Elizabeth. Note: Cue sheet. No music. Typescript (photocopy). Also includes music cues for the film, *The New York Hat*. Filed with The New York Hat. Incomplete.
MOMA   1 p., 26 cm.
Music 3236, Item 592

694
Queen O' Diamonds
Thematic music cue sheet. Film Booking Offices presents Evelyn Brent in *Queen O' Diamonds. Story and continuity by:* Fred Myton. *Directed by:* Chester Withey. *Distributed by:* Film Booking Offices of America, Inc. *Music compiled by:* Dr. Edward Kilenyi. *Note:* Music incipits. "Sunday & Mon 3/14-15" marked in pencil.
MOMA   4 p., 32 cm.
Music 3236, Item 593

695
Quincy Adams Sawyer
A Luz music score. S. L. Arthur Sawyer and Herbert Lubin present *Quincy Adams Sawyer. Film company:* Metro, controlled by Loew's, Inc. *Published by:* Photoplay Music Co., New York, 1922. *Instrumentation:* Piano leader. *Music compiled by:* Ernst Luz. *Copyright:* © C1 E 554974, December 18, 1922.
LC M1527.L95Q7   96 p., 30 cm.
Music 3212, Item 107

696
The Racing Romeo
Thematic music cue sheet. Joseph P. Kennedy presents Red Grange (under the management of C. C. Pyle) in *The Racing Romeo. From the story by:* Byron Morgan. *Production by:* Sam Wood. *Distributed by:* F B O Pictures Corporation. *Music compiled by:* James C. Bradford. *Note:* Music incipits.
MOMA   4 p., 31 cm.
Music 3236, Item 594

697
The Racket
The Racket. Film company: Paramount, July 7, 1928, Feature. *Note:* Cue sheet. No music. Typescript (carbon).
MOMA   1 p., 28 cm.
Music 3236, Item 595

698
The Rainbow
Thematic music cue sheet. Tiffany-Stahl presents *The Rainbow* with Dorothy Sebastian and Lawrence Gray. *Production by:* Reginald Barker. *Directed by:* Reginald Barker. *Film company:* Tiffany-Stahl. *Music compiled by:* James C. Bradford. *Note:* Music incipits.
MOMA   4 p., 32 cm.
Music 3236, Item 596

699

Rainbow Riley

Thematic music cue sheet. C. C. Burr presents Johnny Hines in *Rainbow Riley*. *Film company:* First National. *Music compiled by:* James C. Bradford. *Note:* "Saturday 6/5" marked in pencil.
MOMA   4 p., 32 cm.
                         Music 3236, Item 597

700

Ramona

Ramona. Music composed by: Hugo Riesenfeld. [?]. *Instrumentation:* Piano score.
LC M1527.R26   32 p., 32 cm., Ms.
                         Music 3212, Item 108

701

Ramona

Ramona. Note: Cue sheet. No music. Typescript.
MOMA   1 p., 28 cm.
                         Music 3236, Item 598

701A

Rapsodia Satanica

Rapsodia Satanica. Music composed by: Pietro Mascagni. *Published by:* Società Italiana Cines di Roma, 1917. *Instrumentation:* Piano. *Copyright:* © CL E 400378, May 22, 1917.
LC M35.M   47 p., 28 cm.
                                 No microfilm

702

Razlom

Razlom. Note: Cue sheet. No music. Ms.
MOMA   1 p., 28 cm.
                         Music 3236, Item 599

703

The Reckless Lady

Thematic music cue sheet. Robert T. Kane presents *The Reckless Lady*. *Film company:* First National. *Music compiled by:* James C. Bradford. *Note:* Music incipits. "Tuesday May 4" marked in pencil.
MOMA   2 p., 32 cm.
                         Music 3236, Item 600

704

Red Dice

Thematic music cue sheet. Cecil B. DeMille presents Rod La Rocque in *Red Dice* with Marguerite De La Motte. *Production by:* William K. Howard. *Released by:* Producers Distributing Corporation. *Music compiled by:* Rudolph Berliner. *Note:* Music incipits. "Mon May 24th" marked in pencil.
MOMA   4 p., 31 cm.
                         Music 3236, Item 601

705

Red Hair

Red Hair. Film company: Paramount, March 24, 1928. *Note:* Cue sheet. No music. Typescript. "Henry Falk, Publix Librarian" typed at bottom of cue sheet.
MOMA   1 p., 28 cm.
                         Music 3236, Item 602

706

Red Hot

Red Hot. Film company: Paramount, July 21, 1928. *Note:* Cue sheet. No music. Typescript (carbon).
MOMA   1 p., 28 cm.
                         Music 3236, Item 603

707

Red Hot Rhythm

Red Hot Rhythm. Note: Cue sheet. No music. Typescript. Six copies. Several of the copies appear to be drafts of the cue sheet for the film.
MOMA   6 p., 33 cm.
                         Music 3236, Item 604

708

Red Hot Speed

Greater thematic music cue sheet for *Red Hot Speed* with Reginald Denny. *Production by:* Universal. *Music compiled by:* James C. Bradford. *Note:* Music incipits.
MOMA   8 p., 32 cm.
                         Music 3236, Item 605

709

Red Hot Tires

Warner Brothers presents *Red Hot Tires* starring Monte Blue & Patsy Ruth Miller. *Note:* Cue sheet. No music. "Frid." marked in pencil. *Footage:* 6700. *Projection time:* 73 minutes — 11 minutes per 1000 feet.
MOMA   1 p., 36 cm.
                         Music 3236, Item 606

710

The Red Kimono

Thematic music cue sheet. Mrs. Wallace Reid presents *The Red Kimono*. *Story by:* Adela Rogers St. John [sic]. *Film company:* Vital. *Distributed by:* Vital Exchanges Incorporated…by Davis Distributing Division. *Music compiled by:* Rudolph Berliner. *Note:* Music incipits. "Thurs & Friday 2/25–26" marked in pencil.
MOMA   6 p., 31 cm.
                         Music 3236, Item 607

Dolores Del Rio in the historical melodrama *Ramona* (1928) in which the theme song by Mabel Wayne plays an important part in the picture's plot by jogging the heroine back into reality. Museum of Modern Art, Film Stills Archive.

711
Red Lips
Thematic music cue sheet. Carl Laemmle presents *Red Lips. Production by:* Universal. *Music compiled by:* James C. Bradford. *Note:* Music incipits.
MOMA 2 p., 32 cm.
Music 3236, Item 608

712
The Red Mark
Thematic music cue sheet. James Cruze, Inc. presents *The Red Mark* with Nena Quartaro. *Adaptation and continuity by:* Julien Josephson from the story by John Russell. *Directed by:* James Cruze. *Distributed by:* Pathe Exchange, Inc. *Note:* Music incipits. Two copies.
MOMA 4 p., 31 cm.
Music 3236, Item 609

713
The Red Raiders
Thematic music cue sheet. Ken Maynard in *The Red Raiders. Film company:* First National. *Music compiled by:* Dr. Edward Kilenyi. *Note:* Music incipits. Mutilated.
MOMA 4 p., 31 cm.
Music 3236, Item 610

714
The Red Sword
Thematic music cue sheet. William Le Baron presents *The Red Sword* with Marion Nixon, William Collier, Jr. and Carmel Myers. *Directed by:* Robert Vignola. *Distributed by:* F B O Pictures Corporation. *Music compiled by:* James C. Bradford. *Note:* Music incipits. "Thursday 4/18" marked in pencil.
MOMA 4 p., 31 cm.
Music 3236, Item 611

715
Red Wine
Thematic music cue sheet. Conrad Nagel in *Red Wine. Production by:* William Fox. *Music compiled by:* Michael P. Krueger. *Note:* Music incipits.
MOMA 4 p., 32 cm.
Music 3236, Item 612

716
Redskin
Original compositions from *Redskin. Music composed by:* J. S. Zamecnik and L. De Francesco. *Published by:* Sam Fox Pub. Co., Cleveland, 1929. *Instrumentation:* Piano. *Copyright:* © EP 3459, February 15, 1929; R 175192, Sam Fox Pub. Co., Inc. (PWH), July 17, 1956.
LC M1527.Z22 26 p., 32 cm.
Music 3212, Item 109

717
The Reform Candidate
Paramount photoplay music (P. 136 B 22) *The Reform Candidate. Produced by:* Pallas Pictures. *Music selected and arranged by:* George W. Beynon. *Series title:* Schirmer's Photoplay Series. *Published by:* G. Schirmer, New York, 1915. *Instrumentation:* Piano conductor. *Copyright:* © C1 E 377037, December 23, 1915.
LC M1357.B 59 p., 30 cm.
Music 3212, Item 110

718
Reggie Mixes In
Reggie Mixes In, D. Fairbanks, Triangle, 1916. *Note:* Cue sheet. No music. Ms.
MOMA 2 p., 28 cm.
Music 3236, Item 613

719
The Rejuvenation of Aunt Mary
Thematic music cue sheet. John C. Flinn presents May Robson and Phyllis Haver in *The Rejuvenation of Aunt Mary. Production by:* Erle C. Kenton. *Produced by:* Metropolitan Pictures Corporation. *Directed by:* Erle C. Kenton. *Released by:* Producers Distributing Corporation. *Music compiled by:* Rudolph Berliner. *Note:* Music incipits. "Monday Aug. 1/27" marked in pencil.
MOMA 4 p., 31 cm.
Music 3236, Item 614

719A
Relâche
Relâche. Ballet instantanéiste en deux actes, un entr'acte cinématographique, et "la queue du chien." *Scenario by:* Francis Picabia. *Directed by:* René Clair. *Music by:* Erik Satie. *Published by:* Rouart, Lerolle & Cie., Paris, 1927. *Instrumentation:* Piano score. *Copyright:* © C1 E 657115, January 26, 1927.
LC M1523.S24R3 49 p., 33 cm.
no microfilm

The Baldwin Piano Company used silent films to advertise its pianos. Music Division, Library of Congress.

719B
Relâche

Cinéma. Entr'acte symphonique de *Relâche*. *Music by:* Erik Satie. *Arranged by:* Darius Milhaud. *Published by:* Rouart, Lerolle & Cie., Paris, 1926. *Instrumentation:* Piano four hands. *Copyright:* © C1 E 639703, June 17, 1926.

LC M212.S   25 p., 35 cm.

no microfilm

719C
Relâche

Entr'acte. *Music by:* Erik Satie. *Arranged by:* Arthur Kleiner after Darius Milhaud's piano four-hand arrangement. *Published by:* The Museum of Modern Art, New York. *Instrumentation:* Piano two hands. *Copyright:* © Durand et Cie., Paris.

MOMA   14 p., 28 cm.

no microfilm

720
Le Retour d'Ulysse

Le Film d'Art. *Le Retour d'Ulysse.* Tableaux tirés du poème d'Homère par Jules Lemaître. *Music by:* Georges Hüe. *Published by:* A. Zunz Mathot, Paris, 1909. *Instrumentation:* Piano score. *Copyright:* © C XXC 201430, February 23, 1909.

LC M176.R43   17 p., 31 cm.

Music 3212, Item 111

721
The Return of "Draw"

The Return of "Draw," 1916. W. S. Hart from Triangle. *Note:* Cue sheet. No music. Ms.

MOMA   2 p., 28 cm.

Music 3236, Item 615

722
Revenge

Thematic music cue sheet. Edwin Carewe presents Dolores Del Rio in *Revenge. Story from* The Bear Tamer's Daughter *by:* Konrad Bercovici. *Screenplay by:* Finis Fox. *Production by:* Edwin Carewe. *Film company:* United Artists. *Music compiled by:* Ernst Luz. *Note:* Music incipits. *Number of reels:* 7. *Footage:* 6425. *Maximum projection time:* 1 hour, 12 minutes.

MOMA   6 p., 32 cm.

Music 3236, Item 616

723
Rhapsodie Hongroise

Rhapsodie Hongroise, by Hans Schwarz. *Translation by:* Erich Pommer. *Production by:* U. F. A. (Edition Alliance Cinématographique Européenne). *Music by:* Marcel Delannoy and Jacques

Brillouin. *Published by:* Editions Musicales Sam Fox, Paris, 1929. *Instrumentation:* Piano conductor. *Copyright:* © C1 E for. 8360, November 10, 1929; R 198924, September 12, 1957, Marcel Delannoy (A).
LC M1527.D3R4   149 p., 32 cm.
                        Music 3212, Item 112

724
Richard Wagner
Richard Wagner, eine Film-Biographie. *Music arranged and composed by:* Dr. G. Becce. *Published by:* Messter Film G.m.b.H, Berlin, 1913. *Instrumentation:* Piano score. *Copyright:* © C1 E 332813, August 15, 1913.
LC M176.R5   106 p., 33 cm.
                        Music 3212, Item 113

725
Riders of the Dark
Thematic music cue sheet. Tim McCoy in *Riders of the Dark. Story and continuity by:* W. S. Van Dyke. *Directed by:* Nick Grinde. *Film company:* Metro-Goldwyn-Mayer. *Music compiled by:* Ernst Luz. *Note:* Music incipits.
MOMA   4 p., 32 cm.
                        Music 3236, Item 617

726
The Ridin' Streak
Musical synopsis for *The Ridin' Streak* starring Bob Custer. *Film company:* F.B.O. *Music compiled by:* Dr. Edward Kilenyi. *Note:* Cue sheet. No music. "Thursday Jan 28" marked in pencil.
MOMA   1 p., 30 cm.
                        Music 3236, Item 618

727
The Right to Happiness
Music score for Universal Jewel *The Right to Happiness* starring Dorothy Phillips. *Directed by:* Allan Holubar. *Music prepared and arranged by:* M. Winkler and Sol P. Levy. *Published by:* Belwin Inc., New York, 1919. *Instrumentation:* Piano or organ. *Copyright:* © C1 E 458668, August 30, 1919.
LC M1527.W56R5 (Second copy M1527.R562)
                            71 p., 30 cm.
                        Music 3212, Item 114

728
Riley the Cop
Thematic music cue sheet. William Fox special film production *Riley the Cop. Music compiled by:* Michael P. Krueger. *Note:* Music incipits. Two copies. "Fri & Sat 18–19" marked in pencil on copy 1.
MOMA   6 p., 31 cm.
                        Music 3236, Item 619

729
Rinty of the Desert
Warner Bros. present *Rinty of the Desert* starring Rin-Tin-Tin. *Note:* Cue sheet. No music. "Sat Feb 2" marked in pencil. *Projection time:* About an hour based on a speed of 11 minutes per 1000 feet.
MOMA   1 p., 29 cm.
                        Music 3236, Item 620

730
Ritzy
Ritzy. Note: Cue sheet. No music. Typescript (carbon). Cue sheet typed on "Publix Theatres Corporation Inter-Office Communication" letterhead, dated "June 18–27."
MOMA   2 p., 28 cm.
                        Music 3236, Item 621

731
Ritzy
Thematic music cue sheet. Adolph Zukor and Jesse L. Lasky present Betty Bronson in *Ritzy* with James Hall. *Production by:* Elinor Glyn. *Directed by:* Richard Rosson. *Film company:* Paramount. *Music compiled by:* James C. Bradford. *Note:* Music incipits. Two copies. "Monday July 4/27" marked in pencil on copy 1. "July 4th" marked in pencil on copy 2. *Footage:* 5306.
MOMA   4 p., 31 cm.
                        Music 3236, Item 622

732
The River Pirate
Thematic music cue sheet. Victor McLaglen in *The River Pirate. Production by:* William Fox. *Music compiled by:* Michael P. Krueger. *Note:* Music incipits.
MOMA   4 p., 31 cm.
                        Music 3236, Item 623

733
Road House
Thematic music cue sheet. William Fox Feature Film Production *Road House. Music compiled by:* Michael P. Krueger. *Note:* Music incipits. Two copies.
MOMA   4 p., 32 cm.
                        Music 3236, Item 624

734
Roaring Ranch

Musical setting for Hoot Gibson in *Roaring Ranch. Film company:* Universal Pictures Corp. *Music selected and compiled by:* M. Winkler. *Note:* Cue sheet. No music. Two copies.

MOMA   3 p., 28 cm.

Music 3236, Item 625

735
Robin Hood

Music score for Douglas Fairbank's Production of *Robin Hood. Music composed by:* Victor L. Schertzinger, compiled and arranged by Victor L. Schertzinger and A. H. Cokayne. *Published by:* United Artists Corporation, New York. *Instrumentation:* Piano conductor and orchestral parts (1,1,2,1; 2,2nd cornet,1,0; drums; violin II, viola, cello, bass). *Note: Selections from Robin Hood* (A Comic Opera by Reginald De Koven) and *Musical Synopsis For Robin Hood* (2 page typescript, carbon—two copies) enclosed with piano conductor.

MOMA   83 p., 30 cm.

Music 3236, Item 67

736
The Romance of a Rogue

Musical synopsis for *The Romance of a Rogue. Music compiled by:* James C. Bradford. *Note:* Cue sheet. No music.

MOMA   1 p., 34 cm.

Music 3236, Item 626

737
A Romance of Happy Valley

D. W. Griffith's *A Romance of Happy Valley. Music arranged by:* Harley Hamilton. *Printed by:* Felix Violé, Los Angeles, December 1918. *Instrumentation:* Orchestral parts (flute, clarinets, cornets, trombone, tympani and drums; violin I, cello, bass).

MOMA   34 cm.

Music 3236, Item 68

738
Romance of the Underworld

Thematic music cue sheet. Mary Astor in *Romance of the Underworld. Production by:* William Fox. *Music compiled by:* Michael P. Krueger. *Note:* Music incipits.

MOMA   4 p., 32 cm.

Music 3236, Item 627

739
La Ronde de Nuit

La Ronde de Nuit. Film en trois actes et un prologue. *Scenario by:* Pierre Benoit. *Screenplay by:* Marcel Silver. *Sets by:* R. Mallet-Stevens. *Film company:* International Standard Film Co. *Music by:* Ch. Silver. *Orchestra under the direction of:* A. Leparcq. *Published by:* Choudens, Paris, 1926. *Instrumentation:* Piano score. *Copyright:* © C1 E 638821, February 18, 1926.

LC M1527.S58R5   165 p., 34 cm.

Music 3212, Item 115

740
Rose Marie

Rose Marie. Note: Cue sheet. No music. Ms. Cue sheets written on the verso of first E flat alto saxophone and tenor banjo parts of "The Whisper Song" by Cliff Friend.

MOMA   2 p., 34 cm.

Music 3236, Item 632

741
Rose-Marie

Thematic music cue sheet. *Rose-Marie* with Joan Crawford, James Murray and House Peters. Based on the famous stage production. *Continuity by:* Lucien Hubbard. *Directed by:* Lucien Hubbard. *Film company:* Metro-Goldwyn-Mayer. *Music compiled by:* Ernst Luz. *Note:* Music incipits. "April 1–2" marked in pencil. *Number of reels:* 8. *Footage:* 7535. *Maximum projection time:* 1 hour, 27 minutes.

MOMA   8 p., 32 cm.

Music 3236, Item 631

742
Rose of Montery

Rose of Montery. Note: Cue sheet. No music. Typescript.

MOMA   1 p., 28 cm.

Music 3236, Item 633

743
Roses of Picardy

Thematic music cue sheet. Samuel Zierler presents *Roses of Picardy,* the anguish of a woman's love written in tears of blood. *From:* Rex Ingram Studio. *Music compiled by:* James C. Bradford. *Note:* Music incipits.

MOMA   2 p., 33 cm.

Music 3236, Item 634

Films, accompanied by recordings, were projected out of doors as part of the advertising campaigns of business and government. General Collections, Library of Congress.

744
Rose of the Golden West

Thematic music cue sheet. Richard A. Rowland presents A George Fitzmaurice Production *Rose of the Golden West* with Mary Astor and Gilbert Roland. *Film company:* First National. *Music compiled by:* Eugene Conte. *Note:* Music incipits. "Thurs 17" marked in pencil. "Monday Nov 7/27" written in pencil and crossed out in pencil.

MOMA   4 p., 32 cm.
Music 3236, Item 635

745
Rose of the World

Warner Brothers presents Patsy Ruth Miller in *Rose of the World. Note:* Cue sheet. No music. "Sat Jan 30" marked in pencil. Mutilated. *Projection time:* 1 hour, 19 minutes based on a speed of 11 minutes per 1000 feet.

MOMA   1 p., 32 cm.
Music 3236, Item 630

746
Rough House Rosie

Rough House Rosie. Note: Cue sheet. No music. Typescript (carbon). Typed on "Publix Theatres Corporation Inter-Office Communication" letterhead, dated "Paramount May 21/27."

MOMA   1 p., 28 cm.
Music 3236, Item 628

747
The Rough Riders

The Rough Riders. Note: Cue sheet. No music. Typescript.

MOMA   2 p., 28 cm.
Music 3236, Item 629

748
Running Wild

Running Wild. Note: Cue sheet. No music. Typescript (carbon). Typed on "Publix Theatres Corporation Inter-Office Communication" letterhead.

MOMA   2 p., 28 cm.
Music 3236, Item 636

749
Rupert of Hentzau

Musical setting to the Bluebird Photo-Play No. 7 *Rupert of Hentzau* by Anthony Hope. *Adapted and produced by:* George L. Tucker. *A sequel to: The Prisoner of Zenda. Music selected and arranged by:* M. Winkler. *Series title:* Carl Fischer Photo-Play Series. *Published by:* Carl Fischer, New York, 1916. *Instrumentation:* Piano

or organ (1,1,2,1; 2,2,1,0; drums, strings). *Copyright:* © C1 E 379011, March 7, 1916.
LC M1527.W56R9 (Second copy M1357.W)

                                        62 p., 31 cm.
Music 3212, Item 116

750
The Rush Hour

Thematic music cue sheet. John C. Flinn presents Marie Prevost in *The Rush Hour* with Harrison Ford. *Produced by:* DeMille Pictures Corporation. *Directed by:* E. Mason Hopper. *Distributed by:* Pathe Exchange, Inc. *Music compiled by:* Rudolph Berliner. *Note:* Music incipits. "Mon Mar 5" marked in pencil.

MOMA   4 p., 31 cm.
Music 3236, Item 637

751
Rustlers' Ranch

Musical setting for *Rustlers' Ranch. Music compiled by:* M. Winkler. *Note:* Cue sheet. No music. "Tuesday 3/30" marked in pencil.

MOMA   1 p., 30 cm.
Music 3236, Item 638

752
Rustling for Cupid

Thematic music cue sheet. George O'Brien in *Rustling for Cupid. Production by:* William Fox. *Music compiled by:* Michael P. Krueger. *Note:* Music incipits. "Mon & Tuesday 5/31-6/1" marked in pencil.

MOMA   2 p., 38. cm.
Music 3236, Item 639

753
Sable Lorcha

Musical setting to *Sable Lorcha,* photoplay dramatization. *Music selected and arranged by:* J. A. Raynes. *Published by:* G. Schirmer, New York, 1915. *Instrumentation:* Piano conductor (1,1,2,1; 2,2,1,0; tympani and drums; strings). *Copyright:* © C1 E 373197, October 20, 1915.
LC M1357.R   63 p., 31 cm.
Music 3212, Item 117

754
Sadie Thompson

Sadie Thompson. Note: Cue sheet. No music. Typescript (carbon).

MOMA   3 p., 28 cm.
Music 3236, Item 640

755
Sailor's Holiday
Sailor's Holiday. Note: Cue sheet. No music.
Typescript and manuscript.
MOMA   6 p., 33 cm.
Music 3236, Item 641

756
Sal of Singapore
Thematic music cue sheet. Pathe presents Phyllis
Haver in *Sal of Singapore. Adapted by:* Elliott
Clawson from Dale Collins' *The Sentimentaliste.
Directed by:* Howard Higgin. *Distributed by:*
Pathe Exchange, Inc. *Music compiled by:* James
C. Bradford. *Note:* Music incipits. Two copies.
MOMA   4 p., 32 cm.
Music 3236, Item 642

757
Sally's Shoulders
Thematic music cue sheet. William LeBaron pre-
sents Beatrice Burton's mighty story *Sally's
Shoulders* with Lois Wilson, Huntley Gordon and
George Hackathorne. *Directed by:* Lynn Shores.
Distributed by: F B O Pictures Corporation.
Music compiled by: Howard T. Wood. *Note:* Music
incipits.
MOMA   4 p., 31 cm.
Music 3236, Item 643

758
Samson
Incidental music for Universal Film Mfg. Co. Pro-
duction of *Sampon* [sic]. *Music by:* Noble
Kreider. *Published by:* Noble Kreider, Goshen,
Ind., 1914. *Instrumentation:* Piano score. *Copy-
right:* © C1 E 338414, February 25, 1914.
LC M176.S19   25 p., 31 cm.
Music 3212, Item 118

759
Sandy
Thematic music cue sheet. William Fox special
production *Sandy. Music compiled by:* Michael
P. Krueger. *Note:* Music incipits. "Wednesday June
30" marked in pencil.
MOMA   4 p., 32 cm.
Music 3236, Item 644

Many silent films were accompanied by the selected
and arranged works of classical composers. Here a
minuet by Beethoven is featured on the sheet music
cover for the movie *Scaramouche* (1923). Music Division, Library of Congress.

Alice Terry, Ramon Novarro, and the Loew's State Syn-
copators on the sheet music cover associated with the
film *Scaramouche.* A. Joseph Jordan's orchestra is
fairly representative of the medium-sized, twenty- to
twenty-two piece, theater orchestra. Music Division,
Library of Congress.

760

Satan in Sables

Warner Brothers presents Lowell Sherman in
Satan in Sables. Note: Cue sheet. No music.
"Thurs. Jan. 28" marked in pencil. Mutilated. *Pro-
jection time:* 1 hour, 15 minutes based on a speed
of 11 minutes per 1000 feet. *Number of reels:* 7.
MOMA   1 p., 35 cm.
                                   Music 3236, Item 645

761

The Savage

Thematic music cue sheet. First National Pictures, Inc. present Ben Lyon and May McAvoy in
The Savage. Film company: First National.
Music compiled by: Eugene Conte. *Note:* Music
incipits. "Mon & Tues Aug 23–24" marked in
pencil.
MOMA   4 p., 32 cm.
                                   Music 3236, Item 646

762

The Sawdust Paradise

Thematic music cue sheet. Adolph Zukor and
Jesse L. Lasky present Esther Ralston in *The
Sawdust Paradise* with Hobart Bosworth. *Story
and adaptation by:* George Manker Watters.
Screenplay by: Louise Long. *Produced by:* B. P.
Schulberg, Associate Producer. *Directed by:*
Luther Reed. *Film company:* Paramount. *Music
compiled by:* James C. Bradford. *Note:* Music
incipits. Two copies. *Footage:* 5928.
MOMA   4 p., 32 cm.
                                   Music 3236, Item 647

763

Say It Again

Thematic music cue sheet. Adolph Zukor and
Jesse L. Lasky present Richard Dix in *Say It
Again. From the story by:* Luther Reed. *Screen-
play by:* Ray Harris and Dick Friel. *Production
by:* Gregory La Cava. *Film company:* Paramount.
Music compiled by: James C. Bradford. *Note:*
Music incipits. *Footage:* 6834.
MOMA   4 p., 32 cm.
                                   Music 3236, Item 648

764

Say Young Fellow

Say Young Fellow, Doug. Fairbanks, Par. *Note:*
This is not a cue sheet as such, but rather an
informal description of the film with suggestions
for musical accompaniment. At the bottom of the

page is noted: "From Moving Pict World July 27, 1918." *Number of reels:* 5.

MOMA   1 p., 28 cm.
                                    Music 3236, Item 649

765

The Scarecrow

Music for the moving picture *The Scarecrow.*
Produced by: The Film Guild. *Distributed by:*
The W. W. Hodkinson Co. *Music composed by:* F.
S. Converse. *Published by:* Frederick Shepherd
Converse, Westwood, Mass., 1923. *Instrumenta-
tion:* Piano score. *Copyright:* © E 569088, Sep-
tember 7, 1923.

LC M1527.C75S3   85 p., 35 cm., Ms.
                                    Music 3212, Item 119

766

The Scarecrow

Scarecrow Sketches, six excerpts from the photo-
music-drama *Puritan Passions. Based upon:*
Percy MacKaye's stage play, *The Scarecrow.*
Music composed by: Frederick S. Converse for
the Film Guild, Inc. *Published by:* Oliver Ditson
Co., Boston, 1924. *Instrumentation:* Piano. *Copyright:* © C1 A 778705, March 1, 1924.

LC M1527.C75S4 (Second copy M1527.C27S4)
                                     32 p., 31 cm.
                                    Music 3212, Item 120

766A

Scarecrow Sketches [Puritan Passions]

Glenn Hunter in *Puritan Passions* from Percy
MacKaye's *The Scarecrow* with Mary Astor and
Osgood Perkins. *Film company:* Hodkinson Pic-
tures. *Produced by:* A Film Guild Production.
Music composed by: Frederick Shepard Con-
verse. *Instrumentation:* Piano score.

Frederick Shepard Converse Collection   98 p., 30 cm.
                                    Music 3449, Item 181A

766B

Scarecrow Sketches [Puritan Passions]

Scarecrow Sketches (Puritan Passions) written
for the film based on Percy MacKaye's stage play.
Instrumentation: Orchestral score. *Note:* Holograph score. Dated and signed at end, "Aug.
11/23. F. S. Converse." Gift of Mrs. Emma Tudor
Converse to the Music Division, May 8, 1941.

ML96.C77. Case   267 p., 35.5 cm.
                                    Music 3449, Item 181D

Glenn Hunter and Maude Hill in *Puritan Passions*
(alternate title *The Scarecrow*) (1923). The composer,
Frederick Converse (1871-1940), was one of several
distinguished American composers who wrote only
one film score. Converse Collection, Music Division,
Library of Congress.

767

The Scarlet Saint

Thematic music cue sheet. First National Pictures presents *The Scarlet Saint* with Mary Astor and Lloyd Hughes. *Film company:* First National. *Music compiled by:* Bert Herbert. *Note:* Music incipits. "Tuesday 3/9" marked in pencil.

MOMA   4 p., 32 cm.
Music 3236, Item 650

768

Scenic Snapshot

Scenic Snapshot. Note: Cue sheet. No music. Typescript (carbon).

MOMA   1 p., 28 cm.
Music 3236, Item 651

769

Schuldig

Schuldig. Film company: Messters Film. *Story based on the play* Schuldig *by:* R. Voss. *Music by:* Dr. G. Becce. *Published by:* Messter's Verlag, Berlin, 1913. *Instrumentation:* Piano score. *Copyright:* © C1 E 332873, July 29, 1913, Messter Film, G.m.b.H.

LC M176.S38   53 p., 33 cm.
Music 3212, Item 121

770

Sea Dreams

Cue sheet of *Sea Dreams* from Nathaniel Finston, July 12, 1928. *Note:* Cue sheet. No music. Typescript (mimeograph copy).

MOMA   1 p., 28 cm.
Music 3236, Item 652

771

Sea Horses

Thematic music cue sheet. Adolph Zukor and Jesse L. Lasky present *Sea Horses* with Jack Holt. *Adapted by:* Becky Gardiner. *From the novel by:* Francis Brett Young. *Screenplay by:* James Hamilton. *Production by:* Allan Dwan. *Film company:* Paramount. *Music compiled by:* James C. Bradford. *Note:* Music incipits. "Sunday 6/6" marked in pencil.

MOMA   2 p., 33 cm.
Music 3236, Item 653

772

Sealed Lips

Thematic music cue sheet. Waldorf Pictures presents *Sealed Lips* featuring Dorothy Revier. *Produced by:* Harry Cohn. *Directed by:* Antonio Gaudio. *Copyrighted and distributed by:*

Columbia Pictures Corporation. *Music compiled by:* James C. Bradford. *Note:* Music incipits. "Sunday Jan-17" marked in pencil.

MOMA   2 p., 36 cm.
Music 3236, Item 654

773

Le Secret de Myrto

Le Secret de Myrto, poème musical. *Music by:* Gaston Bérardi. *Published by:* Heugel & Cie., Paris, 1909. *Instrumentation:* Piano/vocal score. *Copyright:* © C xxc 198561, January 11, 1909.

LC M176.S44   [x], 21 p., 28 cm.
Music 3212, Item 122

774

Secret Love

Musical setting to the Bluebird photo-play no. 2. Miss Helen Ware in *Secret Love* with Miss Ella Hall and Harry D. Carey. *Music selected and arranged by:* M. Winkler. *Series title:* Carl Fischer Photo-Play Series. *Published by:* Carl Fischer, New York, 1916. *Instrumentation:* Piano conductor (1,1,2,1; 2,2,1,0; drums; strings). *Copyright:* © C1 E 377797, February 15, 1916.

LC M1357.W   59 p., 30 cm.
Music 3212, Item 123

775

Secret Orders

Thematic music cue sheet. Film Booking Offices presents Evelyn Brent in *Secret Orders. Continuity by:* J. Grubb Alexander. *Directed by:* Chet Withey. *Distributed by:* Film Booking Offices of America, Inc. *Music compiled by:* James C. Bradford. *Note:* Music incipits. "Thurs & Frid 4/22–23" marked in pencil.

MOMA   4 p., 32 cm.
Music 3236, Item 655

776

The Secret Spring

Thematic music cue sheet. Adolph Zukor and Jesse L. Lasky present *The Secret Spring. From the novel by:* Pierre Benoit. *Produced in France by:* Leonce Benoit. *Film company:* Paramount. *Music compiled by:* James C. Bradford. *Note:* Music incipits. "Wed Aug 25" marked in pencil.

MOMA   4 p., 31 cm.
Music 3236, Item 656

777
See You in Jail
Thematic music cue sheet. First National Pictures, Inc. presents *See You in Jail* with Jack Mulhall, Alice Day and Mark Swain. *Adapted from the story by:* Wm. H. Clifford. *Directed by:* Joseph Henaberry [sic]. *Film company:* First National. *Music compiled by:* Eugene Conte. *Note:* Music incipits. "Thursday April 14/27" marked in pencil.
MOMA   4 p., 32 cm.
Music 3236, Item 657

778
Señorita
Señorita (Bebe Daniels). *Note:* Cue sheet. No music. Typescript (carbon). Typed on "Publix Theatres Corporation Inter-Office Communication" letterhead, dated "May 7/27."
MOMA   1 p., 28 cm.
Music 3236, Item 658

779
Señorita
Thematic music cue sheet. Adolph Zukor and Jesse L. Lasky present Bebe Daniels in *Señorita*. *Story and screenplay by:* John McDermott. *Production by:* Clarence Badger, B. P. Schulberg, Associate Producer. *Film company:* Paramount. *Music compiled by:* James C. Bradford. *Note:* Music incipits. "June 2 to 5th" marked in pencil.
MOMA   4 p., 32 cm.
Music 3236, Item 659

780
Sensation Seekers
Thematic music cue sheet. Carl Laemmle presents *Sensation Seekers*. *Film company:* Universal-Jewel. *Music compiled by:* Eugene Conte. *Note:* Music incipits. "Monday March 21/27" marked in pencil.
MOMA   2 p., 32 cm.
Music 3236, Item 660

781
The Set Up
Musical setting for *The Set Up. Music compiled by:* M. Winkler. *Note:* Cue sheet. No music. "Sunday May 30" marked in pencil.
MOMA   1 p., 31 cm.
Music 3236, Item 661

782
Seven Footprints to Satan
Seven Footprints to Satan. Music compiled by: James C. Bradford. *Note:* Cue sheet. No music.
MOMA   1 p., 28 cm.
Music 3236, Item 662

783
Seven Sinners
Warner Brothers presents Marie Prevost in *Seven Sinners. Note:* Cue sheet. No music. "Wed 2/23" marked in pencil. Mutilated. *Footage:* 6700. *Projection time:* 1 hour, 14 minutes based on a speed of 11 minutes per 1000 feet.
MOMA   1 p., 35 cm.
Music 3236, Item 663

784
Seventh Heaven
Conductor of *7th Heaven. Music compiled by:* [Erno Rapee (?)] *Instrumentation:* Piano.
LC M1527.S48   86 p., 32 cm., Ms.
Music 3212, Item 124

785
The Shadow on the Wall
A Gotham Production. Musical setting for *The Shadow on the Wall. Music arranged by:* Joseph E. Zivelli. *Note:* Cue sheet. No music. "Sat & Sun July 24–25" marked in pencil. *Number of reels:* 6. *Projection time:* 52 minutes.
MOMA   1 p., 31 cm. by 25 cm.
Music 3236, Item 664

786
Shadows of the Night
Thematic music cue sheet. *Shadows of the Night* with Lawrence Gray, Louise Lorraine and "Flash." *Original story by:* Ted Shane. *Adapted by:* D. Ross Lederman. *Directed by:* D. Loss [sic] Lederman. *Film company:* Metro-Goldwyn-Mayer. *Music compiled by:* Ernst Luz. *Note:* Music incipits. *Number of reels:* 7. *Footage:* 5390. *Maximum projection time:* 1 hour, 2 minutes.
MOMA   4 p., 32 cm.
Music 3236, Item 665

787
The Shakedown
Thematic music cue sheet. Carl Laemmle presents *The Shakedown. Production by:* Universal. *Music compiled by:* James C. Bradford. *Note:* Music incipits.
MOMA   2 p., 31 cm.
Music 3236, Item 666

Janet Gaynor and Charles Farrell in *Seventh Heaven*
(1927), a romantic drama set in Paris at the outbreak
of World War I. The title song, "(I'm in heaven when I
see you smile) Diane," by Erno Rapee and Lew Pollack,
was one of the most popular songs of 1927. Museum of
Modern Art, Film Stills Archive.

788
Shanghai Bound
Thematic music cue sheet. Adolph Zukor and Jesse L. Lasky present Richard Dix in *Shanghai Bound* with Mary Brian. *Story by:* E. S. O'Reilly. *Screenplay by:* John Goodrich and Ray Harris. *Produced by:* B. P. Schulberg, Associate Producer. *Directed by:* Luther Reed. *Film company:* Paramount. *Music compiled by:* James C. Bradford. *Note:* Music incipits. "Thursday Dec. 8/27" marked in pencil. *Footage:* 5515.

MOMA 4 p., 31 cm.
Music 3236, Item 667

789
Shanghaied
Thematic music cue sheet. Joseph P. Kennedy presents *Shanghaied* with Ralph Ince and Patsy Ruth Miller. *Production by:* Ralph Ince. *Distributed by:* F B O Pictures Corporation. *Music compiled by:* James C. Bradford. *Note:* Music incipits. "Lyceum Dec. 8-9-10" marked in pencil.

MOMA 4 p., 30 cm.
Music 3236, Item 668

790
She
Thematic music cue sheet. Lee-Bradford Corporation presents Sir H. Rider Haggard's own version of *She* starring Betty Blythe. *Produced by:* A to X Productions. *Directed by:* Leander De Cordova. *Music compiled by:* James C. Bradford. *Note:* Music incipits. "Wednesday 6/2" marked in pencil.

MOMA 2 p., 32 cm.
Music 3236, Item 669

791
Shéhérazade
Shéhérazade by A. Volkoff. *Music by:* Léo Pouget and Victor Alix. *Film company:* Ciné Alliance Film de la U.F.A. *Series title:* Edition Alliance Cinématographique Européene. *Published by:* Editions Musicales Sam Fox, Paris, 1928. *Instrumentation:* Piano conductor; strings. *Copyright:* © E for. 4976, December 31, 1928.

LC M1357.P 170 p., 32 cm.
Music 3212, Item 125

792
The Shepherd of the Hills
Thematic music cue sheet. Richard A. Rowland presents *The Shepherd of the Hills* by Harold Bell Wright with Molly O'Day. *Adaptation and continuity by:* Marion Jackson. *Produced by:* Charles R. Rogers. *Directed by:* Al Rogell. *Film company:* First National. *Music compiled by:* James C. Bradford. *Note:* Music incipits. "April-19-20-21" marked in pencil.

MOMA 6 p., 31 cm.
Music 3236, Item 670

793
A Ship Comes In
Thematic music cue sheet. Pathe presents *A Ship Comes In* with Rudolph Schildkraut, Louise Dresser and Robert Edeson. *Original story and adaptation by:* Julien Josephson. *Continuity by:* Sonyà Levien. *Production by:* DeMille Studio. *Directed by:* William K. Howard. *Distributed by:* Pathe Exchange, Inc. *Music compiled by:* Rudolph Berliner. *Note:* Music incipits.

MOMA 4 p., 31 cm.
Music 3236, Item 671

794
Ship of Souls
Thematic music cue sheet. Associated Exhibitors, Inc. presents *Ship of Souls* with Lillian Rich and Bert Lytell. *From the novel by:* Emerson Hough. *Released by:* Associated Exhibitors, Inc. *Film company:* Encore. *Music compiled by:* James C. Bradford. *Note:* Music incipits. "Friday Jun 29" marked in pencil.

MOMA 4 p., 31 cm.
Music 3236, Item 672

795
Shooting Straight
Shooting Straight. Note: Cue sheet. No music. Typescript.

MOMA 7 p., 33 cm.
Music 3236, Item 673

796
The Shopworn Angel
Thematic music cue sheet. Adolph Zukor and Jesse L. Lasky present *The Shopworn Angel* with Nancy Carroll and Gary Cooper. *Adapted by:* Howard Estabrook and Albert Shelby LeVino. *From the story by:* Dana Burnet. *Production by:* Richard Wallace. *Film company:* Paramount. *Music compiled by:* James C. Bradford. *Note:* Music incipits.

MOMA 4 p., 32 cm.
Music 3236, Item 674

A PRECIOUS LITTLE THING CALLED LOVE

by LOU DAVIS *and* J. FRED COOTS

SONG
WITH UKULELE ARRANGEMENT

Theme Song For The
Paramount Production
"THE SHOPWORN ANGEL"
with
GARY COOPER & NANCY CARROLL

REMICK MUSIC CORP.
NEW YORK CITY
BY ARRANGEMENT WITH FAMOUS MUSIC CORP.

Gary Cooper and Nancy Carroll on the cover of the theme song from *The Shopworn Angel* (1928), "A Precious Little Thing Called Love." Music Division, Library of Congress.

797
Short Shots

Short Shots. Note: Cue sheet. No music. Typescript (carbon).
MOMA   1 p., 28 cm.
Music 3236, Item 675

798
Show-Down

Show-Down. Note: Cue sheet. No music. Typescript (carbon). Dated "Week of March 3rd. '28."
MOMA   2 p., 28 cm.
Music 3236, Item 676

799
Show Folks

Thematic music cue sheet. Pathe presents *Show Folks* with Eddie Quillan, Lina Basquette, Robert Armstrong. *From an original story by:* Philip Dunning. *Adapted by:* Jack Jungmeyer and George Dromgold. *Production by:* Ralph Block. *Directed by:* Paul L. Stein. *Distributed by:* Pathe Exchange, Inc. *Music compiled by:* James C. Bradford. *Note:* Music incipits. Two copies.
MOMA   4 p., 31 cm.
Music 3236, Item 677

800
Show Girl

Thematic music cue sheet. Richard A. Rowland presents *Show Girl* with Alice White. *Production by:* Alfred Santell. *Film company:* First National. *Music compiled by:* James C. Bradford. *Note:* Music incipits. Two copies.
MOMA   4 p., 32 cm.
Music 3236, Item 678

801
Show People

Thematic music cue sheet. Marion Davies and William Haines in *Show People. Production by:* King Vidor, Marion Davies. *Directed by:* King Vidor. *Film company:* Metro-Goldwyn-Mayer. *Music compiled by:* Ernst Luz. *Note:* Music incipits. *Number of reels:* 9 *Footage:* 7505. *Maximum projection time:* 1 hour, 23 minutes.
MOMA   6 p., 31 cm.
Music 3236, Item 679

802
The Showdown

Thematic music cue sheet. Adolph Zukor and Jesse L. Lasky present George Bancroft in *The Showdown* with Evelyn Brent and Neil Hamilton. *Story by:* Houston Branch. *Screenplay by:* Hope

Loring. *Continuity by:* Ethel Doherty. *Directed by:* Victor Schertzinger. *Film company:* Paramount. *Music compiled by:* James C. Bradford. *Note:* Music incipits. *Footage:* 7616.

MOMA   6 p., 32 cm.
Music 3236, Item 680

803
Siberia

Thematic music cue sheet. William Fox special production *Siberia. Music compiled by:* Michael P. Krueger. *Note:* Music incipits. "Thurs & Friday 6/17/18" marked in pencil.

MOMA   4 p., 31 cm.
Music 3236, Item 681

804
The Siege of Petersburg

Special piano music for *The Siege of Petersburg. Music by:* Walter C. Simon. *Published by:* Kalem Co., New York, 1912. *Instrumentation:* Piano. *Copyright:* © C1 E 288953, July 16, 1912. *Number of reels:* 2.

LC M176.S57   26 p., 32 cm.
Music 3212, Item 126

805
Silk Stockings

Thematic music cue sheet. Carl Laemmle presents *Silk Stockings. Film company:* Universal-Jewel. *Music compiled by:* James C. Bradford. *Note:* Music incipits. "Monday Jan 9/28" marked in pencil.

MOMA   2 p., 33 cm.
Music 3236, Item 682

806
Silks and Saddles

Thematic music cue sheet. Carl Laemmle presents *Silks and Saddles. Production by:* Universal. *Music compiled by:* James C. Bradford. *Note:* Music incipits. Two copies.

MOMA   2 p., 32 cm.
Music 3236, Item 683

807
The Silver Slave

Warner Bros. presents *The Silver Slave* starring Irene Rich. *Note:* Cue sheet. No music. Two copies. "Sunday March 3" marked in pencil on copy 1. "Mon Mar 12" marked in pencil on copy 2 (mutilated). *Projection time:* 1 hour, 7 minutes based on a speed of 11 minutes per 1000 feet.

MOMA   1 p., 35 cm.
Music 3236, Item 684

Alice White on the cover of "Buy, Buy for Baby," from the First National Production *Show Girl* (1928). Music Division, Library of Congress.

808
Simon the Jester
Thematic music cue sheet. Metropolitan Pictures Corporation presents *Simon the Jester* with Lillian Rich and Eugene O'Brien. *Adapted by:* Frances Marion from the novel by William J. Locke. *Production by:* Frances Marion. *Directed by:* George Melford. *Released by:* Producers Distributing Corporation. *Music compiled by:* Dr. Edward Kilenyi. *Note:* Music incipits. "4/21" marked in pencil.
MOMA   2 p., 32 cm.
                                Music 3236, Item 685

809
Singapore Mutiny
Thematic music cue sheet. William Le Baron presents *Singapore Mutiny* with Ralph Ince and Estelle Taylor. *From the story by:* Norman Springer. *Production by:* Ralph Ince. *Distributed by:* F B O Pictures Corporation. *Music compiled by:* James C. Bradford. *Note:* Music incipits.
MOMA   4 p., 32 cm.
                                Music 3236, Item 686

810
A Single Man
Thematic music cue sheet. Lew Cody and Aileen Pringle in *A Single Man* with Marceline Day. *From the play by:* Hubert Henry Davies. *Screenplay by:* F. Hugh Herbert and George O'Hara. *Directed by:* Harry Beaumont. *Film company:* Metro-Goldwyn-Mayer. *Music compiled by:* Ernst Luz. *Note:* Music incipits. *Number of reels:* 7. *Footage:* 5530. *Maximum projection time:* 1 hour, 10 minutes.
MOMA   2 p., 32 cm.
                                Music 3236, Item 687

811
Sir Lumberjack
Thematic music cue sheet. Film Booking Offices present Lefty Flynn in *Sir Lumberjack. Produced by:* Harry Garson. *Distributed by:* Film Booking Offices of America, Inc. *Music compiled by:* Edward Kilenyi. *Note:* Music incipits. Two copies, "Sunday 6/13" marked in pencil on both copies.
MOMA   4 p., 30 cm.
                                Music 3236, Item 688

812
The Siren
Thematic music cue sheet. Columbia Pictures presents *The Siren* with Tom Moore, Dorothy Revier. *Story by:* Harold Shumate. *Directed by:* Byron Haskin. *Copyrighted and distributed by:* Columbia Pictures Corporation. *Music compiled by:* James C. Bradford. *Note:* Music incipits. "May 1–2" marked in pencil.
MOMA   2 p., 33 cm.
                                Music 3236, Item 689

813
A Six Shootin' Romance
Musical setting for *A Six Shootin' Romance. Music compiled by:* M. Winkler. *Note:* Cue sheet. No music. "Wednesday Feb 24" marked in pencil.
MOMA   1 p., 30 cm.
                                Music 3236, Item 690

814
Skinner's Big Idea
Thematic music cue sheet. Joseph P. Kennedy presents *Skinner's Big Idea* with Bryant Washburn. *From the story by:* Henry Irving Dodge. *Directed by:* Lynn Shores. *Distributed by:* F B O Pictures Corporation. *Music compiled by:* James C. Bradford. *Note:* Music incipits. "Sunday July 22" marked in pencil.
MOMA   4 p., 31 cm.
                                Music 3236, Item 691

815
The Sky Skidder
Musical setting for *The Sky Skidder. Music compiled by:* M. Winkler. *Note:* Cue sheet. No music. "Thursday 4/11" marked in pencil.
MOMA   1 p., 30 cm.
                                Music 3236, Item 692

816
Skyscraper
Thematic music cue sheet. Pathe presents William Boyd in *Skyscraper* with Alan Hale. *Production by:* DeMille Studio. *Directed by:* Howard Higgin. *Distributed by:* Pathe Exchange, Inc. *Music compiled by:* Rudolph Berliner. *Note:* Music incipits. Three copies. "4/26/28" marked in pencil on copy 1. "May 13–14" marked in pencil on copy 2.
MOMA   4 p., 32 cm.
                                Music 3236, Item 693

817

Skyscrapers

Skyscrapers. Note: Cue sheet. No music. Type-script (carbon). Dated "Paramount April 7, 1928."
MOMA   2 p., 28 cm.
Music 3236, Item 694

818

The Small Bachelor

Greater thematic music cue sheet for *The Small Bachelor* with Barbara Kent and Andre Beranger. *Film company:* Universal. *Music compiled by:* James C. Bradford. *Note:* Music incipits. Two copies. "Monday Oct. 3/27" marked in pencil on copy 1.
MOMA   8 p., 31 cm.
Music 3236, Item 695

819

Smile Brother Smile

Thematic music cue sheet. First National Pictures, Inc. presents *Smile Brother Smile* with Dorothy Mackaill and Jack Mulhall. *Production by:* John Francis Dillon. *Produced by:* Charles R. Rogers. *Film company:* First National. *Music compiled by:* Eugene Conte. *Note:* Music incipits. "Monday Sept 26/27" marked in pencil.
MOMA   4 p., 32 cm.
Music 3236, Item 696

820

Smilin' at Trouble

Thematic music cue sheet. F. B. O. presents Maurice Lefty Flynn in *Smilin' at Trouble. Produced and directed by:* Harry Garson. *Distributed by:* Film Booking Offices of America, Inc. *Music compiled by:* James C. Bradford. *Note:* Music incipits. "Saturday 2/27" marked in pencil.
MOMA   4 p., 31 cm.
Music 3236, Item 697

821

Smilin' Guns

Thematic music cue sheet. Carl Laemmle presents *Smilin' Guns. Production by:* Universal. *Music compiled by:* James C. Bradford. *Note:* Music incipits. "Lyceum July 4-5-6 1929" marked in pencil.
MOMA   2 p., 32 cm.
Music 3236, Item 698

822

The Smiling Madame Beaudet

The Smiling Madame Beaudet. Instrumentation: Piano score.
MOMA   60 p., 30 cm.
Music 3236, Item 69

823

So This Is America

So This Is America. Note: Cue sheet. No music. Typescript (carbon).
MOMA   1 p., 28 cm.
Music 3236, Item 699

824

So This Is Europe

So This Is Europe. Note: Cue sheet. No music. Typescript (carbon).
MOMA   1 p., 28 cm.
Music 3236, Item 700

825

The Social Highwayman

Warner Bros. presents *The Social Highwayman* starring Montague [sic] Love and Dorothy Devore. *Note:* Cue sheet. No music. "Wed Sept . . ." marked in pencil. Partially mutilated.
MOMA   1 p., 36 cm.
Music 3236, Item 701

826

Soft Living

Thematic music cue sheet. William Fox feature production. Madge Bellamy in *Soft Living. Music compiled by:* Michael P. Krueger. *Note:* Music incipits. "April 29-30" marked in pencil.
MOMA   2 p., 35 cm.
Music 3236, Item 702

827

Soil

Soil. Note: Cue sheet. Music. Ms.
MOMA   1 p., 28 cm.
Music 3236, Item 703

828

The Soldier Brothers of Susanna

Special piano music for *The Soldier Brothers of Susanna. Published by:* Kalem Co., New York, 1912. Instrumentation: Piano. *Copyright:* © C1 E 289142, July 19, 1912.
LC M176.S675   13 p., 32 cm.
Music 3212, Item 127

829
Soldiers of Fortune

Soldiers of Fortune. Incidental music to the motion picture presentation of Richard Harding Davis' *Soldiers of Fortune* featuring Dustin Farnum. *Directed by:* Augustus Thomas in Cuba. *Produced by:* The All Star Feature Corporation. *Music composed by:* Manuel Klein, Musical Director of the New York Hippodrome. *Published by:* M. Witmark & Sons, New York, 1914. *Instrumentation:* Piano. *Copyright:* © C1 E 330391, January 20, 1914; R 94474, January 24, 1941, Helen Klein, Hollywood, California.

LC M176. S68   13 p., 35 cm.
Music 3212, Item 128

830
Some Pun'kins

A Chadwick Picture. Musical setting for *Some Pun'kins. Music arranged by:* Joseph Zivelli. *Note:* Cue sheet. No music. "Wed July 28" marked in pencil.

MOMA   1 p., 53 cm. by 35 cm.
Music 3236, Item 704

831
Someone to Love

Thematic music cue sheet. Adolph Zukor and Jesse L. Lasky present Charles (Buddy) Rogers in *Someone to Love. Production by:* F. Richard Jones. *Film company:* Paramount. *Music compiled by:* James C. Bradford. *Note:* Music incipits. Two copies. "17th" marked in pencil on copy 1. "Sat Feb 23" marked in pencil on copy 2.

MOMA   4 p., 32 cm.
Music 3236, Item 705

832
Something Always Happens

Something Always Happens. Note: Cue sheet. No music. Typescript.

MOMA   1 p., 28 cm.
Music 3236, Item 706

833
The Song and Dance Man

Thematic music cue sheet. Adolph Zukor and Jesse L. Lasky present *The Song and Dance Man.* From George M. Cohan's stage success. *Screenplay by:* Paul Schofield. *Production by:* Herbert Brenon. *Film company:* Paramount. *Music compiled by:* James C. Bradford. *Note:* Music incipits. "Sunday May 30" marked in pencil. *Footage:* 6969.

MOMA   4 p., 32 cm.
Music 3236, Item 707

834
Sons of the Saddle

Musical setting for Ken Maynard in *Sons of the Saddle. Film company:* Universal Pictures Corp. *Music compiled by:* M. Winkler. *Note:* Cue sheet. No music.

MOMA   3 p., 28 cm.
Music 3236, Item 708

835
Sophmore

Sophmore. Note: Cue sheet. No music. Typescript (carbon). "Pathe" typed on page 1.

MOMA   7 p., 33 cm.
Music 3236, Item 709

836
Sorrell and Son

Sorrell and Son. Note: Cue sheet. No music. Typescript (carbon).

MOMA   2 p., 28 cm.
Music 3236, Item 710

837
Sorrows of Love

Sorrows of Love. Production by: Thomas H. Ince, 1916. *Note:* Cue sheet. No music. Ms.

MOMA   2 p., 28 cm.
Music 3236, Item 711

838
Sorrows of Satan

Sorrows of Satan. Note: Cue sheet. No music. Typescript (carbon).

MOMA   5 p., 28 cm.
Music 3236, Item 712

839
Souls for Sables

Thematic music cue sheet. Tiffany Productions presents *Souls for Sables* featuring Claire Windsor and Eugene O'Brien. *Adapted and supervised by:* A. P. Younger. *Directed by:* James C. McKay. *Music compiled by:* James C. Bradford. *Note:* Music incipits.

MOMA   4 p., 31 cm.
Music 3236, Item 713

Production shot from *The Spanish Dancer* (1923).
Courtesy of the Astoria Motion Picture and Television
Center Foundation, Astoria, New York.

840

Spangles

Carl Laemmle presents *Spangles* starring Hobart Bosworth, Gladys Brockwell, Marion Nixon. *Production by:* Universal-Jewel. *Note:* Cue sheet. No music. "Monday Dec. 27/26" marked in pencil. *Footage:* 5500. *Projection time:* 1 hour based on a speed of 11 minutes per 1000 feet.

MOMA   1 p., 36 cm.
Music 3236, Item 714

841

The Spanish Revolt of 1836

The Spanish Revolt of 1836. Music by: Walter C. Simon. *Published by:* Kalem Co., New York, 1912. *Instrumentation:* Piano score. *Copyright:* © C1 E 282718, March 28, 1912.

LC M176.S735   10 p., 32 cm.
Music 3212, Item 129

842

A Spartan Mother

A Spartan Mother. Music by: Walter C. Simon. *Published by:* Kalem Co., New York, 1912. *Instrumentation:* Piano score. *Copyright:* © C1 E 279506, March 6, 1912.

LC M176.S74   10 p., 32 cm.
Music 3212, Item 130

843

Special Delivery

Special Delivery. Eddy Kantor [sic]. *Note:* Cue sheet. No music. Typescript (carbon). Typed on "Publix Theatres Corporation Inter-Office Communication" letterhead, dated "April 24–27."

MOMA   2 p., 28 cm.
Music 3236, Item 715

844

Speed

Speed. Note: Cue sheet. No music. Typescript (carbon). Typed on "Publix Theatres Corporation Inter-Office Communication" letterhead.

MOMA   2 p., 28 cm.
Music 3236, Item 716

845

Speed Mad

Thematic music cue sheet. Perfection Pictures presents *Speed Mad,* a thrilling drama of racing and romance featuring William Fairbanks, Edith Roberts. *Copyrighted and released by:* Columbia Pictures Corporation. *Music compiled by:* James

C. Bradford. *Note:* Music incipits. "Sunday Feb 7" marked in pencil.

MOMA   2 p., 31 cm.
Music 3236, Item 717

846

Speedy

Speedy. Note: Cue sheet. No music. Typescript (carbon). Dated "Rivoli, April 6, 1928."

MOMA   3 p., 28 cm.
Music 3236, Item 718

847

The Spieler

Thematic music cue sheet. Pathe presents *The Spieler* with Alan Hale, Renee Adorée. *Adapted by:* Hal Conklin. *Production by:* Ralph Block. *Directed by:* Tay Garnett. *Distributed by:* Pathe Exchange, Inc. *Music compiled by:* James C. Bradford. *Note:* Music incipits.

MOMA   4 p., 31 cm.
Music 3236, Item 719

848

The Splendid Crime

Thematic music cue sheet. Adolph Zukor and Jesse L. Lasky present Bebe Daniels in *The Splendid Crime* with Neil Hamilton. *Production by:* William DeMille. *Film company:* Paramount. *Music compiled by:* James C. Bradford. *Note:* Music incipits. "Frid Feb 12" marked in pencil.

MOMA   4 p., 31 cm.
Music 3236, Item 720

849

The Splendid Road

Thematic music cue sheet. Frank Lloyd presents *The Splendid Road. Film company:* First National. *Music compiled by:* Dr. Edward Kilenyi. *Note:* Music incipits. "Wed 3/24" marked in pencil.

MOMA   4 p., 32 cm.
Music 3236, Item 721

850

Spoilers of the West

Thematic music cue sheet. Tim McCoy in *Spoilers of the West* with Marjorie Daw and William Fairbanks. *From the story by:* John Thomas Neville. *Scenario by:* Madeleine Ruthven and Ross B. Wills. *Directed by:* W. S. Van Dyke. *Film company:* Metro-Goldwyn-Mayer. *Music compiled by:* Ernst Luz. *Note:* Music incipits. "April 12–13–14" marked in pencil.

MOMA   4 p., 32 cm.
Music 3236, Item 722

851

The Sporting Chance

Thematic music cue sheet. *The Sporting Chance by:* Jack Boyle. *Production by:* Tiffany Productions, Inc., M. H. Hoffman, Gen. Mgr., 1540 Broadway, New York City. *Music compiled by:* Dr. Edward Kilenyi, Musical Director, Colony Theatre, New York. *Note:* Music incipits. "Wed Jan 13" marked in pencil.

MOMA   2 p., 37 cm.
Music 3236, Item 723

852

Sporting Goods

Thematic music cue sheet. Adolph Zukor and Jesse L. Lasky present Richard Dix in *Sporting Goods. Screenplay by:* Tom Crizer and Ray Harris. *Production by:* Malcolm St. Clair; B. P. Schulberg, Associate Producer. *Film company:* Paramount. *Music compiled by:* James C. Bradford. *Note:* Music incipits. "Thursday Mar 29/28" marked in pencil. *Footage:* 5951.

MOMA   4 p., 31 cm.
Music 3236, Item 724

853

Sporting Life

Thematic music cue sheet. Carl Laemmle presents *Sporting Life* with an all star cast. *From the play by:* Cecil Raleigh and Seymour Hicks. *Directed by:* Maurice Tourneur. *Film company:* Universal-Jewel. *Music compiled by:* James C. Bradford. *Note:* Music incipits. "Thurs & Friday March 4-5" marked in pencil.

MOMA   2 p., 33 cm.
Music 3236, Item 725

854

The Sporting Lover

Thematic music cue sheet. Conway Tearle and Barbara Bedford in *The Sporting Lover. Film company:* First National. *Music compiled by:* Eugene Conte. *Note:* Music incipits. "Sat & Sun Aug 14-15" marked in pencil. *Forum Weekly* (Saturday and Sunday, July 24-25) published by The Forum Theatre enclosed with cue sheet.

MOMA   4 p., 32 cm.
Music 3236, Item 726

855

The Spotlight

Thematic music cue sheet. Adolph Zukor and Jesse L. Lasky present Esther Ralston in *The Spotlight* with Neil Hamilton. *Adapted by:* Hope Loring from the story *Footlights* by Rita Weiman. *Production by:* Frank Tuttle. *Film company:* Paramount. *Music compiled by:* James C. Bradford. *Note:* Music incipits. Two copies. "Monday Jan 2/28" marked in pencil on copy 1. *Footage:* 4943.

MOMA   4 p., 32 cm.
Music 3236, Item 727

856

Spurs

Musical setting for Hoot Gibson in *Spurs* with Helen Wright. *Film company:* Universal Pictures Corp. *Music compiled by:* M. Winkler. *Note:* Cue sheet. No music.

MOMA   3 p., 28 cm.
Music 3236, Item 728

857

Stand and Deliver

Thematic music cue sheet. Pathe presents Rod La Rocque in *Stand and Deliver* with Lupe Velez and Warner Oland. *Adapted by:* Sada Cowan from the story suggested by S. Ponty. *Production by:* Donald Crisp; DeMille Studio, Ralph Block, Associate Producer. *Distributed by:* Pathe Exchange, Inc. *Music compiled by:* Rudolph Berliner. *Note:* Music incipits.

MOMA   4 p., 31 cm.
Music 3236, Item 729

858

Star of the Sea

Star of the Sea. Note: Cue sheet. No music. Ms.

MOMA   1 p., 32 cm.
Music 3236, Item 730

859

State Street Sadie

Warner Bros. present *State Street Sadie* starring Conrad Nagel, Myrna Loy, William Russell. *Note:* Cue sheet. No music. *Projection time:* 1 hour, 7 minutes based on a speed of 11 minutes per 1000 feet.

MOMA   1 p., 35 cm.
Music 3236, Item 731

860
Stella Dallas

Stella Dallas. Music composed by: Alfred Newman and Raphael Penso. *To be published by:* Irving Berlin, Inc. under special contract with United Artists and can be used by them without fee or license, July 28, 1937. *Note:* Cue sheet. No music. Two copies (typescript and carbon). There are a few music cues by composers other than Alfred Newman and Raphael Penso.

MOMA   2 p., 28 cm.
Music 3236, Item 732

861
Stella Maris

Thematic music cue sheet. Carl Laemmle presents Mary Philbin in *Stella Maris* by William J. Locke. *Directed by:* Charles Brabin. *Film company:* Universal-Jewel. *Music compiled by:* Dr. Edward Kilenyi. *Note:* Music incipits. "Monday & Tuesday May 11-12" marked in pencil.

MOMA   2 p., 33 cm.
Music 3236, Item 733

862
Steppin' Out

Thematic music cue sheet. Columbia Pictures presents *Steppin' Out* featuring Dorothy Revier. *Directed by:* Frank Strayer. *Copyrighted and distributed by:* Columbia Pictures Corporation. *Music compiled by:* James C. Bradford. *Note:* "Sunday Jan 10" marked in pencil. Music incipits.

MOMA   2 p., 38 cm.
Music 3236, Item 734

863
Stick to Your Story

Musical setting for *Stick to Your Story* featuring Billy Sullivan. *Film company:* Rayart. *Character of film:* Lively comedy drama. *Music compiled by:* Joseph E. Zivelli. *Note:* Cue sheet. No music. "Plaza Wed & Thurs Aug. 13 & 14" marked in ink. *Number of reels:* 5.

MOMA   1 p., 30 cm.
Music 3236, Item 735

864
The Still Alarm

Thematic music cue sheet. Carl Laemmle presents *The Still Alarm* with an all star cast. *From the play by:* Joseph Arthur and A. C. Wheeler. *Directed by:* Edward Laemmle. *Film company:* Universal-Jewel. *Music compiled by:* James C.

Bradford. *Note:* Music incipits."[ ] & Tues & Wed Aug 16-17-18" marked in pencil. Partially mutilated.

MOMA   1 p., 37 cm.
Music 3236, Item 736

865
Stocks and Blondes

Thematic music cue sheet. Joseph P. Kennedy presents *Stocks and Blondes* with Jacqueline Logan, Gertrude Astor and Richard Skeets Gallagher. *Written and directed by:* Dudley Murphy. *Distributed by:* F B O Pictures Corporation. *Music compiled by:* James C. Bradford. *Note:* Music incipits.

MOMA   4 p., 31 cm.
Music 3236, Item 737

866
Stolen Love

Thematic music cue sheet. William Le Baron presents *Stolen Love* with Owen Moore and Marceline Day. *From the story by:* Hazel Livingston. *Directed by:* Lynn Shores. *Distributed by:* F B O Pictures Corporation. *Music compiled by:* James C. Bradford. *Note:* Music incipits. Two copies.

MOMA   4 p., 32 cm.
Music 3236, Item 738

867
Stop, Look and Listen

Thematic music cue sheet. John Adams presents Larry Semon in *Stop, Look and Listen. Film company:* Pathépicture. *Music compiled by:* Dr. Edward Kilenyi. *Note:* Music incipits. "Tuesday 3/23" marked in pencil.

MOMA   4 p., 32 cm.
Music 3236, Item 739

868
Stop That Man

Thematic music cue sheet. Carl Laemmle presents *Stop That Man. Production by:* Universal. *Music compiled by:* James C. Bradford. *Note:* Music incipits. Two copies. "Tues & Wed Sept 4-5" marked in pencil on copy 1. "Lyceum—Thurs. Fri. Sat. July 19,-20,-21" marked in pencil on copy 2.

MOMA   2 p., 31 cm.
Music 3236, Item 740

869
The Stork Exchange
Musical cue sheet. *The Stork Exchange* @ 90.
Note: No music. Typescript (mimeograph copy).
MOMA   1 p., 28 cm.
                            Music 3236, Item 741

870
The Storm at Sea
Musical setting *The Storm at Sea. Music by:* Alice
Smythe Jay to be used with roll of inspiration
music. In roll form or piano. *Instrumentation:*
Piano. *Copyright:* © C1 E 397537, February 15,
1917, Alice Smythe Burton Jay, Los Gatos, Calif.
LC M176.S88   20 p., 34 cm., Ms.
                            Music 3212, Item 131

871
The Storm Breaker
Thematic music cue sheet. Carl Laemmle presents
House Peters in *The Storm Breaker. From the
novel* Titans *by:* Charles Guernon. *Film com-
pany:* Universal-Jewel. *Music compiled by:*
Eugene Conte. *Note:* Music incipits. "Tues & Wed
Jan 5–6" marked in pencil.
MOMA   2 p., 32 cm.
                            Music 3236, Item 742

872
Stranded
Stranded, 1916. W. S. Hart. *Note:* Cue sheet. No
music. Ms.
MOMA   2 p., 28 cm.
                            Music 3236, Item 743

873
Street of Sin
Street of Sin. Note: Cue sheet. No music. Type-
script (carbon).
MOMA   3 p., 28 cm.
                            Music 3236, Item 745

874
Streets of Shanghai
Thematic music cue sheet. Tiffany-Stahl presents
Streets of Shanghai by John Francis Natteford
with Pauline Starke. *Story and continuity by:*
John Francis Natteford. *Production by:* Tiffany-
Stahl. *Directed by:* Louis J. Gasnier. *Music com-
piled by:* James C. Bradford. *Note:* Music incipits.
"Lyceum Theatre Thurs. Fri. Sat. Feb 2, 3, 4,
1928" typed on cue sheet.
MOMA   4 p., 32 cm.
                            Music 3236, Item 744

S. M. Berg, English-born musician-conductor, who
prepared one of the earliest musical cue sheets for a
motion picture. He edited the musical section of *Moving Picture World,* established the Motion Picture
Department of the music publisher, G. Schirmer, Inc.,
and was Associate Musical Director for the paper,
Exhibitor's Trade Review. From George N. Beynon,
Musical Presentation of Motion Pictures (New York:
G. Schirmer, 1921).

875
The Strength of the Weak
Musical setting to the Bluebird photoplay no. 8. Mary Fuller in the famous play *The Strength of the Weak* by Alice M. Smith and Lucius Henderson. *Music selected and arranged by:* M. Winkler. *Series title:* Carl Fischer Photo-Play Series. *Published by:* Carl Fischer, New York, 1916. *Instrumentation:* Piano conductor; (1,1,2,1; 2,2,1,0; drums; strings). *Copyright:* © C1 E 382313, March 17, 1916.
LC M1357.W.   48 p., 30 cm.
Music 3212, Item 132

876
The Strong Man
The Strong Man. Note: Cue sheet. No music. Typescript. Three copies.
MOMA   1 p., 35 cm.
Music 3236, Item 746

877
The Stronger Will
Thematic music cue sheet. Samuel Zierler presents Percy Marmon, Rita Carewe and Wm. Norton Bailey in *The Stronger Will,* a story of frenzied love and finance. *Produced and distributed by:* Excellent Pictures Corporation. *Music compiled by:* James C. Bradford. *Note:* Music incipits. Two copies. "April–1–2" marked in pencil on copy 1.
MOMA   2 p., 32 cm.
Music 3236, Item 747

878
Subway Sadie
Thematic music cue sheet. First National Pictures, Inc. presents *Subway Sadie* with Dorothy Mackaill and Jack Mulhall. *Film company:* First National. *Music compiled by:* James C. Bradford. *Note:* Music incipits.
MOMA   4 p., 32 cm.
Music 3236, Item 748

879
Sunrice
Sunrice. Note: Cue sheet. No music. Ms.
MOMA   6 p., 32 cm.
Music 3236, Item 749

879A
Surf and Seaweed
Suite for the Film *Surf and Seaweed. Directed by:* Ralph Steiner. *Music by:* Marc Blitzstein. *Instrumentation:* Full score. *Note:* This is a negative photostat of the original score in the Edwin A. Fleisher Collection at the Philadelphia Free Library.
MOMA   94 p., 28 cm.
no microfilm

880
Surrender
Thematic music cue sheet. Carl Laemmle presents *Surrender. Film company:* Universal-Jewel. *Music compiled by:* Dr. Edward Kilenyi. *Note:* Music incipits. Three copies. All are mutilated. "Thursday Nov 3/27" marked in pencil on copy 1.
MOMA   2 p., 36 cm.
Music 3236, Item 750

881
Sweet Daddies
Thematic music cue sheet. M. C. Levee presents *Sweet Daddies. Film company:* First National. *Music compiled by:* Eugene Conte. *Note:* Music incipits. Two copies. "Thurs & Friday Aug 12–13" marked in pencil on copy 1. "Aug 12–13" marked in pencil on copy 2.
MOMA   4 p., 31 cm.
Music 3236, Item 751

882
Syncopating Sue
Thematic music cue sheet. Asher, Small and Rogers presents Corinne Griffith in *Syncopating Sue. Film company:* First National. *Music compiled by:* Eugene Conte. *Note:* Music incipits. "Coming Monday Nov. 22/26" marked in pencil.
MOMA   4 p., 32 cm.
Music 3236, Item 752

883
Take It from Me
Thematic music cue sheet. Carl Laemmle presents Reginald Denny in *Take It from Me* by Will Johnstone and Will R. Anderson. *Production by:* William A. Seiter. *Film company:* Universal-Denny. *Music compiled by:* James C. Bradford. *Note:* Music incipits. Two copies. "Coming Thursday Nov. 18/26" marked in pencil on copy 1. "Thursday Oct. 18/26" marked in pencil on copy 2.
MOMA   2 p., 33 cm.
Music 3236, Item 753

884
Take Me Home
Thematic music cue sheet. Adolph Zukor and Jesse L. Lasky present Bebe Daniels in *Take Me Home* with Neil Hamilton. *Story by:* Harlan Thompson and Grover Jones. *Screenplay by:* Ethel Doherty. *Production by:* Marshall Neilan; B. P. Schulberg, Associate Producer. *Film company:* Paramount. *Music compiled by:* James C. Bradford. *Note:* Music incipits. Mutilated. *Footage:* 5614.
MOMA   4 p., 32 cm.
Music 3236, Item 754

885
Tangled Hearts
Musical setting to the Bluebird photo-play no. 11 *Tangled Hearts* featuring Louise Lovely, Lon Chaney, Hayward Mack. *Music selected and arranged by:* M. Winkler and F. Rehsen. *Series title:* Carl Fischer Photo-Play Series. *Published by:* Carl Fischer, New York, 1916. *Instrumentation:* Piano conductor; (1,1,2,1; 2,2,1,0; drums; strings). *Copyright:* © C1 E 379571, March 31, 1916.
LC M1357.W   68 p., 30 cm.
Music 3212, Item 133

886
Tarnish
Thematic music cue sheet. Samuel Goldwyn presents *Tarnish*. *Production by:* George Fitzmaurice. *Film company:* First National. *Music compiled by:* Eugene Conte, Musical Director, Plaza Theatre, New York City. *Note:* Music incipits.
MOMA   4 p., 32 cm.
Music 3236, Item 755

887
Tartuffe
Tartuffe. *Note:* Cue sheet. No music. Ms.
MOMA   1 p., 28 cm.
Music 3236, Item 756

888
Tatters
Tatters. *Instrumentation:* Piano score.
MOMA   28 p., 31 cm.
Music 3236, Item 70

889
Tea for Three
Thematic music cue sheet. Robert Z. Leonard's Production *Tea for Three* with Lew Cody, Aileen Pringle and Owen Moore. *Directed by:* Robert Z. Leonard. *Film company:* Metro-Goldwyn-Mayer.

Music compiled by: Ernst Luz. *Note:* Music incipits. *Number of reels:* 6. *Footage:* 5220. *Maximum projection time:* 55 minutes.
MOMA   4 p., 32 cm.
Music 3236, Item 757

890
Telephone Girl
Telephone Girl. *Note:* Cue sheet. No music. Typescript (carbon). "Publix Theatres Corporation Inter-Office Communication" letterhead, dated "May 14th–27."
MOMA   1 p., 28 cm.
Music 3236, Item 758

891
Tell It to Sweeney
Thematic music cue sheet. Adolph Zukor and Jesse L. Lasky present Chester Conklin and George Bancroft in *Tell It to Sweeney* with Jack Luden and Doris Hill. *Story by:* Percy Heath and Monte Brice. *Screenplay by:* Percy Heath and Kerry Clarke. *Production by:* Gregory La Cava. *Film company:* Paramount. *Music compiled by:* James C. Bradford. *Note:* Music incipits. "Thurs. Nov. 10/27" marked in pencil. *Footage:* 6006.
MOMA   4 p., 32 cm.
Music 3236, Item 759

892
Telling the World
Thematic music cue sheet. William Haines in *Telling the World*. *Story by:* Dale Van Every. *Scenario by:* Raymond L. Schrock. *Production by:* Sam Wood. *Directed by:* Sam Wood. *Film company:* Metro-Goldwyn-Mayer. *Music compiled by:* Ernst Luz. *Note:* Music incipits. Two copies. *Number of reels:* 8. *Footage:* 6965. *Maximum projection time:* 1 hour, 25 minutes.
MOMA   4 p., 31 cm.
Music 3236, Item 760

893
The Ten Commandments
The Ten Commandments. *Music by:* Jack Snyder. *Published by:* White House Bible Society, New York, 1924. *Instrumentation:* Piano/vocal score. *Copyright:* © C1 E 601818, received November 7, 1924.
LC M1527.S67T32   32 p., 31 cm.
Music 3212, Item 161

894
The Ten Commandments
Music composed by: Jack Snyder. *Published by:*
Jack Snyder Pub. Co., Inc., New York, 1924.
Instrumentation: Piano/vocal score. *Copyright:*
© C1 E 591911, received July 17, 1924.
LC M1527.S67T3   31 p., 31 cm.
                              Music 3449, Item 197

895
Ten Modern Commandments
Thematic music cue sheet. Adolph Zukor and
Jesse L. Lasky present Esther Ralston in *Ten
Modern Commandments* with Neil Hamilton.
Based on story by: Jack Lait. *Screenplay by:*
Doris Anderson and Paul Gangelon. *Continuity
by:* Ethel Doherty. *Produced by:* B. P. Schulberg,
Associate Producer. *Directed by:* Dorothy Arzner.
Film company: Paramount. *Music compiled by:*
James C. Bradford. *Footage:* 6497.
MOMA   4 p., 31 cm.
                              Music 3236, Item 761

896
Ten Modern Commandments
Ten Modern Commandments. Note: Cue sheet.
No music. Typescript (carbon). Typed on "Publix
Theatres Corporation Inter-Office Communica-
tion" letterhead, dated "July 9th 27."
MOMA   2 p., 28 cm.
                              Music 3236, Item 762

897
Tenth Avenue
Thematic music cue sheet. Pathe presents *Tenth
Avenue* with Phyllis Haver. *From the stage play
by:* John McGowan and Lloyd Griscom. *Contin-
uity by:* Douglas Doty. *Production by:* William
C. DeMille; DeMille Studio. *Distributed by:* Pathe
Exchange, Inc. *Music compiled by:* Rudolph
Berliner.
MOMA   4 p., 32 cm.
                              Music 3236, Item 763

898
The Terror
Musical setting for *The Terror. Music compiled
by:* M. Winkler. *Note:* Cue sheet. No music. "Wednesday Sept 8" marked in pencil.
MOMA   1 p., 31 cm.
                              Music 3236, Item 764

899
The Terror
Warner Bros. present *The Terror* starring May
McAvoy, Louise Fazenda, Alec Francis. *Note:* Cue

sheet. No music. "Mond–Tues Dec 3–4" marked in
pencil. *Projection time:* About 1 hour based on a
speed of 11 minutes per 1000 feet.
MOMA   1 p., 35 cm.
                              Music 3236, Item 765

900
Terror Mountain
Musical synopsis for *Terror Mountain. Music
compiled by:* James C. Bradford. *Note:* Cue sheet.
No music.
MOMA   1 p., 32 cm.
                              Music 3236, Item 766

901
Texas Tommy
A Syndicate Picture. Musical setting for Bob Cus-
ter in *Texas Tommy. Music arranged by:* Joseph
E. Zivelli. *Character of film:* Western drama. *Note:*
Cue sheet. No music. "Frid & Sat Aug 1 & 2 1930"
marked in ink.
MOMA   1 p., 29 cm.
                              Music 3236, Item 767

902
Thanks for the Buggy Ride
Thematic music cue sheet. Carl Laemmle presents
Thanks for the Buggy Ride. Film company:
Universal-Jewel. *Music compiled by:* James C.
Bradford. *Note:* Music incipits. Two copies. "April
9/28" marked in pencil on copy 1.
MOMA   4 p., 32 cm.
                              Music 3236, Item 768

903
That Certain Thing
Thematic music cue sheet. Columbia Pictures
presents Viola Dana in *That Certain Thing. Story
and adaptation by:* Elmer Harris. *Directed by:*
Frank Capro [sic]. *Copyrighted and distributed
by:* Columbia Pictures Corporation. *Music compiled by:* James C. Bradford. *Note:* Music incipits.
MOMA   2 p., 33 cm.
                              Music 3236, Item 769

904
That's My Baby
Thematic music cue sheet. Douglas MacLean in
That's My Baby by George J. Crone and Wade
Boteler. *Screenplay by:* Joseph Franklin Poland.
Directed by: William Beaudine. *Film company:*
Paramount. *Music compiled by:* James C. Brad-
ford. *Note:* Music incipits. Mutilated. *Footage:*
6805.
MOMA   2 p., 37 cm.
                              Music 3236, Item 770

905
That's My Daddy
Greater thematic music cue sheet for *That's My Daddy* with Reginald Denny. *Film company:* Universal. *Music compiled by:* James C. Bradford. *Note:* Music incipits. Two copies. "Mar 29 1928 Mar 30 1928" stamped in ink on copy 1. "Thursday Friday & Saturday March 29–30–31" marked in pencil on copy 1. Copy 2 incomplete, pages 7 and 8 missing.

MOMA   8 p., 31 cm.
Music 3236, Item 771

906
A Thief in the Dark
Thematic music cue sheet. William Fox special film production *A Thief in the Dark. Music compiled by:* Michael P. Krueger. *Note:* Music incipits. "Sunday Dec 2" marked in pencil.

MOMA   4 p., 31 cm.
Music 3236, Item 772

907
The Thief of Bagdad
Douglas Fairbanks in *The Thief of Bagdad,* a fantasy of the Arabian Nights. *Music composed by:* Mortimer Wilson, Op. 74. *Published by:* Douglas Fairbanks Pictures Corp., New York, 1924. *Instrumentation:* Piano short score; (1, pic.,1,2,1; 2,2,2,0; tympani; harp; strings). *Copyright:* © C1 E 601678, November 3, 1924; R 100045, September 25, 1952, Mortimer Wilson, Jr. (C).

LC M1527.W52T4   190 p., (& 19 supplemetal pages), 30 cm.
Music 3212, Item 134

908
The Thief of Bagdad
Douglas Fairbanks in *The Thief of Bagdad,* a fantasy of the Arabian Nights. *Distributed by:* The United Artists Corporation. *Incidental music by:* Mortimer Wilson, Op. 74. *Published by:* J. Fischer & Bro., New York, 1924. *Instrumentation:* Piano conductor and orchestral parts (pic.,1,1,2,1; 2,2,2,0; tympani and drums; harp; strings). *Copyright:* © C1 E 601678, November 3, 1924, Douglas Fairbanks Pictures Corp., New York; R 100045, September 25, 1952, Mortimer Wilson, Jr. (C).

MOMA   159 p., 30 cm.
Music 3236, Item 71

909
The Third Degree
Warner Bros. present *The Third Degree* starring Dolores Costello, Tom Santschi, Louise Dresser.

Note: Cue sheet. No music. Three copies. "Coming Monday Feb 28/27" marked in pencil on copy 1. *Projection time:* 1 hour, 20 minutes based on a speed of 10 minutes per 1000 feet.

MOMA   1 p., 38 cm.
Music 3236, Item 773

910
13 Washington Square
Thematic music cue sheet. Carl Laemmle presents *13 Washington Square. Film company:* Universal-Jewel. *Music compiled by:* James C. Bradford. *Note:* Music incipits. Two copies. "Thurs. Fri. & Saturday 3/15-16-17/28. Lyceum Theatre Bayonne N. J." marked in pencil on copy 1. "April–24–25" marked in pencil on copy 2.

MOMA   2 p., 32 cm.
Music 3236, Item 774

911
The Thirteenth Juror
Thematic music cue sheet. Carl Laemmle presents *The Thirteenth Juror. Film company:* Universal-Jewel. *Music compiled by:* James C. Bradford. *Note:* Music incipits.

MOMA   2 p., 31 cm.
Music 3236, Item 775

912
Those Who Judge
Thematic music cue sheet. Banner Productions, Inc. presents *Those Who Judge* with Patsy Ruth Miller and Lou Tellegen. *From the story by:* Margery Land May. *Directed by:* Burton King. *Music compiled by:* James C. Bradford. *Note:* Music incipits. "Thurs & Fri Dec 17-18" marked in pencil.

MOMA   2 p., 33 cm.
Music 3236, Item 776

913
Thoughts for Labor Day
Thoughts for Labor Day. Note: Cue sheet. No music. Typescript.

MOMA   1 p., 28 cm.
Music 3236, Item 777

914
Three Faces East
Three Faces East. Note: Cue sheet. No music. Typescript.

MOMA   1 p., 28 cm.
Music 3236, Item 778

Julanne Johnston and Douglas Fairbanks, Sr. in *The Thief of Bagdad* (1924). Mortimer Wilson's score for this film is the finest American score of the entire silent era and among many other unique features contains a virtuoso French horn part. Museum of Modern Art, Film Stills Archive.

915

3 Keys

Thematic music cue sheet. Banner Productions, Inc. presents *3 Keys*. *Production by:* Ben Verschleisen [sic Verschleiser]. *Directed by:* Edw. Le Saint. *Music compiled by:* James C. Bradford. *Note:* Music incipits. "Mon & Tues Feb 1–2" marked in pencil.

MOMA   2 p., 33 cm.
Music 3236, Item 779

916

The Three Musketeers

Music score for Douglas Fairbanks super production of Alexander Dumas' *The Three Musketeers*. *Music compiled by:* Louis F. Gottschalk. *Published by:* United Artists Corp., New York. *Instrumentation:* Orchestral parts (1,1,2,1; 2,2,1,0; drums; strings).

MOMA   31 cm.
Music 3236, Item 72

917

The Three Musketeers

Piano score for *The Three Musketeers*. *Published by:* The Museum of Modern Art Film Library, New York. *Instrumentation:* Piano score.

MOMA   176 p., 29 cm.
Music 3236, Item 73

918

Three Ring Marriage

Thematic music cue sheet. First National Pictures, Inc. presents *Three Ring Marriage* with Mary Astor and Lloyd Hughes. *Production by:* Marshall Neilan. *Film company:* First National. *Music compiled by:* James C. Bradford. *Note:* Music incipits.

MOMA   4 p., 32 cm.
Music 3236, Item 780

919

Three Sinners

Three Sinners. Note: Cue sheet. No music. Typescript.

MOMA   1 p., 28 cm.
Music 3236, Item 781

920

Three Wise Crooks

Thematic music cue sheet. F. B. O. presents Evelyn Brent in *Three Wise Crooks*. *Directed by:* F. Harmon Weight. *Distributed by:* Film Booking Offices of America, Inc. *Music compiled by:* Dr.

Edward Kilenyi. *Note:* Music incipits. "12/20–21" marked in pencil.

MOMA   4 p., 31 cm.
Music 3236, Item 782

921

Thunder Riders

Musical setting for *Thunder Riders*. *Music compiled by:* M. Winkler. *Note:* Cue sheet. No music. "April–22–23" marked in pencil.

MOMA   1 p., 30 cm.
Music 3236, Item 783

922

Thundering Herd

Thundering Herd. Note: Cue sheet. No music. Typescript.

MOMA   1 p., 28 cm.
Music 3236, Item 784

923

The Tigress

Thematic music cue sheet. Columbia Pictures presents *The Tigress* with Jack Holt, Dorothy Revier. *Scenario by:* Harold Shumate. *Directed by:* George B. Seitz. *Copyrighted and distributed by:* Columbia Pictures Corporation. *Music compiled by:* James C. Bradford. *Note:* Music incipits.

MOMA   2 p., 32 cm.
Music 3236, Item 785

924

The Toilers

Thematic music cue sheet. Tiffany-Stahl presents *The Toilers* by L. G. Rigby with Douglas Fairbanks, Jr. and Jobyna Ralston. *Production by:* Reginald Barker; Tiffany-Stahl. *Directed by:* Reginald Barker. *Music compiled by:* James C. Bradford. *Note:* Music incipits.

MOMA   4 p., 31 cm.
Music 3236, Item 786

925

Tol'able David

Tol'able David. Instrumentation: Piano conductor.

MOMA   111 p., 30 cm.
Music 3236, Item 74

King Vidor marking the script of *The Three Wise Fools* (1923) with his "tempo stamps." In certain scenes Vidor directed his actors and actresses to move in a strict tempo which was set by a metronome. Courtesy of Scott Simmon.

926
The Toll of the Sea

A Luz music score. Piano Leader. Technicolor presents *The Toll of the Sea* in perfect natural colors. *Distributed by:* Metro Pictures Corporation controlled by Loew's, Inc. *Music compiled by:* Ernst Luz. *Published by:* Photoplay Music Co., New York, 1923. *Instrumentation:* Piano. *Copyright:* © C1 E 553487, January 16, 1923.
LC M1527.L95T4   47 p., 30 cm.
Music 3212, Item 135

927
The Tongues of Men

Paramount Photoplay Music (P 126 M9) *The Tongues of Men. Produced by:* The Oliver Morosco Photoplay Co. *Music arranged by:* George W. Beynon. *Series title:* Schirmer's Photoplay Series. *Published by:* G. Schirmer, New York, 1916. *Instrumentation:* Piano conductor. *Copyright:* © C1 E 377025, January 5, 1916.
LC M1357.B   58 p., 31 cm.
Music 3212, Item 136

928
Too Much Money

Thematic music cue sheet. First National Pictures, Inc. presents *Too Much Money. Film company:* First National. *Music compiled by:* Eugene Conte, Musical Director, Plaza Theatre, New York. *Note:* Music incipits. "Wednesday Apr 21" marked in pencil.
MOMA   4 p., 32 cm.
Music 3236, Item 787

929
Too Much Money

Too Much Money. Note: Cue sheet. No music. Ms.
MOMA   2 p., 27 cm.
Music 3236, Item 788

930
Top Sergeant Mulligan

A Crescent Picture musical presentation *Top Sergeant Mulligan. Character of film:* War farce comedy. *Locales:* America and wartime France. *Music arranged by:* Gisdon True. *Note:* Cue sheet. No music.
MOMA   1 p., 25 cm. by 23 cm.
Music 3236, Item 789

931
The Tough Guy

Thematic music cue sheet. F. B. O. presents Fred Thomson with his famous horse Silver King in

The Tough Guy. Distributed by: Film Booking Offices of America, Inc. *Music compiled by:* James C. Bradford. *Note:* Music incipits. "Thurs & Friday 3/11–12" marked in pencil.

MOMA 4 p., 32 cm.
Music 3236, Item 790

932
Tracked

Musical synopsis for *Tracked. Music compiled by:* James C. Bradford. *Note:* Cue sheet. No music.

MOMA 1 p., 32 cm.
Music 3236, Item 791

933
Tracked by the Police

Warner Bros. present *Tracked by the Police* starring Rin-Tin-Tin. *Note:* Cue sheet. No music. "Monday May 16" marked in pencil. *Number of reels:* 6½. *Projection time:* 62 minutes based on a speed of 11 minutes per 1000 feet.

MOMA 1 p., 35 cm.
Music 3236, Item 792

934
The Traffic Cop

Thematic music cue sheet. Film Booking Offices presents Lefty Flynn in *The Traffic Cop. Produced and Directed by:* Harry Garson. *Distributed by:* Film Booking Offices of America, Inc. *Music compiled by:* James C. Bradford. *Note:* Music incipits. "Tuesday 3/9" marked in pencil.

MOMA 4 p., 32 cm.
Music 3236, Item 793

935
Tragedy of the Desert

Special piano music for *Tragedy of the Desert. Music by:* Walter C. Simon. *Published by:* Kalem Co., New York, 1912. *Instrumentation:* Piano. *Copyright:* © C1 E 288569, June 26, 1912. *Number of reels:* 2.

LC M176.T76 25 p., 32 cm.
Music 3212, Item 137

936
Trailing Trouble

Musical setting for Hoot Gibson in *Trailing Trouble* with Margaret Quimby. *Film company:* Universal Pictures Corp. *Music compiled by:* M. Winkler. *Note:* Cue sheet. No music.

MOMA 3 p., 28 cm.
Music 3236, Item 794

Erno Rapee (1891-1945), conductor of the Roxy Theater Symphony Orchestra (1926-31) and music director at Radio City Music Hall. His symphonic concerts were heard over the radio by millions of people as part of the "Roxy" hours. Music Division, Library of Congress.

937
Trent's Last Case

Thematic music cue sheet. William Fox Film Production *Trent's Last Case. Music compiled by:* Michael P. Krueger. *Note:* Music incipits.

MOMA 4 p., 32 cm.
Music 3236, Item 795

938
Le Tresor d'Arne

Le Tresor d'Arne. Music score by: Gaby Coutrot. *Note:* Cue sheet. No music.

MOMA 1 p., 31 cm. by 21 cm.
Music 3236, Item 796

939
Trail Marriage

Thematic music cue sheet. Columbia Pictures presents *Trail Marriage* with Norman Kerry, Sally Eilers and Jason Robards. *Directed by:* Erle C. Kenton. *Copyrighted and distributed by:* Columbia Pictures Corporation. *Music compiled by:* James C. Bradford. *Note:* Music incipits. "Thursday 4/11" marked in pencil.

MOMA 4 p., 32 cm.
Music 3236, Item 797

940
A Trick of Hearts

Thematic music cue sheet. Carl Laemmle presents *A Trick of Hearts. Production by:* Universal. *Music compiled by:* James C. Bradford. *Note:* Music incipits. "April-15-16" marked in pencil.

MOMA 2 p., 32 cm.
Music 3236, Item 798

941
Trifling Women

A Luz music score. Rex Ingram's *Trifling Women. Production by:* Metro controlled by Loew's, Inc. *Music compiled by:* Ernst Luz. *Published by:* Photoplay Music Co., New York, 1922. *Instrumentation:* Piano leader. *Copyright:* © C1 E 552098, November 17, 1922.

LC M1527.L95T6 99 p., 30 cm.
Music 3212, Item 138

942
Trigger Tricks

Musical setting for Hoot Gibson in *Trigger Tricks* with Sally Eilers. *Film company:* Universal Pictures Corp. *Music compiled by:* M. Winkler. *Note:* Cue sheet. No music.

MOMA 3 p., 28 cm.
Music 3236, Item 799

943
A Trip to Chinatown

Thematic music cue sheet. William Fox special production *A Trip to Chinatown. Music compiled by:* Michael P. Krueger. *Note:* Music incipits. "Thurs & Frid Sept 9-10" marked in pencil.

MOMA 4 p., 31 cm.
Music 3236, Item 800

944
Triple Action

Musical setting for *Triple Action. Music compiled by:* M. Winkler. *Note:* "Monday & Tues, Jun 11-12" marked in pencil. Cue sheet. No music.

MOMA 1 p., 30 cm.
Music 3236, Item 801

945
Tropical Nights

Thematic music cue sheet. Tiffany-Stahl presents *Tropical Nights,* suggested by the Jack London story *A Raid on the Oyster Pirates,* with Patsy Ruth Miller and Malcolm McGregor. *Production by:* Tiffany-Stahl. *Directed by:* Elmer Clifton. *Music compiled by:* James C. Bradford. *Note:* Music incipits.

MOMA 4 p., 32 cm.
Music 3236, Item 802

946
True Heaven

Thematic music cue sheet. William Fox feature film production. George O'Brien and Lois Moran in *True Heaven. Music compiled by:* Michael Krueger. *Note:* Music incipits.

MOMA 4 p., 31 cm.
Music 3236, Item 803

947
The Turmoil

Musical setting for *The Turmoil. Music compiled by:* M. Winkler. *Note:* Cue sheet. No music.

MOMA 1 p., 30 cm.
Music 3236, Item 804

948
Twin Flappers

Music cue sheet. *Twin Flappers. Music arranged by:* Saunders Kurtz. *Note:* No music. "Fri & Sat Nov 30-Dec 1" marked in pencil.

MOMA 1 p., 31 cm.
Music 3236, Item 805

949
Two Arabian Knights

Two Arabian Knights. Note: Cue sheet. No music.
Typescript.
MOMA   1 p., 28 cm.
                             Music 3236, Item 806

950
Two Arabian Knights

Thematic music cue sheet. Howard Hughes &
John W. Considine, Jr. present *Two Arabian
Knights* with William Boyd. *Story by:* Donald
McGibney. *Directed by:* Lewis Milestone. *Film
company:* United Artists. *Music compiled by:*
Ernst Luz. *Note:* Music incipits. "Thur–Fri Oct
11–12" marked in pencil. *Number of reels:* 9.
Footage: 7880. *Maximum projection time:* 1
hour, 32 minutes.
MOMA   6 p., 32 cm.
                             Music 3236, Item 807

951
Two Can Play

Thematic music cue sheet. Associated Exhibitors,
Inc. presents *Two Can Play* with Clara Bow. *From
the* Saturday Evening Post *story by:* Gerald
Mygatt. *Directed by:* Nat Ross. *Released by:* Asso-
ciated Exhibitors, Inc. *Music compiled by:* James
C. Bradford. *Note:* Music incipits. "Sunday June
20" marked in pencil.
MOMA   4 p., 32 cm.
                             Music 3236, Item 808

952
Two Days

Two Days. Note: Cue sheet. No music. Ms. Possibly incomplete.
MOMA   1 p., 24 cm.
                             Music 3236, Item 809

953
Two Fisted Jones

Musical setting for *Two Fisted Jones. Music
compiled by:* M. Winkler. *Note:* Cue sheet. No
music. "Mon & Tues Jan 18–19" marked in pencil.
MOMA   1 p., 30 cm.
                             Music 3236, Item 810

954
Two Sisters

A Rayart Picture. Musical setting for Viola Dana in
Two Sisters. Music arranged by: Joseph E. Zivelli.
Character of film: Drama. *Note:* Cue sheet. No
music. "Wed & Thur Feb 19–20" marked in pencil.
Scenes from the film on verso. *Number of reels:* 6.
MOMA   1 p., 32 cm.
                             Music 3236, Item 811

955
Uncle Tom's Cabin

Music score. Edison film *Uncle Tom's Cabin.
Published by:* The Museum of Modern Art Film
Library, New York. *Instrumentation:* Piano
conductor.
MOMA   31 p., 30 cm.
                              Music 3236, Item 75

956
Under a Flag of Truce

Special piano music for *Under a Flag of Truce.
Music by:* Walter C. Simon. *Published by:* Kalem
Co., New York, 1912. *Instrumentation:* Piano.
Copyright: © C1 E 284865, May 16, 1912.
LC M176.U55   11 p., 32 cm.
                             Music 3212, Item 139

957
Under Western Skies

Thematic music cue sheet. Carl Laemmle presents
Norman Kerry in *Under Western Skies. Written
and directed by:* Edward Sedgwick. *Film com-
pany:* Universal-Jewel. *Music compiled by:* James
C. Bradford. *Note:* Music incipits. "Tuesday &
Wednesday 3/16/17" marked in pencil.
MOMA   2 p., 37 cm.
                             Music 3236, Item 812

958
Undertow

Musical setting for Mary Nolan in *Undertow* with
John Mack Brown and Robert Ellis. *Film company:* Universal Pictures Corp. *Music compiled
by:* M. Winkler. *Note:* Cue sheet. No music. Two
copies.
MOMA   3 p., 28 cm.
                             Music 3236, Item 813

959
Underworld

Underworld. Instrumentation: Piano score.
MOMA   126 p., 31 cm.
                              Music 3236, Item 76

960
Undine
Musical setting to the Bluebird Photoplay No. 3 *Undine. Adapted and directed by:* Henry Otto from the story *De La Motte Fongue. Music arranged by:* M. Winkler. *Series title:* Carl Fischer Photo-Play Series. *Published by:* Carl Fischer, New York, 1916. *Instrumentation:* Piano conductor (1,1,2,1; 2,2,1,0; drums; strings). *Copyright:* © C1 E 377798, February 15, 1916.

LC M1357.W 63 p., 30 cm.

Music 3212, Item 140

961
Undressed
Sterling Productions, Inc. present Bryant Washburn, Hedda Hopper, David Torrence in *Undressed. Note:* Cue sheet. No music. Typescript (copy). "Norman R. McKeon" stamped in ink at bottom of page. *Projection time:* An hour at the speed of 10 minutes per reel.

MOMA 1 p., 28 cm.

Music 3236, Item 814

962
The Valley of Bravery
Musical synopsis for Bob Custer in *The Valley of Bravery. Music compiled by:* James C. Bradford. *Note:* Cue sheet. No music. "Wednesday July 14" marked in pencil.

MOMA 1 p., 30 cm.

Music 3236, Item 815

963
Vamping Venus
Thematic music cue sheet. Richard A. Rowland presents *Vamping Venus* with Charlie Murray supported by Louise Fazenda and Thelma Todd. *Film company:* First National. *Music compiled by:* James C. Bradford. *Note:* Music incipits.

MOMA 4 p., 31 cm.

Music 3236, Item 816

964
The Vanishing Pioneer
Thematic music cue sheet. Adolph Zukor and Jesse L. Lasky present Zane Grey's *The Vanishing Pioneer* with Jack Holt, William Powell and Fred Kohler. *From the novel by:* Zane Grey. *Adapted by:* John Goodrich and Ray Harris. *Screenplay by:* J. Walter Ruben. *Produced by:* B. P. Schulberg, Associate Producer. *Directed by:* John Waters. *Film company:* Paramount. *Note:* Music incipits. *Footage:* 5834.

MOMA 4 p., 32 cm.

Music 3236, Item 817

965
Vanity
Thematic music cue sheet. C. Gardner Sullivan presents Leatrice Joy in *Vanity* with Charles Ray and Alan Hale. *Adaptation and continuity by:* Douglas Doty. *Produced by:* DeMille Pictures Corporation. *Production by:* Donald Crist [sic]. *Released by:* Producers Distributing Corporation. *Music compiled by:* Rudolph Berliner. *Note:* Music incipits. "Thursday June 30/27" marked in pencil.

MOMA 4 p., 32 cm.

Music 3236, Item 818

966
Variety
Music *Variety. Published by:* Museum of Modern Art Film Library, New York. *Instrumentation:* Piano conductor.

MOMA 107 p., 31 cm.

Music 3236, Item 77

967
Varsity
Thematic music cue sheet. Adolph Zukor and Jesse L. Lasky present Charles (Buddy) Rogers in *Varsity* with Mary Brian and Chester Conklin. *Story by:* Wells Root. *Screenplay by:* Howard Estabrook. *Production by:* Frank Tuttle; West Coast Productions, B. P. Schulberg, General Manager. *Film company:* Paramount. *Music compiled by:* James C. Bradford. *Note:* Music incipits. *Footage:* 5802.

MOMA 4 p., 31 cm.

Music 3236, Item 819

968
Verdun
Verdun, Visions D'Histoire (Film de Léon Poirier). *Music by:* André Petiot. *Arrangement by:* A. Bernard. *Published by:* Editions Musicales Sam Fox, Paris, 1928. *Instrumentation:* Piano conductor; strings. *Copyright:* © E for. 4977, December 31, 1928.

LC M1357.P 170 p., 32 cm.

Music 3212, Item 141

969
The Virgin of Stamboul
Music score for *The Virgin of Stamboul,* Universal-Jewel $500,000 production de luxe starring Priscilla Dean. *Directed by:* Tod Browning. *Music by:* M. Winkler. *Published by:* Belwin, Inc.,

New York, 1920. *Instrumentation:* Piano score.
Copyright: © C1 E 473192, March 15, 1920.
LC M1527.W56V5   76 p., 30 cm.
Music 3212, Item 142

970
The Vision
The Vision. Note: Cue sheet. No music. Typescript.
MOMA   2 p., 28 cm.
Music 3236, Item 820

971
Visions d'Orient
Ciné Collection Sam-Fox *Visions d'Orient. Music
by:* Roger Guttinguer. *Orchestration by:* Ph.
Parès. *Published by:* Editions Musicales Sam Fox,
Paris, 1927. *Instrumentation:* Piano conductor
(2,1,2,1; 2,2,1,0; tympani, percussion; strings).
Copyright: © E 669385, July 25, 1927.
LC M1357.G   8 p., 27 cm.
Music 3212, Item 165

972
Volcano!
Thematic music cue sheet. Adolph Zukor and
Jesse L. Lasky present *Volcano!* with Bebe
Daniels, Ricardo Cortez and Wallace Beery. *From
the play* Martinique *by:* Laurence Eyre. *Screenplay by:* Bernard McConville. *Production by:* William Howard. *Film company:* Paramount. *Music
compiled by:* James C. Bradford. *Note:* Music
incipits. "Mon Tues & Wed Aug 16–17–18" marked
in pencil. *Footage:* 4770.
MOMA   2 p., 34 cm.
Music 3236, Item 821

973
The Wagon Show
Thematic music cue sheet. Ken Maynard in *The
Wagon Show. Film company:* First National.
Music compiled by: Eugene Conte. *Note:* Music
incipits. Two copies. "April–8–9" marked in pencil
on copy 1. "March–29–30–31" crossed out in
pencil.
MOMA   4 p., 32 cm.
Music 3236, Item 822

974
La Wally
La Wally, musical arrangement in 3 parts from
the opera. *Music by:* Alfredo Catalani. *Arrange-
ment by:* Pietro Sassoli. *Published by:* G. Ricordi
& Co., Milan, 1932. *Instrumentation:* Piano, vocal
score. *Copyright:* © Eu 52604, February 1, 1932.
LC M1527.C35W3   127 p., 27 cm.
Music 3212, Item 143

975
Wandering Footsteps
Banner Productions present Bryant Washburn,
Estelle Taylor and Alex Francis in *Wandering
Footsteps. Music compiled by:* Michael Hoffman.
Note: Cue sheet. No music. "Tuesday 3/2" marked
in pencil. Promotional material for the film on
verso.
MOMA   1 p., 31 cm.
Music 3236, Item 823

976
Warming Up
Thematic music cue sheet. Adolph Zukor and
Jesse L. Lasky present Richard Dix in *Warming
Up. Story by:* Sam Mintz. *Adaptation and
screenplay by:* Ray Harris. *Production by:* Fred
Newmeyer; B. P. Schulberg, Associate Producer.
Film company: Paramount. *Music compiled by:*
James C. Bradford. *Note:* Music incipits. Three
copies. "Fri & Sat Nov 30–Dec 1" marked in pencil
on copy 1.
MOMA   4 p., 31 cm.
Music 3236, Item 824

977
The Warning
Thematic music cue sheet. Columbia Pictures
presents Jack Holt in *The Warning* with Dorothy
Revier and Norman Trevor. *Production by:*
George B. Seitz. *Copyrighted and distributed by:*
Columbia Pictures Corporation. *Music compiled
by:* James C. Bradford. *Note:* Music incipits.
"Thurs Fri & Saturday 3/8-9-10/28" marked in
pencil.
MOMA   2 p., 31 cm.
Music 3236, Item 825

978
Watch Your Wife
Thematic music cue sheet. Carl Laemmle presents
Virginia Valli and Pat O'Malley in *Watch Your Wife*
by Goesta Segerkrants. *Directed by:* Svend Gade.
Film company: Universal-Jewel. *Music compiled
by:* Dr. Edward Kilenyi. *Note:* Music incipits. "Sat-
urday May 8" marked in pencil. Slightly mutilated.
MOMA   2 p., 38 cm.
Music 3236, Item 826

979
Water Hole
Water Hole. Note: Cue sheet. No music. Typescript
(carbon). Dated "Paramount, Sept. 1, 1928."
MOMA   1 p., 28 cm.
Music 3236, Item 827

980
Waterfront
Thematic music cue sheet. Richard A. Rowland presents *Waterfront* with Dorothy Mackaill and Jack Mulhall. *Production by:* William A. Seiter. *Produced by:* Ned Marin. *Film company:* First National. *Music compiled by:* James C. Bradford. *Note:* Music incipits.

MOMA 4 p., 32 cm.
 Music 3236, Item 828

981
Way Down East
D. W. Griffith, Inc., Albert Grey, General Manager, presents a magnificent elaboration of *Way Down East. Based on the famous stage play by:* Lottie Blair Parker. *Music by:* Wm. Frederick Peters. *Instrumentation:* Piano score. *Copyright:* © C1 E 693809, June 26, 1928, Julia Peters.

LC M1527.P55W2 2 vols., 77, 83 p., 30 cm.
 Music 3212, Item 144

982
Way Down East
D. W. Griffith, Inc., Albert Grey, General Manager, presents a magnificent elaboration of *Way Down East. Based on the famous stage play by:* Lottie Blair Parker. *Produced by:* D. W. Griffith. *Music composed and selected by:* Louis Silvers and Wm. F. Peters. *Instrumentation:* Piano conductor and orchestral parts (1,1,2,1; 2,2,1,1; tympani, drums; harps; strings). *Copyright:* © C1 E 693809, June 26, 1928, Julia Peters.

MOMA 2 vols., 78, 85 p., 31 cm.
 Music 3236, Item 78 and 78a

983
Way Down East
Way Down East. Note: Cue sheet. No music. Typescript (carbon). "Griffith" appears on page 1.

MOMA 4 p., 33 cm.
 Music 3236, Item 829

984
Way Down East
Way Down East. Note: Cue sheet. No music. Typescript (carbon). "Griffith" appears on page 1. "Made by E. Luz Orig" marked in ink on page 1. "(Changed)" marked in pencil on page 1.

MOMA 5 p., 33 cm.
 Music 3236, Item 830

985
We Americans
Greater thematic music cue sheet. Carl Laemmle presents *We Americans* with an all star cast. *Pro-*

duction by: Universal. *Music compiled by:* James C. Bradford. *Note:* Music incipits. "May 17 1928 May 18 1928 May 19 1928" stamped in ink.

MOMA 8 p., 31 cm.
 Music 3236, Item 831

986
We Moderns
Thematic music cue sheet. John McCormick presents Colleen Moore in *We Moderns. Film company:* First National. *Music compiled by:* Eugene Conte. *Note:* Music incipits. "Thursday & Friday 3/25–6" marked in pencil.

MOMA 4 p., 32 cm.
 Music 3236, Item 832

987
We Must Be Thrilled
We Must Be Thrilled. Note: Cue sheet. No music. Typescript (carbon). "Publix Theatres Corporation Inter-Office Communication" letterhead.

MOMA 2 p., 28 cm.
 Music 3236, Item 833

988
Der Weltkrieg
Der Weltkrieg (1. Abend: Des Volkes Heldengang), UFA-FILM von George Soldan und Erich Otto Volkmann. *Directed by:* Leo Lasko. *Music by:* Marc Roland. *Published by:* Marc Roland (Universum Film A.-G.), Berlin, 1928. Printed as manuscript, 1927. *Instrumentation:* Piano conductor. *Copyright:* © C1 E 685648, February 27, 1928, Marc Roland.

LC M1527.R63W3 125 p., 33 cm.
 Music 3212, Item 145

989
Der Weltkrieg
Der Weltkrieg (1. Abend: Des Volkes Heldengang). *Music by:* Marc Roland. *Published by:* Marc Roland, Berlin, 1928. *Instrumentation:* Orchestral parts (1,1,2,1; 2,2,1,0; percussion; organ; strings). *Copyright:* © C1 E 689771, April 23, 1928.

LC M1527.R63W3P 34 cm.
 Music 3212, Item 146

990
We're in the Navy Now
We're in the Navy Now. Note: Cue sheet. No music. Typescript (carbon).

MOMA 3 p., 28 cm.
 Music 3236, Item 834

991
Western Pluck

Musical setting for *Western Pluck*. *Music compiled by:* M. Winkler. *Note:* Cue sheet. No music. "Sat Jan 30" marked in pencil.

MOMA 1 p., 30 cm.

Music 3236, Item 835

992
What a Night!

Thematic music cue sheet. Adolph Zukor and Jesse L. Lasky present Bebe Daniels in *What a Night!* with Neil Hamilton and William Austin. *Story by:* Lloyd Corrigan and Grover Jones. *Screenplay by:* Louise Long. *Production by:* Edward Sutherland; West Coast Productions, B. P. Schulberg, General Manager. *Film company:* Paramount. *Music compiled by:* James C. Bradford. *Note:* Music incipits. *Footage:* 5738.

MOMA 4 p., 31 cm.

Music 3236, Item 836

993
What Every Girl Should Know

Warner Bros. present *What Every Girl Should Know* starring Patsy Ruth Miller. *Note:* Cue sheet. No music. Two copies. "Monday March 21/27" marked in pencil on copy 1. Both copies mutilated. *Projection time:* 1 hour, 6 minutes based on a speed of 11 minutes per 1000 feet.

MOMA 1 p., 35 cm.

Music 3236, Item 837

994
What Happened to Jones

Thematic music cue sheet. Carl Laemmle presents Reginald Denny in *What Happened to Jones* by George Broadhurst. *Directed by:* William Seiter. *Film company:* Universal-Jewel. *Music compiled by:* James C. Bradford. *Note:* Music incipits. "Monday & Tuesday June 21–22" marked in pencil.

MOMA 2 p., 38 cm.

Music 3236, Item 838

995
What Price Glory

What Price Glory. Note: Cue sheet. No music. Typescript. "The Museum of Modern Art Film Library" stamped in ink.

MOMA 4 p., 28 cm.

Music 3236, Item 839

996
What Price Glory

Thematic music cue sheet. William Fox special production *What Price Glory. Music compiled by:* Erno Rapee. *Note:* Music incipits. "Please return to Museum of Mod. Art/ 11 West 53 Str/ N. Y. C. 19, N. &." marked on page 1. Cue sheet is a photocopy.

MOMA 8 p., 33 cm.

Music 3236, Item 840

997
When Duty Calls

Musical synopsis for *When Duty Calls. Music by:* James C. Bradford. *Note:* Cue sheet. No music. Typescript (mimeograph).

MOMA 2 p., 28 cm.

Music 3236, Item 841

998
When Husbands Flirt

Thematic music cue sheet. Waldorf Pictures presents *When Husbands Flirt,* a sparkling drama of daring sweethearts and trusting wives, featuring Dorothy Revier and Forrest Stanley. *Produced by:* Harry Cohn. *Directed by:* William Wellman. *Copyrighted and distributed by:* Columbia Pictures Corporation. *Music compiled by:* James C. Bradford. *Note:* Cue sheet. Music incipits. "Sunday & Monday 3/28/29" marked in pencil.

MOMA 2 p., 32 cm.

Music 3236, Item 842

999
When the Clouds Roll By

Piano score for *When the Clouds Roll By. Published by:* The Museum of Modern Art Film Library, New York. *Instrumentation:* Piano score.

MOMA 120 p., 29 cm.

Music 3236, Item 79

1000
When the Devil Drives

Thematic music cue sheet. *When the Devil Drives* by and with Leah Baird. *Production by:* Leah Baird. *Distributed by:* Associated Exhibitors, Inc. through Pathe Exchange Inc. *Music compiled by:* James C. Bradford. *Note:* Music incipits.

MOMA 4 p., 32 cm.

Music 3236, Item 843

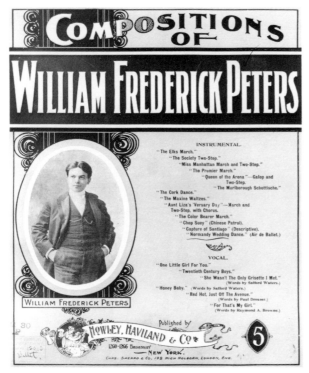

William Frederick Peters (1871-1938), American violinist and composer, studied at the Leipzig Conservatory before returning to the United States where he was the musical director for David Belasco, Mrs. Leslie Carter, and Maude Adams. He composed a number of film scores, most notably *When Knighthood Was in Flower* and D. W. Griffith's *Orphans of the Storm* and *Way Down East,* as well as thirteen operettas for radio. Music Division, Library of Congress.

1001
When We Were Kids

When We Were Kids. Note: Cue sheet. No music. Typescript (mimeograph).
MOMA   1 p., 28 cm.
Music 3236, Item 844

1002
Where the Pavement Ends

A Luz music score. Piano Leader. Rex Ingram Production *Where the Pavement Ends* featuring Alice Terry and Ramon Navarro. *Film company:* Metro, controlled by Loew's Inc. *Music compiled by:* Ernst Luz. *Published by:* Photoplay Music Co., Inc., New York, 1923. *Instrumentation:* Piano. *Copyright:* © C1 E 558614, March 15, 1923.
LC M1527.L95W4   63 p., 30 cm.
Music 3212, Item 147

1003
While London Sleeps

Warner Bros. present *While London Sleeps* starring Rin-Tin-Tin and Helene Costello. *Note:* Cue sheet. No music. Two copies. "Coming Thursday Dec 16" marked in pencil on copy 1. *Number of reels:* 6. *Projection time:* 1 hour, 3 minutes based on a speed of 11 minutes per 1000 feet.
MOMA   1 p., 35 cm.
Music 3236, Item 845

1004
The Whip

Thematic music cue sheet. Richard A. Rowland presents *The Whip* with Dorothy Mackaill. *Production by:* Charles J. Brabin. *Film company:* First National. *Music compiled by:* James C. Bradford. *Note:* Music incipits.
MOMA   4 p., 31 cm.
Music 3236, Item 846

1005
The Whip Woman

Thematic music cue sheet. Robert Kane presents Allan Dwan's Production *The Whip Woman* with Estelle Taylor, Antonio Moreno and Lowell Sherman. *Story by:* Forrest Halsey and Leland Hayward. *Directed by:* John C. Boyle. *Film company:* First National. *Music compiled by:* Eugene Conte. *Note:* Music incipits. "April–12–13–14" marked in pencil.
MOMA   4 p., 32 cm.
Music 3236, Item 847

1006
Whirlwind of Youth
Whirlwind of Youth. Note: Cue sheet. No music. Typescript (carbon). Typed on "Publix Theatres Corporation Inter-Office Communication" letterhead, dated "June 4th 27."
MOMA   2 p., 28 cm.
Music 3236, Item 848

1007
White Mice
Thematic music cue sheet. Associated Exhibitors, Inc. presents Jacqueline Logan in *White Mice. From the famous novel by:* Richard Harding Davis. *Produced by:* Wetherald for Pinellas Film, Inc. *Directed by:* Edward H. Griffith. *Released by:* Associated Exhibitors, Inc. *Music compiled by:* James C. Bradford. *Note:* Music incipits. "Wed July 7" marked in pencil.
MOMA   4 p., 32 cm.
Music 3236, Item 849

1008
The White Rose
D. W. Griffith presents *The White Rose. Music composed and adapted by:* Joseph Carl Breil, as conducted by Albert Pesce. *Published by:* D. W. Griffith, Inc., New York, 1923. *Instrumentation:* Piano conductor and instrumental parts (1,1,2,1; 2,2,1,0; drums; harp; celeste; strings).
MOMA   109 p., 31 cm.
Music 3236, Item 80

1009
The White Rose
D. W. Griffith presents *The White Rose. Music composed and adapted by:* Joseph Carl Breil, as conducted by Albert Pesce. *Published by:* D. W. Griffith, Inc., New York, 1923. *Instrumentation:* Piano conductor.
LC M1527.B73W4   109 p., 30 cm.
Music 3212, Item 148

1010
White Shadows in the South Seas
Thematic music cue sheet. *White Shadows in the South Seas* with Monte Blue and Raquel Torres. *Production by:* Cosmopolitan. *Directed by:* W. S. Van Dyke. *Film company:* Metro-Goldwyn-Mayer. *Music compiled by:* Ernst Luz. *Note:* Music incipits. *Number of reels:* 9. *Footage:* 7765. *Maximum projection time:* 1 hour, 30 minutes.
MOMA   6 p., 31 cm.
Music 3236, Item 850

1011
Whitewashed Walls
Musical setting for *Whitewashed Walls. Music by:* Joseph O'Sullivan, Director of Music Service. *Note:* Cue sheet. no music. "Monday Tuesday" marked in pencil. Various descriptions and promotional material for the film on verso. Slightly mutilated.
MOMA   1 p., 29 cm.
Music 3236, Item 851

1012
Who Am I
Piano or organ (conductor). *Who Am I. Production by:* Selznick. *Music by:* Dr. Hugo Reisenfeld [sic], Erno Rapee, Carl Edouarde, James C. Bradford, Joseph Carl Briel [sic]. Score No. 138. *Published by:* Synchronized Scenario Music Co., Chicago. *Instrumentation:* Piano conductor.
MOMA   52 p., 30 cm.
Music 3236, Item 81

1013
Why Girls Go Back Home
Warner Bros. present *Why Girls Go Back Home* starring Patsy Ruth Miller and Clive Brook. *Note:* Cue sheet. No music. "Thurs & Frid Sept 2-3" marked in pencil. *Projection time:* 62 minutes.
MOMA   1 p., 35 cm.
Music 3236, Item 852

1014
Why Sailors Go Wrong
Thematic music cue sheet. William Fox special film production. Sammy Cohen, Ted McNamara, Sally Phipps and Nick Stuart in *Why Sailors Go Wrong. Music compiled by:* Michael P. Krueger. *Note:* Music incipits. "May-10-11-12" marked in pencil.
MOMA   4 p., 32 cm.
Music 3236, Item 853

1015
Why Women Love
Thematic music cue sheet. Edwin Carewe presents *Why Women Love. Film company:* First National. *Music compiled by:* James C. Bradford. *Note:* Music incipits. "Wednesday 3/31" marked in pencil.
MOMA   4 p., 31 cm.
Music 3236, Item 854

1016
Wickedness Preferred
Thematic music cue sheet. Lew Cody and Aileen Pringle in *Wickedness Preferred*. *Screenplay by:* Florence Ryerson and Colin Clements. *Production by:* Hobart Henley. *Film company:* Metro-Goldwyn-Mayer. *Music compiled by:* Ernst Luz. *Note:* Music incipits. *Number of reels:* 6. *Footage:* 4965. *Maximum projection time:* 1 hour.
MOMA   2 p., 31 cm.
                                          Music 3236, Item 855

1017
Wife Savers
Thematic music cue sheet. Adolph Zuker [sic] and Jesse L. Lasky present Wallace Beery and Raymond Hatton in *Wife Savers* with ZaSu [sic] Pitts and Ford Sterling. *Produced by:* B. P. Schulberg, Associate Producer. *Directed by:* Ralph Cedar. *Film company:* Paramount. *Music compiled by:* James C. Bradford. *Note:* Music incipits. "Thur Mar. 22" marked in pencil. *Footage:* 5434.
MOMA   4 p., 31 cm.
                                          Music 3236, Item 856

1018
Wild & Woolly
Piano score for *Wild & Woolly*. *Published by:* The Museum of Modern Art Film Library, New York. *Instrumentation:* Piano score.
MOMA   86 p., 29 cm.
                                          Music 3236, Item 82

1019
Wild Beauty
Thematic music cue sheet. Carl Laemmle presents *Wild Beauty*. *Film company:* Universal-Jewel. *Music compiled by:* James C. Bradford. *Note:* Music incipits. "Feb 10 & 11" marked in pencil.
MOMA   2 p., 33 cm.
                                          Music 3236, Item 857

1020
The Wild Girl of the Sierras
The Wild Girl of the Sierras (Mae Marsh, Rob. Harron), 1916. *Note:* Cue sheet. No music. Ms.
MOMA   2 p., 28 cm.
                                          Music 3236, Item 858

1021
The Wild West Show
Thematic music cue sheet. Carl Laemmle presents *The Wild West Show*. *Film company:* Universal-Jewel. *Music compiled by:* James C. Bradford. *Note:* Music incipits.
MOMA   2 p., 32 cm.
                                          Music 3236, Item 859

1022
Win That Girl
Thematic music cue sheet. William Fox feature film production. David Rollins and Sue Carol in *Win That Girl*. *Music compiled by:* Michael P. Krueger. *Note:* Music incipits.
MOMA   2 p., 32 cm.
                                          Music 3236, Item 860

1023
The Wind
The Wind. *Instrumentation:* Piano score.
MOMA   123 p., 31 cm.
                                          Music 3236, Item 83

1024
Winds of Chance
Thematic music cue sheet. Frank Lloyd presents *Winds of Chance* by Rex Beach. *Film company:* First National. *Music compiled by:* Eugene Conte. *Note:* Music incipits. "Tues Dec 16" marked in pencil.
MOMA   6 p., 30 cm.
                                          Music 3236, Item 861

1025
The Winged Idol
Musical setting for the photoplay *The Winged Idol*. *Production by:* Thomas H. Ince. *Music composed and arranged by:* Joseph E. Nurnberger, Victor Schertzinger and Wedgewood Nowell. *Series title:* Triangle Plays. *Published by:* G. Schirmer for the Triangle Film Corp., 1915. *Instrumentation:* Piano conductor (1,0,2,0; 0,2,1,0; drums; strings). *Copyright:* © C1 E 373894, October 26, 1915.
LC M1357.N   46 p., 30 cm.
                                          Music 3212, Item 149

1026
Wings
Wings. *Film company:* Paramount. *Music composed by:* J. S. Zamecnik. *Published by:* Paramount Famous Lasky Corp. (under the supervision of Sam Fox Pub. Co.), New York, 1927.

Instrumentation: Piano conductor. *Copyright:* ©
C1 E 679249, December 8, 1927; R 140301,
December 10, 1954.
LC M1527.Z24   246 p., 30 cm.
                          Music 3212, Item 150

1027
The Wise Guy

Thematic music cue sheet. Frank Lloyd presents
The Wise Guy. Film company: First National.
Music compiled by: James C. Bradford. *Note:*
Music incipits. "Thurs & Frid Sept. 2–3" marked
in pencil.
MOMA   4 p., 32 cm.
                          Music 3236, Item 862

1028
The Wise Wife

Thematic music cue sheet. William C. DeMille
presents *The Wise Wife* with Phyllis Haver. *Produced by:* DeMille Pictures Corporation. *Directed
by:* E. Mason Hopper. *Distributed by:* Pathe
Exchange, Inc. *Music compiled by:* Rudolph Berliner. *Note:* Music incipits. Three copies. "Sunday
4/21" marked in pencil on copy 1. "Monday Dec
19/27" marked in pencil on copy 2.
MOMA   4 p., 32 cm.
                          Music 3236, Item 863

1029
Without Mercy

Thematic music cue sheet. Metropolitan Pictures,
Inc. presents a George Melford Production *With-
out Mercy* by John Goodwin with Vera Reynolds,
Dorothy Phillips and Rockcliffe Fellowes.
Released by: Producers Distributing Corporation.
Music compiled by: James C. Bradford. *Note:*
Music incipits. "Wed 4/27" marked in pencil.
MOMA   2 p., 34 cm.
                          Music 3236, Item 864

1030
The Wizard

Thematic music cue sheet. William Fox film production. Edmund Lowe in *The Wizard. Music
compiled by:* Michael P. Krueger. *Note:* Music
incipits.
MOMA   4 p., 31 cm.
                          Music 3236, Item 865

Lillian Gish on the cover of "Love Brought the Sunshine," the theme song by William Axt and David
Mendoza for *The Wind* (1927). Music Division, Library
of Congress.

Charles (Buddy) Rogers in *Wings* (1927), musical
score by J. S. Zamecnik. Museum of Modern Art, Film
Stills Archive.

1031
The Woman Hater
Thematic music cue sheet. Warner Bros. classics of the screen *The Woman Hater* by Ruby M. Ayres. *Scenario by:* Hope Loring and Louis Lighton. *Directed by:* James Flood. *Music compiled by:* James C. Bradford. *Note:* Music incipits. "12/20–21" marked in pencil. Cue sheet was prepared on May 16, 1925.

MOMA   4 p., 31 cm.
Music 3236, Item 866

1031A
Woman of Paris
Music Score for *A Woman of Paris. Music Revised by:* Frederick Stahlberg. *Instrumentation:* Piano conductor score. *Note:* This is a photocopy of a printed score.

MOMA   94 p., 28 cm.
No microfilm

1032
The Woman Tempted
Musical setting for *The Woman Tempted. Note:* Cue sheet. No music.

MOMA   1 p., 30 cm.
Music 3236, Item 867

1033
Woman Wise
Thematic music cue sheet. William Fox superlative special production *Woman Wise. Music compiled by:* Michael P. Krueger. *Note:* Music incipits.

MOMA   4 p., 32 cm.
Music 3236, Item 868

1034
A Woman's Way
Thematic music cue sheet. Columbia Pictures presents *A Woman's Way* with Warner Baxter and Margaret Livingston and Armand Kaliz. *Directed by:* Edmund Mortimer. *Copyrighted and distributed by:* Columbia Pictures Corporation. *Music compiled by:* James C. Bradford. *Note:* Music incipits.

MOMA   2 p., 32 cm.
Music 3236, Item 869

1035
Women They Talk About
Warner Bros. present *Women They Talk About* starring Wm. Collier, Jr., Irene Rich, John Miljan. *Note:* Cue sheet. No music. *Projection time:* About 1 hour based on a speed of 11 minutes per 1000 feet. "58 1/2 min." marked in ink.

MOMA   1 p., 35 cm.
Music 3236, Item 870

1036
Women Who Dare
Thematic music cue sheet. Samuel Zierler presents Helene Chadwick, Charles Delaney and Jack Richardson in *Women Who Dare,* a drama of an heiress who flaunted society. *Produced and distributed by:* Excellent Pictures Corporation. *Music compiled by:* James C. Bradford. *Note:* Music incipits. "May–10–11–12" marked in pencil.

MOMA   2 p., 31 cm.
Music 3236, Item 871

1037
The Wood Nymph
Musical setting for the photoplay *The Wood Nymph* (P. 43). *Production by:* Fine-Arts Feature Co. *Music selected and arranged by:* Joseph Carl Breil. *Series title:* Triangle Plays. *Published by:* G. Schirmer for the Triangle Film Corp., New York, 1916. *Instrumentation:* Piano conductor. *Copyright:* © C1 E 377022, January 4, 1916.

LC M1357.B   69 p., 30 cm.
Music 3212, Item 151

1038
The Wreck of the Hesperus
Thematic music cue sheet. *The Wreck of the Hesperus* with Virginia Bradford, Frank Marion, Alan Hale and Sam DeGrasse. *Produced by:* DeMille Pictures Corporation. *Directed by:* Elmer Clifton. *Distributed by:* Pathe Exchange, Inc. *Music compiled by:* Rudolph Berliner. *Note:* Music incipits. Two copies. "Thursday Jan 5/28" marked in pencil on copy 1.

MOMA   4 p., 31 cm.
Music 3236, Item 872

1039
The Wright Idea
Thematic music cue sheet. C. C. Burr presents Johnny Hines in *The Wright Idea. Story by:* Jack Townley. *Directed by:* Charles Hines. *Film company:* First National. *Music compiled by:* James C. Bradford. *Note:* Music incipits. Two copies. "Mon & Tues Nov 5 & 6" marked in pencil on copy 1.

MOMA   4 p., 32 cm.
Music 3236, Item 873

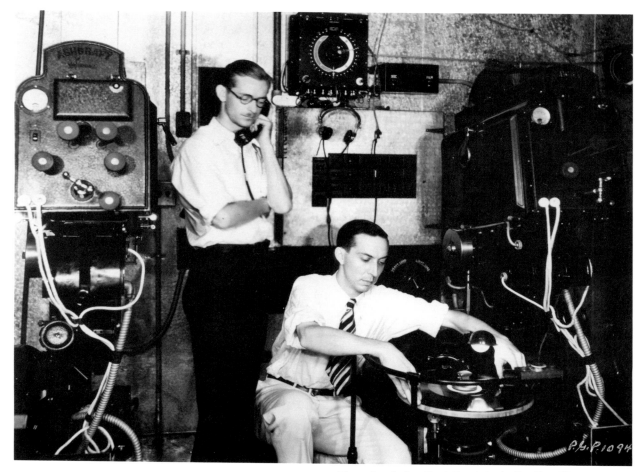

Megaphonic booth at the Astoria Studios. First synchronized recordings, which proved unmanageable, and then sound on film terminated the careers of many silent film accompanists. Courtesy of the Astoria Motion Picture and Television Center Foundation, Astoria, New York.

1040
The Wrong Door

Musical setting to the Bluebird Photo-Play No. 5. Carter De Haven and Flora Parker De Haven in *The Wrong Door. Music selected and arranged by:* M. Winkler. *Series title:* Carl Fischer Photo-Play Series. *Published by:* Carl Fischer, New York 1916. *Instrumentation:* Piano; (1,1,2,1; 2,2,1,0; drums; strings). *Copyright:* © C1 E 379012, March 8, 1916.

LC M1527.W56W8 (Second copy M1357.W)

56 p., 30 cm.

Music 3212, Item 152

1041
The Yankee Girl

Paramount Photoplay Music P 121 M7. Musical setting to the photoplay dramatization of *The Yankee Girl. Produced by:* The Oliver Morosco Photoplay Co. *Music selected and arranged by:* George W. Beynon. *Series title:* Schirmer's Photo-play Series. *Published by:* G. Schirmer, New York, 1915. *Instrumentation:* Piano conductor (1,0,1,0; 0,2,2,0; drums; strings). *Copyright:* © C1 E 373196, October 19, 1915.

LC M1357.B

69 p., 31 cm.

Music 3212, Item 153

1042
The Yaqui

Musical setting to the Bluebird Photo-Play No. 9. Hobart Bosworth in *The Yaqui. Music selected and arranged by:* M. Winkler. *Series title:* Carl Fischer, New York, 1916. *Instrumentation:* Piano or organ; (1,1,2,1; 2,2,1,0; drums; strings—cello missing). *Copyright:* © C1 E 379350, March 21, 1916.

LC M1357.W

44 p., 31 cm.

Music 3212, Item 154

1043
Yellow Fingers

Thematic music cue sheet. William Fox special production *Yellow Fingers. Music compiled by:* Michael P. Krueger. *Note:* Music incipits. "Mon & Tuesday June 21–22" marked in pencil.

MOMA

2 p., 37 cm.

Music 3236, Item 874

1044
The Yellow Lily

Thematic music cue sheet. Richard A. Rowland presents Billie Dove in *The Yellow Lily* with Clive Brook. *Directed by:* Alexander Korda. *Film company:* First National. *Music compiled by:* Eugene Conte. *Note:* Music incipits. Three copies.

MOMA

4 p., 31 cm.

Music 3236, Item 875

1045
Yolanda

Music score *Yolanda. Music by:* Wm. Frederick Peters. *Published by:* Wm. Frederick Peters, 1924. *Instrumentation:* Piano score.

LC M1527.P55Y6

128 p., 31 cm.

Music 3212, Item 155

1046
Yolando [sic]

1st Violin, 2d stand. A Cosmopolitan Production Photoplay *Yolando* [sic]. *Music by:* William Frederick Peters. *Instrumentation:* Violin. *Copyright:* © C1 E 695552, July 7, 1928, Julia Peters, Englewood, N.J.

LC M1527.P55Y

126 p., 35 cm. Ms.

Music 3212, Item 166

1047
Young Desire

Musical setting for Mary Nolan in *Young Desire* with William Janney and Mae Busch. *Film company:* Universal Pictures Corp. *Music compiled by:* M. Winkler. *Note:* Cue sheet. No music.

MOMA

3 p., 28 cm.

Music 3236, Item 876

Appendix 1
Microfilm Contents and Reel Numbers
Library of Congress Collection

Motion Picture Music/Silent Films
Library of Congress Collection
Microfilm, Music 3212

REEL	ITEM	TITLE	EXPOSURES	REEL	ITEM	TITLE	EXPOSURES
1	0	Abie's Irish Rose	17		36	Dan	11
	1	Ach wie ist's möglich dann	55		37	D'Artagnan	37
	2	Aloha Oe	53				
	3	Alt-Heidelberg	61	5	38	A Daughter of the Gods	116
	4	America	38		39	A Daughter of the Gods	110
	5	Antony and Cleopatra	28		40	The Despoilers	45
	6	An Arabian Tragedy	12		41	Don Juan	359
	7	As We Forgive	24		42	Double Trouble	262
	8	The Barrier	63				
	9	The Battle Cry of Peace	65	6	43	Drake's Love Story	20
	10	The Battle Cry of Peace	375		44	The Drummer Girl of Vicksburg	12
2	11	Beau Geste	483		45	The Edge of the Abyss	47
	12	Beau Geste	25		46	L'Empreinte	30
	13	Beau Geste	38		47	Fabiola	431
					48	Fighting Dan McCool	11
3	14	Beau Geste	30		49	The Fighting Dervishes of the Desert	12
	15	The Beckoning Flame	26				
	16	Betrayal	25	7	50	The Flirt	279
	17	Between Men	33		51	The Flying Torpedo	32
	18	Bismarck	42		52	Foolish Wives	43
	19	The Black Crook	26		53	Four Feathers	23
	20	La Briere	259		54	The Gay Lord Waring	256
	21	The Bugler of Battery B & Hungry Hanks Hallucination	14	8	55	The Gentleman from Indiana	246
	22	Captured by Bedouins	14		56	Germania	307
	23	Carmen	248		57	Germania	94
					58	Gloria's Romance	97
4	24	La Chaîne d'Amour	36				
	25	The Chaplin Revue	78	9	59	The Golden Claw	170
	26	City Lights—Les Lumières de la Ville	69		60	The Great Love	50
	27	Civilization	62		61	The Great Problem	268
	28	Comtesse Ursel	34		62	The Green Swamp	36
	29	The Confederate Ironclad	16		63	The Grip of Jealousy	213
	30	The Conqueror	27				
	31	The Corner	32	10	64	Hearts Aflame	56
	32	The Crippled Hand	253		65	Hearts of the World	662
	33	The Crisis	27				
	34	Cross Currents	38	11	66	Honor's Altar	29
	35	The Crown of Lies	7		67	Hop, the Devil's Brew	248

REEL	ITEM	TITLE	EXPOSURES	REEL	ITEM	TITLE	EXPOSURES
	68	Im Kientopp	11		114	The Right to Happiness	47
	69	In Mizzoura	14		115	La Ronde de Nuit	95
	70	Intolerance	36		116	Rupert of Hentzau	255
	71	Iris	287	18	117	Sable Lorcha	224
	72	Jane	48		118	Samson	31
12	73	Janice Meredith	102		119	The Scarecrow	66
	74	Jeanne Dore	239		120	The Scarecrow	29
	75	Joan the Woman	164		121	Schuldig	36
	76	John Needham's Double	218		122	Le Secret de Myrto	26
13	77	Jordan Is a Hard Road	216		123	Secret Love	259
	78	Le Joueur d'Echecs	97		124	Seventh Heaven	53
	79	The Jungle	11	19	125	Shéhérazade	244
	80	Let Katie Do It	55		126	The Siege of Petersburg	19
	81	The Lily and the Rose	252		127	The Soldier Brothers of Susanna	14
	82	Little Old New York	77		128	Soldiers of Fortune	14
14	83	Madame Récamier	124		129	The Spanish Revolt of 1836	12
	84	The Man Nobody Knows	36		130	A Spartan Mother	12
	85	Manon	241		131	The Storm at Sea	19
	86	Martin Luther	41		132	The Strength of the Weak	210
	87	The Martyrs of the Alamo	271		133	Tangled Hearts	240
15	88	Matrimony	226	20	134	The Thief of Bagdad	552
	89	Mawas	33		135	The Toll of the Sea	34
	90	Messaline	45		136	The Tongues of Men	38
	91	Le Miracle des Loups	89		137	Tragedy of the Desert	20
	92	The Missing Links	34		138	Trifling Women	58
	93	Modern Times	176		139	Under a Flag of Truce	10
	94	The Old Nest	85	21	140	Undine	260
	95	One Exciting Night	89		141	Verdum	272
16	96	Paid in Full	16		142	The Virgin of Stamboul	47
	97	La Passion de Jeanne d'Arc	110		143	La Wally	74
	98	The Patriot	98		144	Way Down East	81
	99	Peer Gynt	200	22	145	Der Weltkrieg	79
	100	Peg o' My Heart	54		146	Der Weltkrieg	424
	101	Los Penitentes	57		147	Where the Pavement Ends	42
	102	Pierre of the Plains	13		148	The White Rose	64
	103	Potemkin	231	23	149	The Winged Idol	193
17	103a	Potemkin	60		150	Wings	135
	104	The Prince of Power	41		151	The Wood Nymph	43
	105	The Princess of the Dark	44		152	The Wrong Door	250
	106	A Prisoner of the Harem & Egyptian Sports	14		153	The Yankee Girl	199
	107	Quincy Adams Sawyer	59	24	154	The Yaqui	232
	108	Ramona	21		155	Yolanda	72
	109	Redskin	20		156	Baree, Son of Kazan	28
	110	The Reform Candidate	39		157	Cain	56
	111	Le Retour d'Ulysse	17		158	Carmen	170
	112	Rhapsodie Hongroise	86				
	113	Richard Wagner	64				

REEL	ITEM	TITLE	EXPOSURES	REEL	ITEM	TITLE	EXPOSURES
25	159	Deliverance	290	26	163	Old Ironsides	541
	160	Le Donne di Buon Umore	45		164	Orphans of the Storm	46
	161	The Ten Commandments	24		165	Visions d'Orient	29
	162	Enemies of Women	50		166	Yolando [sic]	67

Appendix 2
Microfilm Contents and Reel Numbers
Museum of Modern Art Collection

Motion Picture Music/Silent Films
Museum of Modern Art Collection
Microfilm, Music 3236

REEL	ITEM	TITLE	EXPOSURES	REEL	ITEM	TITLE	EXPOSURES
1	1	America	518	8	34	Die Geschichte des Prinzen Achmed	614
	2	Arsenal	36				
	3	Ben Hur	47	9	35	Great Actresses of the Past	42
	4	The Big Parade	45		36	The Greatest Question	208
					37	Greed	87
2	5	The Birth of a Nation	310		38	Hamlet	40
	6	The Birth of a Nation	222		39	Hearts of the World	72
	7	The Birth of a Nation	190		40	His Bitter Pill	31
					41	Hotel Imperial	14
3	8	The Birth of a Nation	107				
	9	The Black Pirate	536	10	42	Intolerance	435
4	10	Broken Bossoms	336	11	42a	Intolerance	134
	11	By the Law	55		43	Isn't Life Wonderful	395
	12	The Cabinet of Dr. Caligari	78		44	The Italian Straw Hat	81
	13	Chess Fever	26		45	Juve vs. Fantomas	47
	14	The Clever Dummy	28		46	Kino-Pravda	29
	15	The Cloak	36		47	The Last Card	22
	16	The Covered Wagon	75		48	The Last Command	88
	17	The Crazy Ray	52				
	18	The Doctor's Secret	14	12	49	The Last Laugh	93
					50	The Love Flower	305
5	19	Don Q, Son of Zorro	377		51	The Love of Jeanne Ney	114
					52	Lumiere Films	19
6	20	Dream Street	573		53	Mark of Zorro	80
	21	Dream Street	65		54	Méliès Program	47
	22	Enoch Arden	23		55	Menilmontant	30
	23	The Execution of Mary Queen of Scots	65		56	Metropolis	110
	24	The Fall of the House of Usher	49	13	57	Monsieur Beaucaire	88
					58	Moscow Clad in Snow	24
	25	Father Sergius	75		59	Mother	70
					60	The Mother and the Law	32
7	26	A Fool There Was	68		61	The Mother and the Law	354
	27	The Four Horsemen of the Apocalypse	82	14	62	One Exciting Night	591
	28	Fragment of an Empire	67				
	29	The Freshman	70	15	63	Orphans of the Storm	506
	30	The Fugitive	24		64	The Passion of Joan of Arc	40
	31	The General	56				
	32	German Short Films	58	16	65	Plane Crazy	21
	33	Gertie the Dinosaur	13				

REEL	ITEM	TITLE	EXPOSURES	REEL	ITEM	TITLE	EXPOSURES
	66	Potemkin	55	20	81	Who Am I	34
	67	Robin Hood	269		82	Wild and Woolly	49
	68	A Romance of Happy Valley	234		83	The Wind	68
	69	Smiling Madame Beaudet	36		84	The Iron Mask	269
					85	Der Lebende Leichnam	181
17	70	Tatters	398		86–111	Across to Singapore–The Awakening*	
	71	Thief of Bagdad	398				
	72	Three Musketeers	376	21	112–226	The Baby Cyclone–Compromise	
18	73	Three Musketeers	98	22	227–371	Confessions of a Wife–Gypsy of the North	
	74	Tol'able David	62				
	75	Uncle Tom's Cabin	22	23	372–509	Half a Bride–Midnight Mystery	
	76	Underworld	70				
	77	Variety	61	24	510–656	Midnight Mystery–The Secret Spring	
	78	Way Down East	355				
				25	657–811	See You in Jail–Two Sisters	
19	78a	Way Down East	321				
	79	When the Clouds Roll By	65	26	812–876	Under Western Skies–Young Desire	
	80	The White Rose	453				

*Items 86–876 are thematic music cue sheets arranged alphabetically by title. Most are two to four pages long.

Appendix 3
Film Scores in the Arthur Kleiner Collection University of Minnesota, Austrian Institute

orig. = original score
A. K. = Arthur Kleiner score
[   ] = no longer located

America (orig. Breil and Adolph Fink)
Anemic Cinema
Animated Cartoons
Are Parents People
Arsenal (orig. Ivan Belza)
Asphalt
L'Assassinat du Duc De Guise (orig. orch. and piano)
At the Crossroad of Life
Awful Symphonie

[Ballet mechanique (piano rolls)]
[Balloonatics]
Barney Oilfields Race
The Battle
The Battle of Elderbush
Beau Brumel
Beau Geste (orig.)
Bed and Sopha
Beloved Rogue
[Ben Hur (orig. D. Menoza and W. Axt)]
Berlin (A. K.)
Berlin (orig.)
Between Men
Big Business [A. K.]
[Big Parade (orig. Menoza and Axt)]
Birth of a Nation (orig. Breil)
Black Pirate (orig. Mortimer Wilson)
Le Bled
Blind Husbands
Blood and Sand
Blue Bottles
Blue Light
The Bond
Breakers
The Bride of Glomdale
The Bridge
Bro Lopet Pa (1909)

[Broken Blossoms (orig. Louis F. Gottschalk)]
By the Law

Cabinet of Dr. Caligari (orig.)
Cabiria
Caligiostra
The Cameramen
The Canadian
Chang
The Cheat
Chess Fever
Chien Andalou
Civilization
The Clever Dummy
The Cloak
College
Conquering Power
Cops
Corner in Wheat
Covered Wagon (orig. Riesenfeld)
The Coward
Cowboy Ambrose
Cradle of Courage
Crazy Ray (orig.)

Dance Program
Dancing Fool
Dancing Mothers
Dawn
Deadly 6 (Perils of Pauline)
Dear Old Daddy-Long-Legs
Destiny
Den deutschen Volke
Les deux timid = Unde two timid
Diary of a Lost Girl
Dirnen tragoedie
La dixiéme Symphonie
Docks of N.Y.
Dr. Jeckel and Mr. Hyde
Dr. Mabuse
Dogs Life
Don Q (orig.)

Don't Park Here
Double Whoopee
Doubling for Romeo
A Dozen Fresh Eggs
Dream Street (orig. Louis Silvers)
A Drop of Water
Drums of Love

Earth
Easy Street
Eldorado
En Rade
End of St. Petersburg
Entr'acte
Erotikon
Etoile de Mer
Exit Smiling
Extraordinary Adventures of Mr. West

Fall of Babylon
Fall of the House of Usher
Fall of the Romanov Dynasty
Fanrik Stal Sagner (1909 Swedish)
Fantomas (see Juve vs. Fantomas)
Farmers Wife
Father Sergius
[Faust]
Feud in the Kentucky Hills
Fievre
Fille de L'eau
Fireproof
First Films (Lumiere, etc.)
Flesh and Devil
A Fool There Was (orig.)
Foolish Wives
Forgotten Faces
Forward Soviet
Four Horsemen of the Apocalypse (orig.)
Fragment of an Empire

Freshman (old score)
From Soup to Nuts
Fugitive (old score)

The Gangsters and the Girl
Gaucho
General (old score)
German Short Films:
    Skladanowsky, Primitive
    German films by
    Skladanowsky; Don Juans
    Wedding; Misunderstood (with
    Henry Porten); Sequence from
    Golem
Gertie the Dinosaur
[Geschichte des Prinzen Achmed
    (orig. Wolfgang Zeller)]
Ghost That Never Returns
[The Goat]
Goose Woman
Grandma's Boy
Great Actresses: Cenere, Dure,
    Bernard, etc.
Great Train Robbery
Greatest Question (D. W. Griffith
    orig.)
Greed (orig.)
Gypsy Blood

H2O
[Hamlet (A. Nilsen last three
    reels)]
Handpainted Films (Méliès)
Hands Up
He Who Gets Slapped
The Heart of an Indian
Hearts of the World (orig. Carli
    Densmore Elinor; D. W.
    Griffith)
Hell's Hinges (W. S. Hart)
Hiawatha
High and Dizzy
His Bitter Pill
His Day Out
Home Sweet Home (D. W. Griffith)
Hotel Imperial (first reels)
The House on Trubnaya Squre

Im Anfang War das Wort
In Spring (Russian 1929)
[In the Street (arr. Denyse
    Dixmier)]
In the Street (Helen Levitt film,
    Kleiner score)
The Informer (D. W. Griffith)

Ingeborg Holm
Ins Dritte Reich
Intolerance (orig. Breil)
Iron Horse (orig. Erno Rapee)
Isn't Life Wonderful (orig. Cesare
    Sodero and Louis Silvers)
It
Italian Straw Hat (orig.)
It's the Old Army Game

J'Acuse
Joyless Street
Judith of Bethulia
Juve vs. Fantomas

Keaton Shorts
The Kid
[King of Kings (orig. Riesenfeld)]
Kino Eye (1924)
Kino Pravda (Kombrig Ivanov:
    Rebellion in Odessa)
Kiss for Cinderella

Lady of the Pavement
Lady Windermere's Fan
L'Argent (A. K.)
Last Card
Last Command (orig.)
Last Laugh (orig.)
Late Mathew Pascal (A. K.)
Leaves from Satan's Book (A. K.)
Leonce a la Campagne
Liberty (A. K.)
Life and Death of a Hollywood
    Extra (A. K.)
Life of an American Fireman (A. K.)
Lilac Time (A. K.)
Little Lord Fauntleroy
Lohnbuchhalter Kremke
Lonedale Operator
Long Pants (A. K.)
Love Everlasting
Love Everlasting (A. K.)
Love Flower (orig.)
Love of Jeanne Ney (old score)
Loves of Sunya (A. K.)
Lubitsch Pictures: Madame
    Dubarry (1919) and Die Augen
    der Mumie Ma (1918) and Die
    Bergkaetze (1921)
Lumiere to Langlois See From
    Lumiere to Langlois

Male and Female (A. K.)
Manhandled
Mantel [sic] of Protection (A. K.)
Mantrap (A. K.)
Manxman (A. K.)
Mark of Zorro (old score)
Marriage Circle (A. K.)
Master of the House (Seastroem)
    (A. K.)
Max Linder (shorts, A. K.)
Méliès Program (Trip to the Moon,
    etc.)
Men of Varmland (A. K.)
Men Without Women
Menilmontant (old score)
Menschen am Sonntag (A. K.)
Merry Frolics of Satan (A. K.)
Merry Go Round (A. K.)
[Merry Widow (after Lehar)]
Metropolis
Metropolis (A. K.)
Mickey (A. K.)
Mikael (A. K.)
Miss Lulu Bett (A. K.)
Moana (old score)
[Moment Musicale (Gelser) (A. K.)]
Monsieur Beaucare (old score)
Moscow Clad in Snow, Revenge of
    the Kinematograph
    Cameraman
Mother (A. K.)
Mother and the Law (orig.)
My Best Girl (A. K.)
[My Wife's Relations (A. K.)]
Le Mystéres du Chateau du Dé
Mysterious Island (A. K.)

Nana (A. K.)
Nanook of the North
Napoleon (14 reels)
[Napoleon (24 reels)]
Napoleon (new version Brownlow)
Narrow Trail (A. K.)
Navigator
Never Again (A. K.)
New Babylon (orig. shorts)
New Gentlemen (A. K.)
New York Hat (old score)
Nosferato (A. K.)
Nyu (A. K.)

Officer 444 (A. K.)
Olaf Alom [Olaf; an atom?; Olaf
    alone?]
Old and New (A. K.)
Once Upon a Time (A. K.)

One A.M. (A. K.)
One Exciting Night (orig. Albert Pesce)
Opus 1 (Lichtspiel oft. von Walter Ruttman)
Orchids & Ermin
Orphans of the Storm (orig. L. F. Gottschalk and Wm. Frederick Peters)
Othello (A. K.)
Our Hospitality (A. K.)
Outlaw and His Wife

[Pale Face (A. K.)]
Pandora's Box (A. K.)
Parisian Cobbler (A. K.)
Parson's Widow
Passion (A. K.)
Passion of Joan of Arc (A. K.)
Path to Paradise (A. K.)
Patsy (A. K.)
Pawnshop (A. K.)
[Perils of Pauline (A. K.)]
Le petite Marchande d' Allomettes
Phantom
Phantom Chariot (A. K.)
Phantom of the Opera
Photokina: Newsreels
A Plain Song (D. W. Griffith) (A.K.)
Plane Crazy (old score)
Pleasure Garden (A. K.)
Plunder (A. K.) [Episode 9]
Polikushka (A. K.)
Pollyanna (A. K.)
Poor Little Rich Girl (A. K.)
[Potemkin (Meisel)]
Potemkin (A. K.)
Pretexte (A. K.)
Pride of the Clan (A. K.)
Pueblo Legend (D.W. Griffith; A.K.)
Die Puppe
Putting Pants on Philip (A. K.)

[Queen Kelly (A. K.)]
Quo Vadis

Ramona (A. K.)
Reaching for the Moon (A. K.)
Rebecca of the Sunnybrook Farm (A. K.)
Red Raiders (A. K.)
Rescued from an Eagle's Nest (A. K.)
Return to Reason (A. K.)
Revue de Revue: Follies Bergere
Riders of the Purple Sage (A. K.)

Rien Que les Heures (orig. Yves de la Casiniere)
Robin Hood (orig. Victor L. Schertzinger and A. H. Cokayne)
La Roue (A. K.)
Rumpelstilzchen (A. K.)

Safety Last
Sally of the Sawdust
Salome (A. K.)
Salt for Svanetia
Salvation Hunters
Saturnia Farandola
Scarlet Letter (A. K.)
Sea Beast (A. K.)
The Second One Hundred Years (A. K.)
Seven Chances
The Sheik (A. K.)
Sherlock Junior (A. K.)
Shooting Mad (A. K.)
Shooting Star (A. K.)
Showpeople (A. K.)
A Simple Case (A. K.)
Singer Jim McKay (A. K.)
Sir Arne's Treasure (A. K.)
A Sixth of the World (A. K.)
Sky High
Smiling Madame Beudet (A. K.)
Snatchers
So, This Is Paris
Soilers
Sons of Ingmar
Sorrows of Satan (A. K.)
Sorrow of the Unfaithful (A. K.)
So's Your Old Man (A. K.)
Sparrow (A. K.)
Spies (A. K.)
Stark Love (A. K.)
Steamboat Bill Jr. (A. K.)
Stella Dallas (A. K.)
Stella Maris (A. K.)
Storm over Asia (A. K.)
Straight Shooting (A. K.)
The Street (A. K.)
Strike (A. K.)
Strong Man (A. K.)
The Strongest (A. K.)
Student Prince in Old Heidelberg
Swedish Films: Faust (Murnau); Thomas Graal's Bester Film (1917); Hexen (1922, Benj. Christensen); Captain Grogg (Victor Bergdahl); Captain Grogg (Fischer)

Tatters (old score)
Teddy at the Throttle
Ten Days That Shook the World (Meisel)
Ten Days That Shook the World (A. K.)
Terje Vigen
Testing Block
Theme & Variations
They Would Elope
Thief of Bagdad (orig.)
Third Degree
Three American Beauties
Three Bad Men
Three Musketeers
Three Women
Thundering Hooves
Tire au Flanc
Tol'able David
Toll Gate
Tom Mix (Cactus Jim, etc.—4 shorts)
Le Tournoi
The Tramp
Tramp, Tramp, Tramp (H. Langdon)
Treasure
Trial of the 3 Million
True Heart Susie
Turksib
Two Tars
Two Timid Souls

Ueberall
The Unbeliever
Uncle Tom's Cabin (A. K.)
Underworld (old score)
Unholy 3
The Unknown

Valentino: The Isle of Love; Eyes of Youth; 88 American Beauties; Cobra; Wonderful Chance; The Eagle; Moran of the Lady Letty; All Night; Son of the Sheik.
Les Vampire (31 reels)
Vanishing America
Variety
Voltage, etc. (Méliès)
Vormitagspuck
Voyage ou Travers l'Impossible

Warning Shadows
Wedding March
What Price Glory

What the Daisy Said

When Outlaws Meet

When the Clouds Roll By (old score)

White Oaks

White Rose (orig. Breil instr.)

White Roses

Wild & Wooley

Wild Bill Hickok

Wind (old score)

Wings (orig. J. S. Zamecnik)

A Woman of Affairs

Woman of the World

Won by a Fish

The Young Girl with the Hatbox

The Young Lady and the Hooligan

Zeitprobleme: Wie die Arbeiter Lebt

Zwei Freunde ein Modell und ein Mädchen

Zwenigora

Appendix 4
Cue Sheets for Silent Films in the Department of Film at the George Eastman House
Rochester, New York
Compiled by George C. Pratt

Abraham Lincoln (First National, 1924)

Across the Continent (Paramount, 1922)

Across the Pacific (Warner Bros., 1926)

The Actress (MGM, 1928)

Adam's Rib (Paramount, 1923)

Adventure Mad (Paramount, 1928)

An Affair of the Follies (First National, 1927)

Afraid to Love (Paramount, 1927)

After the Show (Paramount, 1921)

The Amateur Gentleman (First National, 1926)

American Beauty (First National, 1927)

The American Venus (Paramount, 1926)

The Americano (Triangle, 1916)

Ankles Preferred (Fox, 1927)

Anna Christie (Associated First National, 1923)

Annapolis (Pathe Exchange, 1928)

Any Woman (Paramount, 1925)

Anybody Here Seen Kelly? (Universal, 1928)

The Arab (Metro-Goldwyn, 1924)

Are Parents People? (Paramount, 1925)

Argentine Love (Paramount, 1924)

The Arizona Sweepstakes (Universal-Jewel, 1925)

Ashes of Vengeance (First National, 1923)

The Auction Block (MGM, 1926)

The Auctioneer (Fox, 1927)

Avalanche (Paramount, 1928)

The Awakening (United Artists, 1928)

Babe Comes Home (First National, 1927)

Baby Mine (MGM, 1928)

Bachelor Brides (Producers Distributing, 1926)

The Bachelor Daddy (Paramount, 1922)

Back Home and Broke (Paramount, 1922)

Barbara Frietchie (Producers Distributing, 1924)

Barbed Wire (Paramount, 1927)

Bare Knees (Gotham, 1928)

The Bat (United Artists, 1926)

The Battle of the Sexes (United Artists, 1928)

Beau Brummel (Warner Bros., 1924)

Beau Sabreur (Paramount, 1928)

The Beautiful Cheat (Universal-Jewel, 1926)

The Beautiful City (First National, 1925)

The Bedroom Window (Paramount, 1925)

Beggar on Horseback (Paramount, 1925)

Beggars of Life (Paramount, 1928)

Behind the Front (Paramount, 1926)

Behind the German Lines (Paramount, 1928)

Bella Donna (Paramount, 1923)

The Better Role (Warner Bros., 1926)

Big Brother (Paramount, 1923)

The Big Noise (First National, 1928)

Black Oxen (First National, 1923)

Blind Alleys (First National, 1927)

Blindfold (Fox, 1928)

Blonde or Brunette (Paramount, 1927)

The Blonde Saint (First National, 1926)

Blood and Sand (Paramount, 1922)

The Blooming Angel (Goldwyn, 1920)

The Blue Danube (Pathe Exchange, 1928)

The Blue Eagle, (Fox, 1926)

The Blue Streak (FBO, 1926)

Bluebeard's 8th Wife (Paramount, 1923)

Bluebeard's Seven Wives (First National, 1925)

Bluff (Paramount, 1924)

Bobbed Hair (Warner Bros., 1925)

La Boheme (MGM, 1926)

The Bonded Woman (Paramount, 1922)

Boomerang Bill (Paramount, 1922)

Borderland (Paramount, 1922)

Bought and Paid For (Paramount, 1922)

Boy of Flanders (Metro-Goldwyn, 1924)

Braveheart (Producers Distributing, 1925)

Breakfast at Sunrise (First National, 1927)

Brewster's Millions (Paramount, 1921)

The Bright Shawl (First National, 1923)

Bringing up Father (MGM, 1928)

Broadway After Dark (Warner Bros., 1924)

Broadway Rose (Metro, 1922)

Broken Barriers (Metro-Goldwyn, 1924)

The Brown Derby (First National, 1926)

Brown of Harvard (MGM, 1926)

Buck Privates (Universal-Jewel, 1928)

Reprinted from *Image*, Vol. 25, No. 1 (March, 1982).

Buried Treasure (Paramount, 1921)

Burning Daylight (First National, 1928)

Burning Sands (Paramount, 1922)

The Bushranger (MGM, 1928)

The Butter and Egg Man (First National, 1928)

Buttons, (MGM, 1927)

The Calgary Stampede (Universal-Jewel, 1925)

The Call of the Canyon (Paramount, 1923)

The Call of the North (Paramount, 1921)

Cameo Kirby (Fox, 1923)

The Cameraman (MGM, 1928)

The Campus Flirt (Paramount, 1926)

Captain Blood (Vitagraph, 1924)

Captain Lash (Fox, 1929)

The Cardboard Lover (MGM, 1928)

Casey at the Bat (Paramount, 1927)

The Cat and the Canary (Universal, 1927)

The Cat's Pajamas (Paramount, 1926)

Chang (Paramount, 1927)

Charley's Aunt (Producers Distributing, 1925)

The Charm School (Paramount, 1921)

The Charmer (Paramount, 1925)

The Chaser (First National, 1928)

Cheating Cheaters (Universal-Jewel, 1927)

Chicago (Pathe Exchange, 1928)

Chicago After Midnight (FBO, 1928)

Chickie (First National, 1925)

Chinatown Charlie (First National, 1928)

The Chinese Parrot (Universal, 1927)

The Circus Cyclone (Universal, 1925)

Circus Days (First National, 1923)

The Circus Kid (FBO, 1928)

The City (Fox, 1926)

The City Gone Wild (Paramount, 1927)

Clarence (Paramount, 1922)

Classified (First National, 1925)

The Clinging Vine (Producers Distributing, 1926)

Clothes Made the Pirate (First National, 1925)

The Coast of Folly (Paramount, 1925)

Cobra (Paramount, 1925)

Code of the Sea (Paramount, 1924)

The Cohens and Kellys (Universal-Jewel, 1926)

The Cohens and Kellys in Paris (Universal, 1928)

Colleen (Fox, 1927)

Combat (Universal-Jewel, 1926)

Come to My House (Fox, 1927)

The Coming of Amos (Producers Distributing, 1925)

Coming Through (Paramount, 1925)

The Common Law (Selznick, 1916)

Companionate Marriage (First National, 1928)

Confessions of a Queen (MGM, 1925)

The Confidence Man (Paramount, 1924)

A Connecticut Yankee at King Arthur's Court (Fox, 1921)

Contraband (Paramount, 1925)

Cornered (Warner Bros., 1924)

The Cossacks (MGM, 1928)

The Country Beyond (Fox, 1926)

The Country Doctor (Pathe Exchange, 1927)

The Country Kid (Warner Bros., 1923)

The Cradle (Paramount, 1922)

Craig's Wife (Pathe Exchange, 1928)

The Crash (First National, 1928)

The Crowded Hour (Paramount, 1925)

The Crowded Hour (Paramount, 1925)

The Crown of Lies (Paramount, 1926)

A Cumberland Romance (Realart, 1920)

Daddies (Warner Bros., 1924)

Daddy Long Legs (First National, 1919)

Dance Magic (Frist National, 1927)

The Dancer of Paris (First National, 1926)

Dancing Mothers (Paramount, 1926)

The Dangerous Age (First National, 1923)

The Dark Angel (First National, 1925)

The Dark Swan (Warner Bros., 1924)

A Daughter of Luxury (Paramount, 1922)

The Dawn of a Tomorrow (Paramount, 1924)

Declasse (First National, 1925)

Desert Gold (Paramount, 1926)

The Dictator (Paramount, 1922)

Dinty (First National, 1920)

Diplomacy (Paramount, 1926)

The Divine Woman (MGM, 1928)

Do Your Duty (First National, 1928)

The Docks of New York (Paramount, 1928)

Dr. Jack (Pathe Exchange, 1922)

Dr. Jekyll and Mr. Hyde (Paramount, 1920)

Don Juan (Warner Bros., 1926)

Don Juan's Three Nights (First National, 1926)

Don't (MGM, 1926)

Don't Call It Love (Paramount, 1923)

Don't Marry (Fox, 1928)

Don't Tell Everything (Paramount, 1921)

Doubling with Danger (FBO, 1926)

The Dove (United Artists, 1928)

Down the Stretch (Universal-Jewel, 1927)

The Drag Net (Paramount, 1928)

The Dressmaker from Paris (Paramount, 1925)

The Drop Kick (First National, 1927)

Drums of the Desert (Paramount, 1927)

Dry Martini (Fox, 1928)

The Duchess of Buffalo (First National, 1927)

The Eagle (United Artists, 1925)

The Eagle of the Sea (Paramount, 1926)

East is West (First National, 1922)

East of Suez (Paramount, 1925)

East Side, West Side (Fox, 1927)

Ebb Tide (Paramount, 1922)

Ella Cinders (First National, 1926)
The Enemy (MGM, 1928)
The Enemy Sex (Paramount, 1924)
The Escape (Fox, 1928)
The Eternal City (First National, 1923)
The Eternal Struggle (Metro, 1923)
Eve's Leaves (Producers Distributing, 1926)

Fair Week (Paramount, 1924)
The Family Secret (Universal-Jewel, 1924)
The Family Upstairs (Fox, 1926)
The Famous Mrs. Fair (Metro, 1923)
The Far Cry (First National, 1926)
Fascinating Youth (Paramount, 1926)
Fashion Row (Metro, 1923)
Fashions for Women, (Paramount, 1927)
Feel My Pulse (Paramount, 1921)
Feet of Clay, (Paramount, 1924)
Fifty Fifty (Associated Exhibitors, 1925)
The Fifty Fifty Girl (Paramount, 1928)
Fig Leaves (Fox, 1926)
The Fighting Blade (First National, 1923)
The Fighting Buckaroo (Fox, 1926)
The Fighting Coward (Paramount, 1924)
The Fighting Eagle (Pathe Exchange, 1927)
Fighting Love (Producers Distributing, 1927)
Figures Don't Lie (Paramount, 1927)
Find Your Man (Warner Bros., 1924)
Fireman, Save My Child (Paramount, 1927)
The First Kiss (Paramount, 1928)
Flaming Barriers (Paramount, 1924)
The Flaming Youth (First National, 1923)
The Fleet's In (Paramount, 1928)
Fleetwing (Fox, 1928)
Flower of Night (Paramount, 1925)
Fools for Luck (Paramount, 1928)
Fool's Paradise (Paramount, 1921)
For Heaven's Sake (Paramount, 1926)

For the Love of Mike (First National, 1927)
Forbidden Fruit (Paramount, 1921)
Forbidden Hours (MGM, 1928)
Forbidden Paradise (Paramount, 1924)
The Forbidden Woman (Pathe Exchange, 1927)
Foreign Devils (MGM, 1927)
The Foreign Legion (Universal, 1928)
Forgotten Faces (Paramount, 1928)
Forlorn River (Paramount, 1926)
Forty Winks (Paramount, 1925)
The Four Horsemen of the Apocalypse (Metro, 1921)
Four Sons (Fox, 1928)
Four Walls (MGM, 1928)
The Fourflusher (Universal-Jewel, 1928)
Framed (First National, 1927)
French Dressing (First National, 1927)
The Freshman (Pathe Exchange, 1925)

Gang War (FBO, 1928)
The General (United Artists, 1927)
A Gentleman of Leisure (Paramount, 1923)
Get-Rich-Quick-Wallingford (Paramount, 1921)
Getting Gertie's Garter (Producers Distributing, 1927)
The Ghost Breaker (Paramount, 1922)
The Girl from Montmartre (First National, 1926)
A Girl in Every Port (Fox, 1928)
The Girl in the Limousine (First National, 1924)
Girl Shy (Pathe Exchange, 1924)
The Girl Who Wouldn't Work (B. P Schulberg Productions, 1925)
Girls Men Forget (Principal Pictures, 1924)
Glimpses of the Moon (Paramount, 1923)
Go West (MGM, 1925)
The Go-Getter (Paramount, 1923)
God Gave Me Twenty Cents (Paramount, 1926)
The Gold Diggers (Warner Bros., 1923)

The Golden Bed (Paramount, 1925)
The Golden Princess (Paramount, 1925)
Good and Naughty (Paramount, 1926)
The Good Provider (Paramount, 1922)
The Good-bye Kiss (First National, 1928)
The Goose Hangs High (Paramount, 1925)
The Goose Woman (Universal-Jewel, 1925)
The Gorilla (First National, 1927)
The Gorilla Hunt (FBO, 1926)
The Grand Duchess and the Waiter (Paramount, 1926)
Grandma's Boy (Pathe Exchange, 1922)
Grandma's Boy (Pathe Exchange, 1922 reissue)
Graustark (First National, 1925)
The Great Gatsby (Paramount, 1926)
The Great Impersonation (Paramount, 1921)
The Great White Way (Goldwyn-Cosmopolitan, 1924)
The Greater Glory (First National, 1926)
The Green Goddess (Goldwyn-Cosmopolitan, 1923)
The Green Temptation (Paramount, 1922)
Grumpy (Paramount, 1923)
Guilty of Love (Paramount, 1920)

Hairpins (Paramount, 1920)
Half a Bride (Paramount, 1928)
Hands Up (Paramount, 1926)
Hangman's House (Fox, 1928)
Happiness Ahead (First National, 1928)
Hard Boiled (Fox, 1926)
Hardboiled (FBO, 1929)
Harold Teen (First National, 1928)
The Harvester (FBO, 1927)
Headlines (Associated Exhibitions, 1925)
Heads Up (FBO, 1925)
The Heart of a Follies Girl (First National, 1928)
The Heart of a Siren (Frist National, 1925)

The Heart of General Robert E. Lee (MGM, 1928; 2-reeler)

The Heart Thief (Producers Distributing, 1927)

Heart to Heart (First National, 1928)

The Hell Diggers (Paramount, 1921)

Hello Cheyenne (Fox, 1928)

Her Gilded Cage (Paramount, 1922)

Her Honor the Governor (FBO, 1926)

Her Husband's Secret (First National, 1925)

Her Husband's Trademark (Paramount, 1922)

Her Love Story (Paramount, 1924)

Her Man O'War (Producers Distributing, 1926)

Her Sister from Paris (First National, 1925)

Her Temporary Husband (First National, 1923)

Her Wild Oat (First National, 1927)

The Heritage of the Desert (Paramount, 1924)

A Hero for a Night (Universal-Jewel, 1927)

Hero of the Circus (Universal, 1928)

High Hat (First National, 1927)

High Steppers (First National, 1926)

Hiking Through Holland [with Will Rogers] (Pathe Exchange, 1927; 1-reeler)

His Children's Children (Paramount, 1923)

His Dog (Producers Distributing, 1927)

His First Flame (Pathe Exchange, 1927)

His People (Proud Heart) (Universal-Jewel, 1925)

His Private Life (Paramount, 1928)

His Supreme Moment (First National, 1925)

His Tiger Lady (Paramount, 1928)

History of Vaudeville (unidentified)

Hogan's Alley (Warner Bros., 1925)

Hold That Lion (Paramount, 1926)

Hollywood (Paramount, 1923)

Home Made (First National, 1927)

Homeward Bound (Paramount, 1923)

Honeymoon Hate (Paramount, 1927)

Honor Bound (Fox, 1928)

Honor First (Fox, 1922 reissue)

Hot News (Paramount, 1928)

Hot Water (Pathe Exchange, 1924)

The Hottentot (First National, 1922)

How to Handle Women (Fresh Every Hour) (Universal-Jewel, 1928)

Hula (Paramount, 1927)

Human Hearts (Universal-Jewel, 1922)

Human Wreckage (FBO, 1923)

The Humming Bird (Paramount, 1924)

The Hunchback of Notre Dame (Universal, 1923)

I Want My Man (First National, 1925)

Icebound (Paramount, 1924)

The Idle Rich (Metro, 1921)

Idle Tongues (First National, 1924)

Idols of Clay (Paramount, 1920)

If Winter Comes (Fox, 1923)

If You Believe It, It's So (Paramount, 1922)

The Impossible Mrs. Bellew (Paramount, 1922)

The Imposter (FBO, 1926)

In Dublin [With Will Rogers] (Pathe Exchange, 1927; 1-reeler)

In Every Woman's Life (First National, 1924)

In Hollywood with Potash and Perlmutter (First National, 1924)

In Paris [With Will Rogers] (Pathe Exchange, 1927; 1-reeler)

In the Palace of the King (Goldwyn-Cosmopolitan, 1923)

Infatuation (First National, 1925)

The Inside of the Cup (Paramount, 1921)

Inspiration (Excellent Pictures, 1928)

Into Her Kingdom (First National, 1926)

Into the Night (Raleigh Pictures, 1928)

Irish Hearts (Warner Bros., 1927)

Irish Luck (Paramount, 1925)

The Iron Mask (United Artists, 1929)

The Irresistible Lover (Universal, 1927)

Is Matrimony a Failure? (Paramount, 1922)

The Isle of Lost Ships (First National, 1923)

Isobel; or The Trail's End (Davis Distributing, 1920)

It Must Be Love (First National, 1926)

It's the Old Army Game (Paramount, 1926)

Java Head (Paramount, 1923)

Jesse James (Paramount, 1927)

Joanna (First National, 1925)

Johnny Get Your Hair Cut (MGM, 1927)

The Johnstown Flood (Fox, 1926)

The Joy Girl (Fox, 1927)

Just Another Blonde (First National, 1926)

Just Around the Corner (Paramount, 1921)

Just Married (Paramount, 1928)

Just Suppose (First National, 1926)

The Keeper of the Bees (FBO, 1925)

Kick In (Paramount, 1922)

Kiki (First National, 1926)

The King of Kings (Pathe Exchange, 1927)

The King of the Turf (FBO, 1926)

The King of Wild Horses (Pathe Exchange, 1924)

The King on Main Street (Paramount, 1925)

Kismet (Robertson-Cole, 1920)

A Kiss for Cinderella (Paramount, 1926)

A Kiss in a Taxi (Paramount, 1927)

A Kiss in the Dark (Paramount, 1927)

Kiss Me Again (Warner Bros., 1925)

Kosher Kitty Kelly (FBO, 1926)

Laddie (FBO, 1926)

Ladies at Play (First National, 1926)

Ladies Must Live (Paramount, 1921)

Ladies Night in a Turkish Bath
(First National, 1928)

Ladies of Leisure (Columbia
Pictures, 1926)

Ladies of the Mob (Paramount,
1928)

The Lady (First National, 1925)

The Lady in Ermine (First National,
1927)

The Lady of the Harum
(Paramount, 1926)

Lady of the Night (Metro-Goldwyn,
1925)

The Lady Who Lied (First National,
1925)

Lady Windermere's Fan (Warner
Bros., 1925)

The Lane That Had No Turning
(Paramount, 1922)

The Last Command (Paramount,
1928)

The Last Frontier (Producers
Distributing, 1926)

The Last Payment (Paramount,
1921)

The Last Warning (Universal, 1929)

The Latest From Paris (MGM,
1928)

The Law and the Woman
(Paramount, 1922)

The Law of the Range (MGM, 1928)

The Lawful Cheaters (B. P.
Schulberg Productions, 1925)

Lawful Larceny (Paramount, 1923)

Learning to Love (First National,
1925)

Let It Rain (Paramount, 1927)

Let No Man Put Asunder
(Vitagraph, 1924)

Let's Get Married (Paramount,
1926)

The Life of Riley (First National,
1927)

The Light That Failed (Paramount,
1923)

The Lighthouse by the Sea (Warner
Bros., 1924)

Lightning Speed (FBO, 1928)

The Lily (Fox, 1926)

Lily of the Dust (Paramount, 1924)

Little Annie Rooney (United Artists,
1925)

The Little French Girl (Paramount,
1925)

The Little Irish girl (Warner Bros.,
1926)

Little Johnny Jones (Warner Bros.,
1923)

Little Old New York (Goldwyn-
Cosmopolitan, 1923)

The Little Shepherd of Kingdom
Come (First National, 1928)

The Live Wire (First National,
1925)

Long Live the King (Metro, 1923)

Long Pants (First National, 1927)

The Lookout Girl (Quality Pictures,
1928)

Lord Jim (Paramount, 1925)

Lost—A Wife (Paramount, 1925)

Lost at the Front (First National,
1927)

The Lost Battalion (McManus,
1919)

The Lost World (First National,
1925)

Love and Learn (Paramount, 1928)

Love 'em and Leave 'em
(Paramount, 1926)

The Love Gamble (Henry Ginsburg
Distributing, 1925)

Love Hungry (Fox, 1928)

The Love Light (United Artists,
1921)

The Love Mart (First National,
1924)

The Love Master (First National,
1924)

Love of an Actress (Paramount,
1927)

The Love That Lives (Paramount,
1917)

The Love Thrill (Universal-Jewel,
1927)

The Love Toy (Warner bros., 1926)

The Lover of Camille (Warner
Bros., 1924)

Love's Greatest Mistake
(Paramount, 1927)

The Love of Pharaoh (Paramount,
1928)

The Lucky Devil (Paramount,
1922)

The Lucky Lady (Paramount, 1926)

The Lunatic at Large (First
National, 1927)

Lying Wives (Ivan Players, 1925)

Mad Love (Goldwyn, 1923)

Madame Sans-Gene (Paramount,
1925)

Madame Wants No Children (Fox,
1927)

Made for Love (Producers
Distributing, 1926)

Mademoiselle Midnight (Metro,
1924)

Mlle. Modiste (First National, 1926)

The Magic Garden (FBO, 1927)

The Magnificent Flirt ((Paramount,
1928)

Main Street (Warner Bros., 1923)

The Making of O'Malley (First
National, 1925)

Man Bait (Producers Distributing,
1926)

Man Crazy (First National, 1927)

The Man from Home (Paramount,
1922)

The Man from Red Gulch
(Producers Distributing, 1925)

A Man of Iron (Chadwick Pictures,
1925)

Man of the Forest (Paramount,
1926)

The Man on the Box (Warner Bros.,
1925)

Man Power (Paramount, 1927)

The Man Unconquerable
((Paramount, 1922)

The Man Who Found Himself
(Paramount, 1925)

The Man Who Laughs (Universal,
1928)

The Man Who Saw Tomorrow
(Paramount, 1922)

Manhattan (Paramount, 1924)

Manhattan Cocktail (Paramount,
1928)

Manhattan Madness (Associated
Exhibitors, 1925)

Mannequin (Paramount, 1926)

Manslaughter (Paramount, 1922)

The Mark of Zorro (United Artists,
1920)

Marquis Preferred (Paramount,
1929)

Marriage by Contract (Tiffany-
Stahl, 1928)

The Marriage Circle (Warner Bros.,
1923)

The Marriage Clause (Universal,
Jewel, 1926)

Marriage License? (Fox, 1926)

The Marriage Maker (Paramount, 1923)

The Masked Woman (First National, 1927)

The Mating Call (Paramount, 1928)

McFadden's Flats (Paramount, 1927)

The Meanest Man in the World (First National, 1923)

Memory Lane (First National, 1926)

Men (Paramount, 1924)

Men and Women (Paramount, 1925)

Merry Go round (Universal, 1923)

The Merry Widow (MGM, 1925)

Michael Strogoff (Universal-Jewel, 1926)

The Midnight Flyer (FBO, 1925)

The Midnight Kiss (Fox, 1926)

Midnight Lovers (First National, 1926)

Midnight Madness (Pathe Exchange, 1928)

The Midnight Sun (Universal-Jewel, 1926)

Midsummer Madness (Paramount, 1920)

Mighty Lak a Rose (First National, 1923)

Mike (MGM, 1926)

A Million Bid (Warner Bros., 1927)

The Miracle Baby (FBO, 1923)

Mismates (First National, 1926)

Miss Brewster's Millions (Paramount, 1926)

Miss Lulu Bett (Paramount, 1921)

The Missing Link (Warner Bros., 1927)

Mr. Billings Spends His Dime (Paramount, 1923)

Moana (Paramount, 1926)

The Model from Montmartre (Paramount, 1928)

The Mollycoddle (United Artists, 1920)

The Monkey Talks (Fox, 1927)

Monsieur Beaucaire (Paramount, 1924)

Morals for Men (Tiffany, 1925)

Moran of the Marines (Paramount, 1928)

Mother (FBO, 1927)

My American Wife (Paramount, 1923)

My Home Town (Atlas Educational, 1925)

My Official Wife (Warner Bros., 1926)

My Own Pal (Fox, 1926)

My Son (First National, 1925)

My Wild Irish Rose (Vitagraph, 1922)

The Mysterious Lady (MGM, 1928)

The Mysterious Rider (Paramount, 1927)

Name the Man! (Goldwyn-Cosmopolitan, 1924)

Nanook of the North (Pathe Exchange, 1922)

Napoleon (MGM, 1929)

Naughty But Nice (First National, 1927)

The Naughty Duchess (Tiffany-Stahl, 1928)

The Navigator (Metro-Goldwyn, 1924)

Nell Gwyn (Paramount, 1926)

The Nervous Wreck (Producers Distributing, 1926)

Nevada (Paramount, 1927)

Never Say Die (Associated Exhibitors, 1924)

New Brooms (Pararmount 1925)

The New Klondike (Paramount, 1926)

New Lives for Old (Paramount, 1925)

New Toys (First National, 1925)

The Next Corner (Paramount, 1924)

Nice People (Paramount, 1922)

The Night Bird (Universal, 1928)

The Night Bride (Producers Distributing, 1927)

The Night Cry (Warner Bros., 1926)

The Night Flyer (Pathe Exchange, 1928)

Night Life of New York (Paramount, 1925)

The Night Watch (First National, 1928)

No Control (Producers Distributing, 1927)

No Man's Gold (Fox, 1926)

No Place to Go (First National, 1927)

Nobody's Money (Paramount, 1923)

None But the Brave (Fox, 1928)

The Noose (First National, 1928)

North of the Rio Grande (Paramount, 1922)

North of '36 (Paramount, 1924)

Not So Long Ago (Paramount, 1925)

The Notorious Lady (First National, 1927)

The Nut (United Artists, 1921)

Oh, Doctor! (Universal-Jewel, 1924)

Oh Kay (First National, 1928)

Oh! What a Nurse (Warner Bros., 1926)

Old Home Week (Paramount, 1925)

The Old Homestead (Paramount, 1922)

Old Loves and New (First National, 1926)

The Old Soak (Universal-Jewel, 1926)

Old Wives for New (Paramount, 1918)

Oliver Twist (First National, 1922)

O'Malley Rides Alone (Syndicate, 1930)

On to Reno (Pathe Exchange, 1928)

One Increasing Purpose (Fox, 1927)

One of the Bravest (Gotham, 1925)

One Stolen Night (Vitagraph, 1923)

One Women to Another (Paramount, 1927)

One Year to Live (First National, 1925)

Only 38 (Paramount, 1923)

The Only Woman (First National, 1924)

Open Range (Paramount, 1927)

The Opening Night (Columbia Pictures, 1927)

Orchids and Ermine (First National, 1927)

The Ordeal (Paramount, 1922)

Other Women's Husbands (Warner Bros., 1926)

Our Dancing Daughters (MGM, 1928)

Our Hospitality (Metro, 1923)
Our Leading Citizen (Paramount, 1922)
Out All Night (Universal-Jewel, 1927)
Out of the Ruins (First National, 1928)
Out of the Storm (Tiffany, 1926)
Outcast (First National, 1928)
Outcast Souls (Sterling, 1927)
Outside the Law (Universal-Jewel, 1921)
The Outsider (Fox, 1926)
Over the Border (Paramount, 1922)
Over the Hill (Fox, 1920 Reissue)

The Pace that Thrills (First National, 1925)
Paid to Love (Fox, 1927)
Painted People (First National, 1924)
Painted Post (Fox, 1928)
The Palm Beach Girl (Paramount, 1926)
Pals in Paradise (Producers Distributing, 1926)
Paradise (First National, 1926)
Paradise for Two (Paramount, 1927)
Partners Again (United Artists, 1926)
Partners in Crime (Paramount, 1928)
Passion (Madame Dubarry) (First National, 1920)
The Passion Flower (First National, 1921)
The Passionate Pilgrim (Paramount, 1921)
Passionate Youth (Truart, 1925)
The Patent Leather Kid (First National, 1927)
The Patriot (MGM, 1928)
The Patsy (MGM, 1928)
Peacock Alley (Metro, 1922)
Peacock Feathers (Universal-Jewel, 1925)
Peck's Bad Boy (First National, 1921)
Peg o' My Heart (Metro, 1922)
Penrod (First National, 1922)
Penrod and Sam (First National, 1923)

Percy (Pathe Exchange, 1925)
The Perfect Sap (First National, 1927)
Peter Pan (Paramount, 1924)
The Phantom Express (Henry Ginsberg Distributing, 1925)
The Phantom of the Opera (Universal, 1925)
Phyllis of the Follies (Universal, 1928)
Pied Piper Malone (Paramount, 1924)
The Pilgrim (First National, 1922)
The Pinch Hitter (Associated Exhibitors, 1925)
Pink Gods (Paramount, 1922)
The Pioneer Scout (Paramount, 1928)
The Play Girl (Fox, 1928)
The Pleasure Buyers (Warner Bros., 1925)
Poker Faces (Universal-Jewel, 1926)
Pollyanna (United Artists, 1920)
Ponjola (First National, 1923)
The Pony Express (Paramount, 1925)
The Poor Little Rich Girl (Paramount, 1917)
The Poor Nut (First National, 1927)
Poppy (Selznick, 1917)
The Popular Sin (Paramount, 1926)
Potash and Perlmutter (First National, 1923)
Potemkin (Amkino, 1926; cue sheet by V. Heifitz)
Poverty of Riches (Goldwyn, 1921)
Power (Pathe Exchange, 1928)
The Power of the Press (Columbia Pictures, 1928)
The Pride of Palomar (Paramount, 1922)
The Prince of Broadway (Chadwick, 1926)
The Prince of Headwaiters (First National, 1927)
A Prince There Was (Paramount, 1922)
The Prisoner of Zenda (Metro, 1922)
Private Izzy Murphy (Warner Bros., 1926)

The Private Life of Helen of Troy (First National, 1927)
Prodigal Daughters (Paramount, 1923)
Publicity Madness (Fox, 1927)
Puppets (First National, 1926)
The Purple Highway (Paramount, 1923)

Quicksands (Paramount, 1927)
Quo vadis (First National, 1925)

The Racket (Paramount, 1928)
Raffles (Universal-Jewel, 1925)
Rags to Riches (Warner Bros., 1922)
The Rainmaker (Paramount, 1926)
Ramona (United Artists, 1928)
Recoil (Goldwyn-Cosmopolitan, 1924)
Red Dice (Producers Distributing, 1926)
Red Lips (Universal, 1928)
A Regular Fellow (He's a Prince) (Paramount, 1925)
Rent Free (Paramount, 1922)
The Return of Peter Grimm (Fox, 1926)
Revelation (Metro-Goldwyn, 1924)
Rich But Honest (Fox, 1927)
The Riddle: Woman (Pathe, 1920)
The Right That Failed (Metro, 1922)
Riley the Copy (Fox, 1928)
Ritzy (Paramount, 1927)
The Road to Yesterday (Producers Distributing, 1925)
Robin Hood (United Artists, 1922)
Rolled Stockings (Paramount, 1927)
Rolling Home (Universal-Jewel, 1926)
Romola (Metro-Goldwyn, 1924)
Rosita (United Artists, 1923)
Rough House Rosie (Paramount, 1927)
The Rough Riders (Paramount, 1927)
Rubber Heels (Paramount, 1923)
Ruggles of Red Gap (Paramount, 1923)
The Runaway (Paramount, 1926)
Running Wild (Paramount, 1927)
Rupert of Hentzau (Selznick, 1923)

S-O-S Perils of the Sea (Columbia Pictures, 1925)
Sackcloth and Scarlet (Paramount, 1925)
The Sacred Promise (unidentified)
Sadie Thompson (United Artists, 1928)
A Sailor-made man (Associated Exhibitors, 1921)
Sailors' Wives (First National, 1928)
St. Elmo (Fox, 1923 reissue)
A Sainted Devil (Paramount, 1924)
Sally (First National, 1925)
Sally of the Sawdust (United Artists, 1925)
Salome of the Tenements (Paramount, 1925)
Salomy Jane (Paramount, 1923)
The Savage (First National, 1926)
The Sawdust Paradise (Paramount, 1928)
Scaramouche (Metro, 1923)
The Scarlet Letter (MGM, 1926)
School Days (Warner Bros., 1921)
School for Wives (Vitagraph, 1925)
Second Youth (Goldwyn-Cosmopolitan, 1926)
The Secret Hour (Paramount, 1928)
The Secret Spring (Paramount, 1926)
The Secret Studio (Fox, 1927)
Señorita (Paramount, 1927)
Service for Ladies (Paramount, 1927)
Seven Chances (Metro-Goldwyn, 1925)
Seven Keys to Baldpate (Paramount, 1925)
Shadows of Paris (Paramount, 1924)
Shame (Fox, 1921 reissue)
Sharp Shooters (Fox, 1928)
The Sheik (Paramount, 1921)
The Shepherd of the Hills (First National, 1928)
Sherlock Brown (Metro, 1922)
Sherlock, Jr. (Metro, 1924)
The Shooting of Dan McGrew (Metro, 1924)
Shore leave (First National, 1925)
Shoulder Arms (First National, 1918)
The Showdown (Paramount, 1928)

The Show-off (Paramount, 1926)
The Side Show of Life (Paramount, 1924)
The Silent Lover (First National, 1926)
The Silent Partner (Paramount, 1923)
Silk Stockings (Universal-Jewel, 1927)
The Sin Sister (Fox, 1929)
Singed (Fox, 1927)
Singed Wings (Paramount, 1922)
Six days (Goldwyn-Cosmopolitan, 1923)
Skinner's Dress Suit (Universal-Jewel, 1926)
Sky High Corral (Universal, 1926)
Skyscraper (Pathe Exchange, 1928)
Slave of Desire (Goldwyn-Cosmopolitan, 1923)
Slaves of Beauty (Fox, 1927)
The Smart Set (MGM, 1928)
Smile Brother Smile (First National, 1927)
Smilin' Through (First National, 1927)
The Snob (MGM, 1924)
So This is Paris (Warner Bros., 1926)
A Society Scandal (Paramount, 1924)
Soft Cushions (Paramount, 1927)
Someone to Love (Paramount, 1928)
Something Always Happens (Paramount, 1928)
Something to Think About (Paramount, 1920)
A Son of His Father (Paramount, 1925)
The Son of the Sheik (United Artists, 1926)
The Song of Love (First National, 1923)
Sonny (First National, 1922)
The Sorrows of Satan (Paramount, 1926)
So's Your Old Man (Paramount, 1926)
Soul Fire (First National, 1925)
Souls for Sables (Tiffany, 1925)
The Spaniard (Paramount, 1925)
The Spanish Dancer (Paramount, 1923)

Speedy (Paramount, 1928)
The Splendid Road (First National, 1925)
Spoilers of the West (MGM, 1927)
The Spotlight (Paramount, 1927)
Square Crooks (Fox, 1928)
Stage Madness (Fox, 1927)
Stage Struck (Paramount, 1925)
Stand and Deliver (Pathe Exchange, 1928)
Stark Love (Paramount, 1925)
Stella Maris (Universal-Jewel, 1925)
Stephen Steps Out (Paramount, 1923)
Stepping Along (First National, 1926)
The Stolen Bride (First National, 1927)
Stranded in Paris (Paramount, 1926)
The Strange Case of Captain Ramper (First National, 1928)
The Stranger (Paramount, 1924)
Strangers of the Night (Metro, 1923)
The Street of Sin (Paramount, 1928)
The Streets of Forgotten Men (Paramount, 1925)
The Strong Man (First National, 1926)
The Student Prince in Old Heidelberg (MGM, 1927)
Summer Bachelors (Fox, 1926)
The Sunset Derby (First National, 1927)
The Swan (Paramount, 1925)
Sweet Daddies (First National, 1926)
Swim Girl Swim (Paramount, 1927)

Take It from Me (Universal, 1926)
Take Me Home (Paramount, 1928)
Tarnish (First National, 1924)
The Telephone Girl (Paramount, 1927)
Tell It to Sweeney (Paramount, 1927)
Tempest (United Artists, 1928)
The Ten Commandments (Paramount, 1923)
Ten Modern Commandments (Paramount, 1927)

Tenth Avenue (Pathe Exchange, 1928)

A Texas Steer (First National, 1927)

That Royle Girl (Paramount, 1925)

That's My Daddy (Universal, 1928)

A Thief in Paradise (First National, 1925)

A Thief in the Dark (Fox, 1928)

The Thief of Bagbad (United Artists, 1924)

The Third Alarm (FBO, 1922)

Thirty Days (Paramount, 1923)

This Woman (Warner Bros., 1924)

Three Ages (Metro, 1923)

Three Hours (First National, 1927)

Three Live Ghosts (Paramount, 1922)

Three Miles Out (Associated Exhibitors, 1924)

The Three Musketeers (United Artists, 1921)

Three-Ring Marriage (First National, 1928)

Three Sinners (Paramount, 1928)

Three Week Ends (Paramount, 1928)

Three Weeks (Goldwyn, 1924)

Three Wise Fools (Goldwyn-Cosmopolitan, 1923)

Three Women (Warner Bros., 1924)

Three's a Crowd (First National, 1927)

The Thundering Herd (Paramount, 1925)

Tiger Love (Paramount, 1924)

Tiger Rose (Warner Bros., 1923)

Tillie's Punctured Romance (Paramount, 1928)

Time to Love (Paramount, 1927)

Tip Toes (Paramount, 1927)

To Please One Woman (Paramount, 1920)

To the Ladies (Paramount, 1923)

To the Last Man (Paramount, 1923)

Tongues of Flame (Paramount, 1924)

Too Many Crooks (Paramount, 1927)

Too Many Kisses (Paramount, 1925)

Too Much Money (First National, 1926)

The Top of the World (Paramount, 1925)

The Trail of the Lonesome Pine (Paramount, 1923)

The Trap (Universal-Jewel, 1922)

Travelin' On (Paramount, 1922)

A Trip to Chinatown (Fox, 1926)

Trouble (First National, 1922)

True Heaven (Fox, 1929)

Trumpet Island (Vitagraph, 1920)

Truxton King (Fox, 1923)

Tumbleweeds (United Artists, 1925)

Turn to the Right (Metro, 1922)

Two Flaming Youths (Paramount, 1927)

Uncle Tom's Cabin (Universal, 1927)

Under the Lash (Paramount, 1921)

Underworld (Paramount, 1927)

The Unguarded Hour (First National, 1925)

Unguarded Women (Paramount, 1924)

The Untamed Lady (Paramount, 1926)

The Unwritten Law (Columbia Pictures, 1925)

The Valley of the Giants (First National, 1927)

The Vanishing American (Paramount, 1926)

The Vanishing Pioneer (Paramount, 1926)

Vanity (Producers Distributing, 1927)

Variety (Paramount, 1926)

Venus of Venice (First National, 1927)

Very Confidential (Fox, 1927)

Volcano (Paramount, 1926)

The Volga Boatman (Producers Distributing, 1926)

The Waltz Dream (MGM, 1926)

The Wanderer (Paramount, 1926)

Wanderer of the Wasteland (Paramount, 1924)

War Paint (MGM, 1926)

The Water Hole (Paramount, 1928)

We Moderns (First National, 1925)

Weddings Bills (Paramount, 1927)

The Wedding March (Paramount, 1928)

The Wedding Song (Producers Distributing, 1925)

We're All Gamblers (Paramount, 1927)

West of the Water Tower (Paramount, 1924)

What Every Woman Knows (Paramount, 1921)

Where Was I ? (Universal-Jewel, 1925)

While Satan Sleeps (Paramount, 1922)

The Whirlwind of Youth (Paramount, 1927)

White Gold (Producers Distributing, 1927)

White Shadows in the South Seas (MGM, 1928)

The White Sister (Metro, 1923)

Why Girls Leave Home (Warner Bros., 1921)

Why Women Love (First National, 1925)

Why Worry? (Pathe Exchange, 1923)

Wild Bill Hickok (Paramount, 1923)

The Wilderness Woman (First National, 1926)

Wings (Paramount, 1927)

The Winning of Barbara Worth (United Artists, 1926)

The Wise Guy (First National, 1926)

The Witching Hour (Paramount, 1921)

Within the Law (First National, 1926)

The Wolf of Wall Street (Paramount, 1929)

The Woman Disputed (United Artists, 1928)

A Woman of the World (Paramount, 1929)

The Woman on Trial (Paramount, 1927)

Woman-Proof (Paramount, 1923)

The Woman Under Cover (Universal, 1919)

Woman Wise (Fox, 1928)

Womanhandled (Paramount, 1925)

Womanpower (Fox, 1926)

Women and Gold (Gotham, 1925)
The World at Her Feet (Paramount, 1927)
The World's Champion (Paramount, 1922)

The Wreck of the Hesperus (Pathe Exchange, 1927)
Wreckage (Banner 1925)

The Yankee Clipper (Producers Distributing, 1927)

You'd Be Surprised (Paramount, 1926)
Young April (Producers Distributing, 1926)

Zaza (Paramount, 1923)

Appendix 5
Silent Film Scores at the New York Public Library
Music Division
Lincoln Center for the Performing Arts

Arsenal

Belza, Ivan. *Arsenal.* [192-?] JOG 72-32.

Ben Hur

Music score for Ben Hur, based on the famous novel by Lew Wallace. Adapted and arranged by David Mendoza and William Axt. New York, Photo Play Music Co., n.d. *MSP-Amer.

The Big Parade

Music score for King Vidor's Metro-Goldwyn-Mayer production of The Big Parade, based on an original screen story by Laurence Stallings. Adapted and arranged by David Mendoza and William Axt, with original compositions by William Axt. New York, Photo Play Music Co., [1926]. JPG 77-1.

La Bohème

Music score for Metro-Goldwyn-Mayer Production of La Bohème. Original compositions by William Axt; synchronized by David Mendoza and William Axt. New York, Photo Play Music Co., n.d. *MSP-Amer.

Kino-Pravda

Music for Kino-Pravda, Kombrig Ivanov [and] Rebellion, Mutiny in Odessa. The Museum of Modern Art Film Library. [19--]. JOG 72-40.

Potemkin

Music for Potemkin. The Museum of Modern Art Film Library, [194-?] JOG 72-33.

Samson

Kreider, Noble W. *Incidental Music for Universal Film Manufacturing Company's special feature Samson.* [By Noble Kreider] [n.p.] Universal Film Manufacturing Co., [c1914]. JNG 76-109.

Uncle Tom's Cabin

Riesenfeld, Hugo. *Music score of Uncle Tom's Cabin;* a Universal production. Score compiled and synchronized by Hugo Riesenfeld. New York, Robbins Music Corp., c1928. JNG 75-60.

Wild & Woolly

Piano score for Wild & Woolly. [n.p., 193-?] JNG 72-32.

Appendix 6
Silent Film Scores at the
Fédération Internationale des Archives du Film

70 Coudenberg
1000 Brussels, Belgium

Adventures of Prince Achmed (1926) (ensemble de petites partitions)	
Arsenal by Ivan Belza	55 p.
The Birth of a Nation	151 p.
Music written, selected and arranged by Joseph Carl Breil	
By the Law	98 p.
Chess Fever	39 p.
The Clever Dummy	
Score of Alden Beach	
The Cloak	59 p.
Enoch Arden (parts IV, V)	33 p.
Execution of Mary Queen of Scots (1895)	117 p.
Wash Day Troubles	
A Trip to the Moon	
The Great Train Robbery	
Faust	
Queen Elisabeth	
The Fall of the House of Usher (2 copies)	86 p.
Father Sergius	132 p.
A Fool There Was (I-2)	104 p.
A Fool There Was	104 p.
arrangement by Alden Beach	
The Four Horsemen of the Apocalypse	144 p.
Fragment of an Empire	123 p.
The Freshman (Harold Lloyd)	124 p.
Gertie the Dinosaur (II-2) (3 copies)	15 p.
By Windsor McCay	
The Great Train Robbery (1903) (2 copies)	
Greed	158 p.
Hamlet (last 3 reels) (2 copies)	63 p.
His Bitter Pill (Mack Sennett)	48 p.

Intolerance (D. W. Griffith)	224 p.
Isn't Life Wonderful (2 copies)	113 p.
Score compiled and synchronised by Cesare Sodero and Louis Silvers	
The Italian Straw Hat	149 p.
Un chapeau de paille d'Italie (France, 1926)	
The Last Card	30 p.
The Last Command	163 p.
The Love of Jeanne Ney (III-3)	203 p.
Méliès Program	80 p.
Score by Mortimer Browning	
Menilmontant	48 p.
Metropolis	207 p.
The Molly Coddle (ensemble de petits porceaux éparpillés)	
Mother	126 p.
The Mother and the Law (D. W. Griffith)	52 p.
The New York Hat (3 copies)	
Score by Alden Beach	
Orphans of the Storm	136 p.
Score by L. F. Gottschalk and Wm. Frederick Peters	
The Passion of Joan of Arc (3 copies)	65 p.
Plane Crazy	31 p.
The first Mickey Mouse.	
Primitive German Films	77 p.
By Skladanowsky	
La Souriante Madame Beaudet (The Smiling Madame Beaudet)	60 p.
Underworld	126 p.

Bibliography

Adams, Frank Stewart. "On Time or Not At All," *The American Organist* (vol. 9, no. 1, 1926): 14–15.

——————"Photoplaying. Dynamic Values," *The American Organist* (vol. 3, no. 8, 1920): 279–81.

——————"'Way Down East' and the Future," *The American Organist* (vol. 4, no. 1, 1921): 23–27.

Amberg, George, comp., *The New York Times Film Reviews 1913–1970: A One Volume Selection* (New York; Quadrangle Books, Inc., 1971).

"As Broadway Does It. In the Rivoli," *The American Organist* (vol. 6, no. 2, 1923): 107–8.

"As Broadway Does It. The Capitol," *The American Organist* (vol. 6, no. 10, 1923): 623–24.

Baylan, Kenneth. "Points and Viewpoints. Our Terrifying Ignorance," *The American Organist* (vol. 6, no. 4, 1923): 251.

Beynon, George N., *Musical Presentation of Motion Pictures* (New York: G. Schirmer, 1921).

Biograph Bulletins 1896–1908 (Los Angeles: Kemp R. Niver, 1971).

Bitzer, G. W., *Billy Bitzer, His Story: The Autobiography of D. W. Griffith's Master Cameraman* (New York: Farrar, Straus, and Giroux, 1973).

Bordwell, David, *The Films of Carl-Theodore Dreyer* (Berkeley: University of California Press, 1981).

——————*La Passion de Jeanne D'Arc.* (Bloomington: Indiana University Press, 1973).

Brooks, Louise, *Lulu in Hollywood* (New York: Alfred A. Knopf, 1983).

Brown, Karl, *Adventures with D. W. Griffith* (New York: Farrar, Straus, and Giroux, 1973).

Brownlow, Kevin, *Napoleon: Abel Gance's Classic Film* (New York: Alfred A. Knopf, 1983).

——————*The Parade's Gone By* (Berkeley: University of California Press, 1968).

Buhrman, T. Scott, "From New York," *The American Organist* (vol. 12, no. 5, 1929): 293.

——————"Here We Are," *The American Organist* (vol. 13, no. 1, 1930): 34.

——————"Photoplays Deluxe," *The American Organist* (vol. 3, no. 5, 1920): 157–75.

Cameron, Evan William, ed., *Sound and the Cinema: The Coming of Sound to American Film* (Pleasantville, New York: Redgrave Publishing Co., 1980).

"The Capitol, New York," *The American Organist* (vol. 6, no. 11, 1923): 694.

Carter, C. Roy. *Theatre Organist's Secrets: A Collection of Successful Imitations, Tricks and Effects for Motion Picture Accompaniment on the Pipe Organ* (Los Angeles: C. Roy Carter, 1926).

Castillo, L. G. del, "Cue Sheets and Something Better," *The American Organist* (vol. 5, no. 10, 1922): 452–53.

——————"Managers of Heavenly Descent," *The American Organist* (vol. 10, no. 4, 1927): 102–4.

"Cinema/Sound," *Yale French Studies* (no. 60, 1980).

Colwell, Harry, J., "Give the New Baby a Chance," *The American Organist* (vol. 10, no. 5, 1927): 130–32.

Contrib., A. "Roaming the Big Town," *The American Organist* (vol. 8, no. 2, 1925): 25–26.

Cooke, James Francis, *Great Men and Famous Musicians on the Art of Music* (Philadelphia: Theodore Presser Co., 1925).

Cooper, J. van Cleft, "Creation of Atmosphere," *The American Organist* (vol. 5, no. 6, 1922): 240–42.

——————"'The Vagabond'—A Vagabond," *The American Organist* (vol. 6, no. 2, 1923): 109–10.

"Critiques. Brooklyn-Strand," *The American Organist* (vol. 4, no. 8, 1921): 280–81.

"Critiques. Ideas Going to Waste," *The American Organist* (vol. 6, no. 8, 1923): 503–4.

"Critiques. Rivoli," *The American Organist* (vol. 6, no. 6, 1923): 366–67.

"Critiques of the New Art. Loew Family," *The American Organist* (vol. 8, no. 6, 1925): 231.

Curtiss, Thomas Quin, *Von Stroheim* (New York: Vintage Books, 1973).

Darrah, William C., *The World of Stereographs* (Gettysburg: William C. Darrah, 1977).

DeMille, Agnes, *Dance to the Piper* (Boston: Brown and Co., 1952).

Denton, Clive, "King Vidor," in *The Hollywood Professionals,* vol. 5 (London: The Tantivy Press, 1976).

Dreyer, Carl-Theodore, *Dreyer in Double Reflection.* Translation of Carl Th. Dreyer's writings *About the Film (Om Filmen)*, ed. Donald Skoller (New York: E. P. Dutton & Co., Inc., 1973).

——————*Four Screen Plays*, Trans. Oliver Stallybrass (Bloomington: Indiana University Press, 1964).

Edison Films. #288 (Orange, New Jersey: Thomas A. Edison, July, 1906).

Eisenstein, Sergei, *Film Form and The Film Sense,* trans. Jay Leyda (Cleveland and New York: The World Publishing Co., 1965).

Essoe, Gabe and Raymond Lee, *DeMille the Man and His Pictures* (New York: Castle Books, 1970).

Evans, Mark, Soundtrack: The Music of The Movies (New York: Da Capo Press, Inc., 1979).

Fairbanks, Douglas, *Laugh and Live* (New York: Britton Publishing Co., 1917).

Fairbanks, Douglas, Jr., and Richard Schickel, *The Fairbanks Album.* Drawn from the family archives by Douglas Fairbanks, Jr. (Boston: New York Graphic Society, 1975).

Farrar, Geraldine, *Such Sweet Compulsion* (New York: Greystone Press, 1928).

"Film Facts and Fancies," *The American Organist* (vol. 3, no. 8 and 9, 1920): 298-9, 339.

Geduld, Harry M., ed., *Authors on Film* (Bloomington: Indiana University Press, 1972).

"General Notes. The Capitol Theater," *The American Organist* (vol. 7, no. 8, 1924): 482.

"General Notes. Midnight Shows," *The American Organist* (vol. 11, no. 3, 1928): 115.

Giannetti, Louis D., *Understanding Movies* (Englewood Cliffs, New Jersey: Prentice-Hall, 1976).

Gish, Lillian with Ann Pinchot, *The Movies, Mr. Griffith and Me* (London: W. H. Allen, 1969).

Goodrich, Frederick W., "A Review of the Times," *The American Organist* (vol. 12, no. 6, 1929): 370.

Hall, Ben M. *The Golden Age of the Movie Palace. The Best Remaining Seats* (New York: Clarkson N. Potter, Inc., 1975).

Hamrick, George Lee, "Photoplaying. Fundamentals," *The American Organist* (vol. 3, no. 1, 1920): 21-23.

[Hansford, M. M.] "American Conservatory Theatre School," *The American Organist* (vol. 6, no. 7, 1923): 444-50.

Hansford, M. M. "Picturegraphs," *The American Organist* (vol. 4, no. 4 and 5, 1921): 131-32, 169-70.

——————"Picturegraphs," *The American Organist* (vol. 6, no. 4, 1923): 234-35.

——————"Picturegraphs," *The American Organist* (vol. 9, no. 12, 1926): 363-64.

——————"Picturegraphs," *The American Organist* (vol. 10, no. 5, 1927): 129-30.

——————"Strikes and Some Suggestions," *The American Organist* (vol. 4, no. 11, 1921): 385-87.

[Hansford, M. M.] "Wurlitzerizing in the Rialto," *The American Organist* (vol. 5, no. 7, 1922): 292-94.

Hayman, Ronald, *Artaud and After* (Oxford: Oxford University Press, 1977).

Heeremans, Harold, *The Stick: Music the Hard Way* (Harold Heeremans, 1978).

Henderson, Robert, M., *D. W. Griffith: His Life and Work* (New York: Oxford University Press, 1972).

——————*D. W. Griffith: The Years at Biograph* (New York: Farrar, Straus and Giroux, 1970).

Herzog, Dorothea B., "Smiling His Way to the Goal of His Ambition," *National Brain Power Monthly* (November, 1922): 24.

Higham, Charles, *Cecil B. DeMille* (New York: Charles Scribner's Sons, 1973).

Hofmann, Charles, *Sounds for Silents* (New York: Drama Book Specialists, 1970).

Horwitz, Rita and Harriet Harrison with the assistance of Wendy White, *The George Kleine Collection of Early Motion Pictures in the Library of Congress: A Catalog* (Washington: Library of Congress, 1980).

"Hugo Riesenfeld Tells How He Scores a Film," *Musical Courier* (vol. 94, no. 7, Feb. 17, 1927): 48.

"Ideas Going to Waste," *The American Organist* (vol. 6, no. 8, 1923): 503-5.

"J. Van Cleft Cooper," *The American Organist* (vol. 12, no. 6, 1929): 358.

Landon, John W., *Jesse Crawford Poet of the Organ, Wizard of the Mighty Wurlitzer* (New York: The Vestal Press, 1974).

Lang, Edith and J. Harold Weisel, "Cue Sheets: Two Discussions," *The American Organist* (vol. 5, no. 7, 1922): 289-91.

Lauritzen, Elinar and Gunnar Lundquist, *American Film Index 1908-15* (Stockholm, Sweden: Film-Index, 1976).

——————*American Film Index 1916-20* (Stockholm, Sweden: Film-Index, 1984).

Leyda, Jay, ed. *Voices of Film Experiences 1894 to the Present* (New York: Macmillan Publishing Co., Inc., 1977).

Limbacher, James, *Film Music* (Metuchen, New Jersey: The Scarecrow Press, 1974).

Lindsay, Vachel, *The Art of the Moving Picture* (New York: Liveright Publishing Corp., 1970).

The Literary Digest (vol. 82, July 19, 1924): 26-27.

"The Loew Music System," *The American Organist* (vol. 7, no. 6, 1924): 332-36.

London, Kurt, *Film Music. A Summary of the Characteristic Features of Its History, Aesthetics, Technique; and Possible Developments,* trans. Eric S. Bensinger (London: Faber & Faber Ltd., 1936).

Lorenz, Pare, *Lorenz on Film: Movies 1927 to 1941* (New York: Hopkinson and Blake, 1973).

Maitland, Rollo F., "Photoplaying in the Stanley," *The American Organist* (vol. 3, no. 4, 1920): 119-22.

Mebody, S. O., "New York City Notes," *The American Organist* (vol. 9, no. 11, 1926): 330.

Medcalfe, Roy L., "Hollywood Theater," *The American Organist* (vol. 7, no. 11, 1924): 642-44.

"Melodrama," *New York Literary Forum* (New York: 1980): [Guest editor Daniel Gerould]

Merson, Theodore, "Here and There and Everywhere," *The American Organist* (vol. 9, no. 3, 1926): 74-77.

Mills, May Meskimen, *The Pipe Organist's Complete Instruction and Reference Work on the Art of Photo-Playing* (May Meskimen Mills, 1922).

Milne, Tom, *The Cinema of Carl Dreyer* (New York: A. S. Barnes & Co., 1971).

Mr. Curtis Dunham," *The American Organist* (vol. 4, no. 6, 1921): 209.

Munden, Kenneth, *The American Film Institute Catalog of Motion Pictures Produced in the United States: Feature Films 1921-1930* (New York and London: R. R. Bowker Co., 1971).

"New York," *The American Organist* (vol. 12, no. 12, 1929): 756.

The New York Clipper (November 12, 1904): 895.

"News and Notes: The Rivoli," *The American Organist* (vol. 5, no. 2, 1922): 79.

Newson, Iris, ed., *Wonderful Inventions: Motion Pictures, Broadcasting, and Recorded Sound at the Library of Congress* (Washington: Library of Congress, 1985).

Nigma, E., "Sic Semper Tyrannis," *The American Organist* (vol. 10, no. 3, 1927): 65-66.

Niver, Kemp R., *Early Motion Pictures: The Paper Print Collection in the Library of Congress* (Washington: Library of Congress, 1985).

"Organ Again: The Rivoli Organists Find a Way to Keep Alive," *The American Organist* (vol. 12, no. 6, 1929): 358.

Pauli, Hansjoerg, *Filmmusik: Stummfilm* (Stuttgart: Klett-Cotta, 1981).

"Photoplaying: Critiques: Rivoli,"*The American Organist* (vol. 6, no. 3, 1923): 167.

Pickford, Mary, *Sunshine and Shadow* (Garden City, New York: Doubleday & Co., Inc., 1954).

Pratt, George C., "Cue Sheets for Silent Films," *Image* (vol. 25, no. 1, March, 1982): 17-24.

Preston J. Hubbard, "Synchronized Sound and Movie-House Musicians, 1926-29," *American Music* (vol. 3, no. 4, 1985): 429-41.

Publicity with Motion Pictures (Washington: Bureau of Commercial Economics, 1920).

R., T. L. "We're Discovered at Last," *The American Organist* (vol. 6, no. 6, 1923): 382.

"Radio Broadcasting," *The American Organist* (vol. 8, no. 7, 1925): 297.

Rapee, Erno, *Encyclopaedia of Music for Pictures* (New York: Arno Pres and *The New York Times,* 1970).

"Rialto and Rivoli," *The American Organist* (vol. 9, no. 2 and 6, 1926): 40, 182.

Scheirer, James E., "South, South, South," *The American Organist* (vol. 9, no. 9, 1926: 267-68.

Schickel, *Douglas Fairbanks the First Celebrity.* (London: Elm Tree Books, 1976).

Scott, John, "Entertainment the Solution," *The American Organist* (vol. 13, no. 2, 1930): 104-5.

Skinner, Ernest M. "Cinema Music," *The American Organist* (vol. 1, no. 8, 1918): 417-418, 421.

Spehr, Paul C., *The Movies Begin: Making Movies in New Jersey 1885-1920* (Newark: The Newark Museum in cooperation with Morgan and Morgan, Inc., 1977).

Stummfilmmusik gestern und heute: Beitrage und Interviews anlaesslich eines Symkphosiums im Kino Arsenal am 9. Juni 1979 in Berlin (Berlin: Verlag Volker Spiess, 1979).

Talbot, Daniel, ed., *Film: An Anthology* (Berkeley: University of California Press, 1975).

"The Theater World," *The American Organist (vol. 8, no. 2, 1925)*: 69.

Thiel, Wolfgang, *Filmmusik in Geschichte und Gegenwart* (Berlin: Heschelverlag, 1981).

Thomas, Tony, *Film Score: The View from the Podium* (South Brunswick, New Jersey: A. S. Barnes, 1979).

The Trial of Joan of Arc. Being the Verbatim Report of the Proceedings from the Orleans Manuscript, translated with an Introduction by W. S. Scott (Westport, Conn.: Associated Booksellers, 1956).

"Unit vs. Straight," *The American Organist* (vol. 7, no. 1, 1924): 18-26.

"Vitaphone et al.," *The American Organist* (vol. 11, no. 10, 1928): 442-43.

Walker, Alexander, *Dietrich* (New York: Harper & Row, 1984).

—————*Garbo: A Portrait* (New York: Macmillian, 1980).

—————*The Shattered Silents, How the Talkies Came to Stay* (New York: William Morrow and Co., 1979).

Weis, Elisabeth and John Belton, ed. *Film Sound: Theory and Practice* (New York: Columbia University Press, 1985).

Weller, Alanson, "New York," *The American Organist* (vol. 10, no. 6, 1927): 161.

Wescott, Steven D., *A Comprehensive Bibliography of Music for Film and Television* (Detroit: Information Coordinators, 1986).

"White Institute," *The American Organist* (vol. 12, no. 4, 1929): 252.

Wild, Walter, "Variety in the Music Score," *The American Organist* (vol. 5, no. 12, 1922): 546-47.

Wyatt, Geoffrey, *At the Mighty Organ* (Oxford: Oxford Illustrated Press, 1974).

Zierold, Norman, *Sex Goddesses of the Silent Screen* (Chicago: Henry Regnery Co., 1973).

Index

Higgin, Howard, 681, 756, 816
Hill Doris, 34, 891
Hill, George, 46, 127, 197, 321
Hines, Charles, 12, 430, 1039
Hines, Johnny, 12, 117, 164, 699, 1039
Hobart, Henry, 677
Hodkinson, Pictures, 381,, 766A
Hoffman, Aaron, 357
Hoffman, M. H., 851
Hoffman, Michael, 43, 235, 975
Holloway, Sterling, 145
Holmes, Stuart, 146
Holt, Jack, 21, 34, 102, 252, 278, 333, 771, 923, 964, 977
Holubar, Allan, 727
Honegger, Arthur, 611C
Hope, Anthony, 749
Hopper, E. Mason, 94, 606, 750, 1028
Hopper, Hedda, 961
Hopwood, Avery, 490, 629
Hough, E. Morton, 402, 610
Hough, Emerson, 114, 794
Houston, Norman, 112, 504
How to Handle Women. See *Fresh Every Hour.*
Howard, Sidney, 613
Howard, William, K., 363, 548, 704, 793, 972
Howes, Reed, 420
Hubbard, Lucien, 741
Hüe, Georges, 720
Huff, Theodore, 288, 388
Hughes, Howard, 568, 950
Hughes, Lloyd, 19, 408, 767, 918
Hughes, Mr. and Mrs. Rupert, 369
Hughes, Rupert, 595
Hull, George C., 70, 333
Hummel, Ferdinand, 83
Hunt, Jay, 198
Hunter Glenn, 109, 519, 766A
Hunter T. Hayes, 445
Hurst, Paul, 127
Hyland, Frances, 682

Illica, Luigi, 359, 360, 458
Illinois Theatre, Chicago, 291B
Ince, Ralph, 161, 223, 427, 635, 789, 809
Ince, Thomas, H., 15, 26, 60, 69, 173, 174, 192, 195, 226, 236, 272, 343, 437, 442, 687, 837, 1025
Ingraham. Lloyd, 486
Ingram, Rex, 743, 941, 1002

International Standard Film Co., 739
Intolerance, 603
Irving Berlin, Inc., 860
Irwin, May, 674
Ivan Players, Inc., 542

J. and W. Chester, 251
J. Fischer & Bro., 908
Jack Snyder Pub. Co. Inc., 894
Jackman, Fred, 628
Jackson, Joseph, 8
Jackson, Marion, 371, 792
Jaffe Art Film, 115
James Cruze, Inc., 621, 712
Janney, William, 1047
Jay, Alice Smythe Burton, 870
Jeanne, D'Arc. See Joan of Arc
Jess Smith Productions, Inc., 677
Jesse L. Lasky Feature Play Co., 142
Jessel, George, 357, 364
Jesus, 553
Joan of Arc, 657, 658
Johnson, Emilie, 500, 632
Johnson, Emory, 500, 632
Johnston, Calvin, 241
Johnston, Julanne, 216
Johnston, Will, 883
Jones, Buck, 87, 105, 201, 302, 354, 550
Jones, F. Richard, 76, 831
Jones, Grover, 76, 884, 992
Josephson, Julian, 443
Josephson, Julien, 712, 793
Joy, Leatrice, 22, 327, 560, 965
Joyce, Alice, 431
Julian, Rupert, 509
Jungmeyer, Jack, 799

Kahler, Hugh McNair, 519
Kalem Co., 27, 86, 120, 140, 190, 268, 304, 305, 688, 804, 828, 841, 842, 935, 956
Kaliz, Armand, 1034
Kalmus Filmusic Edition, 196a
Kane, Robert, 77, 112, 193, 220, 221, 1005
Kane, Robert T., 615, 703
Kantor, Eddie, [sic] 843
Kaufman, George, S., 125
Keaton, Buster, 185
Keefe, William, 148
Keith, Ian, 193
Kelland, Clarence Budington, 220, 410
Kellermann, Annette, 227, 228

Kelly, Albert, 154
Kelly, George, 202
Kelly, Peggy, 163
Kelly, T. Howard, 535
Kennedy, Joseph, P. 161, 175, 210, 223, 241, 315, 400, 427, 439, 489, 597, 604, 635, 666, 698, 789, 814, 865
Kennedy, Tom, 428, 532
Kent, Barbara, 624, 628, 818
Kent, Larry, 404
Kent, Matty, 376
Kenton, Erle C., 222, 609, 719, 939
Kenyon, Doris, 95, 121, 403, 453
Kerker, G., 65
Kern, Jerome, 369
Kerr, C. Herbert, 389
Kerrigan J. Warren, 351
Kerry, Norman, 46, 330, 533, 939, 957
Kilenyi, Edward, 1, 12, 117, 277, 301, 374, 386, 552, 584, 615, 686, 690, 694, 713, 726, 808, 811, 849, 851, 861, 867, 880, 920, 978
King, Burton, 912
King, Rufus, 634
Kingston, Natalie, 400
Kirkland, David, 13
Kirkwood, James, 126, 535
Klein, Helen, 18, 219, 450, 478, 652, 672, 829
Klein, Manuel, 18, 219, 450, 478, 652, 672, 829
Kleine, George, 369
Kleine-Cines Production, 24
Kleiner, Arthur, 284, 658, 678, 679, 680, 719C
Kohler, Fred, 964
Kohn, Ben Grauman, 492
Kombrig Ivanov Rebellion, 485
Komroff, M., 304
Korda, Alexander, 625, 1044
Koven, Reginald De, 735
Kraly, Hans, 574, 692
Krauss, 574
Kreider, Noble, 758
Krueger, Michael P., 87, 88, 92, 100, 105, 137, 151, 201, 243, 253, 269, 283, 293, 298, 302, 336, 344, 354, 366, 398, 415, 421, 432, 550, 571, 616, 618, 631, 675, 683, 715, 728, 732, 733, 738, 752, 759, 803, 826, 906, 937, 943, 946, 1014, 1022, 1030, 1033, 1043
Kurtz, Saunders, 172, 948